FAITH IN MARKETS

Columbia Studies in the History of U.S. Capitalism

COLUMBIA STUDIES IN THE HISTORY OF U.S. CAPITALISM

Series Editors: Devin Fergus, Louis Hyman, Bethany Moreton, and Julia Ott

Capitalism has served as an engine of growth, a source of inequality, and a catalyst for conflict in American history. While remaking our material world, capitalism's myriad forms have altered—and been shaped by—our most fundamental experiences of race, gender, sexuality, nation, and citizenship. This series takes the full measure of the complexity and significance of capitalism, placing it squarely back at the center of the American experience. By drawing insight and inspiration from a range of disciplines and alloying novel methods of social and cultural analysis with the traditions of labor and business history, our authors take history "from the bottom up" all the way to the top.

The Rise of Corporate Feminism: Women in the American Office, 1960–1990, by Allison Elias
The Dead Pledge: The Origins of the Mortgage Market and Federal Bailouts, 1913–1939,
    by Judge Glock
Unfree Markets: The Slaves' Economy and the Rise of Capitalism in South Carolina,
    by Justene Hill Edwards
Histories of Racial Capitalism, edited by Destin Jenkins and Justin Leroy
Brain Magnet: Research Triangle Park and the Idea of the Idea Economy,
    by Alex Sayf Cummings
How the Suburbs Were Segregated: Developers and the Business of Exclusionary Housing,
    1890–1960, by Paige Glotzer
Threatening Property: Race, Class, and Campaigns to Legislate Jim Crow Neighborhoods,
    by Elizabeth A. Herbin-Triant
Banking on Freedom: Black Women in U.S. Finance Before the New Deal,
    by Shennette Garrett-Scott
City of Workers, City of Struggle: How Labor Movements Changed New York,
    edited by Joshua B. Freeman
Buying Gay: How Physique Entrepreneurs Sparked a Movement, by David K. Johnson
American Capitalism: New Histories, edited by Sven Beckert and Christine Desan
Creditworthy: A History of Consumer Surveillance and Financial Identity in America,
    by Josh Lauer
From Head Shops to Whole Foods: The Rise and Fall of Activist Entrepreneurs,
    by Joshua Clark Davis
Capital of Capital: Money, Banking, and Power in New York City, 1784–2012,
    by Steven H. Jaffe and Jessica Lautin

Faith in Markets

Christian Capitalism in the Early American Republic

Joseph P. Slaughter

Columbia University Press   New York

Columbia University Press
Publishers Since 1893
New York   Chichester, West Sussex
cup.columbia.edu
Copyright © 2023 Columbia University Press
All rights reserved

Library of Congress Cataloging-in-Publication Data
Names: Slaughter, Joseph P., author.
Title: Faith in markets : Christian capitalism in the early American republic / Joseph P. Slaughter.
Description: New York : Columbia University Press, [2023] | Series: Columbia studies in the history of U.S. capitalism | Includes bibliographical references and index.
Identifiers: LCCN 2023014402 (print) | LCCN 2023014403 (ebook) | ISBN 9780231191104 (hardback) | ISBN 9780231191111 (trade paperback) | ISBN 9780231549257 (ebook)
Subjects: LCSH: Capitalism—Religious aspects—Protestant churches—History of doctrines. | Capitalism—United States—History—19th century. | Christian-owned business enterprises—United States—History—19th century. | Protestant churches—United States—History. | United States—Economic conditions—To 1865. | United States—Church history—19th century.
Classification: LCC BR115.C3 S593 2023 (print) | LCC BR115.C3 (ebook) | DDC 261.8/5—dc23/eng/20230505
LC record available at https://lccn.loc.gov/2023014402
LC ebook record available at https://lccn.loc.gov/2023014403

Printed and bound by CPI Group (UK) Ltd, Croydon, CR0 4YY

Cover design: Julia Kushnirsky
Cover illustration: Karl Bodmer (Swiss, 1809–1893), *Economy, Rapp's Colony on the Ohio*, 1832, watercolor on paper, Joslyn Art Museum, Omaha, Nebraska, Gift of the Enron Art Foundation, 1986.49.46. Photograph © Bruce M. White, 2019

Contents

INTRODUCTION
Early Nineteenth-Century Capitalism and Religion 1

PART ONE Christian Communal Capitalism 11

CHAPTER ONE
Communal Industry: Harmonie, Pennsylvania 17

CHAPTER TWO
Industry on the Frontier: Harmonie, Indiana 40

CHAPTER THREE
Republican Industry: Economy, Pennsylvania 64

PART TWO Christian Reform Capitalism 91

CHAPTER FOUR
The Sabbatarians 97

CHAPTER FIVE
The Pioneers 109

CHAPTER SIX
Conflict, Defeat, and Victory 129

PART THREE Christian Virtue Capitalism 151

CHAPTER SEVEN
Methodist Printer-Publishers 157

CHAPTER EIGHT
Creating a Moral Republic 173

CHAPTER NINE
Fostering an American Protestant Identity 190

CONCLUSION
Morality and Markets, Then and Now 217

Acknowledgments 225
Notes 229
Bibliography 335
Index 365

FAITH IN MARKETS

Introduction

Early Nineteenth-Century Capitalism and Religion

> Mister Bissell! Mister Bissell!
> Too short's my epistle
> To do justice to the great "Pioneer"
> Driven by av'rice extreme,
> Your cash has a strong team,
> Drawn by fanaticks, whose blind zeal you steer,
> Mister Bissell,
> Drawn by fanaticks, whose blind zeal you steer.[1]

Published in a Rochester, New York, newspaper just before Christmas Day, 1828, the anonymous poem above refers to a polarizing businessman from upstate New York, Josiah Bissell Jr. It is easy to understand why Bissell was so controversial—he was an early nineteenth-century culture warrior. Even though the term "culture warrior" is anachronistic in this context, it is easy to visualize Bissell right at home amid the cultural conflicts of the late twentieth and early twenty-first centuries. Bissell possessed the resources to fight the cultural battles of his time and place—the early nineteenth-century United States—because he was a successful entrepreneur. However, unlike contemporary culture warriors, Bissell fought a battle to reform not the government or the law but rather the marketplace. Specifically, he believed the increased acceptance of commerce seven days a week—thanks in part to how the Erie Canal connected peripheral communities to market centers—was an abomination. To change this trajectory, Bissell helped found a six-day transportation line—the "Pioneer" referred to in the above-quoted poem—and helped spark a larger movement of market reform that became known as "Pioneerism." In so doing, Bissell sought to stake claim to what the early U.S. marketplace would look like. He never used the term "capitalism," but its characteristics were coalescing all around him, and aspects of it troubled him deeply. (Although the idea and practice of capitalism is contingent and ever-shifting, this book focuses on capitalism's need for legal frameworks that allow economic actors to make autonomous economic decisions; its coordination through markets, prices, competition, coordination, demand, supply, and the exchange of commodities; and the centrality of capital—all of which were unevenly emerging in the early nineteenth-century United States.)[2]

Bissell illustrates the manner in which American Protestantism has wrestled with how to best engage culture, including the marketplace, for more than four hundred years. He chose to fight for reform. Others have chosen to separate to maintain purity, and still others to engage and attempt to redeem culture and the market. This book examines each of these approaches, focusing on how Protestant business ventures reflected these cultural postures (as well as theologies). There is something timeless to the question Christians were wrestling with in Bissell's day. Puritan merchants and ministers debated it in the seventeenth century, and in the twenty-first century American evangelical communities have increasingly come to define themselves according to which "option" characterizes their cultural posture: the "Benedict Option" (separation), the "Wilberforce Option" (fight/reform), or the "Naaman Option" (engage/redeem).[3]

That American Protestants would use their businesses to shape the market and nineteenth-century life more broadly should not be surprising, because there is a long history of American Protestants creating what this study terms Christian business enterprises (CBE) and then using these firms as agents of economic and cultural (and sometimes political) influence.[4] This history is becoming better understood as it relates to the late nineteenth and twentieth centuries.[5] By focusing on the role of CBEs, scholars are undermining the conventional tale of fundamentalist Protestants withdrawing from the broader American culture in the late nineteenth and early twentieth centuries, only to reemerge during the 1950s with the Billy Graham movement.[6] Conversely, no serious scholar would argue theologically conservative Protestants were absent from the culture or politics of the nineteenth-century United States. The story of reform, revivalism, racial oppression, and democratic expansion is well-trodden ground. What is missing from the story is the role of CBEs. Although it is only a preliminary investigation, this study represents an open door through which we can glimpse the ways that businesses "infused with religion" were at the very center of this dynamic period of American history.[7]

The emergence of a full-blown capitalist system is central to this era of U.S. history, and the Christian identity of proprietors such as Bissell was central in shaping what type of capitalism emerged. Scholars have typically traced this linkage through three major transformations related to capitalism and Christianity in the early United States: a "market revolution," the expansion of evangelical Protestantism through a Second Great Awakening, and emergent technology sparking a "communication/transportation revolution."[8] Often, the story goes something like this:

> After the War of 1812, New Yorkers were finally willing to do what the federal government could not: build the Erie Canal, linking previously isolated communities to markets. However, this was destabilizing for many and brought lower-class workers into upstate New York (along the canal) that challenged the dominant Protestant order as villages such as Rochester exploded nearly overnight and small town/agrarian life transformed into factories and mills with restless wage laborers and all their "vices." What was to be done? Religious renewal, courtesy of Charles Grandison Finney and others whose disciples (men such as Bissell), reformed the unruly workforce as they installed a powerful capitalist order.[9]

Despite this narrative's explanatory power, scholars have increasingly come to question and complicate the assumptions that undergird it,[10] specifically the idea that people either resisted the market because it conflicted with their agrarian, democratic, communitarian ethos, or embraced the market because it supported their commercially minded ambitions. Charles Sellers argued one can perceive two kinds of early U.S. Christians—his precapitalist Antinomians (i.e., Methodists) and

Introduction 3

capitalist Arminians (i.e., Presbyterians). Aside from the confusion his labels sow by conflating baggage-laden theological terms with market behavior, Sellers's thesis is fundamentally flawed because it artificially assigns people into "for" and "against" categories. What about those who embraced some aspects of the market while disdaining other characteristics of the emerging capitalist order? How do we categorize them?[11]

Protestants of the early national period did not divide into categories quite so cleanly, and they offered a menu of options for what a Christian marketplace could and should look like. Sellers was right in one regard: for Protestants, the religious orientation of their theology (and eschatology, or study of the end times, which he overlooks completely) was a major factor in shaping their view of the expanding market economy. But which theology? The diversity of Protestant thought explains how and why these Protestants imagined differing visions of an economic system. Religion was not simply playing defense against an expanding capitalist system; neither was it a fringe component of an expanding capitalist system. Instead, this book argues it was at the center of this process as people's religious identities shaped what they imagined the marketplace could and should be in the United States during the early national period. This book explains three such visions, which, with the benefit of hindsight, we can identify as contested forms of capitalism, and which shaped the market in significant ways.

To explore these visions of Christian capitalism, this book offers three case studies from three different under-examined Christian communities in the early United States. The first three chapters focus on German immigrants to America in the opening years of the 1800s. These Lutheran Pietists attempted to purify the marketplace by abolishing private property and emphasizing innovation in textile manufacturing, and in so doing articulated a brand of Christian communal capitalism that achieved fame throughout the Atlantic world. Chapters 4–6 explore how upstate New York Presbyterians strove to reform the market, not through legislation or volunteerism, but through business enterprise. Their strain of Christian reform capitalism offered an alternative marketplace to the consumer who disavowed the seven-day workweek, the consumption of alcohol, or goods produced by enslaved persons. Finally, chapters 7–9 examine how urban Protestants created businesses

4 *Introduction*

for the purpose of producing "virtuous" consumer goods. The upwardly mobile Methodist publishers of this story were quintessential Victorians whose Christian virtue capitalism produced cultural objects that represented a middle-class, Victorian ideal.

These three groups of Protestants deserve further study not only because they were influential, if grossly under-studied, but also because they represent the most significant strains of American Christianity from 1600 to 1850: Pietism, Calvinism, and Arminianism.[12] Calvinism and Arminianism are theological frameworks, named, respectively, after John Calvin (1509–1564) and Jacobus Arminius (1560–1609), and most notably differing over how they address the central tension between God's sovereignty and human free will in the project of salvation. Calvinists historically stress the sovereignty of an all-powerful God and the pervasiveness of sin in the created order, while Arminians emphasize human agency and the ability of people to accept or reject God's call to salvation. Conversely, the historic Calvinist perspective rejects the idea that one can chose to accept Christ (and salvation)—it is God who "elects" a limited number of people for salvation before the dawn of time. Once elected, one cannot reject one's status or lose one's salvation.[13]

Calvinism dominated colonial North America's religious life as the theological underpinnings of Puritans/Congregationalists and Presbyterians. The proliferation during the mid- to late eighteenth century of General Baptists and Wesleyan Methodists portended the massive shift that occurred in the early nineteenth century, as American Protestants increasingly embraced Arminianism. Even historically Calvinist groups such as Presbyterians wrestled with Arminian theology—for example, the phenomenon of Charles Finney's revivalism revolved around his ability to import Arminian notions of personal agency into the pulpits of Calvinist congregations. The transformation in the religious life of North American Protestantism was dramatic, and today dogmatic five-point Calvinists are a minority, as even staunchly Reformed denominations are populated by congregants struggling to reconcile a theology that emphasizes God's sovereignty with the individualistic culture of twenty-first-century America.[14] Scholars of American religion have explored this transformation in depth, with historians often connecting this theological sea change to the broader process of democratization underway in American politics, economics, and society.[15]

Introduction 5

Pietism, on the other hand, is not only a set of theological doctrines; it also is characterized by a specific posture toward one's church and society.[16] Foremost, Pietists strive for holiness or sanctification (becoming more like Christ) in all aspects of their lives, including in their vocations and economic relationships. By living a thoroughly perfected life, Pietists strive to demonstrate to their larger church denomination, state government, and culture at large what an orthodox, sincere Christian life looks like.[17] They emphasize a "personally meaningful relationship of the individual to God," an emphasis on perfectionism or sanctification, an intense biblicism, and an oppositional posture toward the larger society, the government, and the institutional church.[18] Pietism influenced nearly everyone in early North America, as both the aforementioned Puritan Calvinists and Wesleyan Arminians reflected the influence of Pietism, as well as colonial-era religious minorities such as the Dutch Reformed, Mennonites, Moravians, various German sects, and the Brethren.[19]

The central argument of this book is that the beliefs and practices of these theological frameworks shaped attitudes toward economic exchange and ideas about how the marketplace should function within both the local community and the nation. These theologically shaped attitudes led to the formation of businesses that sought, and in some cases succeeded, in shaping what the U.S. market became. The legacy of these businesses is still with us today, in the form of marketplace critiques like "conscious capitalism" and environmental, social, and corporate governance (ESG) investing.

As such, some might wonder if this project is simply an updated spin on the much-maligned Weber thesis: that hard work, vocational calling, and worldly asceticism produced "the spirit" of capitalism in Protestant nations.[20] Max Weber wrote in a religiously polarized Germany, attempting to grasp the origins of the industrial revolution, concluding that Protestantism (really, Calvinism) was a religious system more conducive to producing capitalism. While this project, like Weber's, does distinguish between the theologically influenced marketplace attitudes of various religious groups, unlike Weber, I do not argue that one is more conducive to fostering capitalism or is inherently anti- or pro-market. Additionally, this book is agnostic about the morality or utility of capitalism, even as it takes seriously the religious beliefs of its subjects, and in so doing offers a more complex, rich, and nuanced picture of how

6   *Introduction*

religion shaped the market activities of early national-period Americans than early sociologists such as Max Weber, or influential historians such as Charles Sellers.

Finally, this book centers businessmen in social reform movements in ways that complicate the established narratives of American business in the early national period. Businessmen are often the villains of these tales, sowing seeds of societal crisis, then supplying the shock troops of reform, usually in the form of voluntary associations.[21] This approach, what one might term the "Social Control School," relegates religion to a one-dimensional tool businessmen deployed via religious revivals and moral reform associations to discipline their workers into subservient, capitalist laborers.[22] In contrast, this book builds off the work of scholars who have poked significant holes in the social control thesis by arguing that, for good or for ill, *religious businesses themselves* were every bit as instrumental in shaping early national-period American capitalism and society as the revivals and voluntary associations that have traditionally garnered scholars' attention. For example, scholars have demonstrated that long before Charles Finney brought revivalism to Rochester's churches, the embers of religious renewal were already burning in early nineteenth-century rural America—first in the antiformalist churches of the Methodists and Baptists. These revivals began long before expanding markets ever penetrated these rural communities, complicating the standard chronology by which markets are said to cause revivals. The experience in rural America was far from one of capitalist social control—its story instead was an attempt by the elites to stamp out the revivals pushed by the antiformalist churches. Eventually, the elites lost the battle, and the revivals spread to the more "respectable," bourgeoisie-dominated formalist churches through characters like Finney.[23] This critique reflects the perspective of what one might call the "Democratization School."[24]

Recognizing the role played by CBEs in the early nineteenth-century United States offers an alternative to the competing narratives of the Social Control and Democratization Schools. CBEs stood out in the early national period as firms that possessed a distinctly religious character or purpose—this made some of them, such as the Pioneer Line (a stagecoach line), controversial because of how they transmitted their Christian values into the marketplace. While CBEs predated the early

Introduction 7

national period, as the charters for the Massachusetts Bay and Virginia Companies make clear, CBEs began to stand out more clearly in the early nineteenth century.[25] Partly this was due to the colonial era's blurry line between sacred and secular developing some new boundaries in government and business. For example, the colonial-era ideal of abstaining from work on Sundays began to meet stiff resistance as more Americans were integrated into the country's expanding market economy. This points to the second important difference between colonial-era and early national-period CBEs: by the first decades of the nineteenth century, a capitalist system was emerging, which in turn created the opportunity for CBEs to shape the American system according to their proprietors' religious impulses. In fact, the more distinctive the proprietor's vision, the more the particular CBE stood out.

The CBEs profiled in this study, George Rapp & Associates (Harmony Society), the Pioneer Line, and Harper & Brothers, stood out among their competitors, and observers recognized and commented on the religious identity of these businesses. While none of these companies functioned as platforms for evangelism in the manner of enterprises such as the American Bible Society, each embodied the Christian beliefs of their proprietors. These enterprises did not hold Bible studies, sign checks with Bible verses, or share the gospel of Christ with suppliers, workers, or customers, but instead used religion to shape their lending practices, work schedules, and consumer products.[26]

Ultimately, the defining characteristic of CBEs were (and are still) the ways in which their proprietors chose to integrate faith into their market activities. This market-faith integration takes many forms, manifesting, for example, in unique aspects of corporate culture, governance, activism, and market relations (between customers, investors, suppliers, communities, and employees). Corporate culture included such decisions as the Harpers' choice to not print on Sunday and to always consider the moral value of each new product. CBEs in the early nineteenth century were characterized by tightly controlled governance; the four Harper brothers personally ran their company for decades, while George and Frederick Rapp personally oversaw all the business ventures of Rapp & Associates. Activism does not consistently characterize CBEs, but it certainly did in the case of the Pioneer Line. One can read any published speech by Josiah Bissell Jr. and instantly

8   *Introduction*

understand how the Pioneer Line was a tool of his social activism.[27] Lastly, the focus on market relationships between customers, investors, suppliers, communities, and employees is another important way of measuring, evaluating, and defining CBEs. The Harmony Society restricted property ownership among Rapp & Associates' "employees," endeavored to be a good business partner with its customers and suppliers, and worked to honestly acquire new technology by respecting patent rights. The Harpers prized the way they dealt with their clients (authors) and worked to respect the British copyright laws that most of their competitors disregarded. When critics leveled charges of dishonestly toward authors, those claims stood out because of the firm's reputation for integrity. At the same time, these characteristics of CBEs could be controversial, as when the Pioneer Line's reform agenda alienated many consumers and suppliers, even as it attempted to enforce Christian standards of conduct among its employees.[28]

The stories of early nineteenth-century Christian businesses such as Harper & Brothers, the Pioneer Line, and Rapp & Associates are relatively unknown, despite their contributions to the development of capitalism and social reform in nineteenth-century America. This omission means that even though scholars rightly emphasize the market's transformation of workers, women, families, religion, classes, races, and even political parties and holidays, the role of religion in shaping the early nineteenth-century marketplace is comparatively less understood or acknowledged. The examples of Rapp, Bissell, and the Harpers suggest that the role played by religion during the early national period was much more complicated than has usually been acknowledged in the established narratives. For example, inventor Samuel Morse's less famous brothers Sidney and Richard started a newspaper, the *New York Observer*, which served as the mouthpiece of Old School Presbyterians in the early national period. In September 1831, the *Observer* ran an anticapitalist declaration by the Committee to Ministers of the Gospel and Christians and Patriots in Massachusetts:

> It is alike evident, that the existing course of things, unresisted, will result in the abolition of the Sabbath as a means of moral conservation to our country. The ardor of enterprize [*sic*], the accumulation of business, and the rapidity of movements upon our coasts and

Introduction 9

rivers and canals, by stages and steamboats, withdraw increasing numbers from the ministrations of the Gospel, and threaten the absolute subversion of the Sabbath as a day of religious instruction and influence.[29]

As this quotation suggests, for some Protestants of the early nineteenth century, the very nature of capitalism—its tendency toward growth in accumulation, enterprise, and trade networks—was an agent of spiritual and national destruction. Yet, Old School Presbyterians were often successful business owners themselves.

"The ardor of enterprize, the accumulation of business, and the rapidity of movements" in many ways reflects the capitalist visions of Rapp, Bissell, and the Harpers, who did not regard these characteristics of the market as inherently threatening. Far from rejecting technological innovations, each embraced the latest communication, transportation, and manufacturing technologies to achieve their economic and spiritual goals. They did think these characteristics needed boundaries, and in so doing offered different visions of capitalism to their fellow early nineteenth-century Americans: Christian communal capitalism, Christian reform capitalism, and Christian virtue capitalism.

Ultimately, the three CBE case studies included in this book—Rapp & Associates, the Pioneer Line, and Harper & Brothers—represent three important variations of CBE in early national-period America, each enmeshed in a web of faith and the marketplace. Although they serve to illustrate their reflective visions of capitalism, collectively, these three examples suggest we need to rethink the relationship between religion and business in the early national period and consider the role CBEs played in shaping American capitalism.

10 *Introduction*

PART ONE

Christian Communal Capitalism

Industrial towns were all the rage in the early republic United States. Alexander Hamilton and the Society for the Establishment of Useful Manufactures established Paterson, New Jersey, in 1791.[1] Samuel Slater instituted his Rhode Island system of family-staffed mechanized cotton production at Pawtucket, Rhode Island, in 1793.[2] So-called mill girls were the foundation of the vertically integrated Waltham-Lowell system of Waltham, and later Lowell, Massachusetts, in the years immediately following the War of 1812.[3] Owners and workers lived side by side in the 1820s at mill hamlets such as Rockdale, Pennsylvania.[4] Collectively, they represented Americans' attempt to institute manufacturing processes while avoiding the squalor and immorality they believed characterized the great mill towns of England.[5] Essentially, these towns attempted to balance the pursuit of profit with republican virtues, typically reinforced through Christian instruction, practice, and norms.

At the same time that these well-known, thoroughly studied, and oft-cited examples of republican mill towns were springing up in New England, Americans with similar goals yet different solutions were creating communal capitalist villages elsewhere in the new United States. These societies were organized like businesses, integrated into the market economy, but distinguished by an absence of private property and by the centrality of religion to their most basic organizational and philosophical principles. As in Winfred Barr Rothenberg's concept of the "moral economy," individual members of such communities submitted to community values and abided by an internal exchange system based on the primacy of need over profit.[6]

Originally, these industrial communities were explicitly Christian in one form or another. Moravians, Shakers, Amana, and Mormons are just a few examples of the groups who established villages throughout New England, upstate New York, Pennsylvania, Ohio, Kentucky, and Indiana.[7] By the mid-nineteenth century, the most materially successful of these Christian communal capitalists was the Harmony Society, located in Economy, Pennsylvania. No mere reaction to the market disruptions of the early national period, religious imperatives and a search for a moral economic order drove Harmony.[8] Harmony and other Christian communal capitalist villages were legitimate visions of what the emerging U.S. capitalist order could, and according to some observers, should be.[9]

Citizens of the Atlantic community wrestling with how to reconcile economic development, manufacturing technology, inequality, and urban distress looked to these communities for inspiration. For example, J. S. Buckingham, a member of the British Parliament, visited Economy in 1840 and reflected on how its villages did not appear "over-worked," had their material needs met, and did not suffer fear of "loss of employment, a reduction of wages," or other such anxieties that plagued the English working class.[10] Prominent American publisher Mathew Carey agreed with Buckingham's analysis that Economy offered a potential model of how to balance profit and human "happiness." Amazed at what he found when visiting the Harmonists, Carey marveled that they had found a way to create the ideal agricultural-industrial symbiosis: "[Harmony] holds out a most instructive lesson on the true policy to promote human happiness, and to advance the wealth, power, and resources of nations. . . . The Harmonists were true practical political economists."[11]

For observers such as Buckingham and Carey, the Christian communal capitalist villages springing up in America in the early decades of the nineteenth century provided a viable vision of a more equitable, just, and productive economic system. The next three chapters tell the understudied story of the Harmony Society, beginning with the journey of some eight hundred immigrants from Württemberg to the new village of Harmonie in western Pennsylvania between 1803 and 1805.[12] These German Americans established an agricultural and textile manufacturing enterprise that operated under the name Rapp & Associates, after the leader of the society, George Rapp. The Harmonists initially struggled to establish themselves in their Pennsylvania village from 1804 to 1815, before a combination of spiritual and material issues caused them to move to southwest Indiana in stages, from 1814 to 1815. They gradually expanded operations for ten years in southwestern Indiana, building more elaborate textile factories before selling the second Harmonie to utopian industrialist Robert Owen in 1824. Moving back to western Pennsylvania in 1824–1825, they established their third and final site, Economy. Here the Harmonists achieved renown as sophisticated manufacturers whose work force lived in relative comfort and equality, attracting the attention of Karl Marx and Friedrich Engels. By 1850, Economy was one of the wealthiest textile factory towns in the entire antebellum United States, and the town's citizens were well on their way to establishing what Harmonists called their "divine economy."[13] Of course, Economy's wealth was communal, as its villagers owned almost no private property, instead sharing things in common through their association. It boasted efficient textile factories, a school, library, music program and band, printing press, and museum of natural history. The Harmonists also happened to be intensely religious, somewhat reclusive, and yet thoroughly integrated into the expanding American market economy. Economy was a vibrant village that offers multiple lessons about the evolution and possibilities of early American capitalism.

Harmony is a useful case study because it is one of the earliest of these nineteenth-century societies and as such provides a template for understanding subsequent communities, including non-religious communes such as Robert Owen's New Harmony. Like other similar groups, Harmony attempted to hold the surrounding culture at a distance for religious reasons, yet also welcomed market integration and aggressively embraced technological innovation. Finally, Harmony enjoyed longevity and material success, and therefore presents a fascinating wealth of archival material. This makes it an ideal case study of Christian communal capitalism.

Part One: Christian Communal Capitalism   13

Additionally, the Harmony Society functioned as a Christian business enterprise. Although Pennsylvania refused to incorporate Rapp & Associates because of its policy of communal property ownership, the society's marketplace entity reflected a standard business in many other ways.[14] Rapp & Associates embraced the nineteenth-century market and its tools, including stocks, bonds, leases, mortgages, patents, trademarks, licenses, litigation, agents, and contracts. The firm traded in twenty-two states and ten countries.[15] It was this juxtaposition that made Harmony so fascinating to outsiders. In fact, one British visitor criticized the Harmonists' leaders for being too materially focused. He pointed to their "excessive spirit of trade" as compared with other communal capitalist groups, such as the Shakers.[16] As such visitors quickly realized, Harmony certainly combined business with communalism in surprising ways.

Harmony is also a useful case study because of all the visitors it attracted, drawn by its reputation for industrial equality (and eccentric community). While the reality was more complicated, Harmony seemed a truly equitable industrial community; as Englishman Richard Flower claimed, "perfect equality prevails, and there are no servants; but plenty of persons who serve."[17] Visitors like Flower discovered that, in addition to serving as chief proprietor, George Rapp was a Christian "economist-philosopher," responsible for both the political and spiritual spheres of life in his commune.[18] As Rapp explained in his *Thoughts on the Destiny of Man*, communal life could never work apart from a spiritual motivation and foundation: "This can be rendered practicable, only by the sublime spirit of Christianity, which must influence the conduct of a large majority of the members, or nothing of the kind can ever be accomplished."[19] Rapp was a Christian utopian who thought Harmony would play an important role in ushering in Christ's return and reign on earth, "where the true principles of religion, and the prudent regulations of industry and economy, by their united influence, produce *a heaven upon earth—A true HARMONY*."[20] Rapp's goal in founding Harmony was a fusion of the spiritual and material. Rapp used the name "Harmony" to symbolize the "unity of conjunctive powers of many members to the promotion of *one Whole* for the welfare of all, and that is HARMONY."[21]

Despite Rapp's declarations, visitors such as Buckingham, Carey, and Flower often missed the degree to which Lutheran Pietism underpinned

14 *Part One: Christian Communal Capitalism*

the very foundations of the Harmonists' industrial order. This is yet another reason Harmony is such a relevant case study. Pietism represents one of the three major streams of early American religion, heavily influencing the other two: Puritan Calvinism (covered in chapters 4–6) and Wesleyan Arminianism (chapters 7–9).[22] Reformed theology, or Calvinism, earns the bulk of attention from early Americanists as the literature on Puritan America is enormous. Likewise, Wesleyan Arminianism's ascendency and eclipse of Calvinism in the early national period is increasingly well-trodden territory. In comparison, Lutheran Pietism often serves as a forgotten side tale that usually only assumes a limited relevance in the late nineteenth century with the emergence of the Pentecostal holiness movement, even though Franklin H. Littell argues that along with Puritanism and utopian socialism, Pietism is one of the "three most influential sources of intentional community in American religious history."[23]

The Harmonists' Christian communal capitalism was not without tensions and conflicts. The nature of George Rapp's patriarchal leadership style, George's adopted son Frederick's monopoly on Rapp & Associates' day-to-day operations, and the lack of democratic participation in the society's decision making drove some members to abandon the commune, sue for damages, and charge the Rapps with abuse of power. In fact, this tension almost destroyed the society multiple times throughout its one-hundred-year history. The dynamics of Harmony's internal relationships are an important part of its story, and they illuminate the challenges Christian communal capitalists faced in translating their theories of equality into practice.

Part One: Christian Communal Capitalism 15

CHAPTER ONE

Communal Industry

Harmonie, Pennsylvania

George Rapp surveyed the fields surrounding Economy, Pennsylvania, with pride. Well tilled and fruitful, they were not only feeding his town, but also producing a healthy export profit. As his gaze panned, he caught sight of Economy's hotel-tavern, well-known for the simple yet warm hospitality it extended to travelers and curious visitors. Within the town, streets were laid out in an organized, mulberry tree–lined fashion. Solid, practical, comfortable homes surrounded the town's center: the church. Not far away, cotton, flour, and woolen mills reflected the industry for which Economy was famous.[1]

By the 1820s, economists and social commentators from America and Europe alike discussed the amazing productivity of Rapp's Harmony Society and their unique brand of Christian communal capitalism. "Great capitalists" and "extremely wealthy" is how one of the more critical visitors described Harmony and its citizens—not what one would expect of a rural commune in the early national period.[2] The nineteenth-century father of British socialism, Robert Owen, while unimpressed with Rapp's religious views, was so inspired by his industrial success that he purchased Rapp's Indiana village and set up his own utopian commune, New Harmony, Indiana. But, while Owen dreamed of a secular commune where equality and industry could exist side by side, a desire to replicate the first-century followers of Jesus Christ motivated the Harmonists.[3] More so than any other early American religious communal society, however, Harmony consistently fused industrial manufacturing with communal principles, all the while embracing the latest technological advances in power generation, textile production, and transportation.[4] The philosophical underpinnings of what they came to call their "divine economy" was their apocalyptic brand of Lutheran Pietism, which fused a communal ethos onto a system of innovative textile manufacturing.

The Rapps' decision to establish an industrial commune in western Pennsylvania during the first decade of the nineteenth century was a risky proposition. It was a time of rampant land speculation, undependable credit and currency, and a near complete absence of domestic textile manufacturing. In fact, the United States was a relatively unimportant economic entity at the time, numbering a mere five million persons (just under a million of them enslaved) crowded along a narrow Eastern Seaboard. From 1800 to 1850, the purchase of the Louisiana Territory, military conquest, the violent displacement of Native Americans, a rising birth rate, and waves of immigration (voluntary and forced) doubled the size of the nation's territory, while quadrupling its population (and tripling its slave population). Economic growth was not nearly so exponential, but it enjoyed a gradual expansion over the first fifty years of the nineteenth century, spurred in no small measure by the cotton boom and the expansion of America's slave system.[5] As chapter 2 explains, despite Harmony's public stance against enslavement, it clearly benefited from and depended upon antebellum cotton plantation slavery.

The society's emphasis on technological innovation kept it viable until the end of the nineteenth century, nearly a hundred years—rare for the utopian societies of the nineteenth century. The longevity of the Harmony Society is particularly noteworthy considering that like the Shakers, it gradually turned against sex and childbirth, relying on new immigrants to populate its labor force and association. This union of industry and piety is what makes the Harmonists an intriguing case study: these were people who eagerly embraced market activity, contextualized within the social system they devised to prevent the "corruptions" of the market from undermining their piety. At the center of these corruptions were material possessions, which according to George Rapp led to a host of other evils that would jeopardize the special role he and his followers would play in the new millennium. This millennialism, fused with Harmony's brand of Pietism, led them on their odyssey to

18   *Part One: Christian Communal Capitalism*

Pennsylvania, where they arrived just as the market economy was beginning to destabilize life for Americans in profound ways.

THE ORIGINS AND RELIGION OF GEORGE RAPP AND THE HARMONISTS

Despite its heritage of welcoming German Protestants, Pennsylvania was not the site George Rapp originally envisioned for his band of separatists. Born October 28, 1757, in Iptingen, Württemberg, Rapp "ranked among the middle class," and with his wife and two children grew grapes and did some textile work on the several looms he owned.[6] By the late 1780s, he had formed a dissenting group of Lutheran Pietists enraptured by his personality and teachings. Attracting the concerned attention of leaders of the Lutheran Church as well as government officials, Rapp began planning for the emigration of his growing community. Throughout the eighteenth century, Rapp, like other Germans, dreamed not of Penn's Woods, but rather a place far to the south: Louisiana.[7] Thanks to the marketing efforts of Scottish financier John Law, Europeans envisioned in Louisiana an exotic paradise that formed a sharp contrast with Rapp's home, the war-torn, economically depressed, and overpopulated Duchy of Württemberg.[8] Promotional materials, such as the letter in a February 1718 edition of *Le Mercure de France*, described Louisiana as "one of the most beautiful and fertile countries of the world," with "lush greenness and variety of flowers" punctuated by "an infinite number of creeks and streams."[9] John Law founded the Mississippi Company as part of his ambitious plan to enrich the French crown, and a critical part of his plan was encouraging immigration to the colony.[10] Consequently, Law assumed the role of consummate salesman of what he described as "the magnificent land LOUISIANA."[11]

Even after the failure of Law's company in the "Mississippi Bubble" of 1720, the vision described in his promotional materials continued to capture the attention of Europeans dreaming of a better life. In fact, as late as February 1804, Rapp intended to set out for Louisiana, a plan Napoleon foiled by selling the territory to the United States. (Rapp claimed he had a land grant from Napoleon in Louisiana that the emperor transferred to the Pyrenees after the sale of Louisiana.)[12] Promoters like Law faced stiff competition by the mid-eighteenth century, and deceitful

Communal Industry 19

travel agents were all too common.[13] Agents in Massachusetts, New York, and Pennsylvania especially targeted Germans, enticing them with promises of free travel, tobacco, and loans.[14] Despite ongoing attempts by Württemberg government officials throughout the eighteenth century to discourage emigration by separatists, economic conditions in Württemberg and disenchantment with the Lutheran Church convinced many that immigration to America was the only answer for those seeking a stable livelihood and spiritual purity.[15]

Separatism appealed to radical German Pietists such as Rapp, because they believed Jesus Christ and the Holy Spirit supplied all the life one needed, whereas corrupt societies and institutional churches only served to compromise the process of sanctification.[16] Consequently, withdrawal from society was a means to preserve and increase one's holiness. This orientation was an offshoot of the Lutheran Pietists who emerged from the seventeenth-century international religious revivals led by German Philipp Jakob Spener, who himself culminated a hundred-year-old movement within Lutheranism that began with John Arndt (1555–1621), and was particularly influential in Württemberg, Rapp's home region.[17] Eventually the movement spread to England, where it influenced the Wesleys, and to North America, where it was a part of the Great Awakening of the 1730 and 1740s.[18] In one sense Pietism was, as one of the Harmonists' letters declared, a way "to become similar to its model Jesus," and to stamp out vices such as "cursing, drinking, cheating, [and] lying."[19] However, in a larger sense, it was also a response to the notion, born during the Scientific Revolution and the Enlightenment, that humans are independent actors, capable of discerning truth on their own through scientific, rationalistic inquiry. God naturally receded to the background as men and women discovered the moral and natural laws that governed the world.[20] Separatism appealed as a means for cultivating moral purity for Pietists living amid the wreckage of the Napoleonic Wars. The resulting destabilization of rural village life, combined with the growing frustration with an Enlightenment-influenced church, caused many to consider leaving their homelands. For the followers of Rapp, this Pietistic vision went beyond reforming the German church and envisioned the remaking of society itself.[21] As Rapp's group of Württemberg Pietists came into increasing conflict with the established Lutheran church over

20   *Part One: Christian Communal Capitalism*

doctrine, education, military service, sacraments, and spiritual authority, migration to America seemed like the only alternative.[22]

Pietism did not mandate separatism, nor did it lead inevitably to communal living. Rapp's interpretation of a few New Testament passages led his followers in this direction. Inspired by the apparent communal ethos of Christ's early followers, Rapp interpreted Acts 2:45 and 4:32–35 (as did other Christian communes in early America, including the Shakers, Moravians, and Seventh Day Baptists) to mean that the first-century church had forsaken personal property, and that this action should be a model for Christians, in all times:

> Acts 2:45: And sold their possessions and goods, and parted them to all men, as every man had need.
> Acts 4:32, 34–35: And the multitude of them that believed were of one heart and of one soul: neither said any of them that ought of the things which he possessed was his own; but they had all things common. Neither was there any among them that lacked: for as many as were possessors of lands or houses sold them, and brought the prices of the things that were sold, and laid them down at the apostles' feet: and distribution was made unto every man according as he had need.[23]

These New Testament passages formed the core of the Harmonists' vision of a perfected Christian city.

Separatism and communalism were important manifestations of the Harmonists' theology, but they are far from the only example of how religion shaped their lives. Enumerating his society's beliefs in 1798, Rapp listed the following articles of faith (summarized here for clarity):

1. Church should be modeled after the first church of apostles.
2. Baptism should be conducted after one comes to faith in Christ. (Harmonists, while generally skeptical of infant baptism, left the decision to parents.)
3. Communion should be held several times a year after a "love feast" and the resolution of all disagreements. (A love feast replicated the Last Supper of Christ and his disciples.)

Communal Industry 21

4. Education is important, but the intermixing of children at school is dangerous and thus it is better to "homeschool."
5. Confirmation should be dispensed with as the purchase of new, fine clothes for the child places an undue financial burden on poor parents and distracts children with worldly trappings. (Confirmation of an individuals' faith and church membership often occurs in formal services where participants wear new, expensive clothing.)
6. Support the government wholeheartedly but refuse to swear oaths.
7. Military service is impossible for true Christians.[24]

As historian of religion Alice Ott points out, these articles were less a conventional, comprehensive statement of faith, and more a clarification of the areas in which Rapp and his church were in conflict with local religious and political leadership.[25] In other words, Rapp's articles helped distinguish his group and separated them physically and materially from their neighbors. These were not just organizational "markers," such as uniforms, to the Harmonists. Rather, the Harmonists believed that the world was headed for imminent catastrophe, and that only the "true church" would survive the looming destruction. So, the articles served as "spiritual markers"—the most vital variety—indications of who would survive the coming apocalypse. Economic upheaval, the disintegration of the village social structure in Germany, and the French Revolutionary and Napoleonic Wars only seemed to reinforce the importance of separating from an unraveling world.[26]

This belief in a narrative of rapid global declension derived from the premillennial eschatology of the Harmony Society. The Württemberg Pietists who birthed the Harmonists were noted for their belief in a literal thousand-year millennium—a departure from the amillennial eschatology that had predominated for centuries in Christendom.[27] Premillennialism views the world through the lens of declension—the world is spiraling downward toward a final cacophony of earthquakes, floods, fire, evil, and an Antichrist figure. Jesus Christ then returns and sets things right, ruling for a thousand years before finally banishing evil to hell in a final judgment. Postmillennialism, on the other hand, views the world as improving and becoming more virtuous and Christian until Christ returns.[28]

22 *Part One: Christian Communal Capitalism*

Like his brand of Pietism more generally, George Rapp's premillennialism grew out of Philipp Jakob Spener's writings. For Rapp and other Pietists in Württemberg, the unrest in Europe produced by the French Revolutionary and Napoleonic Wars created the context for an emerging doctrine of utopian premillennialism.[29] Rapp applied mystical numerology to Revelation 13:18 to predict that Christ's return was imminent. For the Harmonists, this lent a sense of urgency to their efforts to establish an economic model that would be the template for human organization in the new millennium. What makes Rapp's premillennialism unique is that it was not as pessimistic as the outlook of most other premillennialists. He rejected absolute declension, believing humanity had improved in some ways over time, even pointing to the Constitution of the United States as proof.[30] All the same, he thought the return of Christ and his thousand-year reign on earth was imminent, and he did cite examples of cultural decline as signposts for this event.

Furthermore, Rapp and his followers were convinced they were fulfilling biblical prophecy, chiefly Revelation 12:1–6. This passage paints a scene in which a pregnant woman ("clothed with the sun") flees a vicious dragon by escaping into the wilderness, where God will have prepared a safe haven for the so-called Sunwoman and her child. Rapp's followers, like those of many other Pietist communities, identified with this apocalyptic woman, and were convinced this apocalyptic imagery prophesied how God would preserve them in America as a remnant to enjoy the coming millennial kingdom of Christ.[31] This picture of deliverance was powerful for pious believers, perhaps especially for the many women who made the trip, pregnant themselves, including the three that gave birth en route during the summer of 1805.[32]

ESTABLISHING CHRISTIAN COMMUNALISM: HARMONIE, PENNSYLVANIA

George Rapp and three other associates disembarked from the *Canton* in Philadelphia on October 7, 1803. Their purpose: to find a spot in America suitable for the immigration of Rapp's separatists—some one hundred and fifty families.[33] Rapp was immediately impressed with the quality of the land, the character of the people, the religious

Communal Industry 23

freedom, abundance of food, and financial opportunities. (Missing was any discussion of the displacement of Indigenous peoples that enabled such impressions. Harmony records are also devoid of evidence that the new settlers traded with or had other interactions with Native peoples.) He had abandoned his earlier designs to buy land in Louisiana, and now concentrated on securing property for the society in Virginia, Pennsylvania, Maryland, or Ohio.[34]

Rapp was particularly smitten with the lands of Ohio, calling on President Thomas Jefferson on July 12, 1804, and again in January 1806, to purchase forty thousand acres on the Muskingum River, but the plan failed for insufficient cash.[35] Rapp also petitioned Congress to have the time of payment extended for a tract of land in the Indiana Territory. Rapp was nearly successful in this gambit, as the Senate passed a bill to sell him a township near Vincennes, Indiana Territory, but after a vigorous debate, the House narrowly rejected the petition, with the Speaker casting a tiebreaking vote.[36] Rapp's failure to secure land did nothing to stem the tide of Württemberg Pietists immigrating to America, as three hundred of Rapp's followers onboard the *Aurora* landed in Baltimore July 4, 1804.[37] Subsequent ships arrived throughout the fall of 1804, carrying hundreds more of Rapp's followers, who along with other German separatists settled in several locations across Ohio and Pennsylvania. (Some, such as the community in Zoar, Ohio, became rivals.)[38] Obviously, if Rapp did not quickly find some land, his vision for a new communal society would perish. Fortunately for the Harmony story, a fellow German, D. B. Muller, provided a solution. On October 17, he persuaded Rapp not to settle as far west as Ohio, but instead to purchase 5,700 acres in Butler County, Pennsylvania, about twenty-five miles north of Pittsburgh. George Rapp could finally begin the project of building his first Sunwoman utopia on the banks of the Connoquenessing Creek: Harmonie.[39]

The seller, D. B. Muller, was a colorful character who had only recently bought the land from the U.S. government himself. Consequently, it required much work to turn it into a viable settlement. One of the first issues to tackle was an economic one: how to pay for the land purchased by Rapp on behalf of the society. Rapp himself did not possess assets to pay the one-third down payment of $3,405.91. In a preview of how the society would handle individual wealth, Rapp billed each member according to his means. Some paid for fifty acres, some twenty,

24 *Part One: Christian Communal Capitalism*

others over a hundred, while the most destitute paid nothing at all.[40] It is not completely clear when Rapp embraced communal ideas, as there is no evidence of such practice in Württemberg. While the other American Protestants described in this study had little trouble reconciling their faith and the acquisitive nature and excesses of the emerging market economy, George Rapp seems to have eventually found them in conflict with the teachings of Christ. His view of personal property rested on two foundations: first, on how the early church handled personal property, and second, on the group's theology of self-will.

Rapp's theology of self-will was straightforward: the annihilation of one's self-will was essential to become like Christ. Rapp absorbed this principle through the teachings of the eighteenth-century German revivalist Gerhard Tersteegen, who argued that egoism undermined the process of sanctification and inhibited one's relationship with God. Consequently, the answer for Tersteegen was radical action—one must deny all that was most important to the individual, including one's reputation, family/friends, and possessions, to find true communion with God.[41]

The emerging democratic and individualistic dynamics of early national-period America were not only in conflict with Tersteegen's teachings, they were especially troubling to Rapp, who as previously mentioned, taught Acts 4:32–35 as a model for perfected society. Consequently, the first of the Harmony Society's February 15, 1805, Articles of Agreement stipulated that members of the society would

> Deliver up, renounce, and transfer all our estate and property consisting of cash, land, cattle, or whatever else it may be, to George Rapp and his Society in Harmony, Butler County, Pennsylvania, as a free gift or donation, for the benefit and use of the congregation there, and bind ourselves on our part, as well as on the part of our heirs and descendants, to make free renunciation thereof, and to leave the same at the disposal of the superintendents of the congregation, as if we never had nor possessed the same.[42]

The second article continued with this communal spirit:

> George Rapp and his Society promise to supply the subscribers jointly and severally with all the necessaries of life, as lodging, meat,

Communal Industry 25

drink, and clothing, etc., and not only during their healthful days, but also when one or several of them should become sick or otherwise unfit for labor, they shall have and enjoy the same care and maintenance as before; and if, after a short or long period, the father or mother of a family should die, or be otherwise separated from the community and leave a family behind, none of those left behind shall be left widows or orphans, but receive and enjoy the same rights and care as long as they live or remain in the congregation, as well in sick as healthful days, the same as before, or as their circumstances or needs may require.[43]

For Rapp, the assumption that society was now unraveling shaped his attitude toward property, and it was supported by New Testament prophesy. Referencing such prophesy, Rapp wrote, "all must fall which is called property, within and without throughout, Christ had nothing except that he served his brethren. So naked, so poor, so deprived of all things inwardly and outwardly the church of Christ must stand . . . so that no one likes to possess or hold on to anything that is his own."[44] Practically, this apocalyptic view of private property took the form of deeds that entering members drew up, handing over their property to George Rapp & Associates.[45] For some, this amounted to a small fortune, while others entered nearly destitute and so had little to sacrifice.

Such a communal society was inevitably controversial. As one critic succinctly put it, Rapp preached a doctrine that "stinks."[46] Even within his own group, dissent over the communal structure of Harmonie induced a small number of followers to break with Rapp and form a rival settlement at Columbiana, Ohio, where they maintained individual property rights.[47] Among those who stayed, the spirit of communalism was embraced gradually, despite the presence of many poor and destitute members.[48] The Rapps were ruthless in their communalism, showing no flexibility in demanding that new members hand over all possessions, including their most sentimental and personally meaningful ones, such as pocket watches and firearms.[49]

Outside the community, the move toward communalism was a cause for alarm. When a committee of the Pennsylvania Legislature considered the Harmony Society's request for incorporation in 1807, it reacted with skepticism. Noting that the prohibition on property ownership was

26 *Part One: Christian Communal Capitalism*

potentially in violation of federal and state constitutions, the committee concluded that granting incorporation to the Harmonists would be "extremely impolitic, inasmuch as it would tend to damp and discourage that spirit of individual exertion and enterprize [sic], that self-dependence, that conscious dignity and consequence, which each individual should attach to himself in a free republic."[50] The Pennsylvania Legislature foreshadowed the classic capitalist's critique of communism: Who would work without the incentive of private property? Would anyone really work solely for the good of the whole? How could individuals act freely in the marketplace without legal protections of their property?

Not surprisingly, some Harmonie residents expressed second thoughts once faced with the reality of communal living. It did not take long for some members to decide that communal living under Rapp was not what they had expected. George Rapp lamented one such disgruntled family that "wanted a comfortable living," including meat, which was scarce in the society's leaner initial years. Departing members demanded the funds they contributed upon entering Harmony, which in the early years Rapp could not pay, even when he was so inclined. Frederick Rapp, George's son, wrote in 1822 that "poor" members were supposed to receive a donation upon leaving. The actual implementation of this was doubtful, and divisive. For the specific case above, George was able to repay the family departing over a lack of creature comforts thanks to a loan from a friend, something George attributed to divine deliverance.[51]

Families often sued to recoup their initial contributions to the communal treasury and unpaid wages for their years of work on behalf of Rapp & Associates.[52] The resulting disagreements sometimes lasted years. Consequently, the Rapps became much more careful in admitting new members because they felt too many people "deceived" them into believing they could adhere to their way of life, only to find "the path to follow Jesus too narrow."[53] Not only was the prospect of reimbursing departing members a problem, but Frederick lamented the time lost in training the members to be productive, skilled workers.

George Rapp struggled to tame the sense of entitlement of the largest contributors to the common treasury, so much so that when the group eventually migrated to Indiana, he had the records of initial property ownership destroyed.[54] This act served to erase, symbolically and literally, the financial profile of members' pre-Harmony lives. Furthermore,

Communal Industry 27

the elimination of the records made it much harder for those leaving the society to reclaim their pre-Harmony property, something the Rapps strenuously resisted, although there is some evidence the Rapps maintained a secret record of accounts, known only to themselves and a few trusted members.[55]

As if communalism was not controversial enough, following a revival within Harmony in 1807–1808, George began preaching that one could only achieve full sanctification through celibacy. (This revival was primarily one of deepening religiosity and spiritual commitment, rather than conversion, as was the case with the many other revivals of this period, such as the Cane Ridge and Stone-Campbell movements.) Rapp advanced the ideas, common among Philadelphia Pietists who followed the teachings of Jakob Böhme, that sex organs were a result of the Fall of Adam, and so sexual activity likewise was emblematic of humanity's fallen nature. Although not going as far as to forbid marriage and sex, Rapp's message was clear: those who were "most pious" should forsake marriage, or sexual relations with one's spouse if already married.[56] Unlike the Shakers, celibacy never became a requirement, and Rapp continued to perform weddings. Approximately 250 weddings took place at Harmony in the years after Rapp began to preach against marriage and sexual relations. Marriages exploded from the late 1820s to the mid-1830s as the second generation of Harmonists came of age (see figure 1.1) and rejected Rapp's marriage doctrine. Marriages continued at a significant rate until the second half of the nineteenth century, reflecting the maturity of Harmony's membership.[57]

Ultimately, celibacy functioned as something of a higher ethic that the most serious and pious Harmonists might aspire to embrace. Consequently, some married couples continued to live together in the same house, while forsaking the sexual aspect of their relationship. Rapp's teaching was that celibacy elevated one to the level of a priest who would help lead in Christ's millennial kingdom.[58] In any case, the record of births in Harmony was robust after 1807, slowly tapering as the membership aged and fewer new members joined after the 1820s, reinforcing the fact that the practice of celibacy was never mandatory.

Like their fellow Christian communal capitalists, the Shakers, the Harmonists' sexual ethic soon attracted that attention of outsiders and was added to the growing curiosity over what sort of community the

28   *Part One: Christian Communal Capitalism*

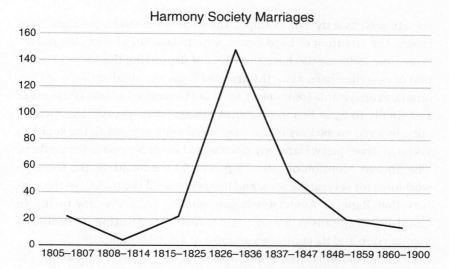

FIGURE 1.1 Harmony Society marriages. By author, data from Eileen English, *Demographic Directory of The Harmony Society*, 2nd ed. (Clinton, NY: Richard W. Couper Press, 2016), 257–267.

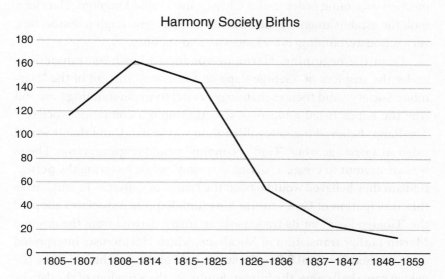

FIGURE 1.2 Harmony Society births. By author, data from Eileen English, *Demographic Directory of The Harmony Society*, 2nd ed. (Clinton, NY: Richard W. Couper Press, 2016), 177–192.

society was, exactly. For example, the society's sexual reputation even caught the attention of Lord Byron, who poked fun of it in *Don Juan*.[59] Over time, celibacy did have the effect of depressing the society's addition of new members, as births dropped from 262 children born at Harmonie, Pennsylvania (1805–1814), to 69 at Harmonie, Indiana (1815–1824), and finally to 25 at Economy, Pennsylvania (1825–1830).[60] Skeptical of outsiders and suspicious of their potential commitment to the society's vision of "true" piety, Harmony never added many new outside members. The uneven adoption of celibacy protected the health of the society's workforce for several decades, and it was not until the middle of the century that Rapp & Associates began shifting from manufacturing to investment capitalism, a pragmatic transition reflecting its declining membership and its enormous amount of available capital.[61]

Furthermore, Harmony never expected to be worrying about the perpetuation of its society in the 1850s, as Rapp taught that the return of Christ was eminent. So, little question was ever given to how the society would replace dying (or departing) members. This expectation of an imminent millennium did not affect their approach to business. Since they expected their "divine economy" would form the basis of the new purified economic order under Christ's millennial kingdom, Harmony took the establishment of their business enterprise, Rapp & Associates, very seriously, building it for longevity and stability.

From the beginning, Harmony conducted business transactions under the auspices of "George Rapp & Associates" instead of the "Harmony Society," and their eschatology is vital to understanding how and why the Rapps fused a business structure onto a communal society.[62] The Rapps believed the new millennium was at hand, and that it would usher in a new age when "God's economy" would reign supreme. Theirs was an attempt to create a "divine economy" while fostering the perfectionism they believed would hasten the return of Christ.[63] To emphasize this anticipation of God's future kingdom, Rapp & Associates adopted the "Golden Rose" for its trademark, an image derived from the original Martin Luther translation of Micah 4:8, which Harmonists interpreted as, "And thou Tower of Eden, the stronghold of the daughter of Zion, thy golden rose shall come, the former dominion, the Kingdom of the daughter of Jerusalem."[64] Here, the Harmonists were adopting the imagery of

30 *Part One: Christian Communal Capitalism*

FIGURE 1.3 Golden Rose lintel. Photo by author, New Harmony, IN, June 27, 2018.

a future blessing and millennium embraced by other eighteenth-century separatist and radical Pietists. Harmonists also regarded the Golden Rose as a symbol of true believers, which enabled them to brand their consumer goods with their piety.[65]

Outsiders consistently struggled to comprehend this union of religion and business, incredulous that they could coexist in "harmony." Instead, critics suspected Harmony was far from a holy utopia, but in fact was dominated by "avarice, envy, hatred, disunity and even the most disgraceful vice of grasping for yourself the property of others."[66] Much of this criticism derived from the character of George Rapp himself, a man powerful in personality and stature—there was no question who was in charge at Harmonie. He was the spiritual foundation as well as unquestioned head proprietor. It was probably inevitable that he would make enemies through the course of building his holy commune. Critics accused Rapp of bullying, greed, megalomania, and even fraud—going so far as to use anti-Semitic slurs to describe their behavior.[67] As Moravian Jacob Eckensperger wrote to his Harmonist brother Friedrich (elected an elder in 1832), "I would rather live among the Indians, there

Communal Industry   31

I would not see such horrors as among you."[68] In an otherwise glowing account of a visit to the society in 1831, the German-American botanist David von Schweinitz described how George ruled "absolutely," and claimed that he "speaks in a rough and commanding tone with everybody."[69] As the head proprietor, not only did Rapp oversee the religious and economic decisions of the commune, he also determined the shape and character of the workforce. As an autocratic leader, he possessed the absolute power to evict persons if they did not adhere to his theology, religious discipline, or work ethic. Sometimes this provoked violence. Butler County records vaguely refer to a "riot" in 1807 when the Rapps possibly tried to forcibly evict someone from the village. Frederick pled not guilty, but was found guilty of fomenting a riot (but not guilty of assault), and assessed a hundred-dollar fine.[70] While violence may seem incongruous with a pious commune, George's attitude toward prospective members who did not pull their own weight and/or demonstrate proper piety could be starkly dismissive at best, if not cold and cruel.[71]

The departure of one member did not always include the exit of the entire family, however, and parents mourned the breakup of their families in language that often painted the Harmony Society in an unpleasant, even cultish light: "The so-called Harmonie Society I left four years ago . . . Rapp, this concentrated monk, allows himself to be honored as divine . . . and when I left them my wife stayed back, my children I had to take with force . . . Rapp has built a silver wall around his slave colony and a person must be happy to get away with empty hands."[72] Jacob Schieck married his wife at Harmonie in 1806 before fleeing the society in 1812. After Schieck absconded with his family, his wife left him to return to Harmonie, where she filed for divorce. In this quote, Schieck, who worked as a shepherd and tanner at Harmonie, underscores the fact that some families disintegrated, as well as the degree to which Rapp used the proceeds of Rapp & Associates to fight his battles in court.[73] Mercy and grace rarely described George Rapp. Furthermore, Rapp's imposing stature reinforced his dominant personality; he was described by a visitor as "tall, above six feet, his whole frame erect and robust, his countenance ruddy, his long hair and flowing beard perfectly white, and he looked at once the most vigorous and most venerable man at eighty-four that could be seen or conceived."[74]

32   *Part One: Christian Communal Capitalism*

He may have been the head of Rapp & Associates, but George did not have a keen business sense. For this, he leaned on his sole business partner and adopted son, Frederick. Johann Friederich Reichert moved to Iptingen on July 9, 1798. Not long after his move, he was made treasurer of Rapp's church and eventually adopted by Rapp, changing his name on the voyage to the United States. Early on, it was clear that Frederick possessed the superior business acumen, and although his official role was "society treasurer," in actuality he was what in the twenty-first century one would call the chief operating or financial officer of Rapp & Associates.[75] While George Rapp was the unquestioned leader, Frederick oversaw the daily business of the commune and its enterprises, including ordering supplies, collecting debts, developing new ventures, and staying informed of economic conditions in America and Europe.[76] In fact, he was so trusted that when Harmony prepared to sell its second location in Indiana, George directed all the members of the society to give Frederick power of attorney to conduct the sale by himself. The power of attorney is interesting because it contains a long list of signatures by all the "subscribers" of Rapp & Associates, sketching out a principle of joint ownership, albeit one that leaned heavily on centralized decision making.[77] In reality, Harmony members were not involved in the society's finances and, legally speaking, they had almost no claim to the company's assets, something that was litigated numerous times over the ensuing years.

The Rapp & Associates records bear witness to Frederick as the sole manager, with an amazing attention to detail, leaving behind thousands of memorandums, including detailed notes on business contacts. Frederick established a precise, shrewd business culture that persisted even after his death. For example, an entry from 1835 (one year after his passing) outlines the important contacts at a cotton factory, including the manager, head of the machine shop, and head of the counting room, whom he described as "very kind." Other notations assessed the mechanical performance and experimentation of Harmony and its competitors in the textile sector.[78] Frederick imbibed much of his adopted father's persona. His reputation outside the society was that of an aggressive businessman who built Rapp & Associates into a highly successful and efficient business enterprise through an astute business sense and cold, hard bargaining. Despite the society's pious mission, Frederick had no problem using power plays and tough bargaining tactics (including lawsuits) to advance his economic goals.[79]

The aforementioned power of attorney was unusual for Rapp & Associates, which in general was not very transparent regarding its decision making and finances, in keeping with George's leadership style. Two examples include the 1805 Articles of Agreement and a contested 1825 statement by Frederick disclaiming ownership of property and business conducted in his name. Evidence suggests that the Rapps postdated the 1805 articles for an 1821 lawsuit against Harmony by a former member, while George created and registered the 1825 disclaimer after Frederick's death to reassure the society during a period of crisis.[80] These foundational documents reveal the extent to which George Rapp viewed himself as a biblical patriarch, invested with unquestioned spiritual and temporal authority on all matters—including business and economic ones. He did not think he owed any explanations of his decisions or actions to the members of the society, and in moments of acute crisis he used his patriarchal position to justify his means.

Despite its lack of transparency, Rapp & Associates was a well-organized and clearly structured operation. Below Frederick, superintendents directed artisans, factory workers, and farmers. Family units lived in simple houses situated on acre lots. Families maintained their own milk cows, hogs, and poultry, while the society furnished all else. The output of a family's labor, excepting that involving one's livestock, went into the society's common economy. Frederick stressed the community's solidarity and unity, claiming that, since "the interest of each lies in the whole," each must work "according to ability."[81] The superintendents also signed paperwork when workers needed clothing or other personal items, so the individual could "purchase" the item from the society's members-only store (it also had a public store). Of note, the name "Rapp" never appears in the store's account records, so it seems as though George and Frederick were living under different terms than the rest of the society. Interestingly, the many disbursements in the accounts are listed under men's names, suggesting they were signing for their families. Although this implies patriarchal gender subjugation, the experience of women in Harmony was a complex and often contradictory one.[82]

Below the superintendents were the family units.[83] At the Indiana site, the society experimented with "community houses," or *Bruderhäuser*,

34   *Part One: Christian Communal Capitalism*

for individuals; evidence suggests they were single young adults, perhaps the children of founding members or those made single from the disease that plagued the Indiana town in its early years. Observers noted that "galleries run through the center of them," with female apartments on one side and males on the other, each opening into one another. Eating took place communally, with approximately forty individuals living in one building.[84] Later, in the society's third location, this system became even more communal, and even the milk from the family cows went into a common reservoir for distribution.[85]

This common economy quickly proved productive. Within five years, the Harmonists (who now numbered one hundred and forty families) had built more than 50 log homes, a 220-foot bridge, 2 barns, 2 gristmills (one with a three-quarter-mile racetrack), an inn/tavern, 2 oil mills, a tannery and dryer's shop, 2 brick storehouses, 2 sawmills, a brewery, a fulling mill, a beehouse, a large brick wine cellar, and a hemp mill. In a symbolic union of the Harmonists' spiritual and material objectives, the upstairs of the church doubled as a granary capable of storing several thousand

FIGURE 1.4 Community House No. 2. Photo by author, New Harmony, IN, June 27, 2018.

Communal Industry 35

bushels of grain.[86] This was also reflective of Harmony's initial focus on agriculture, exporting corn, potatoes, wheat, whiskey, and wine, which it augmented with income from the contract work of its skilled laborers. These included 12 shoemakers, 6 tailors, 12 weavers, 3 wheelwrights, 5 coopers, 6 blacksmiths, 2 nail smiths, 3 rope makers, 10 carpenters, 4 cabinetmakers, 2 saddlers, 2 wagon makers, 12 masons, 2 potters, 1 soap boiler, 1 hatter, 1 doctor, and 1 apothecary. Hiring out these tradesmen to the surrounding county was an important early source of revenue, bringing the society $3,800.59 in 1808 and $5,841.27 in 1809. Since agricultural endeavors such as wine and whiskey production only yielded $670 in 1808, the hiring-out income was especially significant, amounting to 67 percent of Rapp & Associates' total income of $5,676.47 in 1808.[87] The output of the tradesmen was also vitally important in the cash-poor early national-period West, as Rapp used their output to trade and barter for commodities such as iron and gudgeons (cylindrical devices used to hang shutters, among other applications).[88] In fact, by 1809 the society was proving increasingly profitable in its agricultural and trades work, although the decision to produce whiskey garnered predictable criticism, as some outsiders concluded the Harmonists were "going down stream with the corrupted world, in order to get rich soon."[89] However, whiskey was an important bartering item in western Pennsylvania, and the Harmonists were never participants with the broader Protestant reform movements of the early national period. Temperance or abstinence from alcohol was not their concern.[90]

The year 1810 was significant because it marked Harmony's emergence from indebtedness and its entry into the textile market, with the purchase of Merino sheep and the construction of a wool factory that, when completed, contained a wool-carding machine, six spinning jennies, and sixteen looms for the production of wool cloth.[91] In less than two years, regional herdsmen were petitioning the society to process their wool (the society had already been milling its own).[92] Frederick was demonstrating his increasing expertise in evaluating the quality of wool, while purchasing a cotton-carding machine to expand production into that fabric as well.[93]

Recognizing the limitations of his technical expertise and the need to improve the production efficiency and quality of the Harmony textiles, Frederick sought out expert instruction—specifically "a good European

36   *Part One: Christian Communal Capitalism*

workman who understands the Cloth manufactoring [*sic*] business from the Beginning to the End of it."[94] The expansion into textile manufacturing caused the Rapps to grow increasingly concerned with their access to the wider regional and East Coast market. Specifically, they wanted access to the all-important western Pennsylvania postal routes. From the request that the postmaster general establish a post office in Harmonie, to their petition for the creation of postal routes that would include the town, the Rapps understood that the postal service was vitally important to those who wanted access to the financial information necessary for success in the expanding market economy.[95]

By 1811, the Rapps' large and attractive homes reflected the material success of Rapp & Associates (see figures 1.5 and 1.6). In a trend that suggested a hierarchy within the otherwise egalitarian society, prominent members also built new homes that were larger, more comfortable, and more handsome than their original cabins. Meanwhile, a visitor's account from August of that year, John Melish's widely read *Travels in the United States of America*, made the commune famous in America, Great Britain, and Europe when it was published in 1812. Melish detailed how Harmony now consisted of approximately 9,000 acres (2,500 of them cultivated), 800 persons (100 of which were farmers), and had dramatically increased its net worth from approximately $20,000 to $220,000.[96] Frederick consistently embraced technological innovations in the textile industry. By the end of 1813, he was financing the construction of a first-of-its-kind sheering machine, one that was the envy of other manufacturers.[97] At the same time, he was working to obtain a fire engine and purchase a significant share in the Bassenheim Furnace and Iron Works (a water-powered cold-blast charcoal iron furnace located on Connoquenessing Creek).[98]

By fall 1813, Pennsylvania's governor was joining Melish in admiring Harmony's combination of "practical Christianity" and "flourishing manufacturers."[99] Frederick used this growing reputation of Rapp & Associates to establish relationships with other prominent early national-period businessmen, such as the du Ponts, who knew Frederick Rapp as the "owner of the Cloth Factory at Harmony."[100] As a sign of the growing reputation of Harmony's textiles, Frederick fielded an increasing number of requests to buy his sheep and process the region's wool (from as far away as Kentucky).[101]

Communal Industry 37

FIGURE 1.5 George Rapp's Harmonie, PA, home. Photo by author, June 8, 2017.

FIGURE 1.6 Frederick Rapp's Harmonie, PA, home. Photo by author, June 8, 2017.

Concurrently, Rapp & Associates was building a network of agents to market its textile products in the major markets of the eastern United States. Early attempts to market its wool cloth in Baltimore met resistance, as merchants deemed the Harmony products too expensive and not of the right type to be competitive.[102] However, Harmony woolens found an eager market in Philadelphia, at least when their colors conformed to current fashion.[103] Additionally, the proximity to Pittsburgh made it a natural destination for Harmony manufactures (iron as well as textiles).[104] Frederick continued to engage the more resistant markets, such as Baltimore's textile and whiskey sectors. Faced with skeptical merchants, he argued that Harmony's textiles had acquired "such a good renown . . . that it was sold till now as fast as we been able to make it."[105] Such was the duality of Harmony: a community that strove to separate physically from the surrounding culture and thereby preserve its spiritual purity, while at the same time pursuing business opportunities aggressively, keeping abreast of current events, political as well as economic.[106] However, navigating the tension between assertively trading *with* the world while living separate *from* it was difficult. And so, despite their growing material success the Rapps began contemplating a move westward, as recent developments caused the Rapps to worry that the purity of their holy experiment was at risk.

Communal Industry   39

CHAPTER TWO

Industry on the Frontier

Harmonie, Indiana

The first hint that Harmony leadership was pondering a westward move appears in reports George Rapp sent to Frederick in April 1814.[1] George was away investigating new sites for the society, because as Frederick wrote two years later in reflection, western Pennsylvania had "quite a few inhabitants and no more land could be purchased except at very high prices . . . the climate was not quite suitable to us because the winter was somewhat too long which made the raising of sheep and viniculture somewhat difficult."[2] Additionally, Frederick lamented Harmonie's location twelve miles from the nearest navigable waters, which made it more difficult to market its surplus produce and manufactured goods.[3] Critics, however, mused that the real issue was that George Rapp feared losing control of his followers as the surrounding population increased around Harmonie.[4] The tension the Rapps felt between market access and the desire to preserve the purity and holiness of the society was a lasting tension for Harmony, as it was for Christian communal capitalism in general. For such groups, the desire to hold "corrupting" influences at bay was a fundamental goal. Yet for Harmony, this was particularly problematic since the creation of a robust manufacturing "divine economy" was not only a material goal, it was a spiritual one as well. It would do no good for the society to become materially wealthy and yet lose the holiness and "special" status it held as God's chosen remnant to restart human civilization after the apocalypse. Conversely, their definition of a "divine economy" meant efficient and balanced agriculture, industry, and trade, undergirded by a religious system that projected capitalist behaviors while internalizing communal attitudes toward property and wealth accumulation.

It was up to the Rapps to manage this tension between market integration and cultural purity as best they could. Moving every so often seemed to be the answer. Harmony could regain physical distance from the "corrupting" influences of American society, while taking advantage of cheap land (thanks to the violent dispossession of Indigenous peoples) and the expanding market economy that resulted from the growth of transportation networks, such as the National Road and the Erie Canal. In fact, this was a period of tremendous expansion for America's manufacturers. Domestic production grew approximately eight times in value and twelve times in volume from the time Harmony moved to Indiana to the middle of the century. Additionally, the emergence of an expansive domestic trade network helped drive a 230 percent increase in foreign trade. In the early nineteenth century, household manufacturing dominated this production, supplemented by artisans and journeymen. Small, locally owned water-powered mills augmented this household-craftsman system, while a few produced textiles and iron products that supplied not only their localities but regional and overseas markets as well. Two-thirds of Americans wore household-manufactured clothing during the War of 1812, demonstrating the local nature of this system prior to its expansion. The emergence of the domestic (or putting-out) system, where merchants supplied families with raw materials that women and children worked into pieces the merchant then assembled (increasingly in conjunction with the emerging factory system), served as a bridge to the full-fledged factory system that emerged in the second half of the nineteenth century. However, the advent of laborsaving machinery, steam engines, streamlined manufacturing processes, market-oriented production, the concept of limited liability, expanding general incorporation, and the emergence of the factory system fundamentally transformed the nature of work and production. The Rapps comprehended this shift in the economy and embraced it, riding a wave of manufacturing expansion that by mid-century had nearly eliminated the household-craftsman manufacturing system in many counties of America. For those such as Rapp & Associates who focused on the textile

Industry on the Frontier 41

sector in this manufacturing expansion, the growth of the cotton slave system underpinned the entire edifice.[5]

By moving westward, the Harmonists were following the lead of another Christian communal capitalist group, the Shakers, who had established communities just north of Vincennes, Indiana Territory, in Warren County, Ohio (northeast of Cincinnati), and in Logan and Mercer Counties, Kentucky.[6] On May 9, 1814, after touring sites in Ohio and Kentucky that failed to satisfy him, George and his scouting team of three Harmonists finally executed a series of purchases for land on the banks of the Wabash River that would become the society's spacious new commune in the Indiana Territory.[7] According to Frederick, the determining factor in selecting the new location was a place where "culture, trade, and situation would offer more advantages for factories of various type."[8] George assured Frederick that the Wabash River would afford them access to New Orleans (and from there to ports in the West Indies, Britain, and Europe).[9] A trusted member of the society accompanying George on the advance scouting mission, John L. Baker, also stressed the nearby coal banks and potential for waterworks, wood for building, and the need to buy up as much land as possible before the society's advertised move caused land prices to rise prohibitively.[10] Frederick responded that they should buy land on both sides of the Wabash (which included the Illinois Territory) in order to "have the command of the River."[11] Harmony was certainly not moving from western Pennsylvania to abandon the market. If anything, it was simply doing something other ambitious folk were already considering: taking advantage of the perceived opportunity of the West, fueled by a relentless process of Indigenous dispossession.[12]

It was several months before Frederick sold the original Harmonie to a man named Abraham Ziegler, for a sum well below the advertised sale price. Frederick had initially sought $135,000 (one-quarter down) to be paid over four years, with a 10 percent discount if the buyer used cash for the purchase.[13] Officially, the deal was for $100,000, although Ziegler never made good on the full amount, causing some manner of financial difficulties for Harmony.[14] Frederick even renegotiated the terms with Ziegler in 1822.[15] It was a bad time to sell, as money was especially hard to come by thanks to the disruption of the War of 1812 and the closure of the Bank of the United States in 1811.[16] The resulting dispute lasted into the 1830s, with David Shields recommending that Frederick send

42 *Part One: Christian Communal Capitalism*

Ziegler a "pressing, nay a threatening letter" to encourage him to pay up.[17] Frederick took Shields's advice; additionally, he considered filing suit against Ziegler, although he never followed through with that measure.[18]

After opening a store (licensed by the Indiana Territory in December 1814),[19] the Rapps' first priorities were linking the new Harmonie to the federal postal service and rerouting water sources to serve Rapp & Associates' manufacturing aims. Congress eventually obliged the former by altering the Vincennes to Shawneetown postal route so that it passed through Harmonie (April 29, 1816), and it established a post office at Harmonie that opened in early September 1816.[20] The Rapps felt a keen sense of urgency to get their manufacturing operations up and running as customers were still looking to Harmony for their textile needs, even as Rapp & Associates was nowhere near ready to resume production, thanks in part to a deadly fever outbreak in the fall of 1814.[21] Although by March 1815, the new settlement had built log homes for every family, tilled more than eight hundred acres, including orchards and vineyards, resumed alcohol distillation (with a machine powered by two dogs), and started construction of a sawmill, textile production was still a ways off.[22] Additionally, the seasonal unpredictability of neighboring creeks proved problematic, and drove Frederick to purchase a steam engine from Pittsburgh to power Harmonie's mills.[23] The seasons were not only unpredictable but much hotter than in western Pennsylvania (driving the construction of a second church when the first church proved too hot in summer months).[24]

FIGURE 2.1 First Harmonie, Indiana, church. Sketched by Charles Alexandre Lesueur, resident of New Harmony from 1825 to 1836. The second church with a Greek cross plan is in the background. Wikimedia Commons, https://commons.wikimedia.org/ wiki/File:New_Harmony_May_1826.

Industry on the Frontier

FIGURE 2.2 Second Harmony, Indiana, church. Sketched by Charles Alexandre Lesueur, resident of New Harmony from 1825 to 1836. Ewell Sale Stewart Library, Academy of Natural Sciences, Philadelphia, PA, by arrangement.

Frederick quickly realized that doing business in the West was different from participating in the market economy of western Pennsylvania, with an established city like Pittsburgh nearby. Frederick's business correspondence and records are replete with frustration over the confusing, unreliable, and occasionally nefarious currency landscape of the Indiana Territory.[25] Specie money was notoriously difficulty to come by (there was approximately $28,000 worth of currency in the United States in 1800), and what coin there was in the U.S. economy was 60 percent foreign (mostly Spanish) in the 1820s. This foreign coin augmented a confusing array of U.S. coinage, fiat (paper) money, bills of exchange, and promissory notes.[26]

Cities such as Boston, Philadelphia, New York, and Baltimore all had well-developed markets with stable, productive financial systems. On the market's periphery, the situation was very different. For example, attempts to open banks that would service rural Pennsylvania met opposition in the state legislature, which refused to charter applicants such as the Bank of Pittsburgh. Continuing under a different name, these "illegal," private, and unchartered banks attempted to fill the growing demand for credit outside of the eastern urban centers. This demand was partly met by the Omnibus Banking Act of 1814 that chartered forty-one new banks throughout Pennsylvania.[27] Curiously, this was the moment Harmony chose to leave the state for a less stable situation in the Indiana Territory. Moreover, Harmony had decided to move during the economic crisis brought on by the War of 1812. This move came amid a blockade of American ports by the Royal Navy, the burning of Washington, DC, and a run on mid-Atlantic banks, who suspended specie payments (refusing to redeem notes for gold or silver) until reserve levels could meet demand.[28] Only after the War of 1812 did the U.S. economy recover and enter a boom phase that would last until the Panic of 1819.

The First Bank of the United States' charter expired in 1811, leaving a gap until the establishment of the Second Bank of the United States in 1816. In 1800, there were 29 state banks, most in major cities, but by 1811 there were 125, then 300 by 1816, and by 1820, there were 327.[29] Indiana was especially unfortunate, as the absence of a bank charter encouraged wildcat banks (uncharted entities) in the West. Although scholars argue over the definition and prevalence, these banks were established in remote regions (hence the name, since wildcats were common in such places), and they printed banknotes in excess of their specie holdings. At some point, after accumulating enough specie, the proprietor absconded, usually once too many people tried to redeem the bank's notes.[30]

One such institution was established in western Pennsylvania after the departure of the Harmonists, and threatened to sully their good financial reputation. A German minister named Jacob Schnee established the bank under the name the "Harmony Institute," so chosen because of the reputation for honesty that Rapp's group had established locally (see figure 2.3). Schnee had purchased a portion of the original Harmonie property from Abraham Ziegler after failing to purchase the property outright from Frederick. Schnee was not much better than Ziegler at honoring financial obligations, and his notes were quickly denounced as worthless, and his bank failed "monstrously." He ultimately fled west to Indiana in 1818 to escape his creditors.[31] Such instability in the credit landscape was the main reason Frederick became a stockholder in the Bank of Vincennes (which became the State Bank of Indiana in January 1817).[32] Surely trying to stabilize the local credit system, Frederick was also

Industry on the Frontier 45

FIGURE 2.3 Three- and five-dollar notes, issued by the "Harmony Institute" (1817). Note "F. Rapp" and "G. Rapp" on the respective bills. Image courtesy of Old Economy Village, Ambridge, PA.

heavily involved in organizing local branches of the state bank, including the Farmers' Bank of Harmony.[33]

While the establishment of Second Bank of the United States in December 1816 led to the stabilization of the monetary system overall (specie payments resumed in the spring of 1817), Rapp & Associates' experience with banking and trade in Indiana was anything but stable. Indiana was one of several states that retaliated against the opening of Second Bank branches, leading to the *McCulloch v. Maryland* decision that upheld the federal government's prerogative to establish such entities over states' objections. Most impactful for the Rapps was how some western banks continued to resist the Second Bank policies, as cautious Americans feared the expansion of credit, banknotes, and speculation that characterized the years of 1817 and 1818.[34]

Frederick's involvement in the state banking system is particularly interesting given the society's misgivings toward lending and interest. In a letter dated December 3, 1821, Frederick declined to extend a loan to the founder of Vandalia, Illinois, explaining the practice was "against our Rule."[35] In another instance, Frederick refused a loan to the governor of Indiana, even though just days before Frederick had proposed to loan the State of Indiana his stock in the Bank of Vincennes. This was quite a scheme: Rapp's proposal was to loan back to the state its own bank's stock in payment of debt owed the state bank.[36] A few years later, Rapp was again lending money to the state at nearly 15 percent interest.[37] Evidently, the Rapps were not averse to extending loans to public institutions, just private individuals. Even close business associates, relatives of George Rapp, and longtime society friends need not apply.[38] Eventually, Frederick even dispensed with the society's practice during its Indiana days of extending credit to its business partners.[39] The practice of institutional loaning was not just a product of the financial landscape of Indiana, but continued after the society's eventual move back east, such as when Frederick loaned the City of Pittsburgh $20,000 and the City of Wheeling $8,000.[40] Frederick offered fiscal reasons behind the lending policy: Rapp & Associates preferred to reinvest its capital into their community, rather than loan it out to interested individuals, especially given the poor state of the economy in the 1820s.[41]

Ultimately, more important than biblical rules on lending was the Rapps' view of the end times. Their eschatology saw little benefit in helping neighbors or their community in general, since they would not survive to see the new millennium. Instead, since Harmony would rebuild the new "divine economy," it needed to be as robust and well positioned as possible to make its way in the remade world to come. This was their spiritual duty, and it evidently outweighed New Testament imperatives to help one's neighbor. This indifference toward Harmony's materially struggling neighbors would lead to friction—conflict that played a significant role in pushing the society back eastward.

Rapp, like other entrepreneurs in the Northwest Territory, was also forced to deal with the reality that transportation of the items and supplies necessary for industrial work was often painfully slow. The general absence of roads, turnpikes, and canals in 1805 accentuated this problem for western firms like Rapp & Associates. What few roads did exist

Industry on the Frontier   47

were of poor quality, consisting of bumpy dirt (or mud) paths containing the occasional tree stump. (Wood plank roads did not appear in America until 1844, and never caught on due to the cost and upkeep required.) Consequently, access to water that was accessible for as much of the year as possible was essential, a fact the Rapps understood all too well. Steamboats did make an impact on the western rivers, with sixty-nine such vessels working the waterways by 1820, prompting the Rapps to consider building their own. The roads of the early nineteenth century typically ran north–south, not east–west, as would benefit western firms like Rapp & Associates. Despite the obvious need, there was little consensus (or available funds) at either the national or state levels for such projects until the construction of the Erie Canal sparked competing state-level internal improvement projects.[42]

The example of Rapp & Associates' attempts to procure a steam engine and replacement carding machine soon after setting up manufacturing operations in the Indiana Territory illustrates the logistical challenges it faced. River ice impeded the delivery of the steam engine, and when replacement pieces for his carding machine were not included on the boat carrying the steam engine, Frederick resigned himself to the likelihood that his carding machine would sit idle another four to six weeks. Even this proved to be false optimism, as the engine did not become operational until mid-May 1816, limiting Rapp & Associates to finishing cloth it brought from the Pennsylvania Harmonie.[43]

In fact, just getting a simple letter to and from the new Harmonie was an often surprisingly slow process (especially in the winter), as Frederick's associates discovered when a letter he mailed on January 6, 1816, did not arrive in Pittsburgh until February 9, 1816.[44] Five weeks was fast compared with the saga of the letter he sent another associate on January 17, 1816, which did not arrive at its destination in western Pennsylvanian until April 22, 1816![45] Unprofessional postmasters and letter carriers only served to exacerbate the situation.[46] By 1822, Frederick had grown so sick of the poor mail service that he petitioned Indiana's governor to intervene because "the injury occasioned through neglect of Postmasters & Mail carriers in this Western District is very great to its inhabitants and particularly to those engaged in Mercantile business."[47] For businessmen such as Frederick, timely postal service was of the utmost importance in the expanding market economy. This commercial imperative animated Frederick's complaint to Governor Jonathan Jennings: "Not long since I recd. Two Letters at different times from Cincinnati (Ohio) one four-and the other five Month on the Way coming, Each containing urging matters of great importance ... at present we have been for three Weeks without a Mail from Corydon, and are thereby debarred of every Necessary Commercial advise [sic] from the East."[48]

Even more significantly, moving west did not solve Harmony's central tension in trying to find the proper balance between living "in the world" but not "of the world." In 1816, the society increasingly involved itself in matters "of the world" when Frederick was elected to represent Gibson County at the Indiana Territory constitutional convention.[49] His role at the convention included serving on the "committee relative to the executive department" and "committee relative to the militia"—the latter position especially ironic considering Frederick frequently paid the territorial exemption tax to excuse male members of the society between the ages of eighteen and forty-five from military service (which they opposed on religious grounds).[50] Frederick also played a role in picking the site of Indiana's new capital city, serving on the board of commissioners that ultimately selected Indianapolis.[51] This foray into politics was not an exception, but a consistent trait of the Rapps in Indiana and their second Pennsylvania site, although their political involvement usually came to focus on economic issues.

Frederick's voting record at the convention also reflected the society's attitude toward slavery. Despite Rapp & Associates' production of cotton textiles being enmeshed in the Atlantic slave system, Harmony embraced antislavery positions publicly. During its time in Indiana, Harmony admitted several enslaved persons under indentured contracts, setting them free after their terms of service. The society treated them like indentured German immigrants (whose contracts Harmony assumed from Atlantic merchants), with at least one family of former enslaved persons remaining in the society upon the fulfilment of their contracts.[52] Like other northern manufacturers, Rapp & Associates took advantage of the southern market, listening to advice on the proper cloth to market to plantations, including the provisioning of enslaved persons themselves.[53]

While serving as a delegate to the state constitutional convention, Frederick Rapp took a public stance against slavery. Unfortunately, the

Industry on the Frontier   49

convention did not record minutes of its debates, although a failed amendment to the constitution's article regarding revisions further reinforced Harmony's abolitionist position. The amendment sought to explicitly prevent future revision to the state's ban on slavery by stating the convention's opinion that slavery should never be introduced into the state. Frederick voted in the minority on this amendment (13–29), as well as a similar, follow-up amendment that also failed to pass (16–26). These public votes helped establish the Harmony position on slavery, even as they failed to acknowledge any inconsistency in Rapp & Associates' profiteering as beneficiaries of the slave-supported textile boom.[54]

At the same time, the Harmony archives are generally devoid of much reflection or commentary on slavery. For all the incredible amount of correspondence Harmony produced, no one seems to have spilled much ink worrying about the slave trade or the status of enslaved persons of the Atlantic community within which Rapp & Associates traded. Harmony's public stance against slavery and its friendship with antislavery activists such as Frances Wright, and the absence of commentary on the subject in the letters of Frederick, George, or Rapp & Associates' trustees, such as the Bakers, is best understood within the context of Whig politics. The development of the national economic system was too enmeshed for reform-minded Whigs to contemplate a complete disentanglement from the system of slave labor. As will be discussed further, the Rapps were ardent supporters of the Whig agenda, putting them in the company of other business-minded Americans who could oppose slavery's expansion, while continuing to embrace it as part of the national economic system.[55]

THE SEARCH FOR REPUBLICAN MANUFACTURING: VISITORS AND HARMONIE

While Frederick was absent at the constitutional convention, Harmonie began receiving a stream of curious visitors searching for a way to reconcile republican values with successful manufacturing. As early national-period economist Mathew Carey wrote in one of several publications that raised Harmony's profile in England and America, "The settlement of Harmony . . . is probably the only settlement ever made in

50   *Part One: Christian Communal Capitalism*

America, in which from the outset agriculture and manufacture preceded hand-in-hand together."[56] This quest reflected a growing awareness that the nature of work was entering a period of transformational change in the Atlantic world. For example, in 1800 approximately 76 percent of the U.S. workforce was engaged in agriculture, a figure that declined to less than 53 percent by mid-century. Many of these workers shifted to manufacturing jobs in one of the more than 123,000 establishments operating by 1850.[57] Specialization, division of labor, wages, changes in the rhythms of work, and the replacement of fraternal organizations with unions are just a few of the many changes American workers adapted to (or protested) in these decades as the nation's population grew from just over 5 million in 1800 to over 23 million by 1850. The changes meant children and adults (or entire families) were now working in cities and manufacturing towns for long hours (seventy hours per week), typically in unsafe and unsanitary conditions for low wages (they were often paid every three to six weeks). Workers in the domestic system retained more control over their work schedules, but this was offset by relatively small compensation.[58]

All this change to the nature of work made Harmonie (and later, Economy) a source of curiosity. As a productive, healthy industrial village, how did it care for its labor force while earning a reputation for efficiency in production? Visitors from the Atlantic community came to Harmonie and Economy hoping to find the answer, perhaps uncovering principles or a model that could be replicated in other manufacturing towns in Europe and North America. Those who could not visit Harmony in person resorted to correspondence, such as the curious and admiring merchant John Bedford, who wrote in 1816,

> I have examined with admiration . . . the product of the ingenuity and industry of your society upon the Wabash . . . the equal perfection at least, exists among your society, in other branches of mechanical industry & the usefull [sic] arts; from which, (your association) as from a focus, I hope and pray they may diverge and be diffused throughout our land, contributing to & securing, with accumulating force, our national independence and individual comfort & happiness.[59]

Industry on the Frontier 51

Prominent publications such as *Niles' Weekly Register* also took an active interest.[60]

Given this concern with the changing nature of work and plight of manufacturing workers, guests of Harmony often remarked on the society's labor system, wondering how it encouraged industriousness, despite the society's prohibition on private property. As one skeptical New Englander, the missionary Samuel Worcester, put it to Frederick, "Many among us, who think a Society established upon principles analogous to those of the Harmonists, would be useful and delightful, *if possible*, believe also that a prohibition of individual and exclusive property would operate as an inherent and irresistible principle of disorder & decay; and consequently, that all schemes, which act upon such a prohibition must be visionary and impactable."[61] According to Frederick, since "the interest of each lies in the whole," each worked "according to ability."[62] He agreed with Worcester that people were plagued by self-interest—it was a manifestation of the Fall of mankind detailed in the third chapter of Genesis. Frederick argued that the key to Harmony's successful transition to communal living was a desire to care for one's brothers and sisters and for the good of the community, an attitude only produced by "the Religion of Jesus Christ, which teaches to renounce and do without what ever may cause a hindrance, to obstain [*sic*] from what is only a habit and no Necessary of Life and deny self to be usefull [*sic*] for others . . . all Schemes to form Societies similar to Harmonie without practicing the Religion of Jesus Christ and prohibiting indivitual [*sic*] property have gone to wreck."[63] Frederick continued by explaining that before the Fall the nature of man and woman was "activity" that "this primitive Instinct exists yet in the essence of man, and (becomes predominant) as soon as the inner feeling Mediatly [*sic*] or immediately are unfolded through the Light of truth, then this Stimulus for activity and Social life awakes with it."[64]

Additionally, the society's members earnestly believed in the eternal significance and urgency of their holy endeavor: they were ushering in the kingdom of God and would form the foundation of Christ's millennial rule. However, if a member did not have this set as their "chief object," then they would find the community and subjugation to their superintendents very difficult.[65] Visitors were often surprised to learn there was no prescribed workday for this labor force. Despite outsiders

52 *Part One: Christian Communal Capitalism*

who marveled at the work ethic of Harmonists, members of the society contended that "they did not work hard, but were always working at their leisure & just as they liked it."[66] This was surely overstating things, but it speaks in general to the sense of equity in the work routine at Harmony. For example, while there were no wages in Harmony, if workers were sick, they were not forced to work. Essentially, they were entitled to an unlimited number of sick days.[67]

Work was gendered in ways that disoriented some visitors, such as Henry Schoolcraft, who, as a good Victorian, thought fieldwork was inappropriate for young girls and women. This contrasts with visitors like Donald MacDonald, who applauded women working outside their homes.[68] Work for both women and men reflected the increasing labor specialization, as Schoolcraft described Harmony's labor system as one where "Every individual is taught that he can perform but a single operation, whether it be in the various manipulations of the cotton or woollen manufactury [sic], or the simple business of the farmyard. By this means, no time is lost by changing from one species of work to another: the operator becomes perfect in his art, and if he possess any ingenuity, will contrive some improved process to abridge or facilitate his labor."[69] Adam Smith could not have explained it more clearly, and efficiency of work was clearly part of how Rapp & Associates increased its output.

Despite the trend toward efficiency, workers retained some of their preindustrial habits, such as song. Singing was an important part of the cultural life of Harmony's work day, and the Rapps seemed to take special pride in the company's end-of-day singing when they showed off the society to outsiders.[70] Of course, presiding over all of this, and the ultimate source of labor discipline, was George Rapp, who both Frederick and visitors described as an all-powerful "king-priest" of the community in the order of Melchizedek.[71] Visitors at Harmony always had to parse its dualities and carefully intuit what tensions lurked beneath what they saw on the surface.

Philadelphian Georg Friedrich Krimmel, in correspondence with the king of Württemberg, also held up the Harmonists as solving another early nineteenth-century societal problem—emigration. The years immediately following the final defeat of Napoleon were difficult for Württemberg, as prices for barley, oat, spelt, and rye skyrocketed, in part due to the crop failures of 1816 following the eruption of Mount Tambora

Industry on the Frontier 53

(Indonesia) in 1815. The king of Württemberg, William I, had recently succeeded Frederick I and immediately loosened prior restrictions on emigration from his realm.[72] With the surge in emigration came abuse as dishonest agents and merchants took advantage of many desperate emigrants, leaving them destitute in foreign ports, or in long-term bondage or urban poverty in America.[73] Worse yet, the captains charged with transporting the emigrants also cheated their passengers, and at least one denied them food in violation of their contracts, leading to the loss of many emigrant lives.[74] Krimmel held up the Harmonists as a contrasting model of orderly, equitable, and productive emigration.[75]

Harmony's agents struggled to pay the indentures and secure the release of numerous families attempting to make their way to the second site in the Indiana Territory. By 1817, Harmonie experienced its second (of three) great membership additions, as 172 individuals joined over the next three years, with 126 entering in 1817 alone. The average age of the new members was twenty-two, with 59 under the age of ten (17 were born to existing members or members under probational status). In 1827, Harmony experienced its third and final great migration, as 238 were admitted over the course of five years (peaking with 102 in 1830). The nature of Harmony's membership requirements included children under their parents' signatory to the Articles of Agreement after a period of probation (typically a few months). These children were then expected to sign for themselves upon reaching age the age of twenty-one.[76]

What observers appreciated most about the Harmonists' system of emigration was that the Rapps offered a way to incorporate the new arrivals into a community that would care for them, help them acclimate to their new environment, and then turn them into productive labor units in America's economy. Men and women spoke Swabian, wore simple, homespun, uniform clothing, and shared work in the field, much as they had done in Württemberg. J. S. Buckingham, a member of the British Parliament, described in 1840 the Harmonist workforce's traditional demeanor, with men dressing in light woolen grey, black, and brown jackets, pants, and hats, while women wore similarly colored gowns, white or checked aprons, a silk or cotton handkerchief over the shoulders, and either a white or black cap. Men wore beards of various lengths, but shaved their cheeks and upper lips, and women parted their hair in the

54 *Part One: Christian Communal Capitalism*

middle. Most importantly, "in both sexes the characteristics are simplicity, neatness, comfort, and economy; but there is not the slightest particle of taste or elegance in their apparel."[77]

By spring 1817, George Rapp resided in "by far the best" brick home in Indiana, and Harmony had resumed all the industries of the first settlement—including both wool and cotton textiles.[78] Early nineteenth-century tourists valued aesthetics, and visitors to Harmonie marveled at its order, cleanliness, and the construction of its "pretty little town," though some also noted suspiciously that George Rapp and his closest advisers seemed to live better than their followers did.[79] Surrounded by the society's cornfields, the village was organized along two main north–south (Mount Vernon to St. Louis) and east–west (Shawneetown to Vincennes) streets that divided the community into a series of squares; these were abutted by two additional north–south and four east–west parallel streets.[80] Unsurprisingly, the aforementioned churches sat near the center of Harmonie. Indicative of the society's view of alcohol, the second church contained two wine cellars.[81] As a traveling companion of Robert Owen described it, taken as a whole, Harmonie's aesthetics served to bolster the argument for the superiority of communal life:

> To a traveler just emerging from a forest where little or no improvement has taken place, and remembering the many days he has spent in wandering through a thinly peopled & badly cultivated country, the view from these hilly pastures down upon a rich plain, flourishing village, and picturesque river winding through a magnificent forest, is highly gratifying. Then are his eyes opened to the benefits attending the union of numbers, and he hastens on with desire to enjoy the society of beings who, having made so great an improvement, he expects must be of a superior order.[82]

Beyond its workforce and ascetics, the society's technology impressed visitors, particularly its thirty-horsepower steam engine, which carded, combed, and cleaned the wool before spinning on a machine run by children.[83] The engine then powered the weaving and cutting processes. An eight-horse-driven threshing machine was equally impressive, which was also operated by children.[84] Harmony was often a dumping ground for orphans, but rather than hire them out, as outsiders frequently

Industry on the Frontier 55

propositioned the society, Harmony instead trained them in a trade and put them to work within the society.⁸⁵

To deal with wool-processing demands, in 1818, Frederick purchased two weaving looms from Frankfurt, Germany, and explored acquiring a steamboat for trade with New Orleans.⁸⁶ Overall, Frederick seemed satisfied with the progress of the pious capitalist commune, described by one observer as soon to be "the most beautiful city of western America,"

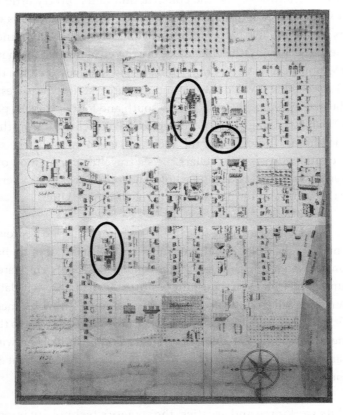

FIGURE 2.4 Harmonie, Indiana (ca. 1825). Harmonie resident W. Weingartner drew this map of Harmonie on November 12, 1832 (in Economy). Left circle indicates the industrial section of Harmonie, containing a weaver shop, steam house, old granary, factory, mill, dye house, lime house, and washhouse. In the lower left, Weingartner wrote, "Thus was situated new Harmonie, on the Wabash, which was begun in the year 1814 and finished 1825." Middle circle: two church buildings. Right circle: Rapp homes. Courtesy of Old Economy Village: OEVA, MG-185, Map #19, 06.72.17.84.

although Frederick privately lamented the fact that his sheep did not grow as large and produced an inferior quality of wool in Indiana.[87] Before long, even the governor of Indiana was a customer of the society's textiles.[88]

All of this took place despite the worsening economic climate in the United States as the Panic of 1819 unhinged the American economic system. Driven by a combination of land and currency speculation, the rapid expansion of credit by central, state, and local banks, and exacerbated by the Bank of the United States' decision to restrict credit and Britain's ban on U.S. trade with the Caribbean, countless farmers, businessmen, and merchants experienced economic ruin.[89] Locally, Frederick struggled with the lack of circulating currency, and worried specifically about the health of the Bank of Vincennes. Revealing his savvy, and perhaps his crafty nature, he used his status as a director to secure outstanding debts owed the society from the bank's debtors before the U.S. Treasury could seize the bank's assets.[90] By summer 1821, the market was still depressed, constrained by the currency crisis in the West and exacerbated by abnormally low water levels, which collectively made trade extremely difficult.[91]

While historians continue to argue over who or what was to blame for the Panic of 1819, the American public believed irresponsible banking was at fault.[92] As public trust dissolved, bank runs ensued. Credit and specie constricted, lenders called in loans, and many merchants, farmers, and speculators defaulted. Unemployment skyrocketed as businesses laid off their workers. It took until 1822 for the economy to begin recovering, but by this time, George and Frederick Rapp most assuredly recognized that they were at a distinct disadvantage after having moved so far westward in 1814. Desiring to trade throughout the East Coast markets such as Pittsburgh, Philadelphia, and Baltimore, southern ports such as New Orleans, as well as overseas, the Rapps were hampered by the tyranny of distance.

Within these ports, the nature of trade was undergoing fundamental change. "Merchant capitalists" who oversaw nearly every phase of exchange no longer dominated the marketplace. In addition to owning (or even building) their own ships, providing for their own insurance, and acting as their own agents, many merchant capitalists were even involved in the manufacturing process as well. However, by the time Harmony

Industry on the Frontier 57

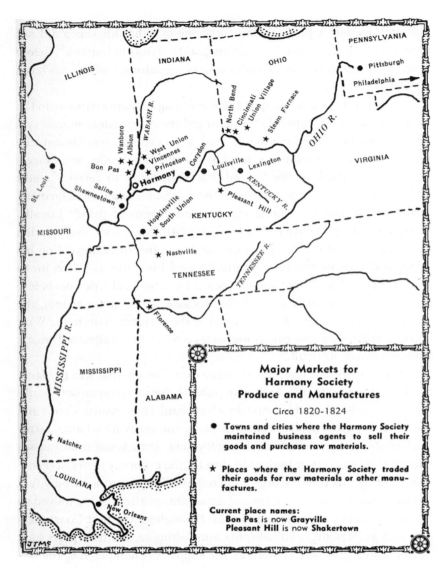

FIGURE 2.5 Rapp & Associates' regional trade network. *DHID2*, 80. Map used by arrangement with the Indiana Historical Society.

established its first location, market specialization saw merchant capitalists displaced by exporters, bankers, insurers, manufacturers, financiers, brokers, investors, wholesalers, retailers, and auctioneers.[93] This change dictated how Rapp & Associates conducted its textile business. Once it manufactured its cotton, silk, or woolen goods, it sent them to agents in Pittsburgh, Baltimore, Philadelphia, or New Orleans for sale at auction. Consequently, the Rapps were constantly in communication with their agents, although the decision to move westward only made it more difficult to stay abreast of the latest developments.

Not surprisingly, the cost to transport goods in the nineteenth century was high, and tended to vary dramatically, depending on access to some of the few turnpikes in existence, although the fees to use these roads were not insignificant added costs. Wagon transport varied between 30 to 70 cents per mile prior to the Panic of 1819, falling dramatically to between 7 and 20 cents, reflecting the general deflation of the period, since road construction was still relatively minor. By moving to Indiana in 1814, Rapp & Associates committed to what has been described as a 3,000-mile counterclockwise irregular circle of trade. Goods from producers such as Rapp & Associates floated downstream to New Orleans (where the boats were sold, the boatmen having to find their way back north on foot), before embarking on a short trip to the West Indies or a slow trip along the coast to Philadelphia, New York, Boston, or across the Atlantic to Europe. Finished goods had to make the expensive westward trip overland. Steamboats and canals did dramatically cut transportation costs on the Mississippi-Ohio river system, so important to Rapp & Associates in its Indiana location. Prices dropped by as much as 75 percent (downstream) and 95 percent (upstream) by mid-century from the rates the Rapps paid in their Indiana years. Additionally, these technologies allowed goods to flow northward to settlements like Harmonie. Wagons and large canal boats averaged around twenty miles per day, something steamboats and railroads improved fivefold by mid-century. It took fifty days on average for goods to travel from Pittsburgh (just a few miles from Harmonie, Pennsylvania) to New York City at the start of Rapp & Associates' operations, whereas by mid-century, a similar shipment could make it to Cincinnati in nearly half the time (twenty-eight days).[94]

Industry on the Frontier 59

Even after the construction of the Erie Canal, the average travel time between New York and the Ohio River was ten days in 1831, while publications from the East took an average of seven days to reach the Ohio in 1841. The National Road (present-day U.S. Route 40) did not reach the Ohio River until 1833 and its terminus in Vandalia, Illinois, until 1839. The simple challenge of redeeming banknotes over such a vast territory was daunting and expensive (in 1830 the cost of transporting specie from banks on the Ohio River to those in New York City was 4 percent of the specie value). The U.S. Post Office only had 903 offices in 1800, expanding to over 13,000 by 1840, and a mere 3,341 officers in 1816, growing to 14,290 officers in 1841. Even so, the costs were still high, as a letter traveling over 400 miles cost 25 cents (compared to 6 cents within 30 miles). A second sheet of paper doubled the cost. (These rates were in effect until 1845, when the cost was lowered to 3 cents within 300 miles.)[95] Newspapers' special rates dramatically helped western businessmen like the Rapps gain market information, however, most of this information was out of date by the time the papers arrived. Consequently, a major change in the economy by the 1850s was the widespread emergence of banknote clearinghouses and consortiums such as New England's Suffolk System, which lowered the cost and time of shipping notes.[96]

Remarkably, Harmony experienced comparatively little pain during the Panic of 1819, apart from falling prices for its agricultural and manufacturing products, and a difficulty paying off its debts due to the failure of many of its business associates and customers to pay what they owed to Rapp & Associates (both of which were due to lack of circulating currency).[97] Throughout the crisis, Rapp & Associates continued to operate 2 water-powered sawmills, 2 grinding mills (1 water, 1 steam), 1 oil mill, 1 hemp mill, 4 wool carding machines, 2 cotton carding machines, 400 wool spindles, 120 cotton spindles, 4 shearing machines, 11 weaving looms (wool and cotton), and 4 stocking weaver looms—making Harmonie by far the most impressive industrial center in the West.[98] Despite the downturn in business, no one was starving, the society was not reduced to selling assets to cover debts, and no one was unemployed, unlike many other places in America in 1819.[99] The Christian communal capitalist model of Harmonie certainly had its undeniable advantages in times of economic crisis, even though Frederick stressed how hard the depression hit the West.[100] By pooling resources, reinvesting Rapp &

60   *Part One: Christian Communal Capitalism*

Associates' profits into the society, and avoiding risky financial deals and loans, Harmony's model offered an alternative to the speculative, individualistic capitalism characterized by such early national-period figures as Andrew Dexter Jr.[101] Here the religious values of the community expressed themselves economically, as the Rapps took a long-term view, with the new millennium at the forefront of their planning. This was distinct from the individualistic, get-rich-quick schemes that led to many of the cautionary tales of the early U.S. capitalist system.

The success of Harmony amid economic panic also underscored how commercial exchange took place on Frederick's terms, which were seldom generous. The society angered its neighbors to the point that they circulated a petition to the Indiana Assembly over Frederick's refusal to accept his neighbors' wheat for grinding at customary prices, the Harmonists' failure to serve in the militia, and their voting "en masse" at the direction of the Rapps.[102] On top of these grievances, Frederick's practice of taking Harmony's neighbors to court over debts fed local anger toward the society. It all came to a head on January 20, 1820, when a local man, William Harris, assaulted two Harmonists. The society's tavern keeper, Friedrich Eckensperger, was in turn charged with assault on Harris, as were eight other Harmonists, including Frederick Rapp. A day later, Harris returned with a small mob and attacked six Harmonists working in the fields east of the town before moving to Eckensperger's dwelling house and threatening him.[103] A separate indictment charged Frederick's confidant John L. Baker with assault on William Harris on January 21, 1820. Eventually, a total of seventeen Harmonists and their neighbors were charged with assault, four were brought to trial, and three were found guilty and fined.[104] Outside observers suspected jealousy toward the Harmonists was to blame, considering the relative luxury they enjoyed, while the Rapps' confidant and trustee, Romelius L. Baker, claimed the fracas was an attempt to free indentured servants.[105] This explanation has merit, considering Frederick Rapp had also sued one of the assailants for unpaid debts.[106] Frederick and five additional Harmonists plead guilty and paid fines ranging from $10 (John L. Baker) to 1 cent (the court assessed Frederick $5), as well as court costs. A seventh Harmonists pled not guilty and was assessed a fine of $25, while Eckensperger was the lone Harmonist found not guilty.[107] Frederick bitterly claimed injustice as one of the outsiders was found not guilty, while

Industry on the Frontier 61

three were found guilty and assessed fines ranging from $5 to $3. Frederick was probably most upset that five men, including William Harris, never appeared for trial at all, and eventually the county dismissed their charges.[108] Whatever the true root of the "Harmony riot," the episode proves the friction between Harmony and its neighbors was real. Englishman William Blane claimed in 1822 that such friction was widespread, in part because the society's communal system gave it a competitive advantage:

> The settlement was once a benefit to the neighborhood; but at present most of the Americans consider it as injurious. At first the people, for a great distance around the Settlement, being supplied with goods that they could not easily procure elsewhere, considered it advantageous to them; but they now think precisely the contrary; for the Harmonites, not having to pay their workmen, are enabled to under-sell every one [sic] who would wish to set up a store, and thus prevent competition. Moreover, as in exchange for their cloths, linens, hats, whiskey, &c., they receive vast sums of money which they never spend, and thus diminish the circulating medium of the country.[109]

These episodes also reveal the tension that characterized Harmony's relationship with its neighbors. On one hand, the Rapps wanted to maintain their distance so as to preserve their spiritual purity, and yet they saw the economic potential of doing business within the regional community. Milling was a good example of this as Rapp & Associates was willing to mill for its neighbors when it served the Rapps' financial purposes, but only on their terms. Two sawmills were in operation by 1817, with a third, along with an oil mill, soon on the way. Frederick planned to construct a gristmill during the summer while also expanding the scope of the society's financial dealings with the region by opening stores in Shawneetown (Illinois) and Vincennes, the latter of which quickly became more profitable than the original store in Harmonie.[110] The establishment of these stores led to envy as residents of other regional villages and towns, including the city of St. Louis, petitioned the Rapps to open stores in their communities.[111] At the same time, Frederick also took over a tavern in Vincennes and contracted to manufacture distillation vessels

62   *Part One: Christian Communal Capitalism*

and help set up a Tennessee distillery—that is, until the apparent holder of the patent behind Rapp's chosen technique showed up in Tennessee and intimidated the prospective distiller into withdrawing his contract.[112] In any case, by the 1820s, Harmonie's distillery produced thirty-six gallons of whiskey a day and its brewery produced five hundred gallons of beer every two days.[113]

An additional way in which Frederick expanded the society's financial dealings with its neighbors was to lease some of Harmonie's peripheral landholdings. These small farms, typically between forty and eighty acres, paid their rents in grains, with slight variation, at a rate between eight to twelve bushels per acre of corn per year. A few also owed one-third of the farm's wheat harvest.[114] Harmony did not utilize all its lands, so the leasing provided revenue to offset the taxes the society had to pay on the unused sections of its lands.[115] Of course, the danger was obvious, for by inviting settlement along the society's periphery, Harmony risked the "crowding" that caused it to seek a new location in the first place.

Ultimately, fear of its neighbors seems responsible for the society's dual use of its granary as a fortress (and the purchase of a cannon).[116] Thanks to his eschatology, Frederick had less concern for the common good of his county neighbors than his larger economic goals, such as his new business partnership in New Orleans, with an eye toward Havana, Cuba, and Liverpool, England.[117] George summed up the society's attitude toward those outside the commune as follows: "And what of it then, if a considerable part of our decadent generation should be lost, what sort of fruit can a spoiled tree and branch still bring . . .?"[118] And yet, despite all this, there were locals who were sad to see Harmony leave southern Indiana. As one Harmony associate wrote, "the people here (with a few exceptions) regret the removal of your society, and begin to estimate your value to the state & community."[119]

Industry on the Frontier 63

CHAPTER THREE

Republican Industry

Economy, Pennsylvania

The beginning of Harmony's end in Indiana came unremarkably, in the form of a letter of inquiry in the summer of 1820 from Welsh industrialist Robert Owen.[1] Owen's awareness of the Harmony Society demonstrates the fame Rapp and his followers had acquired by the 1820s, for as Frederick wrote in early 1823, Harmonie was "attracting the attention of many people in America, especially in the eastern states" thanks to its spiritual and material successes.[2] Owen was specifically interested in George Rapp's experience in the "practical inconveniences which arise from changes to society from a state of private to public property."[3] Of course, it was curious that Owen sought a religious leader's wisdom, considering his view of religion as "absurd and irrational" and, along with marriage and private property, "the only Demon, or Devil, that ever has, or most likely, ever will torment the human race."[4] Despite his disdain for the religious and social organization of the society, Owen's son believed that Harmony fascinated his father because

> Their experiment was a marvelous success in a pecuniary point of view; for at the time of their immigration their poverty did not exceed twenty-five dollars a head, while in twenty-one years (to wit, in 1825) a fair estimate gave them *two thousand dollars* for each person, —man, woman, and child; probably *ten times* the average wealth throughout the United States; for at that time each person

in Indiana averaged but a hundred and fifty dollars of property, and even in Massachusetts the average fell short of three hundred dollars for each adult and child.[5]

Owen had big plans for Harmonie—it was central to his plans to radically reshape American society along the lines of his vision of secular communalism.[6] This was good timing for the Rapps, as they came to realize that southwestern Indiana was not the best place to realize their divine economy. The sale to Robert Owen facilitated their return to western Pennsylvania. In effect, the risk of moving back to a region with higher population density (which could threaten Harmony's communal purity) was worth the chance to more effectively plug Rapp & Associates into the market.

At the same time, by the early 1820s, the location of the second Harmonie was giving Frederick second thoughts. Although the climate of southern Indiana was better than western Pennsylvania for some types of agriculture, Frederick increasingly complained of the poor market access, while George complained of the intense heat.[7] Both he and George had come to realize that Rapp & Associates needed a site located on a major river such as the Ohio, and near a large city such as Pittsburgh, in order to participate more actively in the manufacturing sector.[8] Although George was willing to admit this privately to Frederick, in public he was more opaque as to the motivations for the move, particularly in his discussions with Robert Owen. To the latter, George avoided material explanations and emphasized the spiritual, asserting that divine revelation had foretold and directed him to lead the move back to Pennsylvania. The most he would divulge to curious inquirers was that the climate was not well suited to their society, and that they tended to move every ten years to keep life fresh and challenging, and "in order to do some good."[9] As early as January 1824, Frederick was exploring land in other states that fit this description, while pursuing the sale of Harmonie.[10] On May 4, 1824, the society purchased a new plot of land, which was located, ironically, only fifteen miles from the first Harmonie, approximately twenty miles from Pittsburgh.[11] The society began planning its move even though Harmonie, Indiana, was still for sale.[12]

The irony—that Harmony moved from western Pennsylvania to avoid the corruptions of an increasingly populous neighborhood and to

Republican Industry 65

seek a fortune in the West, only to return to western Pennsylvania—is one of the more intriguing parts of the Harmony story. Harmony's move did not avoid the tensions encroaching upon the society at the original Harmonie, as members experienced more strident conflict with their neighbors in Indiana than they previously had in western Pennsylvania. Likewise, the idea that Rapp & Associates could engage the market more effectively in the West quickly proved erroneous. The Rapps were ahead of their time, moving to Indiana before the construction of a more complete transportation infrastructure, and then moving away just as the needed infrastructure was starting to fall into place (such as the Erie Canal, finished in 1825). In Indiana, the Rapps experienced the worst of the market in terms of lack of infrastructure and a horrendous credit and banking landscape. In contrast, when Harmony moved back to Pennsylvania, it returned to a state bit by "canal fever," most notably the unprofitable Main Line Canal that linked Philadelphia with Pittsburgh.[13] This so-called first wave of national canal building was augmented by a second wave that saw the construction of 3,326 miles of canals by 1840. There was then a smaller third wave that further integrated southern and western regions by 1840 and 1855, respectively, before giving way to the railroads.[14] Additionally, by the time of Harmony's return, Pennsylvania had built a total of 1,800 miles of roads, although most were in the eastern part of the state and built by private corporations.[15] Spiritual reasoning aside, the contrast between the financial and logistical infrastructure of the eastern and western United States in the early 1820s made the decision for the Rapps quite obvious.

The first of eight river trips began on May 24, 1824, with approximately seven hundred Harmonists traveling to their new home on the Ohio River, which the Harmonists named Economy.[16] The completion of Harmony's own steamboat, *William Penn*, facilitated the move.[17] George's decision to name the boat after an enterprising and pious Pennsylvanian suggests a deep symbolism, and he boasted it would prove to be "one of the best and most beautiful boats that runs on the river."[18] Rapp's boasting was justified, as the *Penn* did quickly earn a reputation for uncommon speed, perhaps "the most fast running boat on the Lower Waters" (of the Mississippi).[19] Interestingly, George prohibited members of Harmony from working on the *William Penn* out of fears they would become "spoiled"—that is, become worldly through exposure to the

66   *Part One: Christian Communal Capitalism*

culture of the river trade.[20] Ultimately, Frederick abandoned the steamboat business after just a few months, thanks to constant problems with ice, low water levels, the Ohio Falls, and conflict with river merchants.[21] Once the move back to Pennsylvania was complete, Frederick sold the *William Penn* for $15,000 on September 6, 1825.[22]

It is interesting that the society did not name the third location Harmonie, in keeping with the convention established with the first two settlements. Certainly, using the earlier name for the new location would have caused confusion given its location so close to the first site. Also, the name "Economy" perfectly reflected the goal of Christian communal capitalism, as George explained: "All inventions are contributions to genuine freedom, in which all mechanical powers, arts, & sciences are appropriated for the common good, and restoration of true Philanthropy. This divine Economy, which has been so long neglected is now coming to light in its true and noble characters, exhibiting the image of God in man. . . . This divine *Economy* is the mainpoint [*sic*] of noble & human sentiments."[23] The idea of a "divine economy" connected to their exceptionalism and eschatology is central to understanding why the Rapps fused communal living to the early national-period capitalist system. As George believed, theirs was a more perfect vision of economic exchange: "And therefore all good men, however few in number, must unite tighter to obtain this aim & withdraw from the degraded scenes of life, and associate for nobler purposes."[24]

By virtue of his location further east at Economy, George was the first to meet Robert Owen on his journey in 1824 to take possession of Harmonie, Indiana. Frederick was already satisfied with Owen as the new owner of the second Harmonie, writing to Richard Flower that he was a "proper Gentleman . . . and I am included to believe that Mr. Owen and his Community would carry on the different Branches of Bussiness [*sic*] with success."[25] George likewise had a positive first impression of Robert Owen, surprised as he was that they had so much in common ideologically.[26] Their first meeting went so well, in fact, that George envisioned a flourishing mutual trade between the two societies, further bolstering the communal capitalist model.[27] Owen continued westward and eventually reached Harmonie on December 16, 1824. He and his companions were immediately impressed, and on January 3, 1825, Owen and Frederick finalized the sale of Harmonie for $150,000.[28] The sale

Republican Industry 67

also included an undetermined quantity of Harmonie's livestock and some of its technology, most notably its cotton gin and two woolen carding machines.[29]

Harmony's success certainly reinforced George's belief that they were forging a divine economy that functioned as God intended (at least since the Fall of Adam). However, the growth that Harmony had undergone meant the second move would prove even more difficult than the first. It was a long, arduous process, with the final group not departing Harmonie until a year later, when Robert Owen took control following an emotional ceremony on May 5, 1825.[30]

Meanwhile, George was already in Pennsylvania overseeing the development of Economy.[31] Rebuilding was not easy, even though it was the Rapps' third time. Chief among the challenges was sustaining Rapp & Associates' ventures while building Economy, some five hundred miles away. Frederick decided to transfer the proceeds of the society's stores at Vincennes and New Harmony to Economy, where George could use the cash to make purchases and fund the ongoing construction project. The limitations of the financial system in the West meant the only solution was to find a way to transport specie from Indiana to Louisville to be exchanged for bills honored in Pittsburgh and Philadelphia, usually approximately $2,000 or $3,000 at a time, by way of steamboat. Obviously, this method was tenuous, as it depended on both trustworthy captains and a minimum water level in the rivers.[32]

During the move, the geographic split between George and Frederick strained their working relationship. In general, George completely deferred to Frederick on financial matters, but the separation put George in control of the finances of Economy. Less organized, he did not produce (or preserve) an end-of-year report, as was the custom of the more structured and conscientious Frederick. Due to low water levels slowing down the move east, Frederick continued to preside over the larger group of society members back in Harmonie, something that seemed to eat at George.[33]

The strain deepened over Frederick's reliance on several trusted society men when conducting business, such as John L. Baker, who helped run Rapp & Associates' store in Shawneetown and was now working on behalf of Frederick in Pittsburgh. Men such as Baker acted as agents of Rapp & Associates, and with Frederick stuck at Harmonie, he relied on

68　*Part One: Christian Communal Capitalism*

these men to advance his work back east, especially since George's Swabian dialect complicated his attempts to conduct business.[34] It is an understatement to say this did not sit well with George, who interpreted Frederick's reliance on these agents as a threat to his authority. This was a sensitive matter for George because he took pains to create an aura in which "all the people believe that things depend upon me."[35] George chastised Frederick to stop sending the Louisville money drafts to agents, threatening to destroy a $2,000 draft he found because Frederick had failed to address it to George. Additionally, he forbade further direct correspondence between Frederick and any other Rapp & Associates men—it all had to run through George.[36] Frederick disregarded his adoptive father and continued to correspond with his business agents, but the tension over how to run Rapp & Associates was an ongoing source of strife between them.

While Harmony was inspiring Robert Owen, it was also attracting the attention of the controversial, outspoken socialist freethinker Frances Wright.[37] She visited Harmonie on March 19, 1825, on her way to meet the Revolutionary War hero Marquis de Lafayette in New Orleans.[38] Wright was impressed to the point that she maintained an unlikely friendship with Frederick Rapp, bonding with him over their shared revulsion at slavery. The agent Frederick engaged to broker the sale of Harmonie fell in with Wright and later sought technical guidance and material support from Frederick as Wright established her own utopian commune, Nashoba (Tennessee). Wright envisioned Nashoba as a slave refuge built on the ideal of open, egalitarian relationships—a vision her visits to Harmony helped inspire.[39] This association between Wright and the Rapps is especially intriguing given her antipathy toward religion in general (and that of many American Protestants toward her).[40] Nashoba, like Owen's New Harmony, was a short-lived failure, marked by controversy and an inability to translate idealism into reality.

Another interesting development concurrent with the early phase of rebuilding at Economy and the visits of Owen and Wright was Frederick's entry into the world of financial speculation.[41] In August 1825, Frederick's agent in Philadelphia, J. Solms, opened an account solely in Frederick's name for speculative purposes, principally in stocks, but also commodities such as cotton, and employing practices such as note shaving.[42] This account was large, with an initial deposit of $20,000,

Republican Industry 69

and when necessary, Frederick authorized Solms to access Rapp & Associates' accounts in Shawneetown and Louisville. In an obvious contradiction, the man who would not loan to others allowed some of this speculative money to earn interest on loan.[43]

Frederick's secret speculation game is difficult to contextualize. Clearly, he knew the rest of the society (and most certainly George) would condemn the practice, and yet he did it anyway. One is left with the conclusion that either Harmony's espoused religious values were losing their grip over Frederick, or he had rationalized the practice in some fashion, perhaps thinking that "the ends justified the means." Either way, Frederick's actions humanize him, showing him as a complex person struggling to live "in the world," but not "of the world," at a time when so many of the other enterprising men with whom he did business embraced speculation. Certainly, the temptation to put some of Rapp & Associates' excess profits into speculative investments would have been tremendous.

The decision to move back to Pennsylvania proved wise, financially speaking.[44] George quickly realized there was more money in circulation in western Pennsylvania than in the West.[45] This facilitated Frederick's establishment of a new textile factory at Economy—an L-shaped brick building containing a steam engine to power the cotton and woolen manufacturing processes.[46] He considered various designs before finalizing a contract for two new seventy-horsepower engines, one each for the cotton and wool factories.[47] By early December 1825, Frederick was testing his engines and preparing to open the society's textile factories for production.[48] The expanding factory work changed the nature of the society, and by the fall of 1827 Economy had 150 persons (out of 750 inhabitants) working in the cotton and wool factories (which were up to 2,500 spindles) alone, and the Rapps were telling visitors in 1831 that their mills yielded $32,000 in net profit per year.[49]

By 1828, Frederick was moving beyond cotton and wool textile production into silk, which gained the society tremendous attention—including from Pennsylvania officials who wore Harmony cravats.[50] In a well-publicized account, Frederick explained how Economy had expanded from a few thousand silkworms and the production of a limited number of handkerchiefs to a full-fledged manufacturing endeavor that made the society the leading center for silk production in America:

70   *Part One: Christian Communal Capitalism*

> We have erected a two story house, 24 by 44, particularly arranged and adapted for the worms, as well as the various operations of the silk manufacture, and have at this time, near one million of worms, in a prosperous condition. . . . Females from 12 to 15 years of age, are amply sufficient to attend to the worms within doors; the leaves [of white and black mulberry trees] are gathered, and brought in by the school children after school hours. Upon the whole we are highly pleased with the experiment.[51]

Naturally, this account (along with the silk vests Frederick wore on business trips to Baltimore and Philadelphia) gained Economy even more fame, and the Rapps fielded numerous requests for advice and help from aspiring silk manufacturing entrepreneurs.[52]

As Economy's first year passed, visitors observed a settlement that already resembled the first two Harmonies. Ordered into three clean, tree-lined north–south streets bisected by five east–west streets, it contained brick and wood homes with beautiful gardens, an inn, a large home for George Rapp, a brewery, a distillery, a steam flour mill, and a large, four-story brick factory with two wings for wool and cotton production.[53] By the second year, the factories were in full production, as Prince Bernhard, Duke of Saxe-Weimar-Eisenach, observed in May 1826, a mechanized process powered by a seventy-five-horsepower engine that pumped water from a fifty-foot well. His account is one of the most detailed of Economy's manufacturing process, explaining how the society purchased wool from surrounding farms, which they combined with their own Merino and Saxon sheep. Once the wool was washed, the oldest women of Economy picked it on the fourth floor of the wool factory before sending it down a chute to a lower floor, where it was separated by quality into four classes. At this point the wool left the factory to be dyed in the dye house before being returned for combing, spinning, and winding into yarn by a machine. Next the yarn was placed in a loom, followed by fulling by a steam fulling mill, and finally shorn by a patented shearing machine. Bernhard noted that the "blue middling, grey mixed (principally used for pantaloons) and red and white flannel" were the most popular of Economy's woolen products.[54]

The wool factory was comparable to those of Leeds (the leading woolen center of England), while Economy's cotton factory was set up

Republican Industry 71

in the manner of the great textile mills of Manchester and Lowell, with different stages of production divided between various floors.[55] Economy's cotton production entailed spinning and weaving, while Bernhard claimed the expense of stamps and changing fashion of calicos prohibited printed cottons. While some of the spinning machines (one hundred and fifty spools), power looms, and the cotton factory's dressing machine were manufactured in Pittsburgh, the Harmonists built the majority themselves at Economy. Blue and white cassinette fabric was initially the primary product of the cotton mill.[56]

Young women between the ages of twenty and thirty, noted for their "healthy" appearance, were especially prominent in the cotton factory's approximately one hundred workers, while another hundred men worked in the woolen factory.[57] Bernhard was also impressed by the atmosphere of the factories, which stayed warm from steam pipes during the winter, and which were kept extremely neat, including "sweet-smelling flowers" in vases on the machines. Not surprisingly, workers saluted George as he showed off the factories, displaying a "warm-hearted friendliness" that impressed visitors.[58]

Consequently, for visitors the contrast Economy's factories made with those of a city such as Manchester was stark. Harmony suggested there was a way to industrialize and maintain a sense of beauty, humanity, and equality. The picturesque atmosphere of Economy and its surrounding fields enchanted visitors with a picture of utopia. The reality was not quite so straightforward, however, and serious trouble lurked beneath Economy's seemingly tranquil and harmonious surface.

CRISES: LEGAL AND SPIRITUAL

According to visitors such as Prince Bernhard, Economy was on a pious path to peace and prosperity. However, the reality was more complicated. The first sign of impending trouble occurred when a rival settlement of ex-Harmonists at Bull Creek, near Columbiana, Ohio, prepared to raid Economy and seize indentured children. In 1827, the Columbiana society was in the midst of reorganizing as a Christian communal capitalist settlement called the Society of United Germans, or Teutonia.[59] The conflict revolved around the status of an ex-member's children, still

72   *Part One: Christian Communal Capitalism*

indentured to Rapp & Associates.[60] After a failed early morning attempt to grab the children with the aid of a local lawyer, rumors circulated that a militia was mustering to take the children by force.[61] Although no such armed posse materialized, the incident underscored a recurring critique of Rapp: that he was a leader who often exercised his absolute power in an manner many interpreted as abusive.

These criticisms, combined with other complaints, put George and Frederick on the defensive.[62] The old charge of restricting members' freedom to vote (through block voting) also resurfaced.[63] This had been a sore spot in Indiana, and many in western Pennsylvania were leveling similar charges against Harmony within a few years of their return, including speculation that many Harmonists were not even legal voters.[64] Jealousy and resentment of the society's economic success was nothing new, but an increasing number of charges of monopoly and parasitic business practices caused the Rapps to respond. Frederick released a public rebuttal explaining the extent to which Rapp & Associates bolstered the regional economy through its purchasing of raw material and finished goods.[65]

Another crack in the Harmony edifice was the growing stress in the relationship between Frederick and George. Frederick's use of agents created the initial tension during the return to Pennsylvania, but it boiled over due to Frederick's "favorite occupation" of alchemy. About this time, George seems to have become smitten by a young woman, Hildegard Mutschler, who began to replace Frederick as George's closest confidante. (There is no evidence they were romantically involved, although it is certainly possible.) The first instance of this development involved George's involvement of Mutschler in his own alchemy experiments, encroaching on Frederick's jealously guarded territory. Frederick was so disturbed that George would involve an "impure" person in the experiments that Frederick declared he would abandon his favorite pursuit altogether.[66] Alchemy was common among the more radical German Pietists such as George and Frederick Rapp, who read the works of early modern alchemists such as Theophrast von Hohenheim, also known as Paracelsus (1493–1541). While many only used metaphorical alchemic language, referencing a so-called spiritual alchemy, a minority that included the Rapps conducted laboratory experimentation in an attempt to produce gold.[67] Most importantly for Harmony was the friction it

Republican Industry 73

caused between its two spiritual and business leaders, just as George was attempting to reassert his authority upon the reunited society.

This power play came in the form of George's push to impose new Articles of Association upon the members of Harmony. Frederick had the new articles drawn up in the fall of 1826, but members did not sign them until spring 1827, when George told them they would spend eternity in hell if they failed to sign the new agreement.[68] These articles were much more legally sound than the 1805 articles, reflective of the man who drew them up, the Episcopal bishop and lawyer John Henry Hopkins.[69] It is not exactly clear why George sought the new articles—there are no surviving letters that provide any explanation. However, the new agreement most likely derived from a desire to have a more legally secure foundation for the society's existence. These articles accomplished this goal, and the U.S. Supreme Court subsequently endorsed the society's legality, specifically citing a passage from the 1827 articles in *Baker v. Nachtrieb* (1856).[70]

The motivation to adopt a new set of articles makes even more sense when one considers the petition ex-Harmony members of Teutonia submitted to the Pennsylvania Legislature in the fall of 1827 requesting the investigation of the Harmony Society over its failure to compensate its departing/expelled members.[71] Fortunately for the Rapps, they had some well-placed friends who were able to persuade the Senate to dismiss the petition.[72] In the fall of 1835, the petitioners lost their case against Harmony a second time, a verdict affirmed by the Pennsylvania Supreme Court.[73] Immediately, George led the society in annulling article 6, added in the 1827 articles, which provided for the return to departing members of the property they brought into the society. The absence of such a provision was one reason the Pennsylvania Legislature denied incorporation back in 1807, and this served as the basis of multiple lawsuits. While it made sense for the leaders of Harmony to add such an article in 1827, it ran counter to George's instincts.[74]

But the most destabilizing crisis was spiritual. As previously mentioned, Harmony embraced an eschatology that anticipated the imminent return of Christ. On March 2, 1829, it seemed to Harmony's members that the long-awaited messiah had surfaced in the form of a German alchemist and Mason, Maximillian Bernhard Mueller, also known as Maximillian Ludwig Proli or the Count de Leon.[75] By September 1831, the self-anointed messiah was en route to America, describing in a

74 *Part One: Christian Communal Capitalism*

letter to President Jackson (who answered warmly in a short response) his determination to establish a settlement of "unusual knowledge . . . with the purpose of participating directly in the inner and outer growth of a great society consisting of persons of all levels of society working together to make the United States more prosperous."[76]

George Rapp was convinced of de Leon's legitimacy, in part because the timing of his emergence aligned with his personal calculation that Christ's return to establish his millennial kingdom would come in mid-September 1829.[77] However, the count's wild claims—he boasted, for example, of having caused the great winter of 1812 that halted Napoleon, and told of his plan to establish first a kingdom in Missouri before drawing all of America unto him and marching westward with 144,000 men like a modern day Moses straight through the Pacific Ocean on his way to conquering the Ottomans and "liberating" Europe—gave others ample reason to label him a fraud.[78]

It did not take long before the count's presence in the society was producing problems, as disgruntled members used him to confront George and Frederick with their accumulated grievances. These reflected the dissatisfaction of Harmony's second generation and recent immigrants with George's authoritarianism.[79] Soon, more than one hundred members had affixed their signatures to a declaration rejecting the Rapps in favor of Count de Leon and his secretary, Dr. John George Gontgen.[80] Although the disgruntled members cited vague "disappointment" with Rapp's "Christian obligations as leader of the congregation," teaching, and behavior, which was said to "completely contradict the word and law of God," interestingly, all their specific demands dealt with material and financial grievances, echoing some of the disenchantment Rapp faced during the early years of converting to communalism.[81]

After the anti-Rappists, calling themselves the "New Philadelphia Congregation," appealed in 1832 to the Pennsylvania Legislature with their complaints, the Rapps responded by codifying their governance into a set of bylaws and creating a counsel of twelve elders, which Karl Arndt argues functioned as a "rubber stamp" for the Rapps' decisions. (The Pennsylvania Legislature declined to intervene, citing the society's lack of incorporation.)[82] Although most of the society remained loyal to the Rapps, the crisis threatened Rapp & Associates business dealings—and this is to say nothing of the internal riots that interrupted the standard

Republican Industry 75

work regimen—while attracting national attention.[83] Ultimately, the conflict led to the departure of approximately one-third of the society's members, with the Rapps granting the separatists $105,000, the furniture in their homes, and a few assorted tools.[84] These concessions failed to resolve the crisis, however, and the two groups continued to levy accusations in the press until emotions exploded in a well-publicized attack on April 2, 1833, by seventy separatists (a combination of approximately forty followers of the count and others who had departed earlier) more than a year after their initial move to break with the Rapps. The dissenters took control of the Economy inn, seizing food and drink before targeting George Rapp's home to confiscate written records and cash, but were foiled by locked doors and the building's solid construction. Ultimately, the militia was called in to maintain security, and forty-eight of the dissenters ended up in court.[85] A series of investigations, indictments, and lawsuits occupied the attention of the Rapps for years, despite the eventual breakup of Count de Leon's commune and his attempt to flee his legal troubles.[86]

Of course, this was not the first time that disgruntled members had left Harmony. From the society's earliest years members departed for various reasons, some voluntary, some not, and more than a few even joined other communal groups—including at least one of the count's dissenters, who ultimately joined the Mormons and supposedly taught Joseph Smith the German language.[87] However, in this instance, the sheer number of departures forced the Rapps into making a sizeable monetary concession to the dissenters.[88] The count used this money to purchase more than seven hundred acres a mere ten miles from Economy, on land once owned, ironically, by Harmony. Frederick had sold the land in 1822 to the builders of their steamboat, the *William Penn*, who in turn sold it to the count. It was much too close for Frederick's liking, but ultimately, the society celebrated a return to normalcy.[89]

Things were anything but normal for Rapp & Associates, however. Frederick worked hard to minimize the loss of a third of his labor force and the sizeable monetary concession by selling the remaining lands the society owned in Indiana, including the its Vincennes store.[90] A more serious loss came a year later, in November 1833, when the woolen factory burned down. Given the tumultuous nature of the previous year,

76 *Part One: Christian Communal Capitalism*

Frederick suspected arson and worked to discover the perpetrator, even as his health took a turn for the worse.[91]

WEALTH AND FAME

Despite these legal and spiritual crises, Rapp & Associates continued to prosper thanks to a highly organized, skilled, and subservient workforce, shrewd and cagy business decisions, and an ongoing commitment to innovation.[92] For an example of the latter, Frederick did not let the negative experience of the *William Penn* stop him from building another steamboat to supplement Rapp & Associates' business income. Back in the summer 1827, he contracted with a local builder to construct a smaller, faster steamboat named the *Pittsburgh and Wheeling Packet*.[93] The new boat attracted significant praise for its uncommon speed, but within a year, Frederick again soured on the river transport business and was already trying to sell the *Packet*.[94] This decision is even more puzzling given the vessel's brisk business carrying passengers and trade goods along the Ohio River.[95] But his dabbling in steamboat technology serves as an example of how Frederick was always experimenting with the latest technology to keep Rapp & Associates competitive in the domestic textile industry.

In fact, the society's technology helped it achieve a surprising level of renown and popularity. Travelers continued to make it a required stop on their tours of the developing U.S. economic landscape, while the U.S. Congress summoned Frederick to testify as an expert in wool manufacture.[96] Frederick could confidently boast of the cutting-edge mechanization in Rapp & Associates' woolen factory, which included 2 wool pickers, 5 carding engines, 9 spinning jacks, 1 spooling machine, 1 warping and dressing machine, 9 power looms, 18 cassinette looms, 6 fulling stocks, 4 gig mills, 6 shearing machines, 2 brushing machines, 2 washing machines, and 1 steam engine.[97] Recognized increasingly for its concentration of textile experts, the society participated in industry conferences to discuss wool production.[98] Several years later, Congress contacted Frederick again to provide advice on wool manufacture as the government weighed the merits of protecting American domestic manufactures against British imports.[99] This time Frederick was too sick to appear before Congress.

Republican Industry 77

Such a missed opportunity must have disappointed Frederick greatly, as he increasingly advocated for national policies in support of domestic manufacturing. Despite their claim that the society "always prefers taking as little active part in Politics as possible," the Rapps publicly aligned themselves in the 1820s and 1830s with the Whigs' American System of protective tariffs, internal improvements, and federal banking.[100] George proudly boasted that Harmony had voted for Henry Clay in the 1824 election, even though Andrew Jackson won Pennsylvania. This attitude was indicative of the Rapps' consistent contempt for Jackson.[101] Likewise, Frederick actively corresponded with Clay, attending dinners honoring the powerful politician and sending him a present of their prized Merino sheep.[102] Frederick mourned "that most of the Americans have so little national spirit or patriotism in preferring foreign to domestic manufacturing."[103] Not surprisingly, Whigs courted the Rapps again in 1844, urging the Harmonists to turn out to vote for Clay, despite the threat of violence at the hands of Locofoco Party supporters, who resented the society's habit of "block" voting for Whig candidates.[104]

By this point, Harmony was wealthy enough that George Rapp could do more than deliver a block vote for the American System. He invested the society's money in 110 shares (at $100 per share) of Pennsylvania-Ohio Canal Company stock when it went on sale in 1835, and he strenuously advocated for a silk tariff to foster domestic industry, even sending President Tyler samples of Economy silks as proof that fostering domestic industry was in the country's best interest.[105] Rapp & Associates' share in the canal company was large enough that the company sought its opinion on the selection of representatives to the board, hardly unusual considering the power of shareholders in early American corporations.[106] In the 1840s, when the House Committee on Manufactures looked to Harmony for expertise and advice on how best to foster domestic industry, the society advocated a 33 percent duty on wool and cotton goods, and 25–33 percent duty on silk goods, while calling for the abandonment of the duty on raw silk.[107]

Along these lines, Friedrich List, a well-known spokesman for the American System and domestic manufacturing, likewise encouraged Harmony to open a "Crafts and Agricultural School" since he claimed that Frederick Rapp "could do this better than any other man in the United States."[108] Ironically, in the aftermath of the disintegration of New

FIGURE 3.1 Karl Bodmer (Swiss, 1809–1893), *Economy, Rapp's Colony on the Ohio*, 1832. Watercolor on paper, Joslyn Art Museum, Omaha, Nebraska. Gift of the Enron Art Foundation, 1986.49.46. Photograph © Bruce M. White, 2019.

Harmony, as Robert Owen's sons were picking up the pieces of his failed utopia and trying to restart the industries that had proven so successful under the Harmonists, Richard Owen sought advice from Harmony on wool textile manufacturing.[109] Indeed, manufacturers from as far away as Naples, Italy, visited Economy to inspect their silk production—an example of just how far the fame of Harmony industry had spread.[110]

In June 1834, Frederick lost his battle with intestinal and chest ailments and George assumed control of Rapp & Associates, albeit with two of Frederick's trusted agents still in place.[111] These agents, Jacob Henrici and Romelius L. Baker, were important members of the society and were crucial to ensuring that the change in leadership did not jeopardize Harmony's material success.[112] Having learned the business side of the society from Frederick, Baker took the lead in business matters. Like Frederick, Baker drove a hard bargain, displaying little compassion, and made use of espionage and lawsuits to protect the business interests of Rapp & Associates.[113]

George now oversaw an enterprise worth more than $534,000, a huge figure in 1835, and something the society's leadership was careful to conceal from their own members, as well as the rest of America.[114]

Republican Industry

There was much George did not know about how Frederick ran the business. Some of Frederick's practices, such as his habit of purchasing excess wool from neighbors, were relatively innocent. Although he took a loss on these transactions, they fostered good will, something Frederick was not concerned with in Indiana, and it seems to have been a valuable lesson he learned before moving to Economy.[115] Others, such as Frederick's speculation, must have come as quite a shock to George. Frederick's banker, J. Solms, who in 1831 was elected to the Philadelphia Stock Exchange's board, was unwilling to aid George in speculating, although he proved useful to George in other ways.[116] Alarmed by Jackson's bank wars, increasing speculation in American real estate, and with an eye toward the new millennium, George started stockpiling silver and gold (particularly British sovereigns) as a financial security blanket for the society.[117]

The role Nicholas Biddle, president of the Second Bank of the United States, played in quietly facilitating this endeavor, even amid the Panic of 1837 (a time of intense demand for British sovereigns), is particularly noteworthy and speaks to the shrewd external business and economic relationships Rapp & Associates had cultivated. Biddle agreed to supply the coins, but demanded absolute silence in return.[118] Transporting large quantities of gold in the 1840s presented its own logistical and security challenges, which Romelius L. Baker solved by hiding the gold in barrels containing wood, hardware, and indigo.[119] George's stockpiling of gold suggests he was either becoming materially obsessed or thought it vital to weather the apocalyptic crisis he still thought imminent. Despite pledges of secrecy, a legend of buried gold in Economy began to grow, adding yet another layer of mystery to Harmony's aura.

George Rapp may also have been scarred by the Panic of 1819 and the currency crunch Harmony had experienced in Indiana. However, by returning to Pennsylvania, Harmony was operating in a much different banking world than the one left behind in Indiana. By 1830, banking offices in the United States numbered 429, up from 360 ten years before.[120] Leaving Indiana was especially helpful, as it had 7 state banks (although no branches of the Second Bank of the United States) in 1820, and none a decade later. In contrast, Pennsylvania had 38 banks, including two branches of the Second Bank of the United States, by 1830. The Northwest only had 35 total bank offices in 1820 (18 in 1830), while the Middle

80   *Part One: Christian Communal Capitalism*

Atlantic region had 134 total offices (146 in 1830). Adjusted for population, the Northwest's share of banking offices per 10,000 persons was 4.08 in 1820 (1.12 in 1830) compared the Middle Atlantic's rate of 4.17 in 1820 (3.52 in 1830). The Northwest dramatically lagged the Middle Atlantic in state bank capital per capita, $1.19 to $2.61, a gap that widened over the ensuing decades ($1.41 to $7.71 by 1830; $4.80 to $15.46 by 1850).[121] Aside from any other social or religious considerations, Harmony was returning to a much more stable region financially, one that permitted a greater opportunity for economic success, even as George stockpiled currency in fears of another banking collapse.

George's obsession with gold raises the question of how much Harmony reflected the values of its founding generation. The emergence of something resembling classes reinforces such skepticism. Even if Harmony's lowliest members enjoyed better material conditions than the average citizen of western Pennsylvania, the small forms of inequality that had always been present began growing more obvious by the mid-1830s.[122] From the first site at Harmonie, George set himself apart by dressing in superior fabrics, and with the construction of a large home appointed with "the best of things" on a street populated by "those who originally invested the largest capital" in the society.[123] Subsequent valuations of real estate and eyewitness accounts reinforce the extent to which classes were emerging in Economy during this time:

> The town has beautiful houses—in the first row where the privileged persons live, the houses are of brick, in the second, the residences of the middle class, there are well-painted frame houses, and in the third, the abodes of the lower classes, there are log cabins. In the middle, toward the river, Rapp lives enthroned in a palace. There he has his collections of art, his art gallery, his music room, his reception—and his dining room.[124]

The Rapps reinforced this division between different segments of the society by withholding financial information from all but a few trusted agents. While members could observe the increasing luxury of George's home, they could only guess as to the extent of the wealth Rapp & Associates was accumulating. Whether they feared the corrupting influence of money on their community (as George would assert), or

Republican Industry 81

FIGURE 3.2 Romelius L. Baker's Economy home. Photo by author, June 8, 2017.

FIGURE 3.3 George Rapp's Economy "Great House." Photo by author, June 8, 2017.

were simply corrupt themselves (as their critics would contend), after the society's first two years, the Rapps withdrew the financial status of Rapp & Associates behind a cloak of secrecy.[125] This secrecy, along with the Rapps' uncharitable attitudes toward their neighbors and departing members, reinforced the impression of critics that Harmony's leaders were miserly, greedy, cold-hearted authoritarians.

Manufacturing did not suffer after Frederick's death, but continued to expand so that 1835 estimates put agricultural workers at only one-third, with the rest divided between artisans and factory workers.[126] George pushed for increased mechanization of the textile production, and Rapp & Associates continued to upgrade its technology across the board, switching from teasels to machinery to facilitate the carding process.[127] The fact that Rapp & Associates was facing a looming labor shortage surely lent urgency to the increasing mechanization of its manufacturing. A decline in births (thanks to the doctrine of celibacy), an aging membership, and a refusal to admit new members made it inevitable that the ranks of the society would start to decline. In fact, from the early 1830s onward, Harmony admitted almost no new members, except for those born in the society or brought in as children before George almost entirely closed the society off.[128] Feeling betrayed by more recent members and the second generation of Harmonists, George was increasingly untrustworthy of outsiders. Since the new millennium was close at hand, Harmony's purity and piety was more important than distant concerns over who would operate the factories in another couple of decades.

Before his death, Frederick had even mechanized the silk process by purchasing and constructing silk reeling and twisting machines, powered by steam.[129] One machine in particular impressed J. S. Buckingham as displaying "admirable workmanship." It had been built by Economy's mechanics and was capable of simultaneously producing seven ribbons, the quality of which equaled that of French factories, often regarded as the standard in the field.[130] This machine was unique to America, and it expanded Economy's silk manufacturing into new patterns and styles.[131] By this point, all three of the factories were powered by a seventy-horsepower steam engine, which also powered the flour mill and brought water eighty feet from the Ohio River to Economy.[132]

Republican Industry 83

The increased emphasis on industry and manufacturing was not lost on visitors, as Englishman George Featherstonhaugh remarked in 1835 that one of his first impressions upon approaching Economy was not the beautiful fields that had impressed previous visitors, but "a manufactory with thick coal-smoke reeking from it."[133] Although, after viewing the town itself, Featherstonhaugh did later remark, "I never saw a more satisfactory picture of abundance; it reminded me continually of the gardens of the farmers in Tuscany and Lombardy."[134] He noted that unlike most riverside towns, Economy did not go out of its way to welcome visitors. It certainly did not throw out the welcome mat to visitors in the way of jetties or landings to facilitate the transfer of steamboat passengers, as was the practice in other river towns.[135]

To keep abreast of the latest advances in textile manufacturing, in 1835 and again in 1841, George sent one of his trusted agents and an experienced mechanic on a tour of East Coast textile mills.[136] These trips were fruitful, and indicative of the constantly improving nature of

FIGURE 3.4 *Economy* (ca. 1838). Grenville Mellen, *A Book of the United States*... (New York: H. F. Sumner & Co., 1838), 293.

84   Part One: Christian Communal Capitalism

Harmony's manufacturing.[137] Naturally, the tour included Lowell, Massachusetts, where Rapp & Associates purchased new and improved broadcloth sheering machines.[138] George also welcomed technical experts to Economy to improve and refine the society's silk manufacturing process.[139] This was indicative of the general increase in the society's technical proficiency. As George explained, "At the start we did not even have the common craftsmen, but now machinists and artists are there who not only know how to manufacture wool and cotton goods, but are also able to construct the machines necessary."[140] George was proud of the machinists who built Economy's textile machines, and of the fact that this enabled them to wear "silk clothes of our own make," boasting that "to the present no one in the United States has outdone us" in silk textile production.[141]

Thanks to these gains, by 1836, the wool factory was processing 100,000 pounds a year, producing blankets, broadcloths, satinets, and flannels, while the cotton factory required the importation of 300 bales per year to feed its production of yarns and sheeting. Silk production likewise continued to grow, garnering the society's silk factory attention, advice seekers, awards, and curious visitors.[142] Now under George's granddaughter Gertrude's direction, the operation consisted of 10,000 mulberry trees and 500,000 worms, producing 60 pounds of silk per year, including some items that only Harmony manufactured domestically.[143] J. S. Buckingham estimated in a report on his visit to Economy in 1840 that the society was still worth $500,000, all the more remarkable considering how many lost fortunes in the Panic of 1837.[144]

Fueled by land speculation and easy credit, the Panic of 1837 was a severe shock to the American economy. When the Bank of England raised interest rates and cut credit lines, the result was a collapse of commodities prices (notably, cotton), banks, and companies.[145] Even more so than in 1819, Economy was well positioned to weather the latest American economic crisis, in part because the society was nearly self-sufficient. According to Buckingham, Economy was indifferent to "whether the Banks suspend payment or redeem their notes in specie— whether trade is flourishing or otherwise—whether bankrupts are many or few," and he claimed that Harmonists would just "go on tilling their fields, and reaping their harvests; feeding their sheep, and shearing their wool; growing their fruits, and gathering them in."[146] Buckingham

Republican Industry 85

detailed how the society always stored plenty of its agricultural and industrial products for its own use, and mostly just purchased raw cotton, coffee, tea, and sugar. Additional profit went into new construction, land, and animals.[147]

As Buckingham noted, even though the domestic wool business tanked, American banks stopped issuing specie (and many collapsed), Harmony could afford to sit tight by scaling back its manufacturing and weathering the storm in relative comfort, just as it had during the Panic of 1819.[148] As during that panic, Rapp & Associates struggled to collect its debts, but this did not create a financial crisis for the society. It did not have wages to pay, nor debt payments to make. George's primary concern was to keep his workforce engaged. He was hesitant to cut production too much because "otherwise we know of no other occupation for our many young people for to give them leisure time would have no good effect."[149] This formed a stark contrast with the condition of many Americans, such as the father who pleaded with Rapp in 1837 to take his four children, aged between ten and two.[150] Instead, George was probably the only man in America excited by the economic crisis, as he viewed it as fulfillment of end time prophesies and an indication that Harmony's central role in the new millennium was imminent.[151]

CONCLUSION

George Rapp died on August 7, 1847, in his Economy home. The *Pittsburgh Daily Morning Post* hailed him as "the greatest communist of the age" (coincidentally, this was just a few months before Marx and Engels published *The Communist Manifesto*).[152] Friedrich Engels was well aware of "the Rappites," as he called them in an 1845 German-language article, "Description of Recently Rounded Communist Societies Still in Existence."[153] The article extolled the Harmonists, along with the Shakers and Zoarites, as productive, equitable communities where the only thing one might "criticize are the religious prejudices," which, Engels concluded, "clearly have nothing to do with the ideal of community of goods."[154] The great German economist Friedrich List disagreed. He did not doubt the significance of religion in holding the society together, but he also placed great emphasis on the fearsome power and charisma of George Rapp.[155] Although List may have expected the society to crumble

86 *Part One: Christian Communal Capitalism*

once freed from George Rapp's commanding presence, this was not the case. Rapp had left the business finances of Rapp & Associates in good shape, including the secret stash of gold and silver coins.[156] The senior members of Economy crafted new Articles of Agreement, endorsed a new Board of Elders (including important figures such as Romelius L. Baker) to manage internal affairs, and created a Board of Trustees to manage Rapp & Associates.[157] In the short term, little about the business operations changed, as Baker continued to act as the financial head of the organization, assisted by Jacob Henrici.[158] Each of these men were well regarded by the region's businessmen, referred to as "respected men," with agents of R. G. Dun & Company specifically calling Baker "one of the best businessmen West of the Mountains."[159] Interestingly, these two business leaders were also designated "religious teachers and spokesmen," demonstrating the degree to which religion and business continued to go hand in hand in the Harmony Society.[160]

With its new leadership structure in place, the society continued to prosper, although the nature of its business changed. Over the next two decades, the aging and shrinking society shifted from factory work and invested its significant capital in the purchase of a coal works, the establishment of the Economy Oil Company (which drilled its own wells and refined oil at Darlington, Pennsylvania), and the Darlington Railroad.[161] The shift in its business focus continued Rapp & Associates' impressive growth throughout the first five decades of the nineteenth century. By 1864, R. G. Dun & Company estimated the Harmony Society's net worth at a minimum of $5 million, upping the estimate to more than $10 million just two years later.[162]

Ultimately, George and Frederick Rapp were much more than the spiritual leaders of a group Pietistic German immigrants. History, if it mentions them at all, usually focuses on their spiritual roles, overlooking their success as industrial and manufacturing entrepreneurs. This is a fundamental mistake. From the earliest days of the society, the *Niles Register* described the Harmonists as "among the most persevering and industrious people in the world, and have all things in common. They now have mills and manufactories of many kinds. . . . They make broad cloths, cassimeres, flannels, paper hangings, whiskey, wine, flour, flaxseed-oil, leather, nails, iron-mongery, etc.!! and have a warehouse in Pittsburg [*sic*]."[163] As founders of one of the earliest of the numerous early national-period Christian communal capitalist societies, including the Shakers, Zoarites, Owenites, Mormons, and Hutterities, among many others, they were at the vanguard of an exploding vision of economic communes. Friedrich Engels noted this movement, suggesting in 1845 that it had broad appeal: "The success enjoyed by the Shakers, Harmonists, and Separatists . . . have caused many other people in America to undertake similar experiments in recent years. . . . However, it is not just in America, but in England too."[164]

Harmony's longevity is worth pondering. Long after many nineteenth-century utopian societies disbanded in failure, the economic success of Rapp & Associates allowed the society to endure into the beginning of the twentieth century, despite the self-defeating policies of celibacy and its barring of new members. What led to this success and longevity? Rapp & Associates boasted a skilled, hardworking, generally content workforce. Its market-savvy executives made astute business decisions and resisted the urge to overextend their operations. Consequently, Harmony always weathered the boom-and-bust cycles of nineteenth-century capitalism with ease. Clearly, such engagement with the market economy proved vital to the success of the Harmonists and lay at the root of their ballyhooed financial success. It is telling that the contracts and legal documents always listed "Rapp & Associates" and not "Harmony Society" because the society was a corporation—despite the reluctance of early national-period legislatures to recognize them as such. This was a community that forsook private property yet regularly engaged in many of the other trappings of the nineteenth-century market: stocks, bonds, leases, mortgages, patents, trademarks, licenses, litigation, and contracts.[165] When a farmer named James Anderson entered a lease for 9.5 acres, with whom did he deal? Rapp & Associates, something that sounds more like a twenty-first-century limited liability corporation or a legal firm specializing in contract law than a band of communally minded German Pietists.[166]

The way in which Harmony embraced technological innovation was also vital to its success. Unlike the twenty-first-century Amish or nineteenth-century Luddites, the Harmonists embraced technology, from building their own textile mills to digging oil wells and investing in and purchasing railroads. In fact, the records of Rapp & Associates

88   *Part One: Christian Communal Capitalism*

are replete with patents and trademark applications as they worked to keep up with the rapid pace of technological change in the textile industry. One such example is the agreement George Rapp entered into with Calvin W. Cook of Lowell, Massachusetts, holder of a patent for the dressing of cotton and wool textile blends. Rapp coveted the patent for his textile mills and believed it was well worth the fifty dollars he paid to Cook for the rights to access an improved set of cards used in a steam-powered gig machine. Interestingly, Rapp even used a factory term in referring to himself as "superintendent" in the contract's language. Abreast of emerging technology in the textile industry, Rapp wanted to maintain Rapp & Associates' competitive edge in textiles—an industry that was incredibly competitive and innovative in the 1830s.[167] This was hardly an isolated example: Rapp entered into many of these kinds of contractual agreements as he constantly sought out all manner of technological improvements for his industries, from boring and knitting machines to beehouses.[168]

Yet, for nearly every admirer who thought Harmony offered the perfect republican model for how to stimulate industry while avoiding the "degrading mass" crowding almshouses in Philadelphia, critics instead saw religious zealotry, with an anachronistic, authoritarian despot repressing his naive followers.[169] A Hungarian aristocrat, Alexander Farkas, acknowledged this dichotomy in 1831:

> During our travels we have heard many conflicting opinions about Rapp and his society. . . . Some describe the Rapp Society as a concerted human effort to achieve perfect equality and the purest moral life, while others depict it as a group of gullible Germans deluded by Rapp, who exploits them for his own self-interest and holds them under spiritual domination. They believe that after Rapp's death they will disband. Still others ridicule them and think they are anti-democratic and are under monarchic influence and therefore endanger republican principles and individual liberties.[170]

Americans and Europeans generally admired Rapp & Associates' industry and the peace and order of Harmonie/Economy, but they considered Harmony's religious beliefs aberrant or oppressive. Regardless, it is a mistake to discount the significance of religion in shaping Harmony's market activities, chalking it up to a quirky feature of Rapp's pietist authoritarianism. Owen and his followers assumed they could substitute their humanist philosophies for the biblical worldview of the Rapps and find similar success as they introduced "an entire new state of society; to change it from the ignorant, selfish system, to an enlightened, social system, which shall gradually unite all interest into one, and remove all the cause for contest between individuals."[171] Owen was wrong. Despite his international fanfare, grandiose plans, and sweeping vision, his secular New Harmony lasted only three years.[172] Herein was the rub: religion was central to the lives of Harmonists, both spiritual and material, and it was impossible to separate the sacred and secular within the society. Their brand of Pietism animated everything the Harmonists did, from their decision to immigrate to the United States, to their endeavors to create a communal capitalist society that would redeem the urban industrial order of the late eighteenth and early nineteenth centuries. This fusion of religion and business is why it became increasingly difficult to determine whether Economy, Pennsylvania, was the site of a religious organization or a republican factory town like Lowell, Massachusetts. If towns such as Lowell were an attempt to purify industry and make it morally acceptable to skeptical Americans, then the Harmonists sought to purify industry through more explicitly pietistic measures. The Harmony Society was a spiritual communal refuge and a Christian business enterprise, all wrapped up into one fantastically intriguing place.

90 *Part One: Christian Communal Capitalism*

PART TWO

Christian Reform Capitalism

The purified market and harmonious workforce envisioned by Pietist Americans (and the socialists they inspired) comprised just one vision of a transformed economic order in the early national period. A reformation of the market was likewise on the minds of many Americans of a Calvinist background. The standard historiographic narrative of the early national period and its reform movements connects technological changes (e.g., the Erie Canal) with religious revivalism (e.g., that of Charles Finney), resulting in voluntary associations (e.g., temperance).[1] Some of these reforming Protestants also wielded political power.[2] Political action and voluntary associations were obviously important mechanisms for social reform in the early national period. However, they were neither the only agents of reform nor the only avenue by which reforming Protestants leveraged their religion into vehicles for the transformation of American culture. Christian business enterprises (CBEs) established for the express purpose of reforming the market economy were equally important expressions of the reforming impulse that characterized the early national period. In fact, the creation of reforming CBEs led to some of the most intense revivals in upstate New York, and in general predated the explosion of the voluntary reform associations.

Recently, historians have started recognizing the significance of such business practices, particularly in relation to slavery and abolitionism, convincingly demonstrating how abolitionists sought to harness the power of business to achieve marketplace and societal reform.[3] For example, the American Anti-Slavery Society's reform efforts "resembled a modern business enterprise," one that was innovative and technologically advanced, albeit one whose profits and products worked to end slavery.[4] Atlantic slavery was enmeshed in the emergence of capitalism. This troubled merchants who thought ethical and moral principles should govern their marketplace activities. The Quaker-initiated free produce movement was one such response: an alternate market supplying consumer goods freed of the entanglements of slave labor.[5] Bronwen Everill illustrates another example of reform capitalism in her description of how merchants and consumers pondered ways of practicing a more "ethical commerce," in a serious, if unlikely, bid to end Atlantic slavery. Protestant abolitionists such as Zachary Macaulay (a member of the Clapham Sect) "saw the market as the solution" to the slave system. Ultimately, Protestants such as Macaulay were active agents in reforming the emerging capitalist system into something that was *"acceptable."*[6]

The next chapter focuses on one such reform CBE, the Pioneer Line of upstate New York, established as an alternative to the existing "Old Line" connecting Albany and Buffalo. Like the abolitionist CBEs, the Pioneer was but one of many CBEs formed in the 1820s and 1830s that endeavored to reform the market in some fashion. Some, such as Lewis Tappan's *New York Journal of Commerce*, are still in existence today. A few of these CBEs, such as R. G. Dun & Company, already feature prominently in American scholarship, but historians typically miss the point that, like the abolitionist enterprises, these CBEs were created to rid the marketplace of specific evils.[7] The founders of the Pioneer Line identified a "problem" with the market—companies were increasingly open for business seven days a week thanks to the policies of the federal mail service and the opening of the Erie Canal. Market-minded merchants out west in cities such as Rochester, New York, feared losing workdays to their competition in the market centers of New York, Boston, and Philadelphia. Respect for the Sunday Sabbath was only one way that reforming CBEs sought to mold the market; for example, the proprietors of the Pioneer Line also wanted to promote dry lodging and dining establishments

92   *Part Two: Christian Reform Capitalism*

along their route. They strove for excellence in customer service by building a stage line from the ground up. This meant buying brand-new stagecoaches and hiring a skilled workforce—primarily composed of stage drivers. As the next chapter will explain, the Pioneer Line's boast that it would only hire the best and most godly drivers (who did not curse or drink alcohol) proved difficult to live up to—there were only so many people with the skill necessarily to safely operate a stagecoach in the late 1820s, and many did not fit the Pioneer's image.

As a business entity, the Pioneer Line only operated for four years and was not financially successful, so it is unsurprising that scholars of early America have overlooked its story. The company did not transform the transportation sector to the same degree as other reform CBEs impacted their own respective spheres, as was true, for example, of Lewis Tappan's Mercantile Agency (which created the modern credit rating industry).[8] Yet the Pioneer Line's significance transcends its brief life span and its financial failures. The Pioneer Line provoked a larger public debate over the efficacy and propriety of reform capitalism. It engendered fierce support and virulent opposition. Its critics derisively labeled the larger movement to reform the capitalist system "Pioneerism"—and indeed, the Pioneer Line was part of a much larger effort to reform the market in the early nineteenth century, curing it of the ills of alcohol, seven-day work-weeks, and slave labor.[9] (According to its critics, the term "Pioneerism" seems to have derived from how the leaders of the various strands of the movement designated themselves "the *Pioneers* of the Almighty," since "They have established lines of stages—canal boats—daily, weekly, and monthly journals—missionary societies—tract societies, &c . . . and exercised a controlling and baneful influence over very many of the publick presses!"[10]) Ultimately, a despondent Josiah Bissell Jr., the chief mover behind the Pioneer Line, faced with the demise of his transportation line, turned to the famed preacher Charles Finney, inviting him to address at his church in Rochester, New York. The transformative revivals that followed, which led to the creation of the so-called Burned-Over District of upstate New York, loom large in early U.S. history, even if the reason for Finney's invitation—the Pioneer Line's "failure"—does not.

Consequently, the Pioneer Line challenges the dominant "cause-and-effect" thesis that the Finney revivals produced social reform programs and movements. In fact, the Pioneer Line and the other reforming CBEs

Part Two: Christian Reform Capitalism   93

of the 1820s preceded the Finney revivals by several years, suggesting that enterprises of Christian reform capitalism were already at work before the upstate New York revivals and the subsequent explosion of voluntary associations. For example, the chronology of the Pioneer Line suggests that it led to the formation of the General Union for Promoting the Observance of the Christian Sabbath (an ecumenical association formed to reform the market), not the other way around.[11]

A January 1, 1830, editorial in the *Rochester Observer* identified the primary problem of the early United States as an obsession with money—all fed by the expanding market economy, supported by a government that backed the interests of the business community.[12] Chief among these concerns was the expansion of market activity into Sundays, even though it may be hard to comprehend that reformers like Bissell thought it was central to everything.[13] Consequently, the Pioneer Line and other reforming CBEs emerged as a distinctly evangelical attempt to curb and refashion these perceived excesses of the marketplace, while still embracing the market itself. The three Rochester commissioners of the Pioneer Line, William Atkinson, Josiah Bissell Jr., and Aristarchus Champion exemplified this fusion of faith and the market. They had no interest in destroying the capitalist system even though their goals were also far different from George Rapp's attempt to purify the market via Christian communal capitalism. Instead, reforming Christian businesses of the early national period were created to refashion the marketplace so that it no longer violated God's moral law. Certainly, they were no antimoderns, standing in opposition to the communications and transportation revolutions that spurred the market economy's expansion.[14] Christian reform capitalists were excited about the possibilities presented by the opening of the Erie Canal in 1823. However, this technological revolution presented a dark side for pious entrepreneurs by expanding the workweek to seven days, chiefly because it threatened the nation's divine, covenantal status.

The theology of the covenant, paired with postmillennialism, was at the core of the reforming CBEs. The notion that America had a special relationship with God that the expanding market economy jeopardized was the driving force behind these reform-minded businessmen. Covenantal theology was rooted in the Calvinist tradition, so, unsurprisingly, many businessmen founding reforming CBEs were from

94 *Part Two: Christian Reform Capitalism*

Congregational or Presbyterian backgrounds. Reform-minded business-men warned that doom and destruction—the failure of the republican experiment—was the only possible outcome for a nation that abandoned its covenant with God. Consequently, the stakes were high for the reforming CBEs of the early national period.[15] They were doubly high because of their brand of postmillennialism. This millennial attitude viewed conversion and social reform as ushering in the return of Christ, which would only happen after a thousand-year period marked by increased godliness and peace.[16] Just as the eschatology of the Harmonists drove them to separate from society even as they created a vigorous "divine economy," so, too, did the Christian reform capitalists' millennialism shape the way they interacted with society and the market economy. Since the fate of America and all the world depended on the progression of godliness, the missions of CBEs such as the Pioneer Line were invested with urgent, sacred purpose.

Part Two: Christian Reform Capitalism   95

CHAPTER FOUR

The Sabbatarians

It was breakfast as usual for the Bissell family in their home on South Washington Street, in the village of Rochester, New York.[1] Josiah Bissell Jr. closed his well-worn Bible and looked across at his young son and namesake. The din of the ongoing excavation of the Erie Canal was especially loud this morning, prompting him to consider the ramifications of its eventual opening for the growing village. Clearly, it would not remain a village much longer, and he knew the speculation in the surrounding land tracts would really alter things. What, he wondered, were the chances that—oh heavens! Suddenly, a tremendous crash jolted Bissell from his reverie, as wood splinters showered him and five-year-old Josiah as they watched the breakfast table before them collapse into a heap. Disoriented, Bissell looked around and saw a shocking sight: a hole in the wall of his new house. Peeking through the hole, he could see canal workers rushing toward his home, crying out. Glancing back at the table, it began to dawn on the elder Josiah that a blast charge had gone awry and catapulted a large rock into his house. Rushing around the shattered remains of his table, he grabbed his son, held him tight while looking toward heaven, and offered a prayer of thanks to God for sparing their lives. Perhaps there was a greater purpose for him yet to fill. All the same, the episode was deeply unsettling. Maybe the Erie Canal was not the best place to raise a family, he concluded. Months later, Bissell sold the property to his friend Harvey Ely for $1,775.[2]

Upon completion in 1825, the Erie Canal would shatter more than Josiah Bissell Jr.'s breakfast table, as it served to upend the way people did business and lived their lives in upstate New York. Chief among the "internal improvement" projects of the period, which included the construction of such key pieces of infrastructure as turnpikes, stagecoach lines, and canals, the Erie Canal combined with an expanding Post Office to foster business, migration, the diffusion of international and national news, political participation, and, indirectly, cultural conflict. Not everyone cheered the fact that this new stream of goods (and passengers) was increasingly flowing seven days a week. Certainly not Josiah Bissell Jr., who became one of the chief figures in the Sabbatarian movement in the 1820s and 1830s through the development of a six-day-a-week Albany to Buffalo stagecoach line, illustrating the particular vision of the market espoused by Christian reform capitalists.

Bissell was a founding figure in early Rochester. Before he moved to the growing village from Pittsfield, Massachusetts, Bissell had already formed his first local partnership with his friend Elisha Ely of West Springfield, Massachusetts, in 1813. Together, they constructed a large mill, the so-called Red Mill that came to dominate the village's skyline by 1815. Newly married, Bissell moved to Rochesterville sometime between 1813 and 1817. Along with Ely's brother, Bissell operated a store in Rochester under the name of Bissell & Ely (Bissell built an additional four three-story stores in the 1820s).[3] Like many entrepreneurs of the early national period, Bissell was an aggressive land speculator, the primary landholder of a Rochester neighborhood known as Cornhill (just south of the eventual site of the Erie Canal). He also engaged in manufacturing, specifically skids and slides for moving potash from its manufacturing places in the village to the edge of the Genesee River.[4]

Active in the village's religious community, Bissell was a founding elder of the Third Presbyterian Church of Rochester, perhaps its most evangelistic congregation, and spearheaded construction of the congregation's original building. He was the central backer of the evangelistic *Rochester Observer*, president of both the Monroe County Tract Society and the Genesee Sabbath School Union, and treasurer of the Rochester chapter of the American Board of Commissioners for Foreign Missions.[5] Additionally, his wife Henrietta (known for her daily prayer

98 *Part Two: Christian Reform Capitalism*

meetings at 8:30 a.m.) was the treasurer of the Rochester Female Missionary Society and director of the Female Charitable Society. Bissell taught Sunday school as the superintendent of Third Presbyterian's Sunday school for many years, and supposedly was first to champion the idea of supplying a Bible to every family in America—a goal the American Bible Society soon promoted.[6] Bissell was prone to embrace the extreme among his circle of reformers, once writing his friend and fellow reformer Gerrit Smith, "I have got beyond Temperance to the Cold Water Society—no Tea, Coffee, or any other slops—only pure Water to drink and coarse fare to eat."[7] Finally, and perhaps most significantly, Bissell was instrumental in bringing revivalist Charles G. Finney to Rochester in 1830, sparking the intense revivals that remade the character of the city and the surrounding region.[8] Prior to this he was famous for building his church's first building in just one week's time, and when the congregation had outgrown it, for disassembling the building by segments, which he in turn used to erect new homes.[9] Although he was just one of several proprietors of the Pioneer Line, Bissell was its most public face and spokesman. Along with his fellow Rochester businessmen William Atkinson and Aristarchus Champion, Bissell emerged as the unofficial head proprietor of the Pioneer Line.

William Atkinson, originally from New York City, was a friend of Josiah Bissell Jr., an entrepreneur, and fellow mill owner. Atkinson built his so-called Yellow Mill in 1817, directly across the Genesee River from Bissell's Red Mill, served as director of the Bank of Rochester, and was a member of the city's Board of Manufactures and the Rochester Exchange.[10] Like Bissell, Atkinson engaged in land speculation.[11] His landholdings were important to the construction of the Erie Canal because he co-owned more than two hundred lots along the canal, along with a fellow founding member of St. Paul's Episcopal, Elisha Johnson. Also, in 1828, the state purchased some of their land to construct a new lock.[12] They both went bankrupt in 1832, amid a recession that hit the wealthy and poor alike, with Atkinson's debts rumored at between $60,000 and $80,000.[13]

Like Bissell, Atkinson possessed clear evangelical credentials, even though he was a member of an Episcopalian congregation, St. Paul's, the second Episcopal church established in Rochester, built in 1827. He was also a member of many voluntary religious associations and worked to

The Sabbatarians 99

push St. Paul's in an evangelical direction.[14] Atkinson may have met Bissell serving as the vice president of the Monroe County Tract Society (Bissell was the president). Atkinson would have rubbed elbows with Bissell at the Monroe County Bible Society as well (where he was also vice president).[15] He was also the secretary of the Rochester Seminary, while his wife ran the newly established Atkinson Female Seminary.[16]

The silent partner of the Pioneer Line in Rochester was Aristarchus Champion, who, though he was one of the richest men of the early national period, is absent from histories of the time. Born in New London, Connecticut, and an 1807 graduate of Yale, Champion was not only a business associate of Josiah Bissell Jr., but also his close companion.[17] In fact, Bissell thought enough of Aristarchus that he named one of his four sons Champion Aristarchus.[18] Bissell's financial troubles in 1828, which forced him to default on a mortgage that he used to purchase land from Champion, were not enough to destroy their friendship.[19] Aristarchus inherited an enormous fortune built on speculating in northeastern Ohio lands, benefiting from his father's sizable

FIGURE 4.1 Champion House, Colchester, Connecticut. Photo by author, November 3, 2020.

100 *Part Two: Christian Reform Capitalism*

stake in the Connecticut Land Company. By the 1830s, he was one of the richest men in America, rumored to be worth $300,000.[20] By the 1860s, R. G. Dun & Company estimated Champion's worth at more than $1 million.[21]

Born into a devout Connecticut family, Aristarchus and his twin brother, Aristobulus, had been baptized by their father, General Henry Champion, a second-generation deacon of the Westchester Congregational Church, on October 31, 1784.[22] Aristarchus became a full communing member of the church on May 21, 1809, before moving to Rochester in 1826.[23] He was known as a somewhat reclusive, eccentric individual, and perhaps prone to the schemes of confidence men. (In some quarters, he was regarded as something akin to an Ebenezer Scrooge–type character.) At the very least, he seems to have shared some of Bissell's penchant for alienating people. Upon his death, obituaries pondered who would get the fortune of the lifelong bachelor.[24] It was probably not surprising that he left his complete fortune to the American Bible Society and the Board of Foreign Missions of the Presbyterian Church, since he was known for donating large sums to evangelical groups such as the New York State Temperance Society.[25]

Bissell, Atkinson, and Champion were evangelicals who easily married their religiosity with their business ventures. Reverand Charles Bush remembered Bissell in 1869 as one "that if you saw him in a prayer meeting, you would think he always lived in the sanctuary; or if you met him in his counting room, you would suppose he had never been anywhere else."[26] Bush was not implying Bissell and his type lived inconsistent, bifurcated lives, but rather that they did not feel any conflict between their business and spiritual lives. However, the opening of the Erie Canal created a conflict for them by radically altering the culture of small villages such as Rochester, which saw its population increase from 331 in 1815, to 1,502 in 1820, to 10,863 in 1830, and to 19,061 in 1838.[27] For Atkinson, Bissell, and Champion, no threat was more problematic than the Erie Canal's promotion of seven-day-a-week business, leading the community into potentially grave sin. As Bissell wrote fellow activist Gerrit Smith of Oneida County, "Something must be done or the prevalence of Sabbath breaking will ruin our Churches and our whole land."[28] Just a few months prior, an editorial in Utica's *Western Recorder* described this matter as nothing less than a national urgency: "A righteous Providence, even in this life, will reward national corruptions with national calamities; and no christian land, which shall at length forget her Sabbaths, can expect to escape the tremendous visitations of his rod."[29]

Of course, concerns over the Sabbath did not originate with the opening of the Erie Canal. Going back to colonial times, Sunday activity had been a source of conflict, and the expansion of the U.S. Post Office highlighted the issue in the early national period. More than a simple fight over mail service on Sundays, the debate over the obligations of a federal institution to its citizens, both as consumers and as moral agents, represented one part of the larger battle over Pioneerism.

SABBATARIANISM

Conservative Protestants endeavored to reshape American society in the early national period in a myriad of ways, but foundational to all their efforts was the restoration and protection of the first day of the week, Sunday, as distinct from the Jewish practice of resting on the seventh day, Saturday (according to fourth of the Ten Commandments). New England traditionally observed this twenty-four-hour period from sundown Saturday to sundown Sunday in the traditional Jewish manner of resting on Saturdays. This was in contrast with the dominant practice in Europe and the American South, where the Sabbath was usually celebrated from midnight Saturday to midnight Sunday. Additionally, some groups of American Protestants, such as the Seventh-Day Baptists, continued to observe Saturday as their day of rest. A strict observation of the Sabbath (which extended to sport and recreational activities) stemmed from Puritan disgust with "riotous" sixteenth- and seventeenth-century English cultural practice on Sundays. Although agricultural work never completely stopped on Sundays in early America, it was the gradual increase in commercial activity in the early republic that alarmed those who favored a stricter Sabbath.[30]

Sabbath-minded individuals saw this expansion of the workweek as an unwelcome, if predictable, result of the Post Office's expansion into seven-day service in 1810. Section 9 of the Act Regulating the Post Office Establishment instructed postmasters to keep their offices attended "on every day on which a mail . . . shall arrive by land or water," and claimed that it was the "duty" of the postmaster to deliver "on demand" mail every

102 *Part Two: Christian Reform Capitalism*

day of the week.[31] The first phase of Sabbatarianism, which lasted from 1810 to 1816, was sparked by the experience of Hugh Wylie, a merchant, postmaster, and elder in the Presbyterian Church of Washington, Pennsylvania, whose distribution of the mail from his store on Sundays drew the attention of his synod, resulting in his expulsion from the denomination.[32] Wylie's plight—having to choose between a government directive and the free exercise of his religion—galvanized opposition to the 1810 act as hundreds of petitions flooded Congress protesting the decision to open offices on Sundays.[33]

On the other hand, since newspapers full of the latest financial information dominated this mail, supporters of the 1810 act did not want to lose timely access to valuable news. Since the expanding market economy privileged whoever received the latest economic news first, many businessmen, particularly those in western New York and Ohio, welcomed the advent of seven-day stagecoach lines and daily access to financial news. For Sabbatarian-minded individuals, the Post Office transportation networks, and the market economy collectively pointed to a nation increasingly concerned with chasing dollars at the expense of the community's spiritual health. Sabbatarians regarded the increasing disregard for the Sabbath as symptomatic of a larger declension in civic morality.[34] Despite a slew of congressional petitions in protest of the 1810 act, the mail continued to flow daily, as Congress and the Post Office deemed the continuing seven-day service vital to the nation's interests.[35]

This defeat was hard for men such as Bissell to swallow, because to make matters worse, in the early nineteenth century, the local post office was not simply a place one dropped off and picked up mail; it often functioned as the focal point of the male social scene. Many post offices were located in general stores, drawing in men to relax, tell stories, and catch up on the latest gossip, usually with an alcoholic beverage in hand. As the local post office was the only business establishment open on Sundays, and with the reputation for providing a sanctuary for men to get drunk (and act out in misogynistic and racist ways), it provided a sharp contrast with the only other establishment open on the Sabbath—the church.[36]

The opening of the Erie Canal reignited the Sabbath debate, leading to a revived Sabbatarian campaign against the delivery of federal mail

The Sabbatarians 103

and the formation of a new advocacy association, the General Union for Promoting the Observance of the Christian Sabbath. By 1827, as "A Friend to Enterprize" wrote in the *Rochester Observer*, "The Christian community are beginning to open their eyes a little to the subject of Sabbath-breaking on our canal."[37] Concerned businessmen in nearby Utica seconded these concerns.[38] While perhaps a bit extreme in wishing the canal had never been built rather than encourage seven-days-a-week commerce, conservative Protestants living along the canal would have agreed with scholars who argue that that the influx of workers on projects such as the Erie Canal was instrumental in challenging traditional Protestant social mores. Immigrant labor was key to building the canals, but by the 1830s, people's perception of these waterways was negative.[39] Furthermore, concerned citizens claimed the "rough culture" of the canals produced excessive drinking, gambling, criminality, violence, and Sabbath violations. Fights between boatmen, travelers subjected to obscenities, and bawdy drinking songs caused businessmen such as Bissell to ponder the proper response.[40] In fact, by the 1830s, boatmen of the western canals had earned enough of a reputation that missionary societies specifically targeted them as an urgent mission field.[41]

Rochester found itself at the center of this debate, in part because it was rapidly transforming from a sleepy mill village to a bustling city of manufacturing and trade. In addition to the canal workers, the growing city attracted out-of-town merchants and travelers, which in turn led to the establishment of taverns eager to serve Rochester's visitors.[42] These newcomers included confidence men, prostitutes, pickpockets, and swindlers who found towns such as Rochester a natural stop on their perpetual road act.[43] The rising economic prospects of the town attracted additional migrants who often ended up in tenements and boarding houses, and by the mid-1820s, multiple entertainment establishments opened to cater to the working class. Bissell and other Rochester Protestants did not appreciate how the town's circus and theater (the "chief of Satan's Engines") were a "debasing and demoralizing influence," producing late-night "peals of hooting, howling, shouting, shrieking, and almost every other unseemly noise"—to say nothing of prostitution on the theater's "third tier."[44] We do not have to imagine what Bissell's crowd thought when these establishments requested permission to perform on

104 *Part Two: Christian Reform Capitalism*

Saturday evenings (when those of New England background began their Sabbath).[45]

The fact that Rochester was the site of celebrity daredevil Sam Patch's fatal leap into Genesee Falls on November 13, 1829, only served to reinforce the city's emerging reputation as a boomtown where moral propriety was increasingly fading. Bissell, in Third Presbyterian's Sunday school two days after the tragic event, condemned not only Patch's stunt, but also claimed all who witnessed his demise were murderers in God's sight.[46] While it is going too far to claim Sam Patch's ill-fated final jump "touched off" the entire social reform movement in Rochester, it was certainly one more sign of the cultural decay that made Bissell and company feel their campaign was all the more urgent.[47] After all, it was an "incensed God" who sealed Patch's fate.[48]

Once again, thousands of Sabbath petitions flooded Congress (mostly from northeastern and western states), including one signed by Aristarchus Champion, William Atkinson, and Josiah Bissell Jr.[49] Sabbatarians appealed broadly to Americans by stressing reason and rationality in pressing for observation of the Sabbath.[50] It was common sense for Sabbatarians: disregard for rest on the first day would lead to a collapse of public worship, flourishing of vice, and an end to America's "free institutions."[51] Some went a step further and argued that disregard for the Sabbath specifically fostered vice on the transportation lines.[52] The Presbytery of Onondaga echoed the General Union that the "lamentable declension of vital piety" was tied directly to market activities—"laboring, buying, and selling" on Sundays.[53] It was clear: the market's growth in the early national period seemed to fuel Sabbath breaking.

Sabbatarians argued that the Sabbath was compatible with success in the marketplace. Hardworking people needed a rest, and God modeled this sensibility by resting on the seventh day of His creation. The principle was inherently democratic, as Sabbatarians argued God created the Sabbath to protect the poor from exploitation and oppression—"the Saviour of the world was the friend of the poor man"—thus, "the poorest man on this day feels his own dignity."[54] This was a common argument—that Sabbath observation was in the interest of the working class. The founders of the General Union maintained that a robust Sabbath was key to workers' social mobility: "The Sabbath, duly observed, will raise your families to intelligence, and competence, and all civil

The Sabbatarians 105

honours, as the wheel of Providence rolls; while the violation of it will raise up over you a monied aristocracy, thriving by your vices, and rising by your depression, and dooming you and your posterity to be hewers of wood and drawers of water for ever."[55] Quite simply, the Reverend David Magie argued, "the Sabbath is the poor man's friend," although skeptical critics of the Sabbatarian movement countered that the idle day would lead to "riots" and "playing cards . . . instead of reading the bible [sic]."[56]

Despite this argument, Sabbatarians were concerned that individual, uncoordinated efforts to observe the Sabbath would only serve to damage observant individuals' business prospects. The founders of the General Union for Promoting the Observance of the Christian Sabbath were convinced that the best way to reform the seven-day workweek was not legislative (although they were happy for the government to join the cause), but by "withdrawing our capital and patronage" from those businesses and proprietors who violated the Sabbath.[57] Arguing that "This tide of business is in so many ways interwoven, that individual resistance on the Sabbath, or the resistance of a Town, or City, or State, is hopeless," the only alternative was a "union of effort, and withdrawment from the appalling stream, and in such numbers all over the land" as to transform Americans' market behavior.[58] What they were describing was an alternative, or reformed, marketplace. Sabbatarians argued that this would lead to increased efficiency by providing necessary rest to all the economy's participants.[59]

In addition to fostering a more industrious nation, Sabbatarians believed that observation of the Sabbath would make people more God-fearing and would preserve the nation's republican virtue "because it is the government of God made effectual by his Spirit, which produces that righteousness which exalteth a nation; and the Sabbath is the chief organ of its administration."[60] Alternatively, "[Failing to observe the Sabbath will serve to] corrupt our virtue, and to undermine our republican institutions . . . which will render self-government impossible, and despotism itself the lesser plot."[61] Appealing to the nation's sense of destiny, the founders of the General Union stressed that the stakes were incredibly high because if it did not observe the Sabbath, America would "fail," and "If this nation fails in her vast experiment, the world's last hope expires."[62] Lyman Beecher echoed this concern, in stark, alarming rhetoric:

106   *Part Two: Christian Reform Capitalism*

Give up the Sabbath—blot out that orb of day—suspend its blessed attractions—and the reign of chaos and old night would return. . . . The American character, and our glorious institutions, will go down into the same grave that entombs the Sabbath; and our epitaph will stand forth a warning to the world—THUS ENDETH THE NATION THAT DESPISED THE LORD, AND GLORIED IN WIS-DOM, WEALTH, AND POWER.[63]

This connection between national prosperity, virtue and morality, free government, and religion was nearly an accepted "consensus" among certain intellectual and political circles during the revolutionary and early national periods.[64] The nation was an experiment in free institutions, the argument went, and this form of government, more than any other, required virtue, specifically Christian, republican virtue. The Sabbath was a cultivator of such virtue. Albert Barnes, pastor of First Presbyterian of Philadelphia, argued that even the experience of the Greeks suggested democratic governance called for regular, mandated periods of rest.[65] Preserving the Sabbath was an important component of creating virtue; it fostered social unity, morality, and purity of public conscience. Conversely, nations that failed to respect the Sabbath would not have the virtue necessary to enjoy the liberty and civic freedoms inherent to a republican society.[66]

Sabbatarians trusted that "the common sense" of Americans would see the merits of their movement. They hoped "to persuade" the country by "powerful example," voluntary association, and reformation to rest on the Sabbath.[67] But they also spoke in prophetic rhetoric. Noah Porter and Mark Hopkins, both Congregationalist ministers (the former was the eleventh president of Yale, while the latter was the fourth and longest-serving president of Williams College), used the example of the Hebrew prophet Nehemiah chastising the elites of his society to explain why ministers were justified in calling out their fellow citizens for their desecration of the Sabbath.[68] Like Nehemiah and other Hebrew prophets, Porter and Hopkins were focused on the nation's covenantal status. Stressing a commonly accepted narrative that God favored the moral and cursed the immoral, Sabbatarians argued that resting on the first day was central to preserving "the protection of heaven" over their communities and nation.[69]

The Sabbatarians 107

The influence of Reformed covenant theology upon the reforming Christian business enterprises is unmistakable. Transplanted New Englanders such as Josiah Bissell Jr. and Aristarchus Champion earnestly believed their nation and its covenant with God was drifting toward judgment. The issue was not simply a fear of an unraveling social fabric, or that capitalism demanded a more disciplined community of workers. To understand fully the motivation and spiritual concern of Protestants such as William Atkinson, Josiah Bissell Jr., and Aristarchus Champion requires that we understand their concept of the "covenant."

108 *Part Two: Christian Reform Capitalism*

CHAPTER FIVE

The Pioneers

It was no accident that the first Sabbatarian campaign against Sunday mail service was a joint effort of northern Congregationalists and Presbyterians.[1] Inheriting the covenant theology of seventeenth-century Puritans and Covenanters, many citizens of Rochester (and of the early national-period United States more broadly) viewed their family, church, town, state, and nation through the lens of covenantal communities.[2] This conceptual framework of how God interacts with his people was an internalization of God's covenant made with the ancient nation of Israel, and it formed the theological backbone of Bissell's Christian reform capitalism. Simplified, God's covenant with ancient Israel is as follows: "Walk with Yahweh, follow His commands, and He will protect and care for you and your nation, but turn from Him, follow other gods, and He will remove His hand of blessing and protection from you."[3] Northern Protestants such as Bissell did not interpret this as a onetime contract between Yahweh and ancient Israel. Instead, they viewed it as a timeless model of how God dealt with communities and nations writ large. Some went a step further, drawing continuity with John Winthrop, who viewed America as the New Israel, a nation that would redeem all others.[4] As the Reverend David Magie, pastor of Second Presbyterian of Elizabethtown, New Jersey, cautioned, "*The nation and kingdom that will not serve [God] shall perish.*"[5] Amid national hysteria over the possibility of war with France in 1798, the General Assembly of the Presbyterian Church in the United

States wrote an open letter to its congregants. An "awful dread" possessed the members of the General Assembly because "the eternal God has a controversy with our nation, and is about to visit us in his sore displeasure. . . . With regard to the causes of those national calamities . . . that they may be traced to a general defection from God, and corruption of the public principles and morals. . . . The evidences of our guilt are, unhappily, too numerous and glaring."[6]

Decrees such as this were serious stuff, especially when one considers how influential religious institutional bodies were in the early national period. One scholar describes the General Assembly as the "rival of the federal government for popular influence and esteem" in the early nineteenth century.[7] Fourteen years later, amid another national wartime crisis, the congressional memorial adopted by the General Assembly of the Presbyterian Church in 1812 again expressed the seriousness of the covenant, but now against the backdrop of Sabbath violations: "As [the petitioners] firmly believe in the special providence of God, and that this providence is exercised according to those principles of truth revealed in the scriptures, they fear, and have just reason to fear, that the infractions of the Sabbath allowed by civil law will draw down upon our nation the divine displeasure. God honours those who honour him, and casts down them who forget him."[8] As society became increasingly heterogeneous, Reformed northerners had to confront the reality that while guarding the covenant was relatively easy in homogeneous communities, increasing diversity of race, class, and religion made it challenging to enforce.[9]

For Bissell and other reformers, their angst was less about middle-class values triumphing in a battle of social control over the unruly working classes—it was, rather, about something far more serious, the blessings or curses of an all-powerful God.[10] As Bissell explained to the revivalist Charles Finney, the canal workers were "diseased by their unlawful lives" and were but a small example of the "evil rolling thro our land & among us."[11] This evil had to be confronted if God's covenants with Bissell, Rochester, and America were to be upheld. As an editorial in the *Rochester Observer* argued, observing the Sabbath as a nation "would procure us the blessing of Providence."[12]

This emphasis on covenant theology driving moral reform complicates the hegemonic narrative according to which technology, economics,

110 *Part Two: Christian Reform Capitalism*

and class conflict drove early national-period societal reformers.[13] Notably, the rhetoric of covenant theology was not limited to Congregationalists and Presbyterians. For example, in expressing support for the Sabbatarian transportation movement, a meeting at Second Baptist of Boston declared

> That as the safety and happiness of our country depends on the blessing of that God who ever visits the sins of nations with just retribution, we tremble at every indication of growing corruption in the morals of the community, and esteem it our indispensable duty . . . to promote the observance of the whole law of God. . . . We will to the utmost, abstain from the very appearance of Sabbathbreaking—and will give preference in our patronage to such stages, packets, &c. as observe the Lord's day.[14]

Observation of the Sabbath was central to the covenant because the day was almost a sacrament for the Reformed Protestants of early America. Covenantal language permeated the arguments of the founders of the General Union when they implored Americans to not "forego the means of grace, purchased for you by the blood of Christ; stop in your families the wells of salvation, and put out the light of life, and teach your children to work out their destruction, instead of their salvation, upon the Sabbath."[15] "Means of grace," families as "the wells of salvation," and an emphasis on teaching one's covenant children—this was all rhetoric that the Reformed Christians of early America knew well. Certainly, the founders of the Pioneer Line heard such phrases preached from the pulpits of their churches. Examining the churches that played instrumental roles in the lives of Bissell, Atkinson, and Champion helps us establish the connection between ideas such as the covenant and these believers' vision of Christian reform capitalism.

The church of Aristarchus Champion's youth gives some sense of the significance of the covenant in the mind-set of the reform capitalists. He was born into a rural Connecticut church that exuded covenant theology.[16] The oldest record of Champion's Westchester Congregational Church begins with the founding covenant of the church, where the congregation pledged to follow God's commands, attend church regularly, submit to the church's discipline, and raise their kids to be God-fearing

The Pioneers 111

"so we may obtain the blessings" of the covenant.[17] This covenant is evocative of famous covenantal moments in the life of the ancient nation of Israel, such as Joshua 24, when Moses's successor, Joshua, renewed his people's commitment to serving Yahweh. The Westchester Congregational Church did more than talk about the importance of its covenant—it lived it out through baptisms, membership, excommunications, and other forms of church discipline. These actions by the church were not restricted to immediate family members, but extended to servants and the enslaved, emphasizing the expanded nature of the covenant that included the entire community. This touched Aristarchus's family in particular, because his grandfather's enslaved children and servants were among those baptized during the revolutionary and early national periods.[18]

At Westchester Congregational Church, Aristarchus Champion matured under the teaching of a soon to be famous and controversial early nineteenth-century pastor, Ezra Stiles Ely. Ordained on October 1, 1806, at the tender age of twenty, Ely, a Yale graduate, was sent to the Westchester Congregational Church on his first assignment. (Ely's father gave his ordination sermon and reminded the congregation to "Let no man despise thy youth.")[19] He preached at Westchester for the next four years, where Champion would have heard numerous sermons advocating for the reformation and evangelizing of America. In fact, Ely's very first sermon not only stressed the vital task of evangelism, but argued that "All possible means of gaining the attention of thoughtless souls should be studied, and no lawful, practicable method left untried."[20] In addition to evangelism, Ely had a passion for the poor (his next assignment was as preacher of the New York Almshouse), but he argued that the poor needed moral, not structural transformation.[21] By the time Champion became involved with the Pioneer Line, Ely had shifted his focus toward politics, arguing for the election of Christian leaders and the establishment of a Christian political party. By this time, Ely had such a national profile that he delivered the opening speech of the General Assembly of the Presbyterian Church in May 1829.[22] Much of his rhetoric was very similar to the writings of Josiah Bissell Jr., as both believed that Christian principles needed to permeate all sectors of American life, including the economic and political. While protesting against religious tests for office, Ely certainly did not want a "Jew, Mohammedan, or Pagan" to occupy any of the nation's civil offices, and similar to Bissell's views of

112 *Part Two: Christian Reform Capitalism*

Christians as market actors, Ely argued that Christians needed to uphold their "sacred duty" as Christian voters.[23] It is fascinating that Champion and Ely crossed paths early in their lives, particularly as Ely became one of the chief villains for critics of the moral reform movement of the Second Great Awakening. While Champion never sought the public profile enjoyed by Bissell and Ely, twenty years later they were all key figures in the reform capitalism movement and the larger debate over the place of religion in American life. Ely embraced a form of Calvinism that stressed human agency and placed him in the company with Arminians and other Calvinists, such as the congregants of Rochester's Third Presbyterian.[24]

Like Westchester Congregational, Josiah Bissell Jr.'s spiritual home at Rochester reflected covenant theology and an adherence to the Westminster Confession. However, like Ely, the pastors of his church represented a broader shift in mid-Atlantic Calvinism that "valorized the free-agent American citizen under God the Moral Governor."[25] Bissell was the church's "first elder" (literally and figuratively) and Sunday school superintendent, and despite its small congregation, the church was the fault line of the Rochester reform movements of the late 1820s and early 1830s.[26] Originally, a member of the First Presbyterian Church of Rochester, Bissell and his wife helped found the more evangelistic Third Presbyterian Church of Rochester in December 1826. Their first pastor, Joel Parker, a graduate of nearby Auburn Seminary and the eventual president of Union Seminary (New York City), was a willing and able sidekick to Bissell's activism—critics believed Bissell handpicked him for this exact reason. Bissell's wealth, and the relatively small size of the congregation, meant he was responsible for a good chunk of Parker's salary, which was reputedly $800 per year, a decent sum for the late 1820s.[27]

Third Presbyterian's founding reflected denominational controversies at the local and national levels. The small group of members who left First Presbyterian in 1825 could not agree on a new location for the Second Presbyterian Church (eventually "Brick Presbyterian Church"), and divided again, with yet another breakaway group of twenty-two forming Third Presbyterian on February 28, 1827. Within three years, the church grew to more than two hundred members.[28] In a broad sense, the 1820s and 1830s were a period of upheaval and conflict within Presbyterianism, particularly as New School and Old School Presbyterians fought within their ruling body, the General Assembly. Some of the

The Pioneers 113

issues dividing the ruling body included slavery, theology, revivalism, voluntary societies, and the role of the Westminster Confession. In the case of Rochester, a few of these issues certainly contributed to congregational conflict.[29] For example, regarding theology, Bissell and his allies were sympathetic to Arminianism, which conflicted with the orthodox Calvinism of First Presbyterian's pastor, Joseph Penny.[30] However, local and personal concerns unique to Rochester were also significant. Bissell owned lands on the east side of the Genesee River, which probably influenced his desire to build the church there. Additionally, many of First Presbyterian's founders were strong personalities who gravitated toward controversy, which further accentuated the heightened the opportunity for conflict.

Despite the splintering, Bissell remained an important member within the broader Presbyterian community of Rochester, responsible for bringing the first pastor of Second Presbyterian, William James, to the town, then leading a movement to remove him and replace him with a new pastor in 1830, amid the height of controversy in Rochester over the Pioneer Line. Joseph Penny argued that Bissell was angry with the pastor of Second Presbyterian because he failed to travel on the Pioneer Line on a trip from Buffalo to Rochester. Penny, in criticizing Bissell, decried his entire movement of "Pioneerism" as divisive and disruptive to the peace within the local churches, let alone the greater community. Given Penny's reputation in Rochester, Bissell would struggle to win this fight.[31]

The dispute underscores the fact that Bissell was rarely interested in building consensus, and his public disagreement with the leadership of Rochester's other Presbyterian congregations was fodder for his enemies, while also undermining the assertion that Pioneerism was a unified Presbyterian movement. In fact, more than forty leaders of his denomination opposed Bissell's nomination to the Presbyterian General Assembly.[32] These conflicts surely contributed to the failing financial health of Third Presbyterian, leading to the sale of its magnificent building to the congregation of Second Baptist in 1834.[33]

William Atkinson, like Aristarchus Champion, was never as publicly vocal in his support of Christian reform capitalism as was Josiah Bissell Jr. However, like Bissell, he was no stranger to church controversy. Certainly, the fact that he attended an Episcopalian church, St. Paul's of Rochester, seems an outlier when compared to the Congregationalism

114 *Part Two: Christian Reform Capitalism*

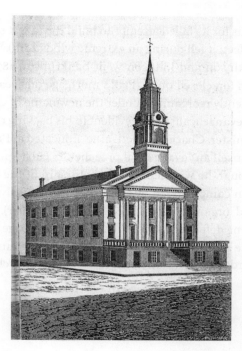

FIGURE 5.1 Third Presbyterian Church. This building was sold off after Bissell's death (for financial reasons), becoming the Second Baptist Church. Henry O'Reilly, *Sketches of Rochester: With Incidental Notices of Western New York* (Rochester: William Alling, 1838), 286.

or Presbyterianism of Champion and Bissell. Denominations are far from uniform, however. Atkinson's church, although adhering to a high-church liturgy, bent toward the same evangelical reform impulses as Third Presbyterian.

In fact, William Atkinson was an important factor in fostering the evangelical posture of St. Paul's. He originally was a member of St. Luke's, the first Episcopalian church of Rochester, where he was a vestryman, but he eventually left with fourteen others to establish St. Paul's in 1827. The division at St. Luke's was primarily logistical—the congregation had grown too large and wanted to plant a church on the east side of the Genesee River.[34] Atkinson, along with Elisha Johnson (with whom Atkinson held title to tracts of land sold to the state in the construction of the Erie Canal), served as wardens in the early years of the congregation, which

The Pioneers 115

was most famous for its failed attempt to build the tallest spire in western New York (277 feet; it fell during an extreme windstorm).³⁵ As previously mentioned, Atkinson and Johnson went bankrupt in 1832. Not coincidentally, lenders foreclosed on St. Paul's mortgage one year later, and the church subsequently reorganized under the new name of Grace Church.³⁶

Atkinson's evangelicalism was evident in his backing of St. Paul's first prospective minister, Charles P. McIlvaine. Educated at Princeton, McIlvaine called himself an "evangelical preacher."³⁷ He helped organize the parish even though he was denied the rectorship of the church thanks to an opposition campaign led by the bishop of Pennsylvania (who, as a missionary, had organized St. Luke's ten years earlier). The spat was public (McIlvaine defended himself in a forty-three-page pamphlet) and centered on the fear that McIlvaine was too "low-church" for Bishop Henry U. Onderdonk, who wanted to preserve high-church liturgy within

FIGURE 5.2 St. Paul's/Grace Church. Henry O'Reilly, *Sketches of Rochester: With Incidental Notices of Western New York* (Rochester: William Alling, 1838), 286.

Episcopalian congregations. McIlvaine, who went on to become the bishop of Ohio, was especially controversial among conservative Episcopalians such as Onderdonk because he had attended Princeton, known as a bastion of Presbyterianism. Conservative Episcopalians not only disproved of Princeton's theology, but also feared an attempt to unite Presbyterians and Episcopalians, as had happened with Congregationalists.[38] When opponents of McIlvaine went public, Atkinson took a vocal stand, defending McIlvaine in a series of public letters in which he claimed the entire parish's support.[39] Of course, it was Atkinson who had initially offered the rectorship to McIlvaine on behalf of St. Paul's, exercising his position as senior warden of the parish. Atkinson ultimately lost the battle over McIlvaine and high-church liturgy, but the conflict foreshadowed his participation in the Pioneerism movement that began the next year.[40]

Atkinson's wife, Elizabeth, provides additional hints to the evangelical impulses of the Atkinson household. For many years she served as the superintendent of a woman's seminary bearing her name. The institution was born amid a movement to educate women on a level equal to that of men, and evangelicals such as Elizabeth Atkinson championed female education to foster global regeneration and bring about the new millennium. In any case, her activism caught the eye of Charles Finney, who she later wed in 1848 (after William had died), yet another intriguing strand in the web linking Pioneerism and the famous revivalist.[41]

PIONEERISM: BEGINNINGS

The second push to persuade Americans to rededicate themselves to the Sabbath provides the context for the establishment of the Pioneer Line in 1828. Whereas the first Sabbath campaign focused on legislative action (revoking the 1810 act), the second campaign (generally marked by the formation of the General Union on May 6, 1828) eschewed political battles in favor of attempts to change public attitudes toward the Sabbath through the use of mass media. As the *Boston Recorder* stated frankly, *"The Press must be enlisted* in the service of the Sabbath."[42] The second campaign was reflective of the democratic mood of the mid-1820s, with its focus on the common citizen, a departure from the first Sabbatarian campaign that emphasized clergy, the state, and the law. For

The Pioneers 117

example, the General Union distributed some 100,000 copies of its inaugural address, an impressive number for 1828.[43] The message was simple: interested individuals pledged to honor the Sabbath and boycott seven-day transportation companies.[44]

Bissell and his friends wanted to go beyond consumer boycotts and create a new, reformed marketplace. The Pioneer Line was just one of many Christian business enterprises (CBEs) created between the 1820 and 1840s aimed at reforming the market. Some, like the Pioneer, focused on the Sabbath, while others targeted excess drinking, and still others tried to avoid all business activity with "immoral" individuals and enterprises—such as slavery. Examples include canal lines (the Hudson & Erie Line, Pioneer Six Day Line, the Albany and Michigan Six Day Line, and the Troy and Michigan Lake Boat Line), hotels (Auburn's Western Exchange and Waterloo's Green Tavern), and periodicals (the *Rochester Observer*, the *Christian Spectator* of New Haven, Connecticut, and the *New York Journal of Commerce*).[45] As an illustration, in addition to covering the "important news of the day" the *Rochester Observer* promised to focus on "the most important and interesting Religious Intelligence," including revivals, missionaries, and the activities of evangelistic and benevolence societies.[46] Initially published twice a month throughout western New York, from Buffalo to Canandaigua, due to popular demand, the paper quickly expanded in size to the standard format of urban papers and in frequency to a weekly publication schedule, while donating profits to evangelical organizations. In its second year, the paper had agents in fifty-eight different cities and villages, including one as far away as central Ohio.[47]

Sensitive to the perception that the first Sabbatarian movement was a Reformed Congregationalist-Presbyterian operation, the second Sabbatarian movement strove to avoid charges of sectarianism. Looking at the movement more broadly, one can find ample evidence of its ecumenicalism.[48] The Pioneer Line itself was a good example of this, because while Presbyterian proprietors owned the majority of the line, Episcopalians and Methodists owned 40 percent of its total mileage.[49] This was consistent with the tendency in the 1820s whereby Methodists, Baptists, Quakers, and Episcopalians served as leaders of other prominent organizations such as the American Bible Society and the American Sunday School Union.[50] In fact, the Methodist *Religious Advertiser and*

118 *Part Two: Christian Reform Capitalism*

Journal celebrated the creation of the General Union with "feelings of delight and gratification" and "rejoice[d] to see so many denominations represented in its board of managers."[51]

Reforming CBEs not only predated the formation of the General Union, they also provided the template for the construction of a movement to restrain and reform the market's arc toward a seven-day workweek. In May 1827, Bissell's *Rochester Observer* called for an economy of Christian consumers, arguing that "Christians will give their influence and custom to such stores and shops as are managed upon *christian principles*."[52] Six-day canal lines fit this description, and Moses Chapin, a Rochester judge and merchant, established one of the first transportation CBEs, the Hudson & Erie Line, in 1827, one year prior to the founding of the General Union (see figure 5.5). (Chapin even boasted his six-day service was every bit as efficient as a seven-day line.)[53] The Hudson & Erie was the original, and most prominent of the six-day canal lines, operating the boats *Herald* and *Waterloo*, which together paid more than $14,000 in tolls during 1829.[54] In fact, the Hudson & Erie Line was still operating the *Herald* in 1845, illustrating the longevity of early reform CBEs.[55]

The viability of the Hudson & Erie surely inspired Bissell and his fellow reformers. The first stirrings of his Pioneer Line began with a small meeting in a mercantile counting room on January 16, 1828, followed by a second meeting two days later, and a third, larger gathering on January 21 that included a collection of influential Rochester businessmen (see figure 5.3). (These meetings predated the establishment of the General Union by three months.) The main purpose of the meetings was to consider how to best reform the market's encroachment into Sundays—specifically on the Erie Canal.

Pledging to support only six-day canal boat lines, their published announcement echoed the concerns of the broader Sabbatarian movement with such issues as the fate of America, a desire for a virtuous citizenry, and the need for a standard American covenantal theology—thereby demonstrating a concern with the morality not just of Christians but also nonbelievers. Rochester businessmen quoted Lyman Beecher in proclaiming that "we will not be accessary to the wrong done by others."[56] In other words, the church would answer to God both for the conduct of its members as well as the actions of the broader community.

The Pioneers 119

"REMEMBER THE SABBATH DAY, TO KEEP IT HOLY!!"

"There must come an era of *more decided action*, before the earth can be subdued to Christ."

"Nothing great on earth, good or bad, was ever accomplished without decisive action."

"There is demanded *more courage* than has, in modern days, been manifested by the church of God."

"Emboldened by the pusillanimity of the friends of virtue, the enemy have become audacious, and scarcely covet the veil of darkness; but seem even to glory in their shame. And if no stand is made, we are undone. The church in this land will go into captivity, and the nation is undone. Our prosperity and voluptuousness will be our ruin; and short and rapid will be our journey from the cradle to the grave. But if resistance is made, then will the waves rise, and foam, and roar, and dash furiously upon those who shall dare to make a stand; and birds of ill omen will flap their sooty wings, and croak, and scream, to intimidate and dishearten the fearful and the unbelieving; and all the engines of bad influence will be applied to prevent that coalition of patriotism and of virtue, which would set bounds to the encroachments of evil.

"And now, *custom*, with silver tongue, will plead *prescription*—' It always has been so, and always will be, and why should we attempt innovation?' And *interest*, too, will plead *necessity*—' How can I withdraw my capital, or alter my course? To refuse to grow a little, would be to take away my children's bread,' And now, *difficulty*, with good wishes and sorrowing face will plead, ' Spare thy servant in this thing—is it not a little one?' While *fear* will see the giants, the sons of Anak, and call out for care, and prudence, lest we should act prematurely, or be righteous overmuch. *Petulance*, too, will lift up her voice, with vexation at our presumptuous meddling, wondering that we cannot mind our own affairs, and let other people alone. And even *charity*, so called, will draw aside her veil, for the archers with poisoned arrows to hit us. While *liberality*, provoked beyond endurance, will hail upon our heads the hard names of ' bigot, enthusiast, fanatick, hypocrite.'

"All this, however, we could easily sustain, were there no treachery within. But our hearts are yet in too close consultation with flesh and blood. ·What will the world think? What will the world say? How will it affect my reputation—my interest—my ambition—or even my usefulness? Suppose I step in as a kind of candid mediator between the world and my too zealous brethren, taking the prudent course, and not carrying matters too far?' O, that *prudent* course !—that middle ground—so crowded, when the lines are drawing between Christ and the world! Satan desires no better troops than neutral Christians. And the Lord Jesus Christ abhors none more. He prefers infidelity to lukewarm Christianity. *I would that thou wert cold or hot; so then because thou art neither, I will spue thee out of my mouth.*

"Two things are required of all who would be found on the side of liberty and evangelical morality. One is, that we will not do wrong in obedience to custom: the other is, that we will not be necessary to the wrong done by others—that we will give to the cause of virtue the testimony of correct opinions—the power of a correct example—and the influence of our inflexible patronage. There are piety and principle enough in the community to put down the usurpations of irreligion and crime, if the sound part of the community will only awake, and array itself on the side of purity and order. But we must come out, and be separate, and touch not the unclean thing. The entire capital in the hands of honest and moral men, which is employed in establishments that corrupt society, must be withdrawn; and that patronage which has swelled the revenue of establishments that lend their aid to the cause of licentiousness, must be turned over to the side of purity and order. Until this is done, we shall not cease to be partakers in other men's sins."—*Dr. Beecher.*

At a meeting of a few of the friends to the observance of the FOURTH COMMANDMENT, held at Rochester, January 21, 1828, the following preamble and resolutions were adopted :—

Whereas the violation of the Sabbath on our Canal has become a most alarming evil in our State ; and whereas we believe the good sense and sound principle of the Christian community is decidedly against such immorality ; and believing that the evil *can be corrected* ; therefore—

Resolved, That we are of one heart and one mind on this subject, and will use our best exertions to prevent the violation of the Lord's day on the Erie Canal.

Resolved, That we will give our business and patronage to such lines of boats as do not travel on the Holy Sabbath.

Resolved, That we invite all the friends of sound morality, in all the villages and towns in the State, to co-operate with us in this important object.

The undersigned concur in the above resolutions.

E. PECK,	W. BREWSTER,	H. RAYMOND,
C. J. HILL,	A. REYNOLDS,	J. WATTS,
I. A. WARD,	B. CAMPBELL,	A. CHAMPION,
S. MURDOCK,	E. D. SMITH,	I. WARD, Jr.,
J. BISSELL, Jr.,	T. EGLESTON,	D. D. HATCH,
THOS. KEMPSHALL,	J. HARRIS,	W. KEMPSHALL,
H. N. LANGWORTHY,	D. SIBLEY,	O. SAGE,
P. SMITH,	S. P. GOULD,	J. K. LIVINGSTON,
A. WAKELEE,	C. DUNNING,	J. H. THOMPSON,
F. STARR,	J. PECK,	O. N. BUSH,
A. CHAPIN,	D. HOYT,	H. ELY.
W. H. WARD,		

FIGURE 5.3 Handbill from January 21, 1828, meeting. Image by author May 13, 2015, Collections of the Seymour Public Library, Auburn, NY (Richard Palmer Collection), by arrangement. (This item has subsequently gone missing from the Palmer Collection.)

Then, on February 5, 1828, more than five hundred citizens of Rochester met to express concern over Sabbath violations on the Erie Canal. Three days later, a circular letter from "influential businessmen" of Utica, New York, called for a convention to discuss six-day transportation. The so-called Utica Circular, dated January 31, 1828, stipulated that delegates should pledge to support a new line for the next two years (through "influence and business"). Additionally, the Utica Circular charged prospective supporters with raising $25,000 in capital, $5,000 each from five regions: Albany/Troy, Utica, Auburn/Geneva/Canandaigua, Rochester, and Buffalo/Batavia.[57]

On February 13, a two-day meeting of "pious and patriotic" businessmen began in Auburn, New York, in response to the circular letter. Twenty-one men (including Atkinson, Bissell, and Champion) signed a series of resolutions that pledged support and patronage to only six-day lines. Auburn was located at the intersection of the main stagecoach line from Albany to Buffalo and lines running north–south. It was an important place in the 1820s, and the meeting spawned similar rallies of support in Albany and Buffalo.[58] The Auburn convention echoed themes of impending doom for America, using language tinged with covenantal imagery combined with an argument that the mission to support six-day lines was essential to preserving republican institutions and the civic virtue that many assumed served as their foundations: "on no institution do practical virtue and morality so much depend; as on that of the Sabbath. . . . The spreading evil which has existed for years, unless counteracting [sic] by some efficient plan, will speedily involve our country in ruin, by annihilating the influence of moral principle."[59]

The Auburn convention quickly inspired similar rallies in other cities along the Erie Canal, including Utica, where Sabbatarians rallied on February 18, 1828, to express support for the convention's declaration of principles. Similar meetings in Albany, Amsterdam, Batavia, Buffalo, Canandaigua, Cayuga, Champion, Greene, Le Roy, Newark, Penn Yan, Saratoga Springs, and Westchester all resulted in statements of solidarity with the Auburn Convention.[60] The meetings in upstate New York did not escape the notice of the newspapers, sparking editorials of support in Connecticut, Massachusetts, Virginia, and New York City, as well as similar meetings in cities such as Boston and Philadelphia.[61] A canal boat line based in Massachusetts declared that it would cease

The Pioneers   121

operations on Sunday in support of the burgeoning movement.[62] A stage line between New York and Ithaca also turned into a six-day operation.[63] Momentum seemed to be building as a stage line based out of Moscow, New York, and one operating in Vermont likewise switched to six-day operations.[64]

Quite simply, the delegates at the Auburn convention believed the Sabbath was essential to fostering a successful society. Their resolutions underscored this by expressing support for the Rochester rally on February 5, a promise to use only six-day transportation lines, and to support the establishment of a six-day steamboat service on the Hudson River. Finally, the delegates designated twelve commissioners (including Atkinson, Bissell, and Champion) from Albany, Auburn, Buffalo, Canandaigua, Geneva, Rochester, and Utica, whose job would be to organize and run a six-day stage line company operating between Albany and Buffalo.[65] The principles of the Pioneer Line, as announced and signed by Atkinson, Bissell, and Champion, were as follows:

1. The duty of the commissioners is, to find proprietors, establish the general principles by which they are to be governed, and procure the pledge and countenance of the community to support the Line of their desired preference.
2. Each proprietor is to own as many miles of the line, as shall be agreed upon, and sustain the whole equipage and expenses of that part of the route, there being no joint stock in the concern.
3. It is our intention, so far as practicable, to have carriages and harness entirely new, and horses first rate, for that business.
4. The drivers are to be men who do not swear, nor drink ardent spirits, and who prefer the house of publick worship on the Sabbath to the noisy bar-room.
5. We are happy to believe that some of our taverns will be *without bars*, and intend that every house where horses are changed, a supply of hot coffee shall always be in waiting, at a low price to the passengers, and *free* to the drivers.[66]

The target date to launch the new line was June 1, an admittedly ambitious time line, but one that revealed the urgency with which the commissioners were to take up their work.[67]

122 *Part Two: Christian Reform Capitalism*

The choice to forgo a joint stock organization between proprietors was common for early national-period transportation lines. The Pioneer owners included two Episcopalians, two Methodists, and three Presbyterians, with the latter controlling 60 percent of the Pioneer Line's mileage.[68] The Old Line's organization was similar, comprised of a collection of individuals who owned portions of its total route. Not surprisingly, the two lines began clashing even before the Pioneer Line began service. The first issue involved the stage lines' practice of affiliating with taverns along the route to provide refreshments for passengers if necessary, and a logistical hub for swapping out teams of horses. When the proprietors of the new Pioneer Line took aim at their rival's taverns, they were not simply denying the Old Line convenient rest stops, but threatening the viability of the line itself. Consequently, all along the route of the Pioneer and the Old Line, taverns had to decide whom they would support.[69]

The new line vowed to offer fair prices to its customers, but the commissioners promised not to underbid rivals or engage in frequent

FIGURE 5.4 Standard "Concord" or "Troy" coach. This version of the Troy coach carried six passengers, three on each of the two interior seats. Luggage was carried in the front, back, or top of the exterior. Basil Hall, *Forty Etchings: From Sketches Made with the Camera Lucida, in North America, in 1827 and 1828* (Edinburgh: Cadell & Co., 1829), xl.

fare manipulation. Additionally, the carriages were branded with a color scheme of white with green trim.⁷⁰ The decision to outfit the Pioneer Line with new, top-of-the-line carriages was important as it signified the seriousness of the new line and challenged the Old Line to respond in kind. This was not going to be a discount service, done on the cheap, forcing those interested in observing the Sabbath while traveling to compromise in their choice as consumers. Rather, the hope was that in offering a superior service in all respects (unless one wanted to travel on Sundays, of course), the Pioneer Line could market excellence in product and piety in execution to prospective consumers. In the first week of June, the Pioneer Line took delivery of the new carriages and prepared to initiate service by mid-month.⁷¹

Aided by the momentum forged by the General Union's publicity campaign and the example of the Hudson & Erie Line (canal boats), Atkinson, Bissell, Champion, and the other regional commissioners

FIGURE 5.5 Hudson & Erie ad. *Western Recorder,* October 9, 1827.

124 *Part Two: Christian Reform Capitalism*

nearly met their target date and launched the Pioneer Line in mid-June 1828, with full service between Albany and Buffalo commencing by the latter part of July.[72] Announcements of the new line triumphantly appeared throughout upstate New York, and even showed up in New York City's newspapers.[73]

Obviously, launching an alternative transportation system complete with new equipment was an expensive proposition. Bissell tapped all his contacts throughout the state of New York to procure the funds required to get the Pioneer Line off the ground and sustain it through its first year of service. His prior fundraising efforts on behalf of groups such as the American Board of Commissioners for Foreign Missions (ABCFM) reveal something of his aggressive tactics and acerbic personality. Selected to head a special ABCFM fundraising committee (along with six others, including Arthur Tappan), Bissell could be pushy, rude, and abrasive in his solicitations. Pressing Gerrit Smith in October 1827, Bissell demanded he cough up major donors from his region of Oneida County (east of Syracuse), "or else."[74] As an ardent abolitionist, supporter of the temperance movement, and future Free Soil congressional representative and leader of the Liberty Party, Gerrit Smith was a prominent individual in the evangelical activist circles that included businessmen such as Bissell and the Tappans. Like these businessmen, he sponsored reforming CBEs, establishing a "temperance hotel" in his hometown of Peterboro, New York, in 1845, which eschewed liquor service, "dancing parties," or office work on Sundays.[75] Even so, Bissell pressed him to raise between $20,000 and $30,000 from his region for the ABCFM. When Smith fell short of his assigned goal by March 1828, Bissell demanded he "go and get your 5 men for 5 M Each per annum. . . . This 10 M must come, and if you do not pay *we will* if we never pay another dollar on earth." Bissell demanded Smith put other matters on hold and raise $10,000 by July 1, 1828.[76]

Similarly, Bissell pressed Smith for money to support the Pioneer Line. Claiming he had already raised $25,000, Bissell hoped that Smith would become a "full toned Pioneer man" by immediately donating to the cause. Bissell stressed he needed $5,000 as soon as possible, as the line was "almost ready." Surely, Smith could join other significant financial supporters such as Arthur Tappan, who was responsible for $5,000 of the $25,000 pledged. Aristarchus Champion had donated twice Tappan's amount, providing a compelling example to his fellow businessmen.

The Pioneers 125

Bissell implored Smith to join "your brother Champion and myself and put in according to your ability."[77] In spite of Bissell's best efforts, Smith was skeptical of the venture, leading Bissell to approach him a month later to plead his case again. The Pioneer Line was up and running by this point and Bissell was pleased to report that "They have stopped multitudes of travelers on the Sabbath—and made men *ashamed* when they rode on."[78] Despite Smith's commitment to the greater reform capitalism movement, there is no evidence he joined the subscribers of the Pioneer Line in financially supporting their cause, but his correspondence with Bissell provides a valuable window into how the Pioneer raised capital.

Lewis Tappan was another important ally of Bissell's in raising funds for the Pioneer Line. Beyond his brother's significant financial stake, Lewis was a member of the General Union's executive committee. Additionally, he worked on behalf of the Pioneer during the spring of 1829, meeting with multiple businessmen to stoke enthusiasm for the Sabbatarian transportation line. Tappan was no stranger to rejection—despite his status as a successful businessman, he was not above handing out religious tracts to "gangs of scoffers" in New York City. Unsuccessful in raising money for the Sabbath lines, he provided spiritual support by leading prayer sessions to beseech God's blessing on the Pioneer Line and its movement.[79]

Multiple sources claim that the total investment in the Pioneer Line amounted to $60,000. One source from 1838, written by one of the founders of the Pioneer Line (most likely Champion), claims that two Rochester men fronted $10,000 each. Since Bissell identified Champion as one, the identity of the other large donor is an interesting question. Atkinson and Bissell are the obvious choices, and considering that the 1838 source claims Bissell lost more than $30,000 in the Pioneer Line, the evidence suggests he was the other "$10,000 man."[80]

Given his significant financial stake in the Pioneer Line, Aristarchus Champion's role begs elaboration, particularly since he is a figure mostly lost to history. While not nearly as publicly polarizing as his friend Josiah Bissell Jr., and ignored by the few historians who have written about the Pioneer Line, Champion's monetary support and contributions were vital. His father, General Henry Champion, one of the original board of directors of the Connecticut Land Company (CLC), purchased the

126   *Part Two: Christian Reform Capitalism*

second-largest number of shares in the CLC for the then staggering sum of $85,675.[81]

Like many men in early America, Henry Champion used his government connections and military service to get his foot in the door of land speculation. He was an active member of the CLC's board, consistently advocating that they should "extinguish" Indigenous land claims so that the proprietors of the Western Reserve could better develop the land, most especially through the construction of roads. Despite the dissolution of the CLC in 1809, some of the investors, like Henry Champion, did not lose the titles of their lands. (Today a township in Trumbull County, Ohio bears Champion's name.)[82]

Aristarchus astutely managed and expanded his father's Western Reserve lands into a real estate empire that stretched from New England to Ohio. While the slow pace of settlement there limited the ability of the original investors to realize a financial windfall, subsequent speculators such as Aristarchus benefitted from the increased investment in transportation and decreased presence of settler-Indigenous violence after the War of 1812.[83] Certainly, the advertisements he placed in newspapers

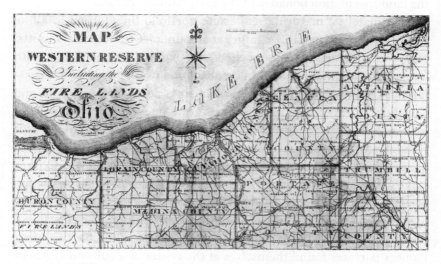

FIGURE 5.6 Western Reserve. Today Trumbull County is considered "Rust Belt America" and contains Warren, Ohio, adjacent to Youngstown, Ohio. https://upload.wikimedia.org/wikipedia/commons/8/8b/Western_Reserve_Including_the_Fire_Lands_1826.jpg. (Original in Connecticut Historical Society, Hartford, CT).

The Pioneers   127

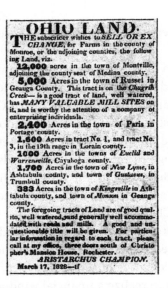

FIGURE 5.7 Champion land sale ad. *Rochester Daily Advertiser and Telegraph*, January 5, 1829.

throughout the region testify to his significance as a powerful agent in the land speculation bonanza of the early national period.

Ultimately, a maturing real estate portfolio (in addition to Ohio, Henry also speculated in a significant amount of land in Massachusetts, New York, Vermont, and Connecticut) began to yield tremendous wealth for Aristarchus and his father in the 1820s and 1830s.[84] Evidence of Aristarchus's growing wealth was his loan of $5,000 to the Wayne and Cuyahoga Turnpike Company in 1826. For a rate of return of 6 percent for ten years, Aristarchus saved the company from going under, as it struggled to raise subscriptions to fund its toll road, which paralleled present day U.S. Route 42 (south of Cleveland, Ohio).[85] Thanks to a large stake in the town of Penfield, New York, this legacy of land speculation brought Aristarchus to the neighboring town of Rochester, where he met like-minded Christians such as his cofounders of the Pioneer Line, Josiah Bissell Jr. and William Atkinson.[86] Soon Champion and his two other Pioneer partners found themselves at the center of a cultural and economic storm of their own creation, a tempest that would produce the rise, temporary fall, and ultimate victory of the reform movement known as "Pioneerism."

CHAPTER SIX

Conflict, Defeat, and Victory

The Pioneer Line polarized upstate New York from the start, even while it experienced growing pains. It was an era of intense political battles over other contentious issues such as Masonry. In fact, one of the lead papers attacking Bissell and the Pioneer Line was Rochester's *The Craftsman*, a short-lived Masonic paper. Interestingly, the Masonic debate surfaced as a subplot surrounding the Pioneer Line, since Bissell was a well-known anti-Mason, as were many of the Sabbatarians. While the issue of Sabbatarianism was in and of itself divisive, it is important to remember that it was bundled together with other cultural conflicts in the early national period, such as that over Masonry. That the Pioneer Line was enmeshed in these conflicts did not help its bid for viability. These self-created headwinds, combined with a failure to secure the federal mail contract, its failure to consistently live up to its own moral code, and the sudden death of Josiah Bissell Jr., led to the Pioneer's demise.

In addition to the cultural conflict it generated, the Pioneer Line had to navigate challenges common to any start-up business. For example, customers had trouble finding the offices of the new stage line, and some fell victim to unscrupulous agents deceptively posing as representatives of the Pioneer Line. Surprised patrons found they merely purchased tickets on the Old Line—often the very business they were trying to avoid.[1] It was especially easy for surreptitious agents to take advantage of the situation in Albany, a place characterized by a confusing, chaotic mess of competitors all jostling with each other and pressuring customers to buy a ticket on their line.[2] Proprietors of public houses disregarded the requests of Sabbath-minded customers by booking seats on the Old Line against their patron's wishes.[3] Stage drivers colluded by posing as part of the Pioneer Line, when in fact they were not.[4] (This was not a one-sided situation, as some Pioneer agents in turn misrepresented themselves.)[5] Advertisements for the Pioneer Line were covered up or pulled down.[6] Citizens praised the Pioneer Line's level of service, only to face charges that the individuals in question had actually traveled on the Old Line.[7] Stages raced each other, sometimes dangerously, to be the first to the next destination.[8] These stories mirrored the experience on the Erie Canal, as six- and seven-day lines competed for customers and to achieve the highest speeds, even resorting to subterfuge and sabotage. One particularly egregious account involved a trip that passengers claimed began with a competitor driving several horses of a six-day line boat, the *Citizen of the Citizens*, into the Erie Canal. Next, the passengers said the *Citizen* had a horse fall through a sabotaged towpath bridge and suffered intentionally severed towlines. Finally, an old scow was set adrift into the oncoming path of the beleaguered *Citizen*, according to its passengers.[9]

Even abiding by the one chief goal of the Pioneer Line—honoring the Sabbath—was not as easy as it might seem. The proprietors had to shift into damage-control mode when the horses of a segment of the Pioneer Line were reshod on a Sunday.[10] Worse yet, one of the stage lines between Lewiston and Niagara Falls actually operated on one of the first Sundays of the line's existence.[11] Even though it was only a distance of ten miles, it was an embarrassing gaffe for a line seeking respectability. Charges of Sabbath violations and misconduct by the Pioneer Line's drivers continued to surface, and despite the questionable nature of some accusations, the venture struggled to fight off charges of hypocrisy.[12] Its founding principles stated that the Pioneer would not underbid its competition, but now that charge, too, was being leveled against Bissell and company by the Old Line.[13] The Pioneer went out of its way to argue that Sabbath work had corrupted drivers, countering with evidence that their line was helping drivers reclaim their virtue, as the presence of six *"well dressed"* drivers of *"good appearance"* in a Sunday church service "surely" suggested.[14] Ultimately, the proprietors of the Pioneer Line had to admit that finding agents and drivers capable of upholding their vision of

130   *Part Two: Christian Reform Capitalism*

Christian morality was difficult, and that they had not been entirely successful in their efforts to do so.[15] A barrage of criticism threatened to drown out positive testimonials, such as the one that ran in the *New York Observer* on September 6, 1828, countering that "The stages are new, spacious and easy, the horses are valuable and fleet, and the drivers sober, careful, and obliging men. . . . It is a safe, quiet, orderly line, where one may travel any distance without fear from drunken, careless drivers, or profane or obscene passengers."[16]

Just two weeks after the February organizing meetings in Rochester and Auburn, critics were outraged to learn of the designs of the commissioners of the new "piety line" of stages. Counterdemonstrations and meetings popped up throughout New York, in places that had previously seen pro–Pioneer Line rallies, such as Auburn, Le Roy, Lewiston, Lockport, Rochester, and Utica.[17] Arguing that Sabbatarians were slandering anyone who did not agree with their view of the Sabbath, the *Gospel Advocate and Impartial Investigator* of Auburn, New York, decried the establishment of an "orthodox line of stages." Rejecting the covenantal argument of the Sabbatarians, the *Gospel Advocate* pulled no punches in labeling them power-hungry, legalistic, freedom-restricting frauds.[18] Certainly, the fact that Josiah Bissell Jr. was associated with the project did not help win over skeptics. Already known within the Rochester community for his business success (though critics charged that it flowed from his "heartless dealings with his fellow men") and generosity toward reform causes (he was reported to have donated $25,000 to the American Bible Society and $10,000 to the American Colonization Society), *The Craftsman* slammed him as "Distrusted by all, and beloved of none—despised by many and respected but by the groveling few whom he controls and leads, he appears to be one of the true descendants of Ishmael, 'whose hand is against every man and every man's hand against him.'"[19]

The proprietors of the Old Line, led by Colonel John Sherwood of Auburn, a giant of a man, literally and figuratively, made a crafty move in April 1828 by publicly offering to sell their operation to the commissioners of the Pioneer Line for $175,000.[20] Defending themselves as "honest men" merely trying to "provide a living for ourselves and families," who "rejoice at every evidence of increasing religion and morality," they claimed to venerate the Sabbath, believing "a due observance of the Sabbath essential to the best interest of society." They called on Christians,

Conflict, Defeat, and Victory 131

as well as every other "well-wisher to society," to observe the Sabbath. The sticking point for the proprietors of the Old Line was "coercion" and their belief that it was impossible to prevent people from traveling on Sunday, given the "present state of public sentiment."[21] To their customers, the proprietors of the Old Line promised that Sabbath-minding individuals could pause their travels on Saturday evenings before continuing Monday morning at no additional charge.[22]

Nineteenth-century upstate New York village histories misinterpret the intent of Sherwood and the Old Line and fail to consider the full context of this offer.[23] It was a clear publicity stunt, addressed not to the commissioners of the Pioneer Line, but to the public. First, the sale price was staggeringly high, far and above what supporters eventually invested in the Pioneer Line. Just coming up with the sum would have been a near impossibility. The statement published by the Old Line, far from conciliatory, offended Sabbatarians like Bissell. Despite the acknowledgment of the Sabbatarians' arguments, the proprietors of the Old Line shrugged their shoulders with the response that it was futile to force people to observe the Sabbath. Perhaps many of the Pioneers would have agreed with this logic, but the fact that the proprietors of the Old Line were still willing to run their stages on Sundays, thereby facilitating widespread Sabbath breaking, would have struck Bissell and his supporters as hypocritical.[24]

Perhaps even more significantly, as Bissell and his friends knew, the offer neglected the reality that the Old Line possessed the federal mail contract. Taking over an operation that mandated seven-day-a-week service would defeat the whole point of the Pioneer Line in the first place.[25] It is clear from correspondence between Bissell and Postmaster General John McLean in 1828 that Bissell did in fact try to renegotiate the federal contract from seven-day to six-day service. Instead, McLean renewed the contract with the Old Line for another term, expressly because they were willing to deliver seven days a week, and Bissell was not. Without a reworked mail contract, Bissell could never take the commissioners of the Old Line up on their offer, and Colonel Sherwood and his partner Jason Parker surely knew this, even as Sherwood's supporters celebrated Bissell's failure to win the federal postal contract.[26]

Sherwood was an astute businessman, and he quickly introduced a new, speedy stage service, the Telegraph Line, in the summer of 1828.

132   *Part Two: Christian Reform Capitalism*

Sherwood's new express service reflected one of the chief modes of competition between the Old and Pioneer Lines: speed. The Telegraph limited its passengers to a maximum of six, did not wait to fill up all its seats, and switched horses every ten miles to minimize travel time. Ads for the Telegraph claimed it would cover the distance from Albany to Utica in twelve hours (almost 8 miles per hour), and the 296 miles from Albany to Buffalo in fifty-six hours (including stops, averaging 5.5 miles per hour). By the fall, ads claimed the Telegraph was completing the total journey in as few as forty-five hours (6.5 miles per hour).[27] In an age when "fast" service achieved a mere 8 miles per hour over "good" roads, theses times were impressive. (In fact, 8 miles per hour was double the typical pace of approximately 4 miles per hour, due to the condition of roads and need to frequently stop and feed or water the horses.)[28] Unsurprisingly, the rival stages raced each other, often finding themselves on the wrong side of the law and facing punitive fines for their violation of village statutes.[29]

The experience of the Old Line's drivers proved extremely important in safely shaving time off a trip. The typical stage driver was part trained professional and part artistic showman, particularly upon arrival in a new town. Drivers liked to announce their arrival with high speeds to underscore their line's velocity, blowing their tin horns in a colorful cacophony. The ego and colorful personalities these men displayed was all part of their appeal, as the most daring passengers might ride outside the coach with the driver to experience the world through their eyes. It was a dangerous world, rife with accidents, which certainly added to their reputation and aura.[30] "Thoroughbraces" (which ran under the carriage to provide a measure of cushion on the uneven roads) or pole straps (which connected the carriage to the team of horses) might snap, wheels could break, and horses risked slipping and falling on descents. Sometimes a coach turned over completely.[31] Consequently, the skill and experience of a driver was of the utmost importance. The experience of the Old Line drivers was on particular display in their handling of their horses amid the battle for speed between the two rival lines. Unaware of the long-term impact this pace would have on their teams, Pioneer drivers tended to push the pace of travel, leading to a diminished capacity in the long term as horses broke down or proved unable to perform at the level of the Old Line teams.[32]

Conflict, Defeat, and Victory   133

Competition was especially intense in Auburn, a cauldron of social reform movements, including abolitionism and women's rights organizations, where the north–south and east–west stage lines converged, making it the epicenter of the Sabbatarian transportation battle.[33] There, in something of a coup, the Pioneer Line succeeded in converting the Western Exchange, Auburn's finest hotel and previously the horse-changing stop for the Old Line, into a temperance hotel—and its chief stop—along the line from Albany to Buffalo.[34]

Colonel Sherwood lived in a large, opulent home on the edge of Auburn, and he was not about to let the Pioneer outwit him on his home turf.[35] From its earliest days, Auburn was the headquarters of the Old Line, and consequently, the conversion of the Western Exchange was incredibly symbolic, necessitating a decisive response by John Sherwood. In a game of one-upmanship, he completed the lavish "American Hotel"

FIGURE 6.1 Western Exchange (top) and American Hotels. Hagaman & Markham, "Map of the Village of Auburn," 1837, David Rumsey Map Collection, David Rumsey Map Center, Stanford Libraries.

134   *Part Two: Christian Reform Capitalism*

on January 1, 1830. Located across the street from the Western, it was intended to service his seven-day-a-week line.[36]

Josiah Bissell Jr. was known for his acerbic and combative rhetoric, which did nothing to dissuade his critics. For example, he claimed that newspapers editors who opposed his movement were guilty of taking "the side of infidels."[37] And in a widely circulated announcement published in the newspapers of upstate New York in late May and early June 1828, he addressed his fellow citizens using pointed, biblically tinged language, arguing they should support his new transportation line because "You have a right to your choice; being responsible . . . not to man, but to *God* . . . Now you are . . . called on *this day* . . . to 'choose *whom* ye will serve,' whether you will serve the God of *Heaven* of *truth* and of the *Sabbath*, or 'the proprietors of the *Old Line*,' and all their companions in transgressions on the Sabbath, in Stage, Canal, or Steam-Boat movements."[38] By quoting from Joshua 24:15, Bissell was exhibiting the influence of covenantal theology on his drive for market reforms. The passage describes the ministry of Joshua, who, according to the Old Testament, led the conquest of Canaan. Chapter 24 documents the occasion on which Joshua gathered the ancient nation of Israel to renew its covenant with Yahweh as he prepared to retire from leadership. Bissell was challenging his nation to do likewise—to remember its special covenantal relationship with God, and to demonstrate its allegiance by reforming its market activities. Bissell singled out newspapers for special criticism: "In this STRUGGLE, you will be known by the . . . *articles you publish or republish.* If you are the friends of the Redeemer, and not ashamed to own him, you will consecrate your presses to the Lord, to truth and righteousness . . .'choose ye this day whom ye will serve.' "[39]

Bissell made support for the Pioneer Line into a litmus test of one's status as a "true" Christian. Words like "consecrate" stressed the spiritual nature of his market reformation, while Bissell's Manichaean approach to the issue allowed no room for earnest Christians to disagree over the Sabbath. Bissell also directed stinging insults at his competitors, the proprietors of the Old Line: "It is too often and incautiously said of the proprietors of the Old Line—*'very respectable gentlemen.'* For what are they respectable? 'They have property'—SO HAVE SWINDLERS. 'They have good manners.' So have ROGUES and DANCING MASTERS."[40] It was the professed piety of the Old Line's proprietors that

Conflict, Defeat, and Victory 135

upset Bissell the most. The fact that professing Christians would work to thwart his plan to fence off the Sabbath—that was simply too much to take. Unsurprisingly, when Bissell evaluated their spiritual lives, he found them grossly wanting:

> But have they PIETY? Are we required to LOVE and RESPECT them, as Christians do one another—NO: because they disobey the commands of Christ, who says, "he that loveth me, keepeth my commandments." Shall, then, we respect whom *God* does not respect? Shall we honour Sabbath-breakers—the disobedient in *heart* and *practice*—the enemies of God—who, after receiving a FAIR WARNING, still persist in being MONEY-MAKING MEN, on the holy Sabbath?[41]

Bissell finished by concluding that if one wanted to obtain "the *favour* of God" one must be "SEPARATE" from all businesses and persons who broke the Sabbath.[42]

Bissell was not the only one leveling charges of apostasy at the critics of the Pioneer Line. His combative stance was common among the cultural reformers of his day, particularly those who saw the covenantal status of the nation hanging in the balance. The short-lived *Albany Christian Register* published a list of newspapers that opposed the Pioneer Line, labeling them "infidel publications."[43] By linking upstanding economic behavior with his transportation plan, Bissell dismissed those who viewed themselves as moral while disagreeing with him on the proper way to live on the first day of the week.

However, by seizing the moral high ground, Bissell set himself and the Pioneer Line up for charges of hypocrisy. Soon, critics were leveling claims of fraud, drunkenness, indecency, and harassment against the Pioneer Line. In addition to the problems noted above, a woman and her elderly relative claimed such horrible treatment by drunk passengers on a Pioneer stagecoach departing from Canandaigua that they abandoned their ride prematurely at Geneva. Another woman charged a Pioneer driver with assault and abuse after refusing his sexual advances.[44] Collectively, these charges clouded the public image of the Pioneer Line and cast serious doubt as to its ultimate mission of redeeming the early national-period marketplace.

136 *Part Two: Christian Reform Capitalism*

Bissell himself, along with his pastor, Joel Parker, was vulnerable to charges of hypocrisy, thanks in part to the bellicosity of the two men's rhetoric. *The Craftsman* ran the following ditty about Parker in December 1829:

Priest Parker! Priest Parker!
Your falsehood's the darker:
Hypocrisy adds to your crime:
To your profession a stain—
Let me not urge in vain—
Repent, if you can, while you've time!
Priest Parker,
Repent, if you can, while you've time![45]

Parker had earned the ire of *The Craftsman* for having taken specific aim at Freemasonry in a published sermon the year prior.[46] The next stanza (quoted at the opening of this book's introduction) took aim at Bissell, alluding to financial improprieties involving a certain "molasses affair" and a "double-mortgage," and threatening to reveal the details of these dealings if he did not temper his rhetoric and disdain toward his opponents.[47]

Orestes Augustus Brownson, a newspaper editor from Auburn, New York, took up the voice of the opposition in the pages of his *Gospel Advocate and Impartial Investigator*, first criticizing the Pioneer Line in mid-March 1828. Brownson was a restless spiritual soul, starting as a Presbyterian, then dabbling in universalism and transcendentalism before becoming a socialist freethinker (he was making the latter transition at the time of his attacks on the Pioneer). Eventually, he settled on Catholicism.[48] Brownson continued his attacks into the summer of 1828, stressing the dogmatism displayed by Bissell and company: "There remains no doubt on the minds of the reflecting part of community, that the 'new line of stages' is *one* of the measures of the orthodox . . . designed to limit our freedom and destroy the rights of the people."[49] Bissell's rhetoric convinced Brownson the Pioneer Line was part of a larger plot by Presbyterian clergy to control American society. Brownson's concerns had little to do with access to the market economy seven days of the week; rather, they reflected a rationalist-deist perspective that was suspicious

Conflict, Defeat, and Victory 137

of clergy (especially Presbyterians) and institutionalized religion and that expected religious enthusiasm to wither and die (making his future standing as one of the foremost Catholic theologians of nineteenth-century America especially ironic).[50]

Brownson spoke for a vocal segment of Auburn's citizens who vigorously opposed the principles of the Pioneer Line's proprietors. A meeting on Auburn's courthouse green on August 23, 1828, reportedly drew a thousand protestors, leading to a series of counter resolutions to those passed by Bissell's convention in Auburn the previous February. Authors of the August counter resolutions expressed anger at the efforts to restrict market activity on Sundays, especially "attacks upon the business, interests and property of such of our fellow citizens as decline to observe the Sabbath in conformity" with the expectations of the General Union.[51] Chief among their concerns was the belief that Sabbatarians like Bissell were secretly angling for political power, a fear fed by sermons such as the one Aristarchus Champion's former pastor, Ezra Stiles Ely, delivered the year before calling for the formation of a Christian political party.[52] Unsurprisingly, Ely's sermon provoked alarm.[53]

Considering that the entire population of Auburn was approximately three thousand in 1828, a thousand protestors, if accurate, represented a significant percentage of the local citizenry.[54] The argument at this meeting, as well as by other opponents of the Pioneer, revolved around its very nature as a Christian business enterprise (CBE): the fusion of religious conviction and market behavior. Critics did not view Pioneer as innocently offering them a new transportation choice in a previously monopolized market. Instead, they argued the true end game of the Pioneer Line was to restrict consumer choice and curtail seven-day market activity.

Bissell's rhetoric and efforts to capture the mail contract roused strident opposition in his hometown.[55] In December 1828, a group of Rochester's business elite gathered for a meeting at which Colonel Nathaniel Rochester's eldest son, William, chaired a discussion of how to respond to Bissell's campaign. The resolutions of the meeting are instructive for several reasons. First, the businessmen stressed their religiosity and respect for the Sabbath but maintained that attempts to coerce people's behavior were counterproductive, and that religion was insincere unless it came from the heart. Second, they stressed the marketplace implications

138   *Part Two: Christian Reform Capitalism*

of Sabbatarianism. In a letter to the postmaster general, Rochester's businessmen emphasized a point echoed elsewhere in upstate New York, that "there is not perhaps within the limits of the Union a village whose business requires a daily mail more than this. Flour, wheat and ashes—our staple commodities—are so fluctuating in price—and so liable to be influenced by the news from abroad—that, if the carriage of the mail every day is expedient any where, it is assuredly not less so here."[56] Finally, William Rochester's group called for their own boycott, this one against the business interests of any individual connected to the Sabbatarian movement.[57]

The criticism by Rochester's own was not without effect. Immediately following the anti-Pioneer boycott, the advertisement campaign for the Pioneer Line assumed a more muted tone. An ad that ran just after Christmas Day buried the Sabbatarian principles underpinning the transportation line, so that a reader might miss that key attribute.[58] Even the paper carrying most of the pro-Pioneer editorials, the *Rochester Observer*, had to reckon with a similar fallout, as subscriptions lagged and its leadership was forced to shuffle its editorial staff.[59]

Labeling Pioneerism "priestcraft," critics such as *The Craftsman* connected Pioneerism to elite-driven plots to rob people of their liberties.[60] Thomas Paine used the term in *Common Sense*, which in the early national period communicated the apparently unholy machinations of

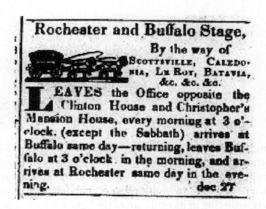

FIGURE 6.2 Pioneer ad. *Rochester Daily Advertiser*, December 27, 1828.

Conflict, Defeat, and Victory 139

the Catholic Church, or similar suspect hierarchies among the Protestant faithful.[61] Throughout 1829 and 1830, the Sabbatarians' opposition echoed Paine's arguments, fearful as they were of a return to the Puritanism of New England, where conformity and coercion threatened the arc of church disestablishment in the early national period.[62] Bissell's efforts to secure the federal mail contract, a renewed effort to petition Congress to overturn Sunday mail service, and the election of 1828 all combined to awaken the opposition forces to organize their own petition campaign and public protests.[63] (Even President John Quincy Adams got mixed up in the controversy when he was accused of traveling on a Sunday in August 1828.)[64] When, on April 19, 1829, Sabbath-minded individuals stopped a shipment of the U.S. Post Office attempting to transit Princeton, New Jersey, the widely circulated story only served to reinforce the fears of the anti-Sabbatarians. Citing local Sabbath ordinances, a local magistrate stopped a wagon carrying the mail, delaying its travels by a day.

FIGURE 6.3 James Akin, "*The 'Holy Alliance' or Satan's Legend at Sabbath Pranks*" (1830). In the picture, a mob of Sabbatarians is attempting to burn at the stake a stagecoach carrying mail on Sunday. A high-resolution copy is on the American Antiquarian Society website and is enlargeable, enabling one to read all the commentary, which is withering in its criticism of the Sabbatarians. American Political Cartoons collection of the American Antiquarian Society, Worchester, MA.

Although evidence suggests the stoppage was a simple misunderstanding resulting from the contractor's failure to mention he was carrying official cargo (which would have superseded the local ordinance), this nuance did not matter to ardent opponents of the Sabbatarian movement.[65] Prints like James Akin's "The 'Holy Alliance' or Satan's Legend at Sabbath Pranks" helped caricature the Sabbatarians as backward, theocratic rubes.

THE PIONEER'S DEMISE

Rumors the Pioneer Line was failing began circulating in early 1829 when some proprietors sold off their segments of the line. By summer 1829, stories of additional sales intensified and Bissell and his allies struggled to counter the damaging narrative.[66] Financial records of the Old Line and Pioneer are nonexistent, but since the Pioneer, like the Old Line, traversed the longest bridge in North America, the mile-long Cayuga Bridge, its toll records afford a mechanism by which to assess the Pioneer's rise and fall. After peaking in 1829 with 41 percent of the market share, the Pioneer declined in the face of Old Line competition and popular opposition to a 32 percent share by 1830.[67] In January of that year, despite plenty

FIGURE 6.4 Cayuga Bridge. Basil Hall, *Forty Etchings: From Sketches Made with the Camera Lucida, in North America, in 1827 and 1828* (Edinburgh: Cadell & Co., 1829), vi.

Conflict, Defeat, and Victory 141

of evidence to the contrary, opponents of the Pioneer celebrated their assumed triumph with a formal gala.[68]

The rumors were inaccurate—the Pioneer continued to run lines once or twice a day (varied across different segments of the line) even as some parts of the line changed hands.[69] Perhaps Bissell's own precarious financial position in 1829 led to the rumors. He had been calling in loans since early 1829, and by 1830 was putting up additional lands in New York and Ohio for sale, signaling an urgent attempt to procure the funds necessary to keep himself solvent.[70] The narrative of failure was also fed by the U.S. Senate report on Sunday mails that decisively ruled against the Sabbatarians' petition campaign in January 1829 (followed by a similar House report in March 1830).[71] Although this dealt a further psychological blow to Bissell and his supporters, it did nothing to end the public debate on the issue.[72]

Another important factor in the Pioneer Line's demise was the fact that several prominent and influential citizens of Rochester came out in opposition to the Pioneer following the congressional reports. The public affirmation of the Senate report and criticism of the Pioneer Line by William Atkinson's business partner and fellow congregant, Elisha Johnson (president of the Village of Rochester's board of trustees), was a personal blow to Atkinson, Bissell, and Champion, and represented a prominent and influential voice of opposition to the Pioneer Line.[73] Jacob Gould, who would eventually become Rochester's second mayor in 1835, also came out in opposition to the Pioneer Line. Both Gould and Johnson connected their criticism of the Pioneer with public support for the Senate report.[74]

Undoubtedly, the toll data suggests that the Pioneer Line was struggling by 1830.[75] The Old Line, by contrast, was adding stage lines in 1830, each offering a certain traveling experience (comfort, speed, etc.).[76] This only further stressed the Pioneer Line. Reinforcing the picture of a business in crisis, Bissell and his pastor at Third Presbyterian, Joel Parker, hit the road to raise additional funds to keep the enterprise afloat. Seeking $20,000, the duo visited churches, raising as much as $2,000 from one congregation alone.[77]

Although "cultural backlash" is the standard explanation for the Pioneer Line's "inevitable" demise as a "national laughingstock," this interpretation causes us to miss other important factors.[78] This backlash was

142 *Part Two: Christian Reform Capitalism*

surely a factor in the Pioneer's collapse, but certainly it was less important than Bissell's failure to win the federal mail contract. Other commentators blamed the inferior customer service skills of the Pioneer's inexperienced workforce, and not its moral stance and political rhetoric. While the Pioneer Line's investors raised significant capital to purchase shiny new coaches, they were less successful in recruiting the Old Line's more experienced drivers. Driving a stagecoach required special skill, honed over years of experience as one learned how to navigate the challenges of early nineteenth-century roads, weather, equipment failures, and most importantly, caring for the horses. The fact that the Old Line was able to retain its drivers meant the Pioneer Line suffered through the mistakes of inexperience, especially when it came to loading and pacing one's horses in what increasingly was a race for speed between the two lines. Knowing when to push, when to pull back, and how to properly rest one's horses was an art honed through experience, and the breakdown of the Pioneer horses from improper care loomed large in the enterprise's demise.[79]

So yes, the market judged the Pioneer Line wanting—it never became the long-term financial success that the founding commissioners envisioned. Consumers were too divided, the rhetoric and personality of Bissell and others were too sanctimonious, and the drivers and operators too inexperienced.

On April 5, 1831, the Pioneer was dealt a decisive blow when its driving force, Josiah Bissell Jr., died soon after his forty-first birthday. Unsurprisingly, the line ceased operations in the same month, a "coincidence" that escapes all the histories of the Pioneer Line.[80] Bissell's lungs became inflamed in late February 1831, and despite this, he still embarked on a business trip to Seneca Falls on March 8, 1831, to organize the construction of a large flour mill. His condition worsened on the trip and his final days were emblematic of the turmoil that always seemed to surround him. He vacillated between confidence that God was going to heal him (evidently, he had word from God that he would recover as his work on earth was not yet complete) and a desire to die and meet his maker. Bissell also debated accepting the services of non-Christian doctors, and chided his fellow elders (and his wife, Henrietta) for praying ambiguously for God's will to be done, rather than for specific prayers that would heal him. In fact, Henrietta told Charles Finney that after her husband died,

Conflict, Defeat, and Victory   143

she was wracked with guilt for not actively praying for his recovery, fearing her lack of faith was to blame for his death.[81] Like Henrietta, some mourned Bissell's death, while others celebrated with joy. Bissell's associate in land speculation, trustee of Bissell's Third Presbyterian, editor of the *Rochester Observer*, and early supporter of Pioneerism, A. W. Riley, remembering his friend, alluded to Bissell's singular ability to polarize: "There never was a man in the city of Rochester so thoroughly hated as was Josiah Bissell; and yet there never was so general mourning at any other funeral as at his. His life was one protest against Sabbath-breaking, liquor-selling, slavery and the secret lodge, and hence he was hated while living, and universally honored and lamented when he was dead."[82]

Josiah Bissell Jr. did not leave Henrietta, Josiah W., or his siblings much money; one sympathetic source from 1838 claims his estate was "insolvent." He left his wife Henrietta the house they were living in, $1,000 yearly income from his stores, a horse, and a few animals. To his children, Bissell initially left $200, with additional payments upon their maturing to the age of twenty-one (sons received $100 each and daughters received $1,000 each). Bissell designated $500 to support the

FIGURE 6.5 Josiah W. Bissell house. Rochester Public Library Local History & Genealogy Division, by arrangement.

144   *Part Two: Christian Reform Capitalism*

anti-Masonic movement and the balance of his estate to the American Board of Commissioners for Foreign Missions, the latter unsurprising as Bissell served as the founding treasurer of its Rochester chapter. Reinforcing the picture of a deeply indebted Josiah Bissell Jr., Henrietta sold the family estate the year after her husband died.[83]

This chapter began with Bissell and his son and namesake, their lives disrupted physically by the Erie Canal. The story is a dramatic allegory for the spiritual disruption the canal represented, and which Bissell dedicated his life to fighting. In an ironic epilogue, Bissell's son Josiah W. went on to create his own share of transportation-related controversy in Rochester. He followed in his dad's footsteps as a "speculator in everything," achieving enough success that he was able to build an impressive house for his family. Josiah W. partnered with the lead engineers who built the second aqueduct carrying the Erie Canal across the Genesee River, completed after six years of construction in 1842. He used his connections to the aqueduct project to acquire stone from the original bridge to build his grand home.[84] Soon, he acquired a pile of debt, and in

FIGURE 6.6 Josiah W. Bissell's Genesee Bridge. Rochester Public Library Local History & Genealogy Division, by arrangement.

Conflict, Defeat, and Victory 145

the words of the agents of R. G. Dun & Company, was "much embarrassed" over his business and financial failures.[85] Josiah W. abandoned his banking dreams and embraced his hobby of bridge engineering full time, starting the architecture and engineering firm Kauffman and Bissell, which worked on several projects throughout the western United States in the 1850s.[86] This work made Josiah W. infamous in Rochester lore by linking him forever to the large and extremely controversial suspension bridge he designed and built across the Genesee River in 1856 while serving as the project's construction engineer. It only lasted one year, collapsing during a spring storm in April 1857, confirming the worst fears of the Genesee Suspension Bridge's many critics.[87] Indeed, transportation-related controversies continued to dog the name of Josiah Bissell.

The Pioneer Line is certainly a colorful story, but it is also so much more than a fascinating vignette. As even the critics of the Pioneer recognized, it was just one small component of a larger movement that sought not just the reformation of the workweek in upstate New York, but a more comprehensive reformation of the American capitalist system. *The Craftsman* of Rochester termed it a "LEAGUE" of "heavy capitalists throughout the union" united by a shared "purpose of REFORMING the structure of our institutions, and re-modelling the grand charter of our rights."[88]

The Pioneer Line died abruptly, but reform CBE transportation lines did not. The Hudson & Erie, the original model for Sabbatarian transportation lines, was still operating well into the 1840s.[89] By then, Sabbatarian lines were beginning to influence their competitors, as other stage lines and canal packet boat lines began to cease Sunday operations.[90] For example, by the 1830s, both the Clinton Line and Commercial Line operated boats named *Temperance*, and by the 1840s, even transportation lines with no other discernable religious characteristics altered their service on Sundays.[91] Other, so-called Opposition Lines, such as the Eclipse, continued to provide six-day transportation alternatives for those seeking to honor the Sabbath during their travels.[92] In any case, the "Sundays Excepted" mark on transportation line schedules persisted. It was only by the end of the nineteenth century, as railroads and other transportation lines began

146   *Part Two: Christian Reform Capitalism*

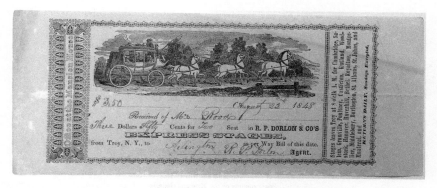

FIGURE 6.7 Express Stage ticket ("Sundays Excepted" on far right). Image by author May 13, 2015, Collections of the Seymour Public Library, Auburn, NY (Richard Palmer Collection), by arrangement.

offering service to recreational sites, that the practice declined and eventually ended.[93]

While Sabbatarians lost the first battles in the early national period to stop mail service on Sundays, it was only the start of a movement that eventually won the "war." Technology became an important ally—particularly the railroad and telegraph, both which relieved some of the market pressure and urgency felt by businesses on the market's periphery. In 1841, mail routes covering approximately 80,000 miles ceased operating on Sundays—conveniently for railroads, of course, which found running mail unprofitable as passenger service was so light on the Sabbath. The telegraph built on this in the 1840s, as its commercial viability meant businesses could access information from the market center in minutes rather than days.[94]

At the same time, the Pioneer Line represented a form of American capitalism that sought reformation through business practice (as opposed to benevolence, local, state, or federal legislation or judicial means). The aims of William Atkinson, Josiah Bissell Jr., and Aristarchus Champion were different from those of Christian communal capitalists such as George Rapp, even though they were united in their sense that the early national-period market could be a corruptive space. The Pietist theology and eschatology of the Harmony Society shaped the market activities of Rapp & Associates, while Calvinism and postmillennialism led

Conflict, Defeat, and Victory 147

72

MERCHANTS AND MILLERS' LINE.

TRANSPORTATION AND COMMISSION.

18 44.

THOMAS PEASE & CO.,

Forwarding & Produce Commission Merchants

77 Exchange St., (up stairs,) opposite the Roch. House,

ROCHESTER, N. Y.,

Dealers in

FLOUR, POT & PEARL ASHES, SALT, TIMOTHY SEED,

And all kinds of Grain, on Commission:

Owners of the "**Merchants and Millers' Line**" of Canal Boats running on the Erie and Genesee Valley Canals:

With an increased number of Boats mostly new, they will forward all kinds of Merchandise from New-York, Albany, Troy, and Greenbush, to the intermediate places on the Canals, Rochester, Dansville, Buffalo, and the ports of the Western States and Canada, and Produce to the various Eastern markets, with promptness and despatch, at rates corresponding with the times. Liberal cash advances made on Produce and other property stored in their own or other safe ware-houses on the Erie and Genesee Valley Canals, for sale or transportation.

Merchants wishing to forward goods from New-York by this Line, will ship by "*Swiftsure Line Tow Boats,*" which leaves foot Broad-street, daily, at 5, P. M., (Sabbaths excepted.)

Mark Packages, "*M. & M. Line.*"

Agents for the Merchants & Millers' Line, and Produce Commission Merchants:

E. T. Pease, 127 Broad-street, New-York.
J. H. Pease & Co., 121 Pier, Albany.
Thomas Pease & Co., 77 Exchange Street, Rochester.
M. S. Hawley, on the Dock, Buffalo.

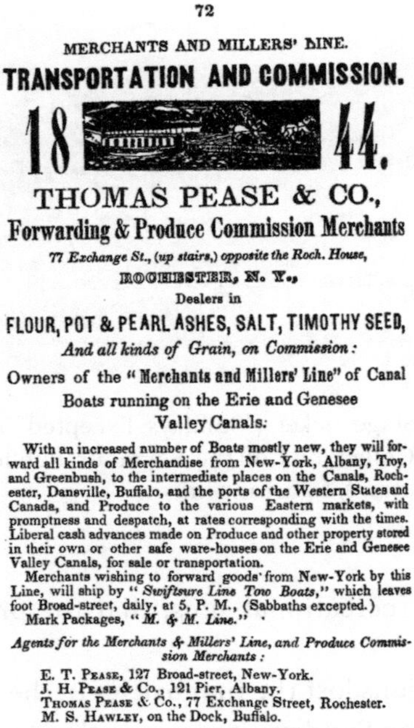

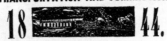

FIGURE 6.8 Ad for Merchants and Millers' Line ("Sabbaths excepted" at the end of main paragraph). James L. Elwood and Dellon M. Dewey, *A Directory and Gazetteer of the City of Rochester* (Rochester: Canfield & Warren, 1844), 72.

Atkinson, Bissell, and Champion to take a different path. Their theology and eschatology pushed them to worry how the vice they associated with an expanding market economy threatened the status of America in the present and forestalled Christ's future return. Accordingly, they created a company that attempted to reform the "ills" of the market while preserving the "good." For these evangelical businessmen, the increasingly impersonal "rules" of the market economy did not dictate how new transportation technology should be employed—that was the purpose of Christian ethics.

The Pioneer was just one of many reforming CBEs in the first half of the nineteenth century, and many of these businesses were financially successful. Some, such as the Tappans' credit monitoring service, created entire new industries. The Pioneer's role in the larger Sabbatarian movement is vital too—the businessmen who launched the line viewed it as a part of a much larger reform project in American economic life. Even though many of its supporters died without seeing the full fruits of their cause, the "blue laws" enacted at the state and local levels in the nineteenth century and the eventual closing of post offices on Sunday should make us reassess the "failure" of the Pioneer Line. Ultimately, the Sabbatarians successfully halted a tide that was moving in that direction two hundred years ago—the shift to a seven-day workweek. Viewed in this light, the Pioneer Line, rather than just a short-term "failure," was in fact the beginning of a larger, long-lasting "victory" of Christian reform capitalism.

PART THREE

Christian Virtue Capitalism

The "culturally conscious" business is common (and controversial) in twenty-first-century America, including diversity, equity, and inclusion offices, environmental, social, and corporate governance (or ESG) investing, and CEO debates over stakeholder capitalism. The next case study demonstrates that businesses attempting to shape culture through their practice and commercial products is nothing new, nor is it unique to twenty-first-century America.[1] Protestant charitable and religious groups' capitalization of new printing technologies and the distributive capabilities of the transportation revolution in creating a mass, evangelical print culture in the nineteenth century is a well-documented story.[2] Conversely, the role of Protestant for-profit publishing companies such as Harper & Brothers has received comparatively little attention from historians looking at the nineteenth century.[3] For example, scholars have demonstrated how twentieth-century publishing firms' religious divisions played an important role in creating a "middlebrow culture."[4] In reality, Harper & Brothers (and many of their competitors) were already doing the very same thing in the nineteenth century, it was just part of their integrated operations, and not relegated to separate corporate divisions. At least one mid-twentieth-century critic has acknowledged this fact, even as he lamented the nineteenth-century literary choices of firms such as Harper, suggesting their effort was nothing more than an effort to pad their bottom lines—resulting in a middlebrow catalogue that weeded out creative geniuses like Poe, Hawthorne, and Melville.[5] (This is only partially true, as Harper published several of Melville's works, including *Moby-Dick* in 1851, which failed to attract much attention in its day. Perhaps publishers such as Harper knew the American public just was not ready for such works.)[6]

The story of Harper & Brothers challenges the assumption that conservative Christian publishers of the nineteenth century were focused on "maintaining purity, being *in* the world but not *of* the world," as opposed to the publishing firms of twentieth-century liberal Protestants who were comfortable living "fully present in the world, redeeming it from the inside out."[7] This characterization of nineteenth-century publishers (the desire first and foremost for "cultural purity") accurately describes the religious presses of the American Bible Society, American Tract Society, and the Methodist Book Concern. But this characterization of twentieth-century liberal Protestants as eager to live "fully present in the world, redeeming it from the inside out," is also an excellent description of the Christian virtue capitalism practiced in the early nineteenth century by such firms as Harper & Brothers.[8] Their approach represented a striving to "preserve the purity of the Word" while "adapting to a changing cultural milieu," since "memoirs, fiction, and Sunday school libraries" could all be "functionally sacred."[9] Ultimately, the goal was the same: transforming American culture into a broadly moral, middle-class milieu.

The foundation of Harper's virtue capitalism was Wesleyan Arminianism (Methodism), a tradition that emphasizes the importance of the written word, and by mid-century, the firm's rising power paralleled the growth and clout of the denomination to which its directors belonged. Arminian theology shaped the Harpers' approach to society, just as Pietism and Calvinism were the foundations of Christian communal and reform capitalism. Arminianism emphasizes the role of human agency in salvation, a view that regards people as free actors, able to choose their spiritual destiny. Consequently, the impulse to persuade, educate, and shape Americans—encouraging them to make moral decisions—is imperative. The Harpers saw their books as accomplishing this task. The early national period was the hinge point in American religion, the

152 *Part Three: Christian Virtue Capitalism*

time when Calvinism gave way to Arminianism as the dominant theology, and Harper was right in the middle of this shift. As Wesleyan Arminianism continued to expand its influence, so, too, did Harper.

Far from an outlier, Harper was one of many Protestant commercial publishers in the early nineteenth century, including Gould & Lincoln (Baptist), Crocker & Brewster (Congregationalist), and E. P. Dutton & Company (Episcopal) of Boston; Robert Carter & Brothers (Presbyterian) and Anson D. F. Randolph (Presbyterian) of New York; and J. B. Lippincott & Company (Episcopalian) of Philadelphia.[10] Of these, fellow publisher John Francis argued in the 1850s that Harper was the most influential, even more so than denominational publishers like the Methodist Book Concern.[11] For these commercial firms, the focus was less on reforming or purifying the market and more about creating a virtuous print culture. Books did not have to be overtly spiritual to contribute to the goals of Protestant publishers like Harper, since in their view, "Histories narrated the progress of God's redemption of the world; biographies offered models for Christian character formation; travel narratives encouraged interest in missions; and science explained God's providence."[12]

The Harpers' era was a time when Protestant Americans were shedding the Puritan unease with fiction (even though many religious journals continued in their outspoken opposition to the genre).[13] Related to this shift, the Harpers were part of a larger transformation occurring within Methodism, as some of the movement's leaders were anxious to shed its artisanal roots and embrace middle-class culture, as evidenced by the construction of impressive churches, the founding of colleges and universities, and the entry of various Methodist leaders into politics.[14] In tandem, Harper & Brothers achieved more cultural power than any other players in the nineteenth-century book trade, as it embraced and fostered an American Victorian middle-class Protestant culture that expressed a "deep concern for morality, respectability, and order."[15] Theirs was a middle-class audience, since virtually all books in the antebellum United States were out of reach of poorer Americans.[16] From its earliest reprints of religious and classical English works, to its Family and School District Library series, to its crowning achievement, the *Illuminated Bible*, Harper & Brothers' production choices determined and produced a sizable portion of the literary consumption of middling Americans throughout the nineteenth century.

Part Three: Christian Virtue Capitalism 153

The Harpers' work reflected a system of "order" predicated on five interrelated characteristics of early nineteenth-century America: faith, science, the Bible, morality, and civilization.[17] Consequently, it is not surprising that Harper found itself on the front lines of a battle in America over how education would reinforce and teach these five ordering characteristics. With the increase in Catholic immigration in the 1830s and 1840s, educational publishing became a contested field. Consequently, Protestant publishers such as the Harpers were an important, if now forgotten, force in determining the direction of American education. As publisher Anson D. F. Randolph noted following the death of the youngest Harper brother, Fletcher, in 1877, "It has always been a surprise to me that in the enumeration of the educational forces of the country, the publishing house is so seldom included."[18]

Harper & Brothers, along with its competing Protestant trade publishers, were quite different from the Christian business enterprises discussed in the preceding chapters. The Harpers were not interested in reforming the market, at least directly, and they certainly did not offer an alternative form of capitalism like that envisioned by the Rapps. Their abstention from running their presses on Sunday in a high-pressure, time-sensitive industry was not a political statement as much as the outcome of a quiet desire to operate according to personal moral convictions, in this case, derived from their Methodism. For example, for the eldest Harper brother, James, the first question regarding a prospective publishing project was always, "Is this a proper book to do?"[19] In an advertisement, Harper described its literary product as follows: "the public may rest assured that no works will be published by J. & J. H. but such as are interesting, instructive, and moral."[20]

Yet the Harpers, like the Harmonists, are largely overlooked, not only by early Americanists, but by U.S. historians more broadly. This is stunning, considering Harper & Brothers was the only American publishing firm established prior to 1820 that thrived in a cutthroat business environment and enjoyed continued success all throughout the nineteenth century, and ultimately surviving into the twenty-first century as HarperCollins.[21] Additionally, as one of the leading scholars of the book-publishing industry argues, "the Harper firm was the first book publisher in New York in the modern sense," one that "appeared to touch off a succession of new starts."[22]

154 *Part Three: Christian Virtue Capitalism*

Despite its status as one of the most important American business enterprises of the nineteenth century, one has to go back to the 1960s to find the most recent works on Harper & Brothers, both written by the head of Harper's religious books division from 1928 to 1965, Eugene Exman. Ironically, Exman's histories pay scant attention to the firm's religious character. Perhaps his own liberal, "searching" brand of Protestantism led Exman to discount (or at the very least unconsciously omit) the evangelical Methodism of the Harpers.[23] This forgotten story of the connection between the Harpers' Methodism and their publishing endeavors is crucial to understanding the evolution of American Protestant middle-class culture in the nineteenth century. As Harper boasted in 1854, "Millions of volumes of the best books of all ages have gone forth from its doors into every corner of our extended country, and have become part of the intellectual life and activity of our people."[24]

The market's growth and expansion in the first half of the nineteenth century generated new tensions that publishers such as the Harpers strove to engage. As members of an evangelical denomination, they believed in the idea of the "priesthood of all believers," and yet the explosion of the American press in the early national period led some Protestants to worry about the ability of the reading public to make discerning choices in its reading material. Not content to leave the American publishing "Wild West" of the 1830s and 1840s to liberal Protestant authors, the Harpers and other like-minded publishers strove to publish works that could "penetrate every space on every day of the week."[25] Harper focused on the emerging middle classes by publishing "at wonderfully cheap rates," part of a "plan for placing within the reach of every American, however humble, the most valuable and instructive books in the language."[26]

The Harpers are particularly compelling because not only are they little studied, but the relationship between their religious framework—Methodism—and American capitalism has been overlooked relative to other areas of American religion.[27] This is particularly jarring when compared to the central place of Methodism in narratives describing the history of British capitalism, thanks to scholars such as E. P. Thompson and Eric Hobsbawm. Methodism was also especially suited to a changing America that was increasingly embracing the concept of a virtuous market economy and economic liberalism. In other words, Methodism

Part Three: Christian Virtue Capitalism 155

in America "was the prototype of a religious organization taking on market form."[28]

But it was not simply that Methodism adapted the methods of the marketplace to its evangelism. Methodism integrated itself into the expanding markets of early nineteenth-century America in a way that undermines the influential narratives of Charles Sellers and Max Weber regarding the growth of capitalism in America. Sellers characterized Methodists as rejecting the growth of capitalism (exhibited by their support for the anti-market politics of the Jacksonians), while Weber dismissed the Methodists' economic spirit outright on account of their emotionalism.[29] The following chapter's description of Harper & Brothers does not fit the Sellers-Weber characterization of Methodism. Instead, its narrative and conclusions support the arguments of those who discover Methodists fostering a "radical, egalitarian counterculture" and "reacting against genteel patriarchalism and aristocratic pretention . . . and not against industrious effort and self-improvement."[30]

Harper & Brothers was the forerunner of a Christian virtue capitalism that became more common in the late nineteenth century; for example, John Wanamaker's eponymous department store, a "public space created and orchestrated with a dual purpose—to make money but also to proffer a mix of religion, genteel manners, and curated goods intended to battle the corrupting moral influences of the city."[31] Although Wanamaker could veer into reform movements more zealously than the staid Harpers, their enterprises shared the same Christian virtue capitalist ethos: "the general uplift of sentiment and refining of all influences and ethics."[32] Wanamaker believed his business could exude Christian "character" and "integrity," while his goods would "lift people up" and fashion a moral citizenry.[33] This approach was based on Wanamaker's "Golden Rule of business," which he derived from the biblical golden rule, along with his conviction that consumer taste could be sanctified so as to reinforce the nation's righteousness, or what the leading historian of Wanamaker terms "aesthetic evangelism."[34] However, as the following chapters demonstrate, Wanamaker's approach, while innovative, did not represent a new expression of Christian enterprise, because the Harpers had already blazed the trail.[35]

156 *Part Three: Christian Virtue Capitalism*

CHAPTER SEVEN

Methodist Printer-Publishers

James Harper gazed down at his publishing house's latest masterpiece to be produced by his publishing house, the 1846 edition of the *Illuminated Bible*. Such a beautiful creation, stunning in its clarity, painstaking craftsmanship, and artistic construction, was a triumph of printing technology and human artistic expression. It had already generated immense sales in a serial release, and Harper was confident that it had elevated the artistic culture of the American public. Making money while producing works of moral value to America: that was the Harper way. The Bible before James embodied those dual goals more clearly than anything his firm had yet produced. He could not wait to show the new edition to his three brothers, his closest confidants and business associates.

The *Illuminated Bible* also illustrated the Christian virtue capitalism by which the brothers integrated their religious views into their marketplace endeavors. From their practice of not printing on Sundays (despite the pressure of competitors printing seven days a week in a race to be the first to resell British authors), to the conviction that their products needed to edify consumers, the Harpers operated a Christian business enterprise (CBE) whose goods were synonymous with nineteenth-century middleclass American Protestant values of morality, virtue, and citizenship. By the time Harper released the 1846 edition of the *Illuminated Bible*, the firm's influence on not only the publishing industry but on American culture writ large was clear to observers on both sides of the Atlantic.

Born over an eleven-year span lasting from 1795 to 1806, James, John, Joseph Wesley, and Fletcher Harper grew up in a home as thoroughly Methodist as any in postrevolutionary America.[1] The New York publisher and friend of the brothers James Derby, when illustrating the character of the brothers' father, Joseph, recounted an apocryphal story of how Joseph quit smoking cold turkey after a neighbor had confronted him about his habit, asserting it was no different than the neighbor's overindulgence in alcohol.[2] Joseph (a farmer, carpenter, and storekeeper) and the brothers' mother, Elizabeth, opened their home to a revolving door of Methodist preachers, to the point that the Harpers' guest bedroom earned the nickname "the Preacher's bedroom."[3] This was a family tradition—Joseph's father, James, had hosted traveling ministers as well. Fletcher's grandson, J. Henry, believed this constant, close exposure to preachers like Francis Asbury was foundational to the formation of the Harper brothers' character, exerting "a lasting influence" on them.[4]

These preachers surely influenced the Harpers' view of money and business. John Wesley and prominent Methodists such as Asbury espoused concerns with wealth, greed, and materialism that would seem to complicate the entrepreneurial drive of the Harpers.[5] But Wesley taught that the problem was not to be found in money itself as much as "in them that use it." It could be "used well" as "a most compendious instrument . . . of business," even "an excellent gift of God, answering the noblest ends," but only if one observed a set of rules, the first of which was "*Gain all you can* . . . by honest industry." This might seem surprising, until one qualifies it with Wesley's subsequent injunction to do this without hurting one's own body, or one's neighbor (or their body). Specifically, one "must not engage . . . in any sinful trade" (something that was up to each individual to discern), "sell anything which tends to impair health," or "sell our goods below the market price. We cannot study to ruin our neighbour's trade in order to advance our own." Wesley preached hard work, encouraging his followers to "use all possible diligence in your calling. Lose no time. . . . Never leave anything till tomorrow which you can do today. And do it *as well* as possible. . . . Put your whole strength to the work. . . . Let nothing be done by halves, or in a slight or careless manner." Finally, Wesley taught improvement: "*You* should be continually learning from the experience of others or from your own experience, reading, and reflection, to do everything you have to do better today than you did yesterday."[6]

158 *Part Three: Christian Virtue Capitalism*

The Harpers' reputation for hard work, astute business decisions, innovation, and for selling products that edified the public derived from Wesley's rules. (Although in keeping records, the brothers were haphazard. They did not adopt double-entry bookkeeping until 1857, a decision that sometimes yielded muddled financial records.)[7] As for Wesley's teachings on what one should do with one's wealth—namely, "*Save all you can*" and avoid "superfluous or expensive furniture, pictures, painting, gilding, books"—the brothers, like all wealthy Methodists, ran afoul of these strict injunctions.[8] Although they were famous penny-pinchers, expensive, luxury products such as the Harpers' *Illuminated Bible* stretched the boundaries of Wesley's teachings. Francis Asbury, who had a reputation for asceticism, and who seemed to distrust the wealthy, visited the home of the Harper brothers' grandfather in 1787.[9] Asbury wrote in his journal, "I came to Harper's, where we have a little new house, and about thirty members. . . . The people on this island, who hear the Gospel, are generally poor, and these are the kind I want, and expect to get."[10]

Yet despite their pedigree as humble Methodists exposed to Asbury and other Wesleyan suspicions of wealth, the Harper brothers came to find little conflict between their market activities and their religion. Central to how they resolved this tension was the influence of the brothers' first church in New York City, John Street Methodist. It was a congregation that exemplified the appeal of Wesleyan Arminian theology "to men and women of ambition" because it "encouraged individual initiative, self-government, optimism, and even geographic mobility." The claim that "Methodism taught people not to fear innovation and ingenuity," and ultimately "encouraged the new values necessary for 'improvement' in a market-driven society," might as well refer to the Harpers themselves.[11] The brothers were not concerned with purifying or reforming the market; instead they used commerce to bring moral and religious truths to Americans through popular, educational, and religious texts. At the same time, the Harpers created a business enterprise that reflected their cultural ethic, one shaped by their religious upbringing. This was evidenced by the core principles of Harper & Brothers:

1. Each brother would oversee his area of expertise, but nothing was done without the approval of all four brothers.

Methodist Printer-Publishers 159

2. "Each step forward should be based on and justified by the steps before."
3. Combine enterprise with "the utmost caution."
4. Never overextend the business in such a way that it was susceptible to "outside shocks."
5. Produce the highest-quality products at the cheapest prices.
6. Hire and retain the best talent, "by careful discrimination in favor of ability, experience, and length of service."
7. Pay employees at rates commensurate with their abilities, and treat them "as one man should treat another."[12]

These principles reflected the "self-control" and "upright" business practices of Methodist tradesmen and artisans in the late eighteenth and early nineteenth centuries, who took their cue from John Wesley. His *General Rules* articulated a Weberian asceticism. Specifically, his injunctions against usury, imprudent and risky borrowing, drunkenness, working on the Sabbath, and ostentatious dress helped inform the business culture of the Harpers.[13] For Wesley, the emerging capitalist system created something of a conundrum, as he preached in Sermon CXVIII: "For wherever true Christianity spreads, it must cause diligence and frugality, which, in the natural course of things, must beget riches. And riches naturally beget pride, love of the world, and every temper that is destructive of Christianity."[14] He even went as far as to argue that the danger was greatest for those who made their money, like the Harpers, through "skill and industry."[15] For Wesley, the only solution was to "*give* all you can."[16]

In an era rife with confidence men, counterfeiting, risky market speculation, and shady financial and business dealings, the brothers' reputation told of an "integrity as unimpeachable as their credit."[17] They were loyal to long-standing booksellers and "made it a rule not to pursue any course that must prove injurious to another publisher, unless driven to it by aggression."[18] Toward prospective authors, they promised only what they believed they could deliver, even though, as the brothers acknowledged, "We know perfectly well that there are publishers, who, having nothing to lose would be willing to incur any risk—agree to any terms—make any promises."[19] R. G. Dun's agents described the Harper culture as one of "strict integrity," "very safe," and "reliable."[20]

Above all, the brothers trusted each other in their business partnership, a fact that was nowhere more aptly illustrated than in their practice of keeping a common account, from which each drew as he found need, a system that seems to have held sway until approximately 1860.[21] The editor of *Harper's Weekly* during the Civil War, George William Curtis, remarked that "it was hard to say where James ended, and John, Wesley, and Fletcher began."[22] The *New Yorker* argued that they proved "the truth of the adage 'in union there is strength,'" and because they were "Tied firmly together by the bonds of fraternal regard no less than those of interest, they have acquired a strength which cannot be broken."[23] One of the most tangible signs of this united front was the fact that the entirety of the Harpers' correspondence, regardless of the actual author, was signed simply "Harper & Brothers." They all spoke as one.

J. Henry believed that the character, morality, and unity displayed by his grandfather and great-uncles began and ended with their Methodism.[24] The eldest brother, James, typified the religious culture of the company. Despite his reputation as a jovial trickster, he was emblematic of the worldly aestheticism that Max Weber famously ascribed to American Protestants: self-discipline, thrift, honesty, and hard work, but never on Sundays.[25] He rose early to spend time reading one of his favorite sections of the Bible (Psalms, Romans, or Paul's letters) prior to breakfast and heading into work. Sources also assert that James faithfully attended church upon his arrival in New York City in December 1810.[26] He was fifteen that year and indentured to a Wesleyan printer, Abraham Paul, on the corner of Burling Slip and Water Street.[27] Soon, he moved to the shop of Jonathan Seymour, located a few doors down from First Methodist Episcopal Church (also known as John Street Church), the country's oldest continuously meeting Methodist congregation. James began attending John Street and also led a prayer meeting a few blocks away on Ann Street.[28] Prayer meetings differed significantly from Methodist class meetings, in that the former grew out of revival camp meetings, which were focused on evangelism (versus sanctification), often skewed toward emotionally charged experiences, and were led by laypersons (rather than board-selected class leaders).[29]

Interestingly, James's obituary in *Harper's Weekly* noted that this prayer meeting took place in the home of a "colored woman."[30] It was not uncommon for prayer meetings to be held outside the church building

Methodist Printer-Publishers 161

itself, but this detail—repeated by several sources and published by *Harper's* in 1869, almost certainly at the behest of James's brothers—is particularly interesting in the context of Reconstruction and the debate over the status of African Americans in the late 1860s. Despite this seemingly open-minded attitude toward accepting free persons of color in their church, the brothers never aligned themselves privately or publicly with the abolitionist movement, and John Street's record on racial matters was mixed at best. Although John Street, like many similar churches, was integrated, white Methodist leaders often did not embrace African Americans in full fellowship—as evidenced by the practice of segregated Sunday worship. Another example of the tension: one of John Street Church's earliest sextons was an enslaved man named Peter Williams. He served the church as sexton and undertaker during the American Revolution, for which he was regularly paid by the congregation. After the war, John Street purchased Williams from his Loyalist owner (who was leaving America) for forty pounds. Evidence suggests that the church purchased Williams at his behest, since he was married with a son and would not have wanted to leave his family and migrate with his Loyalist owner

FIGURE 7.1 John Street Church, also known as Wesley Chapel. J. B. Wakeley, *Lost Chapters Recovered from the Early History of Methodism* (New York: Carlton & Porter, 1858), 108.

after the war. Over a period of several years, Williams purchased his freedom from John Street Church. A more troubling question, indicative of the contradictory ways race played out in early Methodism, is why John Street Church did not simply set Williams free upon purchasing him from his owner. Some records claim that the church treated Williams as a freeman, and that the congregation was slow in following through with obtaining his manumission papers. One must also acknowledge the possibility that the congregation dragged its feet on setting Williams free, not out of the realm of possibility in a city that was increasingly hostile toward free persons of color, even as the policy of gradual emancipation gained support. Ultimately, Williams remained committed to biracial Methodism, attending integrated city churches and resisting pressure from African Americans to join the new African American Methodist churches of New York.[31]

James was enrolled in a John Street class by 1813, a significant step, since membership in a Methodist class was more important in many ways than membership in a Methodist society or church in the early nineteenth century.[32] This was a unique moment for a young apprentice such as James to become involved at John Street Church. A minister named Nathan Bangs was appointed to New York City's Methodist churches in 1810, and he embodied those who wanted to move Methodism from its laboring/artisanal roots to embrace middle-class "respectability." Emphasizing order and intellectualism over emotionalism, Bang's New York City Methodist congregations grew enormously in the early nineteenth century.[33] Congregations multiplied, new buildings were erected, and membership in Methodist classes boomed.[34] John Street was right in the middle of the expansion, building a new, larger structure in 1818—a project John and James both contributed toward, even though they had just started their printing business.[35]

It was during his time as a journeyman, prior to opening his own business, that James met Thurlow Weed (a prominent nineteenth-century newspaperman and Whig politician), who was also working as an apprentice.[36] As his journeyman partner on the presses, Weed especially remembered James's work ethic:

> He and I were both emulous to be first at the office in the morning. . . .
> It was a custom with us in summer to do a half day's work before the

Methodist Printer-Publishers 163

other boys and men got their breakfasts. James and I would meet by appointment in the gray of the morning, and go down to John Street. We got the key of the office by tapping on the window, when Mr. Seymour, the proprietor, would take it from under his pillow and hand it to one of us through an opening in the blind.[37]

It would have been quite natural to find such an apprentice at John Street Church in the early nineteenth century, as the congregation first met in a rigging loft. This was not unusual, since artisans and skilled tradesmen were prevalent in the Methodist congregations of New York City during this period.[38]

By the time James (and then his brother John) began attending John Street Church, the congregation was starting to reflect the growing influence of merchants and retailers. Unlike other Methodist communities, many in the John Street congregation were wealthy. The church also

FIGURE 7.2 John Street's old rigging loft. Samuel Seaman, *Annals of New York Methodism, Being a History of the Methodist Episcopal Church in the City of New York* (New York: Hunt & Eaton, 1892), title page.

164 Part Three: Christian Virtue Capitalism

had a reputation for preferring order and decorum—it was seldom the scene of revivals. John Street reflected the tension between the "producerist" economic critique of the emerging liberal capitalist system by middling Methodist artisans and laborers and its wealthy and economically successful merchants and retailers.[39] In fact, the entrepreneurial character of the congregation in the early nineteenth century would have made it the perfect spiritual community for enterprising capitalist laborers like James and his brothers. (In contrast, the Bowery Methodist congregation was much more exclusively comprised of laborers, and it was known as the site of frequent revivals.)[40] In this way, John Street illustrates Weber's error in dismissing the entrepreneurial potential of Methodists, which was chiefly due to his disdain for the "emotional character" of their religion.[41] Wesley espoused a "progressive, demanding faith" and was convinced that since "God was not lazy, he could see no reason why any of his followers should be, either."[42] James Harper could not have agreed more.

Francis Asbury preached frequently at John Street in the early nineteenth century, and his sermons to the congregation were consistent in their tackling of a single issue: the perils of wealth. On July 25, 1802, Asbury preached on Revelation 3:17–20 at John Street.[43] This scripture is part of the Apostle John's revelation and contains a message for the first-century church at Laodicea: "Because thou sayest, I am rich, and increased with goods, and have need of nothing; and knowest not that thou art wretched, and miserable, and poor, and blind, and naked."[44] The next year, on May 22, Asbury was back at John Street, where he recorded the core of a sermon based on James 3:17 in his journal:

> I. "The wisdom that cometh from above is revealed and inspired," it is "pure"—*negatively*: it is not mixed by its Divine Author with that wisdom which is "earthly, sensual, and devilish"; it is not mixed with the policy, or pleasures, or profits of this world; or of sin, which is of hell. The apostle that written "pure religion," and thus it cannot be when mingled with such qualities, all of which spring form men or devils."[45]

One year later, on August 5, 1804, following the delivery of his sermon, Asbury wrote in his journal, "At the old house in John-street, my subject

Methodist Printer-Publishers 165

was 1 Tim. vi. 6, 7, 8. York, in all the congregations, is the *valley of dry bones.*"[46] In this passage, the Apostle Paul says to his friend Timothy, "For we brought nothing into *this* world, *and it is* certain we can carry nothing out."[47] Clearly, Asbury believed the John Street congregation's wealth and business endeavors were causing it spiritual harm.

Asbury preached at other New York congregations on the same Sundays he was in the John Street pulpit, but those sermons centered on different themes and biblical texts, underscoring the degree to which he believed the primary weakness of John Street was the wealth of its congregation. In fact, when Asbury preached at the Bowery congregation, his records contain no mention of ever delivering sermons focused on money.[48] Indeed, of the four New York Methodist congregations at the time of these Asbury visits, John Street was home to the wealthiest members, who filled the pews alongside the poorer and middling men and women who typically formed the core of early Methodism. Even as its wealthier members started migrating uptown in the 1830s, John Street's tithing (which recorded each giver's class) was consistently one of the top two New York City congregations (which numbered eight by the early 1830s).[49]

John followed his brother into a printing apprenticeship at Seymour's shop, and he also matched his attendance at John Street Church. By the time James's indenture was complete, John had worked enough overtime to buy out the remaining years of his contract. In doing so, the brothers could open J. & J. Harper, Printers, on Dover Street in 1817, with Wesley as their apprentice. James and the more introverted John were twenty-two and twenty years old, respectively. Their firm moved several times over the next few years, adding Wesley and Fletcher as partners in 1823 and 1825.[50] The latter two developed into vital members of the four-brother team, as Wesley, not as "robust" as his brothers, but easily the most "scholarly" and widely read of the four, came to lead the book publishing operations, corresponding directly with authors. Fletcher, the more talented administrator of the four, ran the periodicals, including the highly successful *Harper's Weekly.*[51]

Harper & Brothers (the name changed from J. & J. Harper in 1833) conducted its business in a way that identified it as a CBE. Influential publisher Evert Duyckinck, one of the founding members of the Young America political and literary movement, recorded the following in his diary on January 5, 1842: "They are remarkable men, the Harpers, and have undoubtedly been raised and sustained in their position by their energy and enterprise [sic]. They are keen and wary with little compunction and scent a falling author very rapidly. . . . John Harper is the more godly, for the firm is religious, some people requiring more of this article or what passes for it than others."[52] Known as "the Boss" to his brothers, "a Temperance man" to others, James's religiosity was clear to all who knew him well, but, as Duyckinck's testimony suggests, it was John in particular who earned a reputation for religious fervor.[53] In underscoring that Harper & Brothers did not work on Sunday, several accounts claim John risked his position as an apprentice by refusing to work on the Christian Sabbath, thus establishing the principle by which the brothers operated their future business.[54] In his memoirs of the publishing industry, James Derby recounts an exchange between John and his sons in which John chided them over their Sunday plans, boasting that at their age he attended church and Sunday school twice a day.[55] Unsurprising for one so named, Wesley also imbibed the morality of his parents' Methodism. His children were fond of recounting the time he succumbed to peer pressure and visited the theater, at which point "all the prayers of my mother, all the instructions of my father, rushed across my mind at once," producing such intense guilt and shame that Wesley fled the premises before the final curtain.[56] Likewise, during a funeral rife with evangelical language and doctrine, Fletcher was lauded as a Christian of "spotless character," "unbroken . . . commercial honor," and a model for all young businessmen.[57] Such praise would have pleased James, who told Dr. Davis W. Clark that "the basis upon which we commenced [our business] was *character*, and not *capital*."[58]

Fletcher's grandson, J. Henry, claimed one of the brothers was disciplined for reading a work of the ancient Jewish historian Josephus on the Sabbath—evidently, a violation of their father's prohibition on the consumption of "secular" literature on Sundays.[59] J. Henry also recounted another way in which his grandfather followed the modeling of his parents, by hosting prominent Methodist clergy each Monday night for dinners that also featured prominent literary figures.[60] These social events were illustrative of how the Harpers fused religion, business, and culture, blurring the lines between their personal and public lives, as many of the stories told at these gatherings worked their way into print. *Harper's*

Magazine came to feature a segment entitled "The Drawer" (later the "Editor's Drawer"), referencing Fletcher's habit of writing down especially compelling stories from these Monday-night dinners and placing the accounts in his office desk. According to J. Henry, many of these stories often ended up in the next month's magazine, in the "Drawer" feature, edited by Dr. Samuel I. Prime, a minister and editor of the *New York Observer*.[61]

James and John, the latter the financial expert of the firm (he was also called "the Colonel" for reasons lost to history), practiced a brand of Protestantism that was much different from the evangelicalism of men such as Josiah Bissell Jr., characterized by a "high-minded liberality toward other denominations" and exhibiting "a large Christian tolerance for the views and convictions of others."[62] Not surprisingly, the Harpers' CBE took a different shape than Bissell's. James believed that "it is so much easier to draw than to push" people into moral living (even though, as mayor of New York in 1844, he was every bit the public figure in his community as Bissell was in his).[63] Despite the fact that James aligned himself with evangelical reform movements (in the 1840s he was elected president of the Washingtonian Total Abstinence Society, and in 1851 was named trustee of Matthew Vassar's women's college), he and his brothers endeavored through their literary products to create an ecumenical, if Protestant, culture.[64] As their friend James Derby reflected after the brothers had died, "they were men of broad, catholic minds, and their predilections for their own form of religious worship did not prejudice them against other forms."[65] Consequently, their brand of virtue capitalism was less controversial than either the communal capitalism of Harmony or the reform capitalism of Bissell. Or at least it was until Harper & Brothers grew so large that critics came to fear its power.

MORAL FOUNDATIONS OF THE REPUBLIC: J. & J. HARPER'S EARLY PRODUCTS

Initially, the brothers focused solely on printing. Naturally, one of their early customers was the Methodist Book Concern (which used J. & J. Harper in addition to several other printers to produce its works throughout the 1820s).[66] The close partnership with the Methodist Book Concern during the 1820s was important not only in providing income for

168   *Part Three: Christian Virtue Capitalism*

the Harpers, but also because Nathan Bangs, elected the concern's president in 1820, worked tirelessly over the next forty years to elevate the intellectual life of American Methodism. Sharply critical of the Methodist Church's anti-intellectual "foul blot" on its character, which he argued came deservedly from its indifference to "the cause of literature and science," Bangs represented a faction of Methodists determined to shed the sect's stereotype of an emotional religion led by uneducated clergy.[67] J. & J. Harper was a Methodist firm that could further Bangs's goals.

The focus of J. & J. Harper's early years (printing) was typical and reflective of the infantile state of American publishing in the early nineteenth century, when Philadelphia was the industry leader and most domestic publishing entailed the reprinting of books originally published in England.[68] English literature generally was considered superior, and the U.S. government's failure to acknowledge foreign copyrights made these royalty-free reprints profitable to reproduce. (Although, the largest firms, including Harper, did typically pay a foreign author for "rights," which they "established" by announcing an intent to publish in American newspapers.)[69] Consequently, publishers engaged in cutthroat competition to be the first to print new releases of British titles, even rowing out to meet packet ships as they entered port in order to gain a few precious hours on their rivals.[70] An often-cited story that details this atmosphere involves the Harpers and one of their chief competitors, the main Philadelphia firm of the 1820s and 1830s, Carey & Hart.[71] Both received an advance copy of Edward Bulwer-Lytton's *Rienzi* via the same packet ship, setting off a race to see who would get the book to the public first. Carey & Hart used twelve different printing firms and purchased every open seat on the first stagecoach the following morning to race five hundred copies of *Rienzi* to New York bookstores, beating the Harpers by one day, despite the exclusive contract between Bulwer-Lytton and the Harpers, which should have afforded them first chance at publishing the American edition.[72]

Even before transitioning to publishing, the early Harper products reflected the growing fusion of republican political ideology and common-sense moral philosophy reflective of Bang's brand of Methodism (and American Protestantism more broadly). Their first printed work was an English translation of *Seneca's Morals*, released in August 1817.

Methodist Printer-Publishers 169

Harper printed the book for Evert Duyckinck, who was happy enough with the firm's work that he placed what would be its second order: John Mair's *Introduction to Latin*. John Locke's *An Essay Concerning Human Understanding* signified the brothers' first foray into publishing.[73] These early works were a mix of general religious and moral texts, aimed at furthering the moral foundations of the early republic.

The "secular" Harper titles, including *Seneca's Morals*, *Introduction to Latin*, and *An Essay Concerning Human Understanding*, are instructive because they illustrate that the Harper cultural project was not limited to strictly religious texts. Protestants like the Harpers regarded the Greek philosophy of *Seneca's Morals* as essentially "Christian," as the volume's preface explains:

> We are fallen into an age . . . so desperately overrun with Drolls and Sceptics, that there is hardly any thing so certain or so sacred, that is not exposed to question and contempt, insomuch, that betwixt the hypocrite and the Atheist, the very foundations of religion and good manners are shaken, and the two tables of the *Decalogue* dashed to pieces the one against the other; the laws of government are subjected to the fancies of the vulgar. . . . In this state of corruption who so fit as a good honest Christian Pagan for a moderator among Pagan Christians?[74]

Harper's object was not to purify or reform the American market, but to redeem American culture by producing morally edifying cultural products. The philosophy of a "Christian Pagan" like Seneca fit this description and was reflective of American Protestants' republican political ideology and common-sense moral philosophy in the late eighteenth and early nineteenth centuries.[75] Consequently, when the Harpers made publishing decisions, it was natural for them to ask themselves, "Is this book moral as well as interesting and instructive?" Or, in other words, "does the book contribute to the common good?"[76]

Lastly, it is worth noting that the early years of J. & J. Harper coincided with controversy and upheaval within the Harpers' congregation. John Street Church's original building was old and too small for its growing attendance (see figure 7.1), so the congregation built a new, relatively grander marble structure.[77] By modern standards, the new building was

170   *Part Three: Christian Virtue Capitalism*

quite modest, but compared to the original (with its sand-sprinkled floor, whose simplicity reminded observers of a Quaker meeting house more than a church) it was a dramatic change, representing the transformation taking place within Methodism itself.[78] In fact, although he probably did not approve of the marble, even Francis Asbury himself had called for a new, "larger and better" building to accommodate John Street's growing congregation.[79] This neoclassical building was an appropriate metaphor for the congregation's growth economically and socially, but engendered so much controversy it nearly tore the Methodist community of New York City apart.

The issue reflected a growing divide between "uptown" (artisans, small shopkeepers, and laboring class) members of John Street who were concerned not only about the new John Street building being "too fine" and its "carpet on the altar," but also about the general direction of New York City Methodism. The "downtown" members (wealthier merchants, artisans, larger shopkeepers) of John Street thought these concerns overblown.[80] Uptown members also voiced concern over the rumor that the

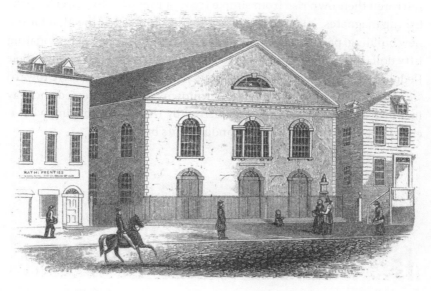

FIGURE 7.3 Second John Street Church. J. B. Wakeley, *Lost Chapters Recovered from the Early History of Methodism* (New York: Carlton & Porter, 1858), 580.

Methodist Printer-Publishers 171

new John Street building would contain pews instead of seats—suggesting the initiation of pew rentals (something common in New York's Episcopal churches), which might serve to push poorer members of John Street to the margins of the fellowship.[81] Since the Methodist churches of New York pooled their resources and submitted to a common governance, it was especially frustrating to the congregants who did not attend John Street to stomach the idea of giving their offerings to a new, "opulent" church that they would never attend. Part of a larger rift over Methodist finances, authority, and leadership within the city's association of churches, a small splinter group of "uptown" members ultimately withdrew from the Methodist churches of New York City and started a small Methodist society of their own, disdaining the move toward "respectability" that they saw in the "opulence" of the new John Street Church.[82] The Wesley brothers' early followers embraced simplicity—meeting in a rigging loft, for example, not as a formal church, but as a "society." As Wesleyanism evolved into the Methodist denomination and some congregations grew wealthier and more bureaucratized, members like the uptown group grew increasingly uneasy with the changes. However, for rising businessmen like the Harpers, the change in their church simply mirrored their own rise from simple trade apprentices to powerful publishing magnates. James and John evidently approved of the plan for the new building, participating in the church's fundraising drive by donating fifty dollars in 1818, no small sum considering they had just opened their fledgling printing business the previous year.[83] As such, the drive toward "respectability" by John Street's "downtown" faction reflected the way in which Harper wanted to be perceived by the public, shaping what it chose to publish and the way it conducted its business.

172   *Part Three: Christian Virtue Capitalism*

CHAPTER EIGHT

Creating a Moral Republic

By 1825, the Harper brothers' business had moved to a four-story building at 82 Cliff Street. The press now employed fifty workers. Looking back from the 1860s, Harper claimed it was already the largest printing firm in New York City.[1] In a sign that the brothers were outpacing their competitors, they converted the bulk of their operations to stereotyping, embracing that technology well before their peers. (Stereotyping created metal plates from papier-mâché molds taken from type settings.)[2] Over the next fifteen years, the Harpers invested more than $280,000 in stereotyping equipment.[3] These years also saw the brothers transition the business from one focused solely on printing to a hybrid operation that did both printing and publishing, and finally to full-time publishing. Their products were a mix of American and British titles and continued the flavor of the first set of Harper works: titles that would enlighten and elevate the public by promoting republican political ideology and common-sense moral philosophy. Such works included medical treatises, historical fiction, adventure novels, poetry, ecclesiastical history, and classics such as Gibbon's *Decline and Fall of the Roman Empire*.[4] Additionally, Harper & Brothers was also building a cadre of salesmen (agents) and booksellers, starting with their publication of the monthly *National Preacher*, which compiled and published sermons of prominent American preachers such as Lyman Beecher.[5]

This emphasis on agents over advertising was typical of Harper's marketing, particularly in comparison to the large British firms.[6]

A mere four blocks from 82 Cliff Street, John Street Church (where all the brothers were members in the 1820s) was undergoing significant change as well. By the 1820s, New York City was growing in a northly direction, and John Street Church suddenly found itself directly downtown. Accordingly, merchants and professionals began to overtake artisans and unskilled laborers within the church's membership.[7] James's personal life reflected this shift. He married Maria Arcularius in 1823, in a union that represented his growing prominence within New York Methodism (and the changing dynamics of his congregation), as his new father-in-law was a trustee of John Street Church and a "pillar" of the congregation, financially and spiritually.[8]

More broadly, Methodism itself was transforming from an emphasis on personal sanctification (the pursuit of holiness, or becoming more Christlike) to community renewal, reflecting the Arminian, reforming, postmillennial thrust of the Second Great Awakening. Consequently, the focus of congregants shifted from introspection and personal spiritual disciplines to active involvement in reform associations, missionary societies, and other forms of institutional evangelism. Methodism was also evolving bureaucratically and culturally from a "society" into a denomination, and from a conference or circuit system into a congregational model of governance. Clergy were increasingly assigned to a single church after they completed a now requisite four-year course of study.[9] Once Methodists founded or took control of institutions of higher education in the 1830s, including Randolph-Macon, Dickinson, Allegheny, McKendree, Emory, DePauw, and Wesleyan, this clerical requirement was a realistic expectation.[10] Additionally, in the spirit of Victorianism, Methodism began focusing more on the family structure. One obvious example was the decline of gender-segregated seating on Sundays in favor of (nuclear) family seating.[11] Another example was the ending of gender segregation in Methodist classes, as increasingly couples began to attend the same classes together. In this regard, John Street was conservative and continued to segregate classes by gender into the 1840s. In fact, after James became a class leader in 1832, he led a female class for more than a decade, which his wife Maria attended well into the 1840s.[12]

174   *Part Three: Christian Virtue Capitalism*

This new emphasis on the family within (and outside) Methodism was not lost on Harper, which began to aggressively market to the family unit. The increased demand for libraries and public education led to the proliferation of "library" series among American publishers in the 1830s. In meeting this demand, the Harpers were keen to find a means for "reducing the quantity of merely fictitious writings" while at the same realizing they would need to supply something that would "be equally entertaining and more instructive."[13]

The result of this new marketing focus, Harper's Family Library, was described by the firm in 1869 as the "most famous work that bears the imprint of J & J Harper," and it represented a new trend in publishing— the serial library.[14] Although they were the first American publishers to use this marketing technique, the brothers did not hide the fact that they borrowed the idea from British publishers who pioneered the concept in 1825, lifting the title "Family Library" from publisher John Murray, specifically.[15] Beginning in 1830, the Family Library series began retailing at discounted rates, and within seventeen years it totaled 187 volumes (131 individual titles), including British and American authors and with a particular emphasis on works of biography, travel, and history.[16] The volumes were relatively small (six by four inches), and affordable to the middle class, making them attainable for a large segment of the American population. The Harpers boasted that their Family Library would "offer to the American public a work of unparalleled *merit* and *cheapness*, forming a body of literature which will obtain the praise of having instructed many, and amused all."[17] The audience for the Family Library was purposefully broad, and the Harpers envisioned it as "equally entertaining to age and instructive to youth; alike profitable to the ignorant, and acceptable to the learned."[18] Although the audience was wide enough that a young Herman Melville could have read seventy-two volumes of the Family Library during his time on board the frigate USS *United States* in the early 1840s, it was not as broad as it might have been. The Harpers were interested in maintaining a certain level of quality and uniformity in their products, and were not willing to skimp on consistency or quality in pursuit of sales; consequently, many Americans would have found the ownership of Family Library volumes out of reach.[19]

Religious themes were prominent in the series; the first three volumes of the Family Library (H. H. Milman's multivolume *The History of*

Creating a Moral Republic   175

the Jews) contained what the *Southern Literary Messenger* argued was "one of the best histories . . . of the Jews," one that "assists to the proper understanding of many passages of the Bible."[20] Religious works by no means predominated, as the books in the Family Library covered a wide variety of secular topics and included such titles as *Two Years before the Mast, History of Egypt, Life of Washington, Philosophy of Living,* and *Life of Sir Isaac Newton.*[21] The Harpers described their new series as "a rich and varied collection of works in the several departments of literature, forming a complete circle of useful, instructive, and entertaining knowledge, adapted for popular use. The utmost care has been taken, not only to exclude all works having an injurious influence on the mind, but to embrace every thing calculated to strengthen the best and most salutary impressions."[22]

The Family Library garnered praise from former president John Quincy Adams, then member of the House of Representatives. Speaking in 1838 to youths at the Franklin Association of Baltimore, Adams stressed that young men should be daily engaged in reading and studying the Bible. However, if one was to branch out from this foundational text, he pointed his young listeners to the Family Library (in addition to monthly reviews and magazines), which contained "useful and of entertaining knowledge" that would provide a "constant supply of profitable reading," the authors of which would "be your wisest counsellors."[23] Newspapers were also profligate in their praise for the Family Library, declaring in one form or another that "It is the duty of every person having a family to put this excellent Library into the hands of his children."[24]

By 1839, observers lauded the Family Library as both a moral achievement and an economic success. There were eighty-five volumes in the collection, each of which sold between 7,000 and 20,000 copies (the biggest seller was volume 37, *Inquiries Concerning the Intellectual Powers, and the Investigation of Truth,* by Scottish physician John Abercrombie).[25] In 1843, the brothers cut the price of the Family Library in half (to twenty-five cents per volume), endeavoring to ensure "every house where there are children to instruct, or adults to edify, may be furnished with a Library of the best and most useful works in the English Language."[26] The *New England Palladium* applauded this, arguing that the price was "moderate," which, combined with the *New York Gazette*'s belief that the works of the library would "prove instructive and amusing to all classes,"

176 *Part Three: Christian Virtue Capitalism*

suggested that the series would help increase the virtue of the American public. The *Charleston Gazette* articulated this sentiment clearly when it wrote of "a Family Library, from which at little expense, a household may prepare themselves for a consideration of those elementary subjects of education and society, without a due acquaintance with which neither man nor woman has claim to be well bred, or to take their proper place among those with whom they abide."[27]

The Family Library also served to advance the careers of American authors by circulating their works at cheaper prices and more widely than if published independently. Although Harper readily acknowledged that the finished product was "not . . . as handsome," the price was half that of a typically published work in the 1840s. As Harper reasoned, this was "an important consideration with all classes of community, the rich as well as the poor." Additionally, given the current state of the publishing industry, Harper concluded that cheaper works were the only ones that could succeed commercially.[28] Ultimately, what was good for Harper's bottom line indirectly benefited a new crop of American authors by expanding their distribution.

Soon, Harper was producing other serial libraries, including the 245-volume School District Library, prominently used by all the early public libraries of New York, and the foundation for the Harpers' foray into educational publishing.[29] The School District Library grew out of a partnership with the American Society for the Diffusion of Useful Knowledge (ASDUK) that aimed to publish books that would be "elevating to the popular mind."[30] This was essentially Harper's mission statement, and the brothers similarly aligned with ASDUK over the role of religion in the "elevation" process. To this end, ASDUK declared Christianity "the great source and the only preservative of all our blessings, individual and national. Its great truths and sanctions are the only foundation of sound morality, the only defence of public and private virtue. . . . Its principles can alone inspire that purity, charity, and order, which are essential to freedom, and without which our free institutions must come to an end."[31] ASDUK envisioned fifty to a hundred volumes in a given "district school library," and it even published a synopsis of the works and subjects such a library should include.[32]

In 1838, New York, in the hopes of putting accessible reading materials in the hands of all New Yorkers, funded school libraries.[33] The hope

Creating a Moral Republic　177

was that through the "diffusion of knowledge" school district libraries would elevate the intellect, "refining the taste, and purifying the morals of the community."[34] While not the equal of modern public libraries, these school district libraries were publicly accessible literary collections, housed within schools or a school trustee's private home. The districts themselves were small, designed to limit the distance young children would have to walk to access such material, each with an average population of a few hundred adults and children. There were approximately eleven thousand of these districts in New York in the 1830s.[35]

Such a project was tailor-made for Harper, and its first two series (1839 and 1840) numbered ninety-five volumes for the "surprisingly low" price of $38, or $0.38 per volume, or a lockable boxed set of fifty volumes for $20 (the case and lock added $1).[36] There is powerful evidence to suggest that these prices were worked out in coordination with the man in charge of establishing the New York school libraries, New York Secretary of State and Superintendent of Common Schools John C. Spencer, who not so subtly suggested that libraries purchase Harper's product—"the best selection that has yet appeared."[37] James was able to utilize the connections of his old press partner, Thurlow Weed, in securing Fletcher Harper an audience with Spencer. This meeting clearly paid dividends. (Weed was emerging as the leader of the New York Whig Party, and his *Evening Journal* was one of the party's most important voices, while Spencer became the U.S. secretary of war in 1841.)[38] The governor also came out in support of Harper's series, expressing his "hope that the books may be extensively introduced into the school districts."[39] *The Knickerbocker* and *The Jeffersonian* likewise threw their weight behind the Harper's School District Library, describing "the enterprise of the Messrs. Harpers as being precisely the thing that was required . . . by securing to the school districts an ample supply of books, . . . of a suitable and uniform size, at the lowest possible cost. . . . We fully unite with our brethren of the press . . . in warmly recommending these series to the public."[40]

Although the state did not require districts to purchase the Harper School District Library, its convenience, along with the endorsements of critics at such publications as *The Knickerbocker*, made it nearly inevitable that it would become a bedrock of these school district libraries, used by children and adults alike.[41] In fact, tucked within Superintendent

178   *Part Three: Christian Virtue Capitalism*

Spencer's regulations for the new district libraries was a "recommendation" that the Harper series was not only the best but also the most economical option.[42]

Within two years of the District Library's debut, the State of New York alone had purchased 422,459 volumes at a cost of $94,988.56, of which the first three Harper series formed the vast majority of volumes purchased.[43] Titles included the *Life and Works of Franklin, Natural History of Birds, The Pleasures and Advantages of Science, Paley's Natural Theology,* and *Napoleon's Expedition to Russia.*[44] *The Knickerbocker* suggested that the entire nation would benefit by the adoption of the Harper School District Library as it would bring "instruction to every door," fostering "a spirit of rational inquiry" and helping Americans to understand their "interests," "rights," and "duties."[45] This fit within the scope of New York's mandate for its school district libraries—namely, that books purchased for these facilities should not be "light or frivolous tales and romances; but works conveying solid information. . . . Works imbued with party politics and those of a sectarian character, or of hostility to the christian religion, should on no account be admitted."[46]

Avoiding politics and sectarianism had the effect of universalizing the School District Library's appeal. The *Southern Literary Messenger* expressed its wish that Virginia would adopt Harper's School District Library for its school districts, since "there is nothing sectional about it," and concluding that there was "nothing cheaper; nothing better" as an educational tool.[47] Virginia did not formally establish a school district library system until 1870, but many states followed New York's example in the next decade, including Massachusetts and Michigan (1837), Connecticut (1839), Rhode Island and Iowa (1840), Indiana (1841), Maine (1844), Ohio (1847), and Wisconsin (1848).[48] In any case, the School District Library expanded the reach of Harper products beyond the urban middle classes who formed the core of the firm's original audience. In an era when the purchasing power and geographic dispersal of rural Americans generally prevented them from participating in the publishing revolution of the antebellum period, the School District Library represents an important exception that has escaped the notice of scholars.[49]

Both the School District and Family Libraries reflected the Harpers' willingness to publish works that other Protestants feared and detested. One of the most prominent examples is the aforementioned

Creating a Moral Republic   179

The History of the Jews by H. H. Milman (1830), which comprised volumes 1–3 of the Family Library. Influenced by German biblical historical criticism, many conservative Christians protested Milman's treatment of Old Testament miracles and historicity—Murray ended up pulling it from his own Family Library series, for example.[50] Similarly, Harper published Robert Chambers's *Vestiges of the Natural History of Creation*, a book that helped pave the way for public acceptance of Darwin's theories. Focusing on what it called "transmutation" of species, *Vestiges* was controversial and published anonymously. (Chambers had already made a name for himself by voicing public skepticism of biblical events such as the flood account in Genesis.) Although generally well received, *Vestiges* upset some Protestants.[51]

There were certainly limits to this acceptance of challenging titles, as the effort to publish *Two Years before the Mast* (volume 106 of the Family Library and volume 127 of the School District Library) by Richard H. Dana Jr. proved.[52] The Harvard student, named after his poet father, wrote a compelling manuscript about his experience at sea on the merchant ships *Pilgrim* and *Alert*.[53] In the finest tradition of seafaring literature, *Two Years* provided a colorful account of the author's exploits, replete with vivid language and description, although the end result was tamer than the original manuscript. Harper used a trusted reader to review prospective manuscripts for questionable material, though Dana's father feared the individual was probably "some dull-head" who would fail to "appreciate" his son's work.[54] In this case, the Harper content screener's primary concern was how "those Christians who look with the same suspicion upon efforts for the diffusion of Popular reading" would regard Dana's descriptions of habitual Sabbath breaking, gambling, drinking, and foul language at sea:

1. Whether, in the frequent notices which the author gives of <u>Sabbath</u> devoted by himself and his companions to amusement on shore, it would not be well for him to occasionally intimate his regret that the day could not be more religiously observed—or at least his sense of its proper sacredness. I am aware, that in the concluding chapter he makes <u>amends honourable</u> on this and other kindred points,—but it must be remembered that many young minds will devour the narrative, but never read the closing reflections—

180 *Part Three: Christian Virtue Capitalism*

2. Whether some similar intimation might not be connected with the mention, on page 189, of a <u>night spent at cards</u>—and with the notice on page 158 of his friend Harris' <u>contempt for the temperance pledge</u>. The reader would be likely to infer, that the author sympathized fully with the <u>contempt</u> in the latter case and had no objection, to cards at any time—It might be considered that this book is likely to have a great charm for the young—that the fine, frank spirit of the meter will secure for him the cordial and unrestrained sympathy of his reader, and that it is on that account peculiarly desirable that he should always appear to be as he surely is, the friend of virtue, and the respecter even of religious prejudices, if they have been found to be salutary.[55]

Dana was a bit more generous toward these suggestions than his father, who contended that the Harpers did not want "to offend the Goodies" who would object to such language in a schoolbook.[56] Dana decided the Harper reader was not suggesting anything he had not already heard from his father, "and I have complied with it so far as is consistent with my [undetermined/damaged letter] from the time of the events."[57] The senior Dana was more skeptical, counseling his son, "don't trouble yourself as to his advice about the Goodies—The next thing they will call for will be an expungated [sic] Bible."[58] An example of Dana's editing is found in the 1840 edition of *Two Years before the Mast*, in which Dana's friend Harris is depicted not as one who would mock the temperance pledge, but instead as the rare sailor who forsake drink altogether because he had witnessed firsthand the destructiveness of the grog—in other words, he did not need a pledge to stay away from alcohol.[59]

Collectively, while concerned with content and language, these works suggest that the Harpers were far from ultra-moralists trying to shove a conservative brand of Protestantism down the throats of the American public. Instead, they took a broad view of what cultural objects were acceptable and positive. Certainly, this was pragmatic from a business sense, as the literary press noted. The *New York Gazette* observed that the Family Library would "prove instructing and amusing to all classes." Pragmatic, yes, but the *New England Palladium* urged that "every family that can afford it" should buy the Family Library because its volumes clearly articulated the values of the emerging American middle class.[60]

Creating a Moral Republic   181

The brothers' pragmatism, then, went hand in hand with their promotion of Victorian values, something the *Boston Masonic Mirror* applauded: "there is no publication in the country more suitably adapted to the taste and requirements of the great mass of community, or better calculated to raise the intellectual character of the middling classes of society, than the Family Library."[61]

The Harper brothers were themselves knocking on the door of the upper-middling class of New York society—something the fellowship of their John Street Church reflected and fostered. While their more militant artisan brethren attended the Bowery Methodist Church (if they attended church at all), John Street artisans such as the Harpers embraced an upwardly mobile, entrepreneurial ethos, leaving behind the preindustrial artisanal and craft world.[62]

MORALITY AND THE MARKET: POE AND DANA

In 1833, the Harpers changed the name of their firm to "Harper & Brothers" and moved exclusively into publishing, trading their horse-driven power presses, originally designed by Daniel Treadwell in the 1820s, for Isaac Adams's newer and more efficient steam presses.[63] The adoption of new technology helps explain Harper's rapid expansion—along with its efficient, four-headed executive team, its location in the country's emerging market center, and the brothers' keen sense for the public's appetite, balanced against their personal convictions. By 1837, all this made Harper chief among New York publishers, enabling it to produce an estimated one million volumes a year, equivalent to the output of all other New York publishers combined.[64] It quickly developed a reputation as a powerful business entity, and the size and scope of Harper's operations in turn attracted hopeful American authors. One such

> **J** **& J. HARPER,** will hereafter transact business
> under the firm of HARPER & BROTHERS,
> at No. 82 Cliff street, New-York.
> JAMES HARPER,
> JOHN HARPER,
> J. W. HARPER,
> oc 29   F. HARPER.

FIGURE 8.1 Harper's name change ad. *New-York Commercial Advertiser*, October 29, 1833.

182   *Part Three: Christian Virtue Capitalism*

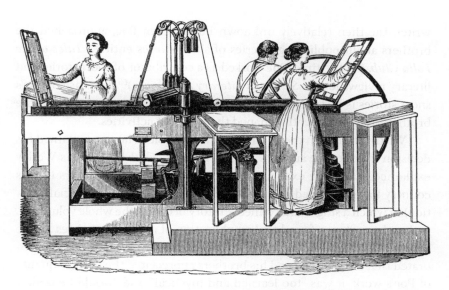

FIGURE 8.2 Treadwell Press. Henry C. Hill, *The Wonder Book of Knowledge* (Philadelphia: John C. Winston Co., 1921), 174

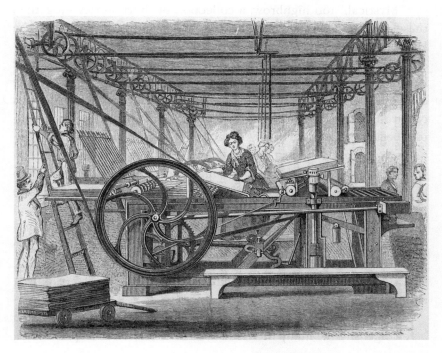

FIGURE 8.3 The Adams press was capable of eight hundred impressions/hour. Abbott, *The Harper Establishment*, 120.

writer, the then relatively unknown Edgar Allen Poe, approached the brothers about publishing a series of short stories entitled *Tales of the Folio Club*. (At the time, Poe worked as a contributor of short stories and literary reviews for the *Southern Literary Messenger*.)[65] The case of Poe's short stories is instructive, because it is yet another example of how the brothers' religious identity shaped their market activities.

Writing to Poe in the summer of 1836, Wesley Harper explained his decision to reject the author's *Tales of the Folio Club* because, as Wesley explained, "our long experience has taught us that . . . readers in this country have a decided and strong preference for works (especially fiction) in which a single and connected story occupies the whole volume . . . and we have always found that a publication of magazine articles . . . are the most unsaleable of all literary performances."[66] Wesley further elaborated that although he and his brothers appreciated the literary quality of Poe's work, it was "too learned and mystical" and "would be understood and relished only by a very few—not by the multitude. The number of readers in this country capable of appreciating and enjoying such writings as those you submitted to us is very small indeed."[67]

"Mystical," too highbrow, a collection of short stories—together, these qualities doomed Poe's *Tales of the Folio Club* in the eyes of the Harpers, who valued cultural objects that would further the moral development of the young nation—as they defined it, of course.[68] The other half of Wesley's comments speak to Harper's financial calculus. The company was not going to make a bad investment, even if the work was culturally valuable. Poe's rejection is hardly surprising as commentators began to take note of how "cautious" Harper was in selecting volumes, a concern born out the "character" of its products. Writer Asa Greene observed that "as certain kings and great men . . . used . . . to keep a *taster* . . . so do Harper & Brothers employ a *reader*, to whose critical judgment and moral taste are subjected all new works . . . and without whose sanction none of these works are ever permitted to see the light." But, Greene, concluded, Harper's selection process "not only insures the purity of the moral, and the briskness of the intellectual, atmosphere . . . but also provides effectually against the assertion that their books 'are never read.' "[69]

The brothers were not legalistic Protestants, nor were they fixated on evangelism like many Methodists of their era. The Harpers took a

184 *Part Three: Christian Virtue Capitalism*

broad view of how their Christianity contributed to the common good, including much in that definition that more conservative Protestants would have excluded. For example, Harper took heat from conservative Protestants for publishing the works of the famous British author Edward Bulwer-Lytton, whose novels some deemed immoral.[70] The Harpers were not ignorant of these criticisms, but they had a more tolerant view of what was acceptable in literature and were therefore willing to publish material that pushed the limits of acceptability for more conservative early nineteenth-century Protestants.

The Harpers' correspondence with authors such as Poe also reveals a concern with their company's bottom line: What, they wondered, would the American public purchase? Poetry, for example, did not enjoy a wide audience, because, as the Harpers wrote to Bulwer-Lytton, "We are too busy in this country to be great readers of poetry."[71] Additionally, while Americans of earlier eras were well versed in British culture and trends, by the 1830s, the Harpers cautioned that American tastes had changed. So, when Bulwer-Lytton tried to pitch the brothers poetry centered on British life, they were doubly doubtful as to its profitability. Conversely, the brothers acknowledged that "'fashionable novels' . . . trashy as some of them are," were extremely profitable in America. Instead, the brothers gently suggested that Bulwer-Lytton write the biography of "some prominent man"—something suitable for their Family Library.[72]

A couple of years later, Poe took the brothers up on Wesley's suggestion by submitting for publication his only full-length novel, *The Narrative of Arthur Gordon Pym, of Nantucket,* although the Panic of 1837 forced Harper to delay its release.[73] At the time, bank failures made it hard for Harper to pay even its outstanding contracts to authors like Bulwer-Lytton.[74] (Despite the economic panic, the brothers continued their giving to their church. James gave special gifts of fifty dollars to John Street Church in 1838 and 1839, while Fletcher responded to the church's call for extra giving by donating twenty dollars.)[75] The Harpers explained their restraint during the economic crisis to Henry Wadsworth Longfellow in the summer of 1838: "The times have been so unfavorable that we have not been able to do much for the last year. Consequently we have still remaining on hand, and engaged, a large number of unpublished works—enough probably to last us until next Spring. We are therefore compelled to decline negotiating for additional works at present."[76]

Creating a Moral Republic 185

Harper finally published Poe's work anonymously and did not explicitly state that it was fiction. The *New York Review* suspected this was intentional, with an eye toward creating the "charm" of works such as *Robinson Crusoe*. However, while *Pym* sold well in England, it was not a success in America.[77]

The 1830s were reflective of Harper's growing literary power, paralleling James's rise within John Street Church. By 1832, the Methodist leadership in New York elected James a class leader, a role that initially saw him take over the Sunday morning men's class he was attending along with Wesley.[78] By the end of the decade, he was leading the Wednesday afternoon class, an all-women group that he helmed for ten years.[79] Designation as class leader by the Methodist Board of Leaders was no small thing in early nineteenth-century New York City. It meant someone was judged sufficiently "equipped" by the clergy to foster spiritual growth and discipline within the church body. In addition to the leadership of a class (sometimes leading the same class for several years), class leaders performed some of the church's administration functions while overseeing the examination of "probationers" (prospective members).[80] James's ascendency to such a position was no small feat, particularly in the most important Methodist congregation in New York City. It signified that both his spiritual and business reputations were on an upward trajectory.

Certainly, the religiosity displayed by James and his brothers existed in tension with the often messy world of contracts and money. Generally, Harper had a reputation for strict payments to authors for their copyrights, particularly compared to its largest competitors in London, although commenters acknowledged Harper was more generous with popular American authors.[81] The company's penchant for playing hardball with its authors emerged in a dispute over the contract for *Two Years before the Mast*. Under his father's guidance, throughout the spring, summer, and fall of 1839, Richard Dana shopped his manuscript around to numerous publishing firms in Boston, New York, and Philadelphia, including Harper, which his father argued would afford the widest circulation and owned a reputation for "more generous terms than most of their brethren."[82] Harper offered 10 percent royalties after one thousand copies sold, which the Danas rejected, mostly likely because they deemed it was inferior to the "half-profits system" Harper offered more

186 *Part Three: Christian Virtue Capitalism*

established authors.[83] The general concept of this agreement was that authors would not see payments until the initial publishing costs were covered, after which Harper would split proceeds fifty-fifty with its authors. Harper first used the half-profits system in an agreement with Theodore Sedgwick Jr. in 1833.[84] In reality, Harper was willing to pay a portion of the costs of manufacturing the plates sooner—as much as half of the amount thirty days after publication.[85] For authors such as Herman Melville, the half-profits system was not the surest way to riches, even if it involved less upfront risk.[86] In contrast, in some publishing contracts the author paid for the stereotype plates, thus retaining ownership over his or her work, leasing the plates to publishers for an established period. This approach, while it was risky in the short term, could perhaps yield larger revenue if the work was a lasting success. In yet other variations, after certain publication runs, authors were able to purchase their plates and copyright for half the plates' initial manufacturing cost, or the publisher and author shared the rights to the plates fifty-fifty.[87] Harper employed all these methods, even though it became identified with the half-profits system in the 1830s.

After nine months passed without any other firms showing interest, Dana Sr. approached the Harpers once more in January 1840, frustrated that he and his son were meeting once again with such "sharp and vulgar men."[88] The Harpers were still willing to publish Richard's work, but now the terms were far less generous: $250 for the copyright and no 10 percent profit sharing. (They argued they needed the copyright if it was to be part of their School District Library series.)[89] The Danas accepted the offer, but when the book enjoyed immediate popularity, they grew unhappy, as acquaintances criticized their decision to surrender the copyright and accept such a small payment for the manuscript.[90] In actuality, the contract was not unlike other contracts between Harper and new, unproven authors. The Harper contract book contains more than 160 contracts for the period 1834 to 1850, and of these, 10 percent were for half-profits, while only 5 percent included ownership of the manuscript copyright and stereotype plates. Additionally, of the latter 5 percent, all granted Harper exclusive ownership of the manuscript copyright for anywhere from three to twenty-eight years.[91] Nevertheless, in the 1840s, publishers came out of the woodwork, happily criticizing their biggest competitor, claiming they would have paid a thousand dollars for

Creating a Moral Republic   187

Dana's book, as *Two Years before the Mast* "must be a handsome affair to the Harpers."[92] Friends of the Danas maintained that they should press Harper either for the copyright or higher compensation. Dana Sr. complained that it was an example of publishers abusing writers by driving hard bargains: the publishers raked in the profits while the writer was "struggling to make his way along in life."[93] Fletcher, while admitting the brothers got the book on the cheap, refused to divulge how many copies it had sold, further raising the suspicions of the senior Dana that they were making money hand over fist. When a rival bookseller pressed Fletcher on Harper's contract for *Two Years before the Mast*, according to Dana Sr., Fletcher countered, "But suppose we had been the losers?"[94]

Despite the pressure, Harper would not give up the copyright to the book. Firstly, the company maintained that it was not possible to yield the copyright once it placed a book in the Family and School District Libraries, as it would lose control over those series. Secondly, it steadfastly argued that it had not yet turned a profit of even $250 (Dana's payment) and that reports to the contrary were much exaggerated and inaccurate.[95] Dana Sr. told his son he did not "like the thought of your having anything more to do with the Harpers," and so Dana approached Little & Brown with his next project (although it only offered him 10 percent profits, not half-profits).[96] The feeling was mutual, as the Harpers did not appreciate Dana playing the tough negotiator, demanding "your highest price, or I shall take up with one of the offers here, unless you go beyond them."[97] (They declined to raise their offer.)[98] Dana and the Harpers mutually went their own separate ways.[99]

The other prominent case of a disgruntled Harper author involved the case of novelist Theodore Sedgwick Fay, who publicly accused the brothers (erroneously, according to Eugene Exman, the first to document the episode) of financial impropriety—something that in fact appears to have been the result of Harper's chief weakness: poor recordkeeping.[100] Such recriminations had the potential to poison the relationship between the company and its authors, as evidenced by correspondence between Francis Lieber (nineteenth-century economist and author) and prominent author William H. Prescott. Having caught wind of Fay's accusations, Lieber wrote to Prescott, who had extensive experience with the Harpers and "found them birds of the right feather."[101] Contrary to Fay's accusations, Prescott explained that the brothers paid him "punctually."

188   *Part Three: Christian Virtue Capitalism*

Additionally, he was very skeptical of intentional deception on the part of the Harpers:

> I do not think there is much danger of such a gross fraud in a house of their standing and character, and where it must be known to the four partners, and to some of the subalterns in the establishment,—at least if carried to any extent. This would be supposing rogues to be more plentiful than usual, even among publishers. I have found, too, that the report of the Harpers from persons who have dealt with them, and know them best has been almost always favorable to their integrity.[102]

Additionally, Prescott maintained that his experience was typical of others who worked with the Harpers, "who think them shrewd and sharp in their bargains, but faithful in the execution of them." Prescott cautioned Lieber not to expect generous gifts should his book hit the best-seller list, and "to be precise in your written contract—and to leave as little in said contract as possible, to contingencies."[103] Prescott struggled to explain Fay's complaints, and although he allowed that he could "easily believe they could be guilty of considerable blunders in their rapid wholesale way of doing business," he was "very slow to suspect them of intentional fraud," as Fay had contended.[104] Harper weathered Fay's accusations far better than the Dana flap (which some rival publishers quietly used to their business advantage). At the end of the day, people might expect four Methodists to be miserly, tight-fisted scrooges who drove a hard bargain, but outright dishonesty just did not ring true to those familiar with the brothers' Christian values and work ethic.

Creating a Moral Republic 189

CHAPTER NINE

Fostering an American Protestant Identity

By the end of the 1830s, observers declared that Harper & Brothers "rightly enjoys a higher distinction than any other [publisher] in the country, from the character of its partners as well as on account of the extent and importance of its operations."[1] The fact that Harper now employed two hundred employees (including seventy-five "very pretty girls") working in two "large" buildings seems to have bolstered this conclusion.[2] In reality, there was so much more to Harper's growth. Its brick-and-mortar enterprise was the physical evidence of how Harper's twelve hundred field agents, along with its strong relationships with booksellers, prescient selection process, strong business reputation, and improvements in transportation networks (the Erie Canal in particular) combined to make Harper & Brothers into an incredible success. The firm now surpassed the Philadelphia publishing giant of Carey & Lea while encouraging the careers of countless American authors, to the point that the *Southern Literary Messenger* declared utterly "foolish" the sarcastic question "Who reads an American book?"[3] Their project to enrich the culture of the American public was also gaining notice. The *American Monthly* congratulated the Harpers for having "done more to render classical literature popular in America, than all the colleges and institutions from Maine to Mississippi," and in the process, sparking a "revolution" in the country's literature.[4] The *New Yorker* declared that over twenty-five years of business, the brothers had earned "most

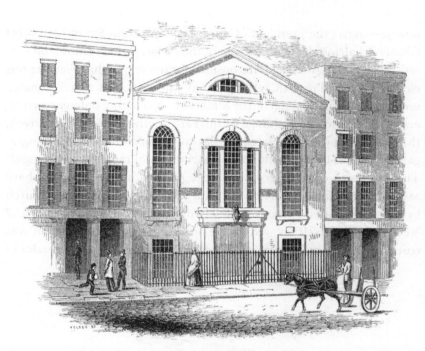

FIGURE 9.1 Third John Street Church. The building is flanked by row houses on either side that the congregation built as rental properties to supplement its declining offerings. J. B. Wakeley, *Lost Chapters Recovered from the Early History of Methodism* (New York: Carlton & Porter, 1858), 584; Raynor Rogers, *The Story of Old John Street Church* (New York: Raynor R. Rogers, 1984), 30–33.

deservedly, a greater reputation than any other bookselling house in the United States.... The Harpers have probably done more for the advancement of literary taste and the advantage of native authorship than all the other publishers."[5] Indeed, the firm's reputation had grown to the point that even when it published a substandard work, reviewers gave it the benefit of the doubt, even to the point of blaming translators and other associates in the publishing world rather than the publisher itself.[6] Certainly not everyone celebrated Harper's literary power and choices, but even its detractors served to underscore the influence wielded by the brothers.

This reputation derived in part from the fact that by the end of the 1830s James Harper had risen in spiritual esteem to the point that he was

Fostering an American Protestant Identity   191

now serving as the president of the trustees for John Street Methodist Church, chairing the construction of the congregation's third (and current) structure.[7] James held this position for ten years, while Fletcher was elected a steward in 1848, serving into the 1850s; he was also designated secretary in 1851.[8] (Elected by the Methodist Quarterly Conference, trustees oversaw land and buildings within early Methodism. Comparatively, the office of steward regulated the day-to-day operations of the congregation, such as the collection and distribution of monetary offerings.)[9] This stands in contrast to the picture painted by scholars who have assumed the Harpers were no longer a presence at John Street Church by the early 1840s, reflecting the changes in the urban landscape of New York City itself (as well as the brothers' moves uptown).[10] It was true that the financial crisis of the late 1830s (and the general squalor of

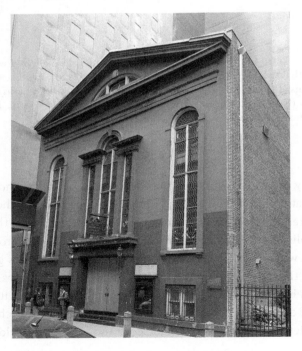

FIGURE 9.2 John Street Church today is surrounded by skyscrapers, and serves more as a museum of American Methodism, even though it is still an active congregation. Photo by author, July 13, 2016.

192 *Part Three: Christian Virtue Capitalism*

the surrounding neighborhood) reduced John Street's membership by half while dramatically increasing the percentage of working-class members. Even after Wesley and John moved uptown, Fletcher and James continued to live near John Street into the 1840s and attended classes at John Street; in other words, they did more than just fill absentee leadership roles. (James and his family moved to the house formerly belonging to Lewis Tappan on Rose Street—scene of a famous anti-abolitionist riot in 1834.)[11] The exodus of wealthy New Yorkers to neighborhoods to the north of downtown affected many churches, not just John Street. As John Street Church's congregation shrunk as a result of these demographic changes, a movement to relocate the congregation uptown emerged, which James narrowly defeated. Consequently, he led the construction of the smaller third structure that still stands today.[12]

Such buildings demonstrated the growing significance of New York City's Methodist community, a development that paralleled Harper & Brothers' expanding influence. A work that demonstrated the brothers' business acumen and cultural power was their 1843 contract with Noah Webster to produce a revised edition of his controversial *American Dictionary of the English Language*, which granted Harper the copyright to the dictionary for fourteen years. Signed two days prior to Webster's death, the original contract established terms of agreement (and reserved ninety cents per copy to White and Sheffield, who transferred the original stereotype plates to Harper for payment of ten thousand dollars).[13] The brothers were purposeful in setting terms that could provide a handsome profit while negotiating with the publishing firm White and Sheffield over the abridged royal-octavo edition of Webster's dictionary.[14] Harper was not shy about pricing its products aggressively in what was often a cutthroat business in the 1830 and 1840s. When sales of the dictionary disappointed the brothers in August 1849, Harper proposed reducing its retail price by a full dollar to $2.50, arguing that reducing the cost "to the lowest point" represented the "only way to compete with the quarto and university dictionary."[15]

Most importantly, *An American Dictionary of the English Language* represented Harper's cultural power. Webster's alternate orthography was controversial in early nineteenth-century America because it was part of his larger campaign to create a distinctive American identity, a

Fostering an American Protestant Identity　193

project the *New York Evening Post* blamed for "corrupting" the English language.[16] Embracing Webster's agenda, Wesley decided that all future manuscripts printed by the Harpers would conform to Webster's spelling innovations. This decision incensed critics such as author and commentator Edward S. Gould, who lamented Webster's "ridiculous" rules, which he claimed had only served to introduce "confusion" and create a national "calamity."[17] Criticism of Webster's "pernicious 'system'" also implicated Harper, since, as Gould maintained in an article published in the *United States Democratic Review*, the publisher was out of step with "educated men and good writers" who "have repudiated the experiment."[18] Furthermore, Gould refused to buy any of Harper's books because he did not want to "encourage their abominable orthography."[19] Others, like Oliver Wendell Holmes, mocked a literary culture where "printers teach them how to spell."[20]

Although Harper was not the only publisher of *An American Dictionary of the English Language*, the firm had sold more than 100,000 copies of its version by 1853, and one can argue that the company played a role in the eventual public acceptance of Webster's system.[21] The company's decision to bring its publications in line with Webster's orthography is a less obvious way in which Harper influenced American culture. By casting its lot with Webster's system, still controversial in the 1840s, the publisher helped ensure this new approach to orthography persevered. This was an important part of the formation of an American national identity in the nineteenth century, and Harper's endorsement, as the largest publisher in the country, played an important, if overlooked, role in the process.[22]

The role of Webster's dictionary in reinforcing an "American identity" in the year of its first Harper edition—1843—must be contextualized alongside the arrival of thousands of Irish Catholics to America in the 1830s and 1840s. The nativist backlash immigrants faced in cities such as New York lent symbolic power to a publication such as Webster's dictionary—even as some conservative Protestants feared a loss of "American identity." James's candidacy for mayor of New York one year later, in 1844, deepens the symbolism of Harper & Brothers' decision to publish the dictionary and convert to Webster's orthography.

James ran as a member of the populist American Republican Party, succeeding where prominent nativist Samuel F. B. Morse had failed eight

194 *Part Three: Christian Virtue Capitalism*

years earlier.[23] James's beginnings as a humble apprentice was part of his appeal to New York City voters, representing a dying capitalist myth of unity between "master and journeyman, merchant and artisan."[24] Added to this was his religious experience, which along with his artisanal roots combined to shape James's vision of unity for New York society and American identity more broadly. Since John Street Church endeavored to unite laboring workers with wealthier congregants, combining them within integrated Methodist classes, James's experience with Christian unity amid diverse socioeconomic groups provided him with a confidence that he understood the template for unity in the city writ large. But for James this unity was an ecumenical one. He did not make sectarian religious appeals, and certainly did not bang the anti-Catholic drum.[25]

Skeptical of James's sense of unity, scholars judge him harshly for running as candidate of the American Republican Party—part of a common tendency to label Harper & Brothers "nativist."[26] The brothers may very well have been nativists, but the fuller context presents a more complicated picture. The brothers' politics typically aligned most closely with those of the Whigs, whose support catapulted James into the mayor's office. If Whigs were those who "poured the new wine of commerce and industrialization into the old bottles of deference, patriarchalism, Scottish moral philosophy, and classical rhetoric," that description applies equally to the Harpers.[27] James's public speeches during the campaign and subsequently as mayor did not reflect the nativism of his party. If anything, they revealed his assertions of piety and patriotism, replete with such passages as "let us ever keep that Book to our hearts which is a lamp to guide the feet of the wary traveler . . . and teach it to our children—May our watch-word ever be—The <u>Bible</u>—<u>Liberty</u>. My country or death."[28]

In part because he was a known advocate of the temperance movement, president of a New York Washingtonian auxiliary, and officer in the Brotherhood of Temperance (a local society), scholars mostly remember James's administration for his attempt to remake New York in the image of the disciplined, hardworking, sober, thrifty, principled Methodist artisan.[29] Most famously, he attempted the reorganization of the city's police department, outfitting officers with blue uniforms, aggressively enforcing laws prohibiting alcohol sales on Sundays, banning the

Fostering an American Protestant Identity   195

sale of alcohol on July 4 (from special booths traditionally erected for the holiday), banishing street vendors, and initiating almshouse reforms. The new municipal police were called either "MPs" after the letters on their collars, or "Harper's Police," since he departed from prior convention in selecting the two hundred additional officers himself (previously wards had selected officers). Notwithstanding these innovations, critics have labeled most of Harper's efforts a failure, in part because the city charter severely limited his power.[30]

Although such evidence complicates simple attempts to label James a nativist, his willingness to tap into the populist movement by running as a candidate of the American Republican Party implies an endorsement of its nativist platform, despite an 1854 letter to Thurlow Weed in which James attempted to distance himself from the descendants of his movement, the "Know-Nothings."[31] (Although it should be noted he won in 1844 with Whig support and lost reelection the following year after being shunned by Whig voters—not as a result of nativist populism.)[32] In fact, this letter contains the most damning piece of evidence against James: his claim to be a member of the Order of United Americans, a nativist, anti-Catholic workers group. He casually mentioned his membership in this group to Weed as something that would "act in my favor, if nominated," for the New York governorship.[33]

Harper avoided nativism in its offerings, although it was ultimately connected to the movement through a work it printed (though it was not published under the Harper imprint—a common practice in the first half of the nineteenth century), the fraudulent *Awful Disclosures by Maria Monk*.[34] Purported to detail the corruption of a Canadian convent, the book was an exposé said to be written by a mysterious Maria Monk, who had supposedly escaped the convent in question.[35] Its revelations of sexual abuse, infanticide, and harsh punishment inflamed anti-Catholic nativism during the 1830s, reinforcing common antebellum tropes of a Catholic conspiracy.[36] Subsequently, it has become the most-cited (if highly problematic) piece of evidence used to accuse the Harpers of nativism.

The claim that the Harpers were secretly behind *Awful Disclosures* seems to have originated with Ray Billington's unsupported speculation in 1938 that the brothers used a dummy front to publish the work. Billington disregards (or is unaware of) evidence to the contrary (such as the

196 *Part Three: Christian Virtue Capitalism*

fact that other works were also published by the "dummy" firm, and its listing in New York registries), while reading nonexistent evidence into his primary sources. Billington's speculation established the persistent narrative attributing the book to Harper as evidence of the firm's unsurprising nativism. The claim has been repeated numerous times, by both scholars and popular sources such as Wikipedia, without question (or further investigation).[37] The Harpers' decision to print (if not publish) the book seems inconsistent and odious, but for the nineteenth-century publisher, it was one's mark on the book that transmitted one's name and reputation. Printing was simply contractual, even if it involved a work such as *Awful Disclosures*. However, once the book was exposed as fraudulent, the brothers were surely glad their name was not on it, although their role in printing and disbursing royalties enmeshed them plenty enough in lawsuits (in which they were defended by Ralph Waldo Emerson's brother, William.)[38] At the very least, one would like to ask James if this indeed was a morally redeeming book, and if printing it was "the right thing to do."

One overlooked piece of evidence in the debate over the Harpers' nativism was their publication of the Apocrypha, a series of books Catholics regard as authoritative scripture, but which Protestants regard as noncanonical. If the Harpers truly believed Catholic immigrants posed an imminent threat to America (as did the concerned citizen who wrote Mayor Harper from Mount Carmel, Illinois), their decision to publish the Apocrypha is puzzling.[39] As an extension of Irish-Catholic immigration angst in the nineteenth century, the battle over whose Bible would dominate American public life was highly contentious—violent in the case of New York—in the 1840s, when Harper published Bibles that included the Apocrypha. (By comparison, the evangelistic American Bible Society's ban on publishing Bibles containing the Apocrypha lasted until 1964.)[40] However, as the Catholic population of America increased dramatically in the 1840s (especially in New York City), producing a Bible that appealed to Protestants and Catholics alike made financial sense and reflected the ecumenical spirit of the Harpers. In the brothers' words, this choice also reflected their desire "To render it *universally* acceptable, the text is the authorized version, given without note or comment, excepting only marginal references, so that no sectarian prejudice can exist against its unlimited circulation."[41] Including the Apocrypha in Bibles made sense to the market-oriented, broadly Christian ethos of the Harpers, but for others this was in "questionable taste."[42] The reality is that any nativist sentiments the brothers harbored—and clearly James had some, as his membership in the Order of United Americans attests—paled in comparison to their desire to market to Catholics and Protestants alike.

PROTESTANTS AND ART: *HARPER'S ILLUMINATED AND NEW PICTORIAL BIBLE*

"These high-priests of Minerva, who have erected here a holy temple, as it were, in the midst of money-changers and shopkeepers. . . . Without them or some such as shall follow in their footsteps, darkness would come over the land."[43] Such was one man's description of Harper by the 1840s. Hyperbolic (or tongue-in-cheek), of course, it nonetheless encapsulates the firm's identity as an entity of Christian virtue capitalism as it sought to produce morally redeeming products amid a cutthroat industry. Harper's rise was so striking that three years later this same observer—Moses Beach, editor and publisher of the New York *Sun*—contended that the firm could turn any book into a profit, a claim evidenced in his mind by how "they had published several of the worst and most stupid books ever issued," which still found ready homes.[44] The Family and School District Libraries, specifically, proved highly successful and profitable, leading the firm through the Panic of 1837 and onto solid financial footing by the mid-1840s, allowing for a significant expansion in Harper's yearly publishing output.[45]

However, Harper products did not necessarily call to mind high quality and fine art, as critics pointed out, since they were the kind of works "one may carry in the hand."[46] By the 1840s, the market for elevated works of culture was growing along with the American middle class, and Harper wanted to catch this trend and ultimately lead the publishing industry's foray into artistic engravings and other embellishments.[47] Much has been made of the contributions of more liberal Christian authors in shaping consumer culture during this period, with the contributions of Unitarians and Universalists playing a prominent role in these narratives.[48] Although theologically liberal Protestant writers and cultural elites did influence culture in significant ways, this story ignores the prominent role played by theologically conservative Protestant

198　*Part Three: Christian Virtue Capitalism*

publishers such as Harper. One example of this influence is *Harper's Illuminated and New Pictorial Bible*, published between 1843 and 1846, a project that one prominent American literary expert deemed the country's "first richly illustrated book."[49] As an 1844 article from a Boston newspaper explains, "no edition of the Bible has been published in this country, approaching that which is now in the course of publication. In the appearance of its typography, the elegance of the engravings, and the exquisite character of the designs, it is certainly unsurpassed."[50]

When Harper contracted with engraver Joseph Adams and the painter John Gadsby Chapman (already famous for his *Baptism of Pocahontas* hanging in the rotunda of the Capitol Building) in April 1843 for "original designs and woodcuts . . . for each chapter of the Bible," the brothers envisioned the project—"the most splendid and richly-illustrated Bible ever published in the world"—as a work of art and culture more than a tool of evangelism.[51] Containing more than fifteen hundred images, when previously illustrated American Bibles only contained at the most one hundred illustrations, the *Illuminated Bible* transformed the way the American public interacted with their most sacred text.[52] Chapman and the brothers seemed to have envisioned a modern, industrially produced version of a premodern illuminated Bible, as Harper's marketing featured reviews that claimed it harkened back to the highly ornamental Bibles of the great seventeenth-century libraries.[53]

The project was possible because of a production process that Adams (whom J. Henry Harper credits with the idea for the *Illuminated Bible*) helped popularize, an innovation in printing called electrotyping, combined with hard end-grain, boxwood engravings. Electrotyping created copper printing plates by immersing a wax mold in a copper solution charged with an electric current, which after ten to twelve hours yielded a mold with a thin coating of copper (from which the wax was removed, leaving a thin copper shell). Ultimately, this yielded a faster production process, and allowed for finely detailed pictures to be put on the same page as text.[54] As Peter Wosh points out, part of the genius of the *Illuminated Bible* was technological, in finding a way to produce such a beautiful item while selling it at a relatively low price. Printed on innovative presses manufactured by R. Hoe and Company, these machines only required one attendant and could print single and double pages.[55] Combined with the decision to first release the Bible serially, this technological

Fostering an American Protestant Identity   199

innovation made the Harpers' work an item of sacred art affordable to the expanding middle class. Numbering fifty-four volumes of between twenty-five and sixty pages, and retailing for twenty-five cents each, Harper released the *Illuminated Bible* over three years. As these volumes ended somewhat randomly (without even finishing chapters, let alone books of the Bible), the project's fifty thousand subscribers had great incentive to continue buying additional volumes. Customers received instructions on the back cover of volume 52 on how to bind the volumes into one keepsake Bible. Volume 54 included the extra sheets (replete with places to record family marriages, births, and deaths) to complete this task. Additionally, in 1846 Harper released a complete, leather-bound, gold-embossed *Illuminated Bible*, which retailed for $22.50 and sold an additional twenty-five thousand copies (amazing considering its price) and was reprinted again in 1859 and 1866.[56] As figure 9.6 demonstrates, Harper's claim that it achieved "the Highest State of Perfection" in its *Illuminated Bible* series was a bit of an overstatement (for volumes 45 through 49, for example, Harper issued some copies with the wrong numbers on their covers).[57]

Such errors were problematic, to be sure, since the Bible was supposed to be authoritative for Protestants. Seth Perry has demonstrated that this was an era when the Bible's status as a basis of authority was changing along with the way Americans engaged with their sacred text. The inclusion of indices, commentaries, and references in early nineteenth-century Bibles reinforced the trustworthiness and authoritativeness of the scriptures, making publishers the new institution of spiritual authority.[58] Harper was part of this trend, including in the *Illuminated Bible* an alphabetical table of the names mentioned in the Bible, tables of various measurements (weights, lengths, time, coinage, liquids), a chronological time line (starting with creation in 4004 BCE), and an index of the Bible's subjects. But the *Illuminated Bible* took this process a step further, by embedding over a thousand images that served as both commentary and a basis of the project's trustworthiness. The *Richmond Advertiser*, for one, celebrated this. Even more so than the quality of the "engraver's skill, and of the perfection of the typographic art," the paper explained that "most of all we are pleased with the distinct, outstanding idea—indeed commentary—they give to the portion of Scripture imbodied in the engraving. It is not so much as an ornamented Bible that we

200 *Part Three: Christian Virtue Capitalism*

thus commend it, but because the ornaments are illustrations, striking and true, of the ideas conveyed by the text."[59]

A specific example of how the illustrations functioned as "commentary" is found in the *Illuminated Bible*'s Isaiah, a book of prophesy that Christians have traditionally interpreted as foreshadowing the coming of Jesus Christ. (For example, Handel's *Messiah* famously uses numerous passages from Isaiah.) To underscore the connection between the ancient Hebrew prophet Isaiah's words and the person of Jesus, the *Illuminated Bible* contains several portraits of Jesus throughout the book of Isaiah (and of Jeremiah).[60] By illustrating the book of Isaiah in such a manner, the *Illuminated Bible* removed the possibility that one might interpret the book in an altogether different manner, and eliminated the opportunity for readers to make such connections themselves. Readers could trust in the pictorial accuracy and reliability of this prophesy (and the depiction of Christ), because as Harper claimed, "Among other features peculiar to this edition of the Sacred Scriptures, one will be

FIGURE 9.3 Jesus depicted in the Old Testament. Clockwise from top left: Jeremiah 23, p. 700; Isaiah 53, p. 671; Isaiah 50, p. 669; Isaiah 52, p. 670. *HINPB*. Courtesy of Special Collections & Archives, Wesleyan University, Middletown, CT. Arranged and formatted by Marijane Ceruti.

Fostering an American Protestant Identity 201

found to consist in the greater accuracy of its Pictorial designs, as to architecture, costumes, localities, and characters." Drawing a contrast with the "paintings of the Old Masters," Harper assured readers that they could trust the authority of its images because these were "in strict accordance with the recent important discoveries of ancient relics in the East." So, they "may be regarded as the *true Commentary* on the text, forming a medium through which much instruction may be communicated to the mind of the reader, at the same time opening up a source of pleasurable entertainment to the eye."[61] Of course, even as Harper claimed artistic accuracy, its depiction of Jesus adhered to the stereotypical "Anglo-European Christ," which derived from a fraudulent medieval manuscript.[62]

Like textual commentaries, the images contained in the *Illuminated Bible* applied a particular perspective—that of maternal Protestantism—in order to interpret the scriptural text for readers. By featuring a mishmash of baroque, neoclassical, rococo, and romantic styles, the *Illuminated Bible* projects an air of refined feminine sentimentality. At the same time, its style and imagery belies the underlying tension between the ideal of middle-class women in the 1840s as pious, maternal, and domestic, and their status as leaders in the era's revivalism and reformism.[63] More important than the raw number of female images depicted (which are not proportionally greater than in other illustrated Bibles of the era) is how the *Illuminated Bible* presents women, specifically in relation to violence, the female form, and an emphasis on maternal piety. The *Illuminated Bible* associates biblical wisdom, courage, and truth with feminine beauty, using the female form to symbolize these virtues. In this vein, the maternal, pietistic, mourning female archetype is the one the *Illuminated Bible* most commonly depicts.[64] Figure 9.4 presents a sample of how women appear in the *Illuminated Bible*, not only as a maternal ideal, but also as a representation of righteousness and pious devotion to God.

The women in figure 9.4 also illustrate how Harper broke with the common depiction of the nude female form in early nineteenth-century American illustrated Bibles. These women emphasize inner beauty over the display of the classically celebrated nude female form. This stands in contrast with the pre-Reformation view of women as

202   *Part Three: Christian Virtue Capitalism*

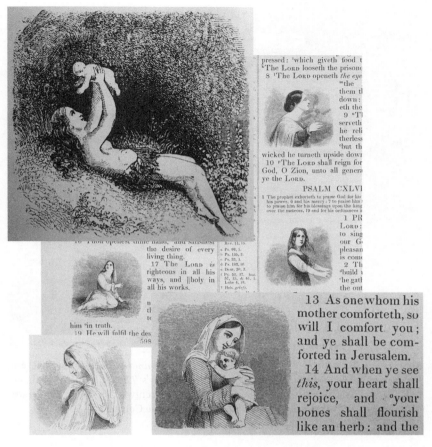

FIGURE 9.4 Maternal Protestantism in the *Illuminated Bible*. Top: Genesis 4, p. 5; center: Psalm 145–147, p. 598; bottom right: Isaiah 66, p. 680; bottom left: Ecclesiastes 7, p. 625. *HINPB*. Courtesy of Special Collections & Archives, Wesleyan University, Middletown, CT. Arranged and formatted by Marijane Ceruti.

temptresses exuding raw sexuality. Figure 9.5 likewise demonstrates this shift, as New York City publisher Thomas Kinnersley's 1833 family Bible depicts Bathsheba publicly bathing, turning her face toward King David as she disrobes and extends a shapely leg into her bath—the premodern temptress, descendent of Eve. In contrast, Harper's Bathsheba is bathing in wooded seclusion. She is doing everything possible to guard her virtue. Instead, it is the man who cannot control his sexuality, and the message

Fostering an American Protestant Identity 203

FIGURE 9.5 Bathsheba in two renderings: in the *Illuminated Bible* (upper left) and Kinnersley's *The Holy Bible. HINPB*, 330; Kinnersley's *The Holy Bible* (Philadelphia, 1833), 308. Courtesy of Special Collections & Archives, Wesleyan University, Middletown, CT. Arranged and formatted by Marijane Ceruti.

embedded in the image is of King David as the surreptitious spy, greedily violating Bathsheba's feminine modesty and virtue.

The *Illuminated Bible*'s gendered imagery suggests the degree to which the female consumer was at the heart of a middle-class consumer culture of sentimentality, religiosity, and gentility. Astutely, the Harpers simultaneously capitalized upon and contributed to this cultural transformation with products like the *Illuminated Bible*—and in this sense, one might call them "aesthetic entrepreneurs."[65] Consequently, the *Illuminated Bible* transcended the realm of sacred wisdom and assumed the qualities of a prized possession every Victorian middle-class urbanite needed to display in her parlor, particularly if she wanted to sacralize the space.[66] These women were an important audience, representing the growing effort among Methodists (and other evangelicals) to create a synthesis between worldly attainment and pious holiness—all within the middle-class parlor, not the local congregation. Methodist women like Phoebe Palmer, who was famous for her weekly in-home Bible study, further blurred the boundaries of sacred spaces, since within her home, she functioned as a priest.[67] Embossing a picture of one's local church on the Bible's cover furthered the transformation of the parlor into a quasi-church, a sacred domestic space where Victorian women presided as proto-clerics, imbuing their families with morality and virtue.[68]

No longer was the Bible merely a sacred scripture—it was also now a status symbol, a luxury item, and a matter of refined "taste." Harper's term for the object that resulted from this synthesis was "sacred token."[69] When the Harper Bible rested in a parlor, it occupied a space used for family devotions, christenings, and funerals, and now increasingly decorated with religious artwork.[70] The *Illuminated Bible* formed the centerpiece of this sacralized parlor. Harper anticipated exactly what *The Knickerbocker* suggested in its review of the 1846 edition, that "the Bible is a book which should be a *family possession*, and every family

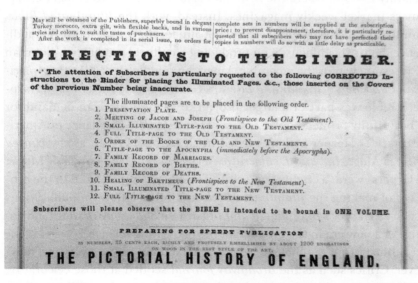

FIGURE 9.6 Volume 53 corrected. *HINPB*, vol. 53. Image by author, courtesy of HLHU.

throughout the Union should possess itself of a copy . . . handed down from generation to generation as an enduring family memorial."[71] The *Illuminated Bible*'s dedication page includes "to" and "from" lines, signaling Harper's intent to market it as a gift book, taking advantage of a growing consumer market for luxurious Christmas presents in the 1840s. The 1846 edition's gold leaves, embossed covers with engraved names or church buildings, large size (nine by twelve and a half inches in size and three inches thick), and significant weight (thirteen pounds) all underscored the *Illuminated Bible*'s status as a luxurious display item. The Houghton Library's *Illuminated Bible* is engraved on the front with "A. C. & Eliza B. Downing," honoring a couple who were married in 1846 and gifted their Bible in 1848, possibly at Christmas.[72]

In summary, Harper took a risk in creating its *Illuminated Bible*, considering how much it invested in the project's development. The company could have pursued a simpler, cheaper, and less elaborate edition. For example, at the same time the Harpers announced their *Illuminated Bible*, New York publisher J. S. Redfield began marketing "the cheapest illustrated Bible ever offered to the American public" in the form of its *London Pictorial Bible*.[73] The decision to market a high-quality artistic product was a departure from Harper's standard offering, such as the Family Library, where the firm cut costs in an effort to combat cheap, mass-market weekly magazines. Instead, with the *Illuminated Bible*, unlike its other works, Harper did not aim for the broadest possible audience, but instead focused on producing a cultural product of Victorian Protestant art for the emerging American middle class.[74] As the *American Publishers' Circular and Literary Gazette* proclaimed in 1855, Harper's Bible was part of a larger project to shape American demand for "beautifully printed books" and contribute to "the excellence of American art."[75] Harper had succeeded in elevating its craft, as the *United States Magazine and Democratic Review* noted; "the hands of Mssrs. Harpers" were "a credit to the city." The advances pioneered in the process of making the *Illuminated Bible* and other follow-on publications such as Harper's *Illuminated and Illustrated Shakespeare* were "indicative of a new era in the progress of the publishing science."[76]

Illustrating the Bible on such a scale did not please everyone, however. Critics such as the *Broadway Journal* scoffed at those celebrating Adams's artwork, and particularly lamented the number of illustrations,

206 *Part Three: Christian Virtue Capitalism*

their supposedly low quality, and the decision to allow one artist sole responsibility for their creation. The cover ornaments ("utterly destitute of artistic merit"), engraving borders ("two of them paltry, and one hideous"), and the initial letters ("meagre, feeble, and paltry") were also targets of the *Broadway Journal*'s derision.[77] The *Broadway Journal* only ran for two years, and while it certainly had a point about the artistic quality of some of the *Illustrated Bible*'s artwork, it was in the minority in voicing such criticism, and had no perceptible impact on the *Illuminated Bible*'s reception, sales, or legacy. Today, scholars uniformly recognize it as one of the most important developments in the history of the American book.[78]

Finally, the *Illuminated Bible* project reflects the transformation of Harper's strand of American Methodism. Beginning as an "outsider" sect, Wesleyan Methodism initially embodied the working class, eschewing formal educational and clerical strictures, and meeting in humble, nondescript buildings. By the late 1840s, not only did Methodism now include wealthy congregations, worshipping in ornate buildings such as the Harpers' John Street Church, but Methodists had established the first Methodist seminary (and a total of thirty-five educational institutions by 1860).[79] Similarly, while the early Harper products were known for providing quality literature at modest prices, the *Illuminated Bible* embodied the aspirations of a new, ascendant Protestant urban middle class that demonstrated just how far the journeymen printers had come.

CONCLUSION: PERIODICALS AND *HARPER'S NEW MONTHLY MAGAZINE*

By 1850, the Harpers were starting to confront the realities of mortality. James's wife, Maria, had died three years earlier, memorialized with a plaque in John Street Church lauding her "meek and quiet spirit."[80] By this time, James had moved uptown to 4 Gramercy Park, where he lived until his death in 1869 (see figure 9.8). Maria's death seems to have been the impetus for James to finally withdraw from active involvement in the John Street congregation in the early 1850s. Although he was still technically the president of the trustees until August 23, 1852, he attended only one meeting from January 13, 1851, until his replacement was secured.[81] Interestingly, James's absence from these meetings coincides

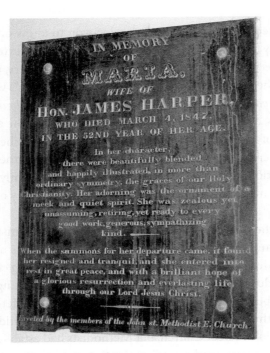

FIGURE 9.7 Memorial to Maria Harper. Photo by author, July 13, 2016, with permission of John Street Church, New York, NY.

with one of the great mysteries of the John Street trustee minutes. From June 11, 1849, to February 8, 1850, John Street Church loaned Harper & Brothers $6,330—a large sum for a congregation in 1850, the equivalent in today's money of about $225,000, and a departure from either the church's or Harper's practice. Harper & Brothers repaid the loan one year later, plus $139 in interest.[82] It is probably not coincidental that James stopped attending trustee meetings shortly after repayment of the debt. The Harpers expanded their facilities tremendously during the 1840s, and it is possible this loan was part of the company's financing during its ambitious building project. Harper's expansion grew to ten multistory buildings (some as tall as six stories), spanning an entire block from Cliff Street to Pearl Street by 1850. The company now employed more than 350 employees (including more than 100 women), while Harper's thirty plus steam-driven Adams presses were a far cry from the two hand-powered Ramage presses originally in operation when

208 Part Three: Christian Virtue Capitalism

FIGURE 9.8 4 Gramercy Park. Photo by Stephen Slaughter, July 13, 2016.

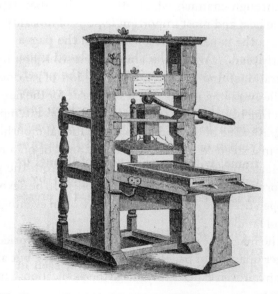

FIGURE 9.9 The Ramage Press. Jacob Abbott, *The Harper Establishment, or How the Story Books Are Made* (New York: Harper & Brothers, 1855), 118.

the brothers first opened for business in 1817.[83] By 1850, even British observers commented that Harper's "unrivaled resources and facilities" were key to their dominance at the end of the previous decade, evidenced by their ownership of half of the bestsellers in the United States from the final three years of the 1840s.[84] The firm was booming, and it seems John Street Church, by extending a valuable loan at a critical moment, played one more significant act in the brothers' rise to prominence.

Looking to expand in a new direction, the brothers waded into periodicals in 1850 with *Harper's New Monthly Magazine* (continuing today as *Harper's Magazine*), which sought "to place within the reach of the great mass of the American people the unbounded treasures of the Periodical Literature of the present day."[85] *Harper's* was designed to reach a wide audience by publishing "the progress and result of the literary genius . . . at so low [a] rate, and to give to it a value so much beyond its price, that it shall make its way into the hands or the family circle of every intelligent citizen of the United States."[86] Although one purpose of the monthly was pragmatic (as Fletcher explained, it began as "tender to our business," meaning that it kept a large volume constantly moving through the company plant), the magazine also fulfilled a moral purpose.[87] A bound copy of the first six months of the magazine explains that Harper sought "in every article, to combine entertainment with instruction, and to enforce, through channels which attract rather than repel attention and favor, the best and most important lessons of morality and of practical life."[88]

In its early years, *Harper's* was almost exclusively literary (with little or no illustrations) and achieved a circulation of 50,000 within six months, while averaging 110,000 copies per issue for the next decade and half.[89] Reflecting back in 1950, the editor of *Harper's* attempted to articulate the significance of the country's first national monthly magazine: "to a family in a steepled town on the Erie Canal, or on a remote Ohio farm, the Magazine was a welcome messenger from the great world, bringing information and ideas and entertainment to be devoured eagerly beside the open fireplace or the Franklin stove of an evening, by the light of a whale-oil lamp."[90]

Key to the magazine's success was not only its low price, high quality, and larger quantity of pages than its competitors, but also Harper's decision to hire proven experts to manage the publication. The magazine's

210   *Part Three: Christian Virtue Capitalism*

first editor, Henry J. Raymond, is better known as the founder of the *New York Times*. Tayler Lewis, a popular Union College professor, contributed regular pieces on social issues, political debates, and philosophical musings. Donald Mitchell, an accomplished nineteenth-century writer, was a regular author in a popular department called "Editor's Easy Chair." The literary editor of Horace Greeley's *New-York Tribune* wrote most of the literary reviews.[91]

Of course, not everyone was enthralled with the success of *Harper's New Monthly Magazine*. While not naming Harper outright, the Methodist Book Concern established its short-lived *National Magazine* in 1852 with the goal of addressing the "morbid appeals to passions" and "tendencies which are at least indirectly adverse to religion" that one found in the fiction of periodicals such as *Harper's*.[92] While both publications strove for "good taste," the *National Magazine* wanted to minimize the

FIGURE 9.10 New Harper complex. Jacob Abbott, *The Harper Establishment, or How the Story Books Are Made* (New York: Harper & Brothers, 1855), 24.

Fostering an American Protestant Identity   211

amount of fiction it published. Allowing that some fiction was acceptable (otherwise Bunyan's *Pilgrim's Progress* was out), the magazine's editors felt that its presence in popular periodicals such as *Harper's* was "unquestionably exaggerated" and "its tendency generally unhealthy."[93] The criticism is intriguing, given the firm's work for the Methodist Book Concern in the early days of J. & J. Harper and the position of James and Fletcher as trustees of the denomination's flagship church. The Methodist Book Concern's fears demonstrate that even as Protestants began to accept that one could harness fiction for good (illustrated by 1852's blockbuster *Uncle Tom's Cabin*), many still held the genre, and its purveyors, in disdain. It speaks once again to the way in which the brothers' Christian virtue capitalism pushed the limits of what their fellow conservative Protestants thought appropriate and redemptive for the nation.

The success of *Harper's New Monthly Magazine* helped Harper overcome a massive fire in 1853 (George Templeton Strong described it as "dramatic and splendid") that caused more than $1.2 million in damage.[94] Rebuilding quickly, within a few years the brothers celebrated a new nine-building, five-story complex in New York City that covered half an acre. There the Harpers combined all their printing and publishing operation under the roofs of two blocks of buildings, connected by numerous iron bridges, lending visual evidence to the claim that Harper was one of the largest, if not the largest, publishing firm in the world.[95] Nineteenth-century sources justify labeling the Harper operation in the 1850s as "industrialized printing"; it took place within a sophisticated "factory" containing the latest in laborsaving technology that churned out an average of twenty-five volumes a minute, ten hours a day, six days a week.[96] Visiting the company's premises, an amazed Dr. Davis W. Clark attested to the grandeur of the jewel of the publishing industry, because even though he had "visited and minutely surveyed many of the vast manufacturing establishments of the east . . . none of them have inspired within us such feelings of awe, almost of solemnity, as the large publishing houses," chief among them the new Harper complex.[97]

Buildings were important, but Harper's workforce is often overlooked. The few visitor accounts to survive emphasize its skill, productivity, and temperament. Combined with the long tenure of many Harper employees, Clark was convinced these workers were "well paid and not overworked" and one of the most "contented-looking class of operatives

212 *Part Three: Christian Virtue Capitalism*

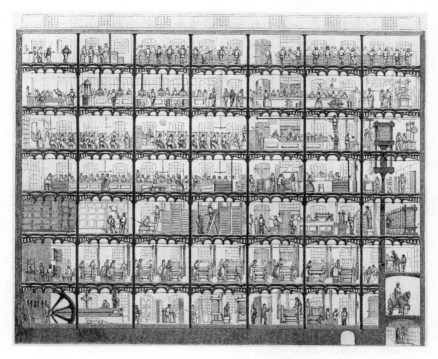

FIGURE 9.11 Interior of the new Harper building. Jacob Abbott, *The Harper Establishment, or How the Story Books Are Made* (New York: Harper & Brothers, 1855), 42.

anywhere." Dr. Clark also made a point of commenting on the appearance of the women as "fine, healthful," with "little of that pale, sallow, exhausted aspect worn by so many in the crowded and confined manufactories of the east."[98] Even if we allow that Clark may not have been the most discriminating visitor, Harper never left behind a reputation for exploiting its workers. The work was of a tremendous volume. G. P. Putnam, secretary of the Publishers' Association, estimated the annual output of the new Harper complex at more than a million volumes, while British observers put the number closer to 2 million. The *New York Daily Times* included *Harper's Monthly* in its annual tally of published volumes and arrived at 4.5 million volumes. Considering the *Daily Times* estimate came prior to the construction of the new complex, Putnam's estimate is surely a gross undercount.[99] (Since the British estimate was made in

Fostering an American Protestant Identity 213

1850, and the *Daily Times* numbers are from 1853, it is possible they are not in conflict.) Harper's reach only grew in the 1850s, thanks to an expanding rail network in America, the new postage law of 1851 that lowered the cost of mailing books, and the firm's expensive national advertising campaign.[100] By this point, the artisanal world the brothers had entered forty years earlier was long gone, transformed by enterprising journeymen, technological change, and the expanding market economy. Their estimated annual sales attested to that reality.

In fact, Methodism had grown just as dramatically as Harper's had. Counting less than 3 percent of all church members in the United States 1776, Methodists rose to more than 34 percent by 1850—the single largest religious group in America.[101] In 1810, the year James arrived in New York City, Methodism counted 2,200 members in five churches in the city. By 1850, there were twenty-five Methodist churches in New York City boasting a collective 7,534 members. The Methodists had transitioned from a Wesleyan "sect" to a full-fledged denomination. As such, Harper's growth and success paralleled the growth of Methodism as an institution and reflected the profound changes occurring within American Christianity.[102]

This incredible growth and longevity suggests that what distinguished Harper from Christian business enterprises such as the Pioneer Line was its posture toward the market. Whereas the Pioneer Line and its proprietors and commissioners wanted to *reform* the market, the Harpers preferred to use the market to *redeem* the culture through its products—the essence of Christian virtue capitalism. For example, both respected the Sabbath, but Josiah Bissell Jr. and the supporters of the Pioneer Line made observing the Sabbath a primary aim of their business. For the Harpers, the observance of the Sabbath was less visible—just part of their business ethos. Far from beating their neighbors over their heads with their religious beliefs, the Harpers—as some competitors were surprised to find—quietly did not print on Sundays.[103] Instead, they focused on selling a cultural vision to the American public—an idea of how to live a proper, upstanding republican life "in which Christian teachings and genteel behavior could coexist with economic success."[104]

Harper's size and control over information made it controversial. The brothers' correspondence with Sir Edward Bulwer-Lytton is an example of their firm's power and influence. Bulwer's relationship with Harper

214 *Part Three: Christian Virtue Capitalism*

dated back to the publication of his first major novel, *Pelham; or the Adventures of a Gentleman*, in 1828. (Condemned by *The Critic* as a "pernicious book" because of its apparent celebration of immorality, the Harpers tried and failed to convince *The Critic* of the book's literary worth.)[105] The brothers (most likely Fletcher) stressed to Bulwer-Lytton in an 1835 letter titled "Strictly Confidential" that he was controversial to work with in the United States and owed his success in the country to their "influence with editors," something they had "acquired by years of judicious management and effort, and is not kept up without constant attention and outlay." For Bulwer-Lytton, they "exerted to the utmost, not only in securing favorable notices, but in preventing those of a different character." The Harpers knew that "you have many and violent enemies in this country," especially "the numerous religious journals and magazines, in particular, which are opposed to all works of fiction, there is great hostility to your writings, and these possess much influence over the minds of their readers." The Harpers emphasized that it was their religious and business reputation and relationships throughout the industry that allowed them to publish controversial works such as *Pelham* while succeeding financially. The Harpers were not always successful, admitting to Bulwer-Lytton they "half succeeded almost universally in keeping them silent." But, even these reviews were not a total failure, as the Harpers argued that such negative attention had "elicited from them notices which did service, either by actual commendation, or by such remarks, as, with nature to excite interest and curiosity." Finishing with one final boast, the brothers reminded Bulwer-Lytton that "as general rule, our name in the title-page of a book, secures favorable criticism, and seldom fails to mitigate the severity of even those censors who do not acknowledge our influence."[106]

The Harpers' spiritual reputation had earned them the benefit of the doubt. In other words, because the broader Protestant community (including those who were more theologically conservative) recognized the Harpers as "genuine" Christians, they could get away with things other publishers could not. Bulwer-Lytton, in response, showed minimal concern over the powerful voice of theologically conservative Protestants, but the Harpers knew their influence was real, and could spell the death of a publishing firm.[107] These unseen battles with the theologically conservative American Protestant community speaks to Harper's

Fostering an American Protestant Identity 215

cultural power. Nineteenth-century Americans such as the politician Samuel Goodrich acknowledged and applauded the firm for its cultural achievements. Writing in 1856, Goodrich declared, "The publishing establishment of the Messrs. Harper, the legitimate result of industry, discretion, energy, and probity, is justly the pride of New York, and one of the reflected glories of our literature, probably surpassing every other establishment of the kind in the world in its extent and the perfectness of its organization."[108]

Not all Americans were so charitable. Henry David Thoreau criticized the size and power of the Harpers' literary and cultural influence, asking, "Why should we leave it to Harper & Brothers and Redding & Co. to select our reading?"[109] For their part, the Harpers were not ashamed of the cultural influence and power they wielded. They were proud of their role in shaping American society, boasting in 1854 that not only had they sold millions of volumes of books and worked their way into the "intellectual life" of America, but their products "have followed the pioneer into the remotest regions. . . . They are to be found upon the student's desk, on the farmer's and the mechanic's table, in the private, the social, and the school library, from one end of the Union to the other. They have imparted useful knowledge to millions of our countrymen, and have done something to render them more intelligent, more energetic, and more virtuous."[110] It was quite a heady rise for four brothers who began as journeymen apprentices, and as this quote reveals, the Harpers were proud that their virtuous vision had penetrated American culture so thoroughly.

216 *Part Three: Christian Virtue Capitalism*

Conclusion

Morality and Markets, Then and Now

American Protestants have debated and argued about the proper relationship between the believer and her or his culture for more than four hundred years. Typically, they have chosen one of three options: flee/separate from the culture, fight/reform the culture, or engage/redeem the culture. For example, faced with defeat on many fronts in the culture wars of the late twentieth and early twenty-first centuries, American evangelicals are engaged in a heated debate over whether to embrace the "Benedict Option" (separation), the "Wilberforce Option" (fight/reform), or the "Naaman Option" (engage/redeem). The decision by fundamentalist Protestants to withdraw from cultural engagement following the Scopes Monkey Trial is a well-established narrative in American historiography. Conservative Protestants split after the Second World War, as some, following Billy Graham's model, reengaged with the culture—the "neo-evangelicals"—while the more fundamentalist conservatives continued to maintain a posture of cultural separation, à la Bob Jones and his school. The late 1960s and 1970s brought the reemergence of political engagement, with the rise of the Religious Right, a movement that incorporated strands of both groups. Yet, when it comes to business, this narrative is misguided at best, and flat-out wrong at worst. Darren Dochuk, Nicole Kirk, Sarah Hammond, and Keven Kruse are just a few of an increasing number of scholars who have demonstrated that fundamentalist Protestants did not really withdraw from American culture, but stayed enmeshed in their communities (local, national, and global) through business activity. Most of these tended to adhere to various forms of virtue capitalism, as was the case for Walt Meloon, founder of Correct Craft and creator of the popular Ski Nautique brand waterski boat, who fostered an earnest, Protestant ethic in his business culture and relationships.[1]

In this way, Protestants in the early American republic can be placed on something of a continuum with those of the present, even if some of their visions of capitalism (communal and reform) are not as commonly practiced today. Faced with sweeping technological and cultural change, they strove to follow a path they believed accorded with their Protestant beliefs. Much of this story has already been told, and in fine fashion. Historians of the early American republic have explored the various paths these religious Americans embraced, not the least of which was transformative social reform, primarily through the mechanism of voluntary associations. Slavery, alcohol, prostitution, seven-day workweeks, crime, and Bible illiteracy were all causes tackled by voluntary associations. While the American public may have only a dim understanding of these movements, U.S. historians know them well.

Missing from this story, however, is the role business, and specifically Christian business enterprises (CBEs), played in this drama. Concerned Protestants formed these economic entities for the express purpose of reconciling their faith to the dynamic emerging market economy of the early national period. For the Harmonists, it involved a process of separation from the world at large, even as they maintained a strong connection to the market, technology, and industrial innovation. Their brand of Lutheran Pietism informed their Christian communal capitalism. It was a direct response to the certainty that early nineteenth-century culture was hopelessly corrupt, even as they believed a strong, balanced economy based on agriculture and manufacturing would be the template of the coming kingdom of God. The Harmonists were not outliers, as many other Pietists, Moravians, Shakers, and other emerging sects fused cultural separation with economic industry and continuing engagement with the surrounding economy.

Advocates of Pioneerism took a combative approach to mainstream American culture and sought to create an alternative economy that they

218 *Conclusion*

hoped would transform the broader market in fundamental ways. Their Puritan, Calvinist-inspired covenant theology, that suggested America's unique relationship with God was in jeopardy, shaped this cultural posture. Even as revivals remade American Calvinism into a more Arminian form of Protestantism, the focus on America's special status as a chosen nation continued to animate Christian reform capitalists such as Josiah Bissell Jr. Only radical action could save the country from ruin and destruction. While for many, this took the form of voluntary associations, or political organizing, others started businesses that aimed to save America while offering a version of capitalism that would not jeopardize America's covenantal status.

Lastly, Harper & Brothers represents a vision of Christian virtue capitalists whose goal was cultural formation, not separation from cultural forms or fighting battles for cultural dominance. Wesleyan Arminianism shaped this vision—one in which all Americans were free actors, able to choose their spiritual destiny. Consequently, the impulse to persuade, educate, and shape American society was imperative. If cultural redemption was possible, then Americans could be encouraged to embrace spiritual, material, and political renewal and salvation as well.

Pietism, Calvinism, and Arminianism were all powerful forces shaping the actions of early national-period Americans, including the republic's business proprietors. Equally as strong, however, were the two major strands of millennialism in the early national period—premillennialism and postmillennialism. The Harmonists' premillennial belief that the judgment of the world was imminent and that they were destined to help Christ build the new millennial kingdom was foundational to the way they embraced industry and the market. The founders of the Pioneer Line, such as Josiah Bissell Jr., agreed that one should prepare for Christ's return, even though they were generally postmillennial. The cultivation and progress of civilization that Bissell and his allies championed was certainly an important component of this effort.[2] Likewise, the Harper brothers lived as functional postmillennialists. Certainly, their life's work suggests as much. By purposefully producing works that in their minds contributed to the cultivation of civilization, education, and civic and private virtue, the brothers mirrored the efforts of postmillennialists who endeavored to usher in an era

Conclusion 219

when Christian notions of peace, harmony, and morality would be the norm everywhere.

The question of business and morality has never been more controversial. Whether formally or informally, under the label of religion, spirituality, ESG (environmental, social, and corporate governance), conscious capitalism, or stakeholder capitalism, Americans continue to incorporate their deepest values into their workplaces.[3] ESG investing garners increasing attention, and it has spawned CBEs that attempt to wed biblical principles to asset management. While some of these Christian investment funds merely promise to avoid investing in businesses that traffic in "sin" (alcohol, tobacco, LGBTQ advocacy), others, such as Eventide, work to ensure the businesses they invest in are engaged in capitalism without "plunder." Their concern extends beyond products to the means of production, believing that a sound company is one that cares for consumers, employees, and the community alike. One could argue that the question of how to do good in the marketplace has never been more earnestly asked.[4] It is a question that people from a diverse set of backgrounds are seeking to answer.[5]

While stories concerning the social values of large companies like Disney and Chick-fil-A grab headlines, it is important to recognize that small businesses make up the core of CBEs today. Some are explicit in their religiosity, such as the small "A Christian Plumber" firm in Griffin, Georgia, which seeks to "make a difference while plumbing for Jesus."[6] Others are less obvious, such the Whey Station(ary) restaurant in Middletown, Connecticut, which on the surface seems like any other quirky, cozy place to enjoy comfort food and a brew. However, near the restaurant's entrance is a picture of their Sunday food and clothing outreach program, captioned with James 2:15–16: "Suppose a brother or a sister is without clothes and daily food. If one of you says to them, 'Go in peace; keep warm and well fed,' but does nothing about their physical needs, what good is it?" A visit to the Whey Station(ary) website provides more details under the "Outreach" tab, which offers additional Bible verses and explains how their conviction that God's desire is for all people to be "fully known, fully loved" is at the heart of their business.[7]

Even as polling indicates that an increasing number of Americans are leaving institutional Christianity, one can locate a persistent residue

220 *Conclusion*

FIGURE CON.1 The Whey Station(ary). Photo by author, June 10, 2022.

of the millennialism and reforming impulse that characterized early national-period CBEs in the endeavors of businesspersons such as Jeff Bezos, Elon Musk, and Ethan Brown. As Mary-Jane Rubenstein perceptively observes, Bezos and Musk view their respective space companies, Blue Origin and SpaceX, as utopian projects that will save humanity, while affording humans exceptional standards of living through a technologically enhanced form of capitalism.[8] The parallels between Bezos, Musk, and George Rapp are startling—each offers a road map to the salvation of humanity while adhering to a purified form of business and marketplace interactions. Their collective certainty that humanity's imminent doom demands a voyage to a "new world" where their utopian experiment can be established is striking.

Ethan Brown, CEO of Beyond Meat, provides a parallel to Josiah Bissell Jr. While they do not share the same polarizing personality traits, both proprietors established businesses in order to reform key components of the marketplace that they identified as central to the flourishing of humanity. Whereas revivalist Calvinism motivated Bissell, Brown promotes "hedonistic altruism" as the animating impulse behind his

Conclusion 221

founding of one of the largest companies producing plant-based meat products. Concerned with the ethics of animal consumption and the issue of climate change, Brown sought to integrate his morals into his business endeavors by creating Beyond Meat in 2009.[9] Despite his humanist bent, when Brown asserts that he wants "to create products that help people feel better about themselves, but also confer benefits to the world," one also hears the echo of Harper's Arminian Methodist vision of creating products that people would enjoy, and that would improve them as citizens.

Brown's desire to integrate his moral convictions into his business enterprise is exactly what CBE proprietors sought to do in the early national period. Bissel and his colleagues on the Pioneer Line started their business for the same reason Brown started his: a sense that the current market was morally corrupt and demanded an alternative economy. For Bissell as for Brown, making money was important, but it was almost secondary to the cultural change they hoped their business would usher in. One might even conclude that religiously motivated proprietors are not particularly exceptional since the idea that one's spiritual identity should be part of one's marketplace activities is not that uncommon.

Additionally, the twenty-first century's widening inequality is forcing corporate leaders to grapple with the ultimate purpose of business enterprise. (Proprietors of early nineteenth-century CBEs might ask them why it took their modern counterparts so long to reexamine the marketplace's moral implications.) Although the debate over who corporations serve—shareholders or a broader set of stakeholders—is not new, it has received updated attention.[10] On August 19, 2019, just under two hundred American corporate CEOs, all members of the Business Roundtable, released a "Statement on the Purpose of a Corporation" in an effort to reorient American businesses away from an exclusive focus on shareholders and toward greater attention to a broader set of constituents, including customers, employees, and suppliers.[11] With its board made up of a "who's who" of industry leaders, such as Mary Barra, Tim Cook, and Jamie Dimon (CEOs, respectively, of General Motors, Apple, and JPMorgan Chase), the statement grabbed the national spotlight.[12] While it is debatable if the Business Roundtable has accomplished any meaningful change since its inception, its declaration gestures at a greater desire to reimagine who businesses serve.[13] Perhaps the Business Roundtable is just trying to save capitalism in some agreeable form, as some historians have concluded was the goal of the welfare capitalists of the early twentieth century. It is certainly valid to conclude that the statement was a way to head off criticism of the contribution that America's corporations have made to the growth of inequality in the United States. A more generous interpretation is that these CEOs are wrestling with morality and the marketplace, as did the subjects of this study.[14] It is certainly possible that all three of these interpretations are true at the same time.

Finally, this book complicates the economic philosophy of twenty-first-century evangelical and fundamentalist Protestants in the United States. Among these groups (and especially among those members over the age of fifty), laissez-faire capitalism or "rugged individualism in business enterprise" is frequently assumed to reflect God's best design for human flourishing.[15] As much as the progressive critique of CBEs as a recent phenomenon is erroneous, the idea that commitment to free markets inevitability flows from theological conservativism is contradicted by early American Protestantism. This dogma—that "true" Bible-believing Christians "must" be (and always have been) ardent capitalists (because socialism is the atheistic alternative)—obscures the multitude of ways in which theologically conservative American Protestants have thought about and engaged with the market economy since the country's founding. This study demonstrates that many such Protestants engaged the market with a focus on shaping American culture according their vision of a virtuous, republican order. Others, fearing the forces of social change wrought by the market, sought to reform the market itself. And still others, concerned with the corrupting influence of the market, sought to hold it at arm's length, living communally even as they successfully enmeshed themselves in the fabric of early American capitalism. None of them considered laissez-faire capitalism to be the biblical and divine norm.[16] And yet, this assumption is powerful enough that students in my undergraduate course on capitalism and Christianity in the early American republic are consistently surprised when they read passages from the Old and New Testaments that discuss money and wealth. Finding that Jesus and the Hebrew prophets consistently viewed wealth

Conclusion 223

as a spiritual liability and spent more time discussing care for the poor than counseling personal industriousness is surprising for students, most of whom have never read the Bible or had much exposure to Christianity. Instead, their assumptions about what the Bible teaches about money come from American evangelicals' embrace of laissez-faire capitalism.

The phenomenon of Christian business enterprise is similarly surprising. While it often shows up where one would expect, such as rural Georgia, it also flourishes where one does not, including liberal New England college towns. It takes many forms, from proudly stated creeds to more subtle touches, easily missed by the less observant. The purposes are varied as well, ranging from a desire for genuine reform to a conviction that orienting the business around Christian principles or teachings simply makes for the most prudent business plan. If American culture continues on its trajectory toward increasing pluralism, CBEs will be increasingly noticeable, and possibly offensive, to some. That will hardly represent a new development, as the history of CBEs in the early United States demonstrates: they have been ever present and ever controversial in American history, shaping our markets and culture in profound ways.

224 *Conclusion*

Acknowledgments

No one completes a book without the generosity of many kind individuals. First, I owe a debt of gratitude to my many friends in the Department of History at the United States Naval Academy. Your friendship and encouragement provided the initial motivation to begin this project. I am especially grateful to department chairs Richard Abels, C. C. Felker, and Rick Ruth, and associate chairs John Freymann, James Rentfrow, and Mark Belson, all of whom afforded me the resources and scheduling to research and write while balancing a full teaching load. I am similarly grateful to Wesleyan University and the Chamberlain Project for a multiyear fellowship that allowed me to both teach and write about Christianity and capitalism. Provost Nicole Stanton, Deans Mark Eisner and Demetrius Eudell, department chairs Ethan Kleinberg, Bill Johnston, and Justine Quijada, and Professor Jennifer Tucker all ensured that I would have an intellectual home at Wesleyan throughout the difficult COVID years, even as many institutions cut similar positions.

Many individuals deserve thanks for helping me uncover the stories of Harmony, Pioneerism, and the Harpers. Mark Noll supplied encouragement early on and deserves credit for recommending the Harpers as a possible avenue of study. Sharon Murphy has been a longtime sounding board and has provided kind mentorship since the project's early phases. I am also thankful for the feedback of her colleagues at the

Providence College Seminar on the History of Early America. Russell Richey pointed me in the right direction regarding the Methodism of the Harpers. Joseph Moore introduced me to the Covenanters, which broadened my perspective on the Sabbatarians. Mary DeCredico told me to look at the records of R. G. Dun & Company. Wendy Woloson provided constant affirmation throughout the project and deserves special recognition as the only person to attend all four of the conference presentations at which I presented my initial archival research. Subsequently, she has provided many valuable leads pertaining to the history of the book. Reverend Ron Thompson of the Westchester Congregational Church, and Alice Csere, clerk at the same institution, responded to a short-fused, same-day request for access to their archives and then provided follow-up support by sending me images of specific requested documents. Reverend Jason P. Radmacher, of John Street Church, generously showed me the collections of his church and offered some interesting insights on early Methodism in New York City. Old Economy Village curator Sarah Buffington was incredibly patient as she humored my obsession with the maps, sketches, and diagrams in the Harmony archives. Kim Taylor at SUNY Fredonia helped me track down a "white whale": Marilyn Haas's paper on the Harper School District Library movement in New York. Aaron McWilliams not only provided helpful guidance at the Pennsylvania State Archives, he also found my lost thumb drive and saved me from something of a research catastrophe! Dan Hinchen at the Massachusetts Historical Society aided my study of the Dana letters, while showing me some additional materials that provided much-needed context on the Dana family. Andrea Rapacz at the Connecticut Historical Society, Nancy Assmann at the Cayuga County Historian's Office, William Keeler at the Rochester Historical Society, Sarah Kozma at the Onondaga Historical Association, and various staff at the Buffalo Historical Society all helped me discover out-of-the-way treasures. Mariam Touba at the New York Historical Society not only responded to my research questions, but also suggested additional sources that proved incredibly rich. Lisa Caprino at the Huntington Library helped me locate a vital letter on Harper's business culture. Numerous staff members at the New York Public Library (and especially the Brooke Russell Astor Reading Room for Rare Books and Manuscripts), the Monroe County Public Library (Rochester, New

226 *Acknowledgments*

York), the Seymour Public Library (Auburn, New York), and the libraries of the University of Rochester, Syracuse University, Columbia University, Yale University, and Harvard University (especially the Baker and Houghton Libraries) went out of their way to help me find materials in my numerous research blitzes. Brandon Fess, archivist of the Central Library of Rochester and Monroe County, helped me track down the Schermerhorn letter and generously scanned it for me. Tom McCutchon of Columbia's Rare Book and Manuscript Library scanned several important Harper letters for me when, sadly, I discovered that the images I had made the year prior were so blurry I could not read them. V. Heidi Hass of the Morgan Library and Museum did the same for a segment of the annotated copy of Eugene Exman's *The Brothers Harper.* Amanda Nelson patiently dug up (on multiple occasions) a host of illustrated Bibles in Wesleyan's Special Collections and Archives, which supplied me with a host of compelling imagery that Marijane Ceruti, thanks to her technical expertise, was able to craft into several informative figures. Finally, the Special Collections and Archives Department of the United States Naval Academy's Nimitz Library helped me locate some first-edition Harper publications. The Interlibrary Loan staffs of the University of Maryland, the U.S. Naval Academy, and Wesleyan University were particularly patient with my constant loan requests, surely numbering in the high hundreds.

Early on, Louis Hyman and Bridget Flannery-McCoy provided advice and encouragement that the seedlings of my project held promise. Bridget helped shape my work over the next several years, and I owe her immense gratitude for helping me write a manuscript framed as a publishable book. Stephen Wesley continued Bridget's work, providing the space to tend to career matters as I got my feet under me after finishing my PhD. I greatly appreciate his advice, grace, and insightful comments and suggestions. Louis was the first scholar to show a keen interest in my project, expressing an enthusiasm at my first academic conference that helped me to believe I might be onto something. His support helped yield an article in *Enterprise & Society* (September 2020) on the Harmony Society, and I am grateful the journal is allowing significant portions of that article to appear in this book. Then as the book project unfolded, Louis continued to provide vital suggestions that helped shape its improved final form. Thanks also to the *Journal of the Early Republic* for allowing parts of an article on *Harper's Illuminated and New Pictorial Bible* (published in their Winter 2021 issue) to appear in this book.

At the University of Maryland's Department of History, Whitman Ridgway was the lone faculty member who responded to the pleas of a lost master's student many years ago, and his willingness to advise and counsel me was an answer to prayer. The fact that we have become friends is an incredible bonus. Professionally, I would not be where I am today without the encouragement, advice, and friendship of David Sicilia. His willingness to function as an unofficial adviser before assuming that official designation is an example of his dedication to graduate students. I am particularly indebted to him for introducing me to the business history community. (Special thanks goes to the Business History Conference and its many welcoming voices for helping me to feel part of a community at the very beginnings of this project.) Holly Brewer's charge to ask big questions challenged my approach to this entire project, while Mark Valeri earned my eternal gratitude by providing guidance and critique despite his incredibly demanding schedule.

Last, but not least, thanks to my family for their love, support, and patience. My brother, Steve, timed his layovers as an airline pilot so we could hang out on several of my research trips and presentations. I grew up with my father, George Slaughter, always discussing the book on behavioral science he wanted to write. (I think that must have seeped into my subconscious somehow.) My mother, Anne Slaughter, always championed my graduate studies. My in-laws, Curt and Ann Kemp, put up with my checking footnotes at holidays. To my wife and kids—Casey, Wren, and Graydon—thanks so much for enduring this multiyear project and for allowing me to go on the many "history trips" that made it possible. I love you all so much and am eternally grateful for your love and support, even though I do not expect you to drop *Percy Jackson* and *House of Robots* to read this anytime soon. (Casey's already read it too many times, in too many forms.)

Notes

ABBREVIATIONS

ACP	Aristarchus Champion Papers, Monroe County Public Library, Rochester, NY
AGUS	*The Address of the General Union for the Promoting the Observance of the Christian Sabbath, by the People of the United States*
AHB	Archives of Harper & Brothers, Center for Research Libraries, Chicago, IL
CRNY	Canal Records, New York State Archives, Albany
DFP	Dana Family Papers, Massachusetts Historical Society, Boston
DHID1	*A Documentary History of the Indiana Decade of the Harmony Society*, vol. 1, *1814–1819*
DHID2	*A Documentary History of the Indiana Decade of the Harmony Society*, vol. 2, *1820–1824*
DS	David Shields
ELB	Edward Bulwer-Lytton
EOTO	*Economy on the Ohio, 1826–1834, George Rapp's Third Harmony: A Documentary History*

FR	Frederick Rapp
GH	Godfrey Haga
GR	George Rapp
GRA	George Rapp & Associates
GRRH	*George Rapp's Re-established Harmony Society: Letters and Documents of the Baker-Henrici Trusteeship, 1848–1868*
GRS	*George Rapp's Separatists, 1700–1803, Prelude to America: A Documentary History*
GRYG	*George Rapp's Years of Glory: Economy on the Ohio, 1834–1847, George Rapp's Third Harmony Society: A Documentary History*
GS	Gerrit Smith
GSP	Gerrit Smith Papers, Bird Library, Syracuse University
HBR	Harper Brothers Records, Butler Library, Columbia University
H&B	Harper & Brothers
HCP	Henry Champion Papers, Connecticut Historical Society, Hartford
HINPB	*Harper's Illuminated and New Pictorial Bible*
HLHU	Houghton Library, Harvard University
HOTC	*Harmony on the Connoquenessing, 1803–1815: A Documentary History*
HOTW	*Harmony on the Wabash in Transition, 1824–1826: A Documentary History*
HSR	Harmony Society Records, 2335, Pennsylvania State Archives, Harrisburg
JBJ	Josiah Bissell Jr.
JDH	John D. Hay
JH	Jacob Henrici
JHP-BL	James Harper Papers, Butler Library, Columbia University
JHP-NYHS	James Harper Papers, New York Historical Society, New York City
JLB	John L. Baker
JS	J. Solms
KAC	Karl Arndt Collection of Harmony Society Materials, Manuscript Group 437, Pennsylvania State Archives, Harrisburg
LOC	Library of Congress, Washington, DC

230 *Abbreviations*

MCLR   Monroe County Land Records, Office of the Monroe
            County Clerk, Rochester, NY
MECR   Methodist Episcopal Church Records, New York Public
            Library, Manuscripts and Archives Division, New York City
RDJ   Richard H. Dana Jr.
RDS   Richard H. Dana Sr.
RGD   R. G. Dun & Company
RHPF   *Rochester Historical Society Publication Fund Series*
RLB   Romelius L. Baker
RPF   Richard Palmer Files, Seymour Public Library, Auburn, NY
SL   Sterling Library, Yale University
WCB   William C. Bryant
WCCR   Westchester Congregational Church Records, Colches-
            ter, CT

INTRODUCTION

1. "Written for *The Craftsman*," *The Craftsman*, December 22, 1829.
2. Jurgen Kocka, "Introduction," in *Capitalism: The Reemergence of a Historical Concept*, ed. Jurgen Kocka and Marcel van der Linden (New York: Bloomsbury, 2016), 4–5. Capitalism's ascendency in the early republic: Paul A. Gilje, "The Rise of Capitalism in the Early Republic," *Journal of the Early Republic* 16, no. 2 (Summer 1996): 159–181.
3. Mark Valeri, *Heavenly Merchandize: How Religion Shaped Commerce in Puritan America* (Princeton, NJ: Princeton University Press, 2010). This is notwithstanding recent victories by conservative Christians at the Supreme Court. Rod Dreher, "Benedict Option," *American Conservative*, November–December 2013, and "Coming to Terms with a Post-Christian World," *Christianity Today*, November 2, 2015, http://www.christianitytoday.com/ct/2015/november/coming-to-terms-with-post-christian-world.html (Catholic-turned-Orthodox Christian Dreher articulated an approach that resonated with many conservative Protestants); Michael Gerson and Peter Wehner, "The Power of Our Weakness," *Christianity Today*, November 2015, 40–46; Gabriel Salguero, Rod Dreher, and Shirley Hoogstra, "Will the Wilberforce Option Work?," *Christianity Today*, November 2015, 47–49; Skye Jethani, "An Evangelical Case for Gay Wedding Cakes," *HuffPost*, February 20, 2014, https://www.huffpost.com/entry/an-evangelical-case-for-g_b_4476307.

Introduction   231

4. Joseph P. Slaughter, "The Virginia Company to Chick-Fil-A: Christian Business in America, 1600–2000," *Seattle University Law Review* 44, no. 2 (Winter 2021): 421–462. Ronald Colombo's description of "religious business corporations" as enterprises "infused with religion" (ranging from a business owner's simple and unobtrusive acknowledgment of the importance of religion in daily life, to the intentional decision to make religion part of the business's decision-making process) caused me to first consider the existence of CBEs. Ultimately, for Colombo a religious business corporation "is a for-profit entity that embraces a particular religious identity." Colombo, "Religious Liberty and the Business Corporation," *Journal of International Business and Law* 17, no. 1 (Winter 2017): 26–28. Colombo now favors the term "religiously expressive corporation." Colombo, "Corporate Entanglement with Religion and the Suppression of Expression," *Seattle University Law Review* 45, no. 1 (Fall 2021): 187–239.

5. Nicole C. Kirk, *Wanamaker's Temple: The Business of Religion in an Iconic Department Store* (New York: New York University Press, 2018); Darren Dochuk, *How Christianity and Crude Made Modern America* (New York: Basic Books, 2019); Sarah Hammond, *God's Businessmen: Entrepreneurial Evangelicals in Depression and War*, ed. Darren Dochuk (Chicago: University of Chicago Press, 2017); Kevin Kruse, *One Nation Under God: How Corporate America Invented Christian America* (New York: Basic Books, 2015); Bethany Moreton, *To Serve God and Was-Mart: The Making of Christian Free Enterprise* (Cambridge, MA: Harvard University Press, 2009).

6. The most nuanced discussion of this is in George Marsden, *Fundamentalism and American Culture*, 2nd ed. (New York: Oxford University Press, 2005), 102–243. Even though some fine works are starting to poke holes in this narrative of evangelical history, it still holds tremendous sway in the history of evangelicalism. An example of a recent work that questions Marsden's thesis is Neil J. Young, *We Gather Together: The Religious Right and the Problem of Interfaith Politics* (New York: Oxford University Press, 2016).

7. Colombo, "Religious Liberty and the Business Corporation," 26–28.

8. I use the term "evangelical" sparingly because of its contested definition, both in the period covered in this book and in current discourse, reserving it for individuals or organizations that identified as such. Marsden, *Fundamentalism*, 231–236; Linford D. Fisher, "Evangelicals and Unevangelicals: The Contested History of a Word, 1500–1950," *Religion and American Culture: A Journal of Interpretation* 26, no. 2 (2016): 184–226; Mark A. Noll, David W. Bebbington, and George Marsden, eds., *Evangelicals: Who They Have Been, Are Now, and Could Be* (Grand Rapids, MI: William B. Eerdmans, 2019), 123–187.

9. For an introduction to the market revolution and its enormous literature, see Daniel Feller, "The Market Revolution Ate My Homework," *Reviews in American*

History 25, no. 3 (September 1997): 408–415, and John Lauritz Larson, "The Market Revolution in Early America: An Introduction," *OAH Magazine of History* 19, no. 3. (May 2005): 4–7.

10. In his chapter in *Religion and the Marketplace in the United States*, E. Brooks Holifield identifies fifteen related scholarly conclusions, including the notion that American Protestantism curbed market excess, that commercial success promoted Christianity (and millennial optimism), and that Christianity created a "haven" from a "heartless" market-driven society. See Holifield, "Why Are Americans So Religious? The Limitations of Market Explanations," in *Religion and the Marketplace in the United States*, ed. Stievermann, Goff, and Junker (New York: Oxford University Press, 2015), 35. See also Martin Bruegel, *Farm, Shop, Landing: The Rise of a Market Society in the Hudson Valley, 1780–1860* (Durham, NC: Duke University Press, 2002); Mark Noll, ed., *God and Mammon: Protestants, Money, and the Market, 1790–1860* (New York: Oxford University Press, 2002); Scott C. Martin, ed., *Cultural Change and the Market Revolution in America, 1789–1860* (New York: Rowman & Littlefield, 2005); Cathy Matson, ed., *The Economy of Early America: Historical Perspectives and New Directions* (University Park: Penn State University Press, 2006); Daniel Walker Howe, *What Hath God Wrought: The Transformation of America, 1815–1848* (New York: Oxford University Press, 2007); Stewart Davenport, *Friends of the Unrighteous Mammon: Northern Christians & Market Capitalism* (Chicago: University of Chicago Press, 2008); John Lauritz Larson, *The Market Revolution in America* (New York: Cambridge University Press, 2010); Michael Zakim and Gary J. Kornblith, eds., *Capitalism Takes Command: The Social Transformation of Nineteenth-Century America* (Chicago: University of Chicago Press, 2012); Brian P. Luskey and Wendy A. Woloson, eds., *Capitalism by Gaslight: Illuminating the Economy of Nineteenth-Century America* (Philadelphia: University of Pennsylvania Press, 2015).

11. Stewart Davenport adds a third category, "accommodation," to Sellers's thesis, but still frames the early U.S. market as something one either supported or opposed. Davenport, *Friends of the Unrighteous Mammon*; Charles Sellers, *The Market Revolution: Jacksonian America, 1815–1846* (New York: Oxford University Press, 1991).

12. Marsden, *Fundamentalism*, 44.

13. Mark A. Noll, *America's God: From Jonathan Edwards to Abraham Lincoln* (New York: Oxford University Press, 2002), is the best at contextualizing these differences within early North America.

14. "Five Point Calvinism" refers to the "TULIP" acronym: T—total depravity of man; U—unconditional election; L—limited atonement; I—irresistible grace;

Introduction 233

P—perseverance of the saints. See F. Ernest Stoeffler, *The Rise of Evangelical Pietism* (Leiden: E. J. Brill, 1965), 113.

15. Nathan O. Hatch, *The Democratization of American Christianity* (New Haven, CT: Yale University Press, 1989). This is an oversimplified, "Americanized" perspective of these theologies; see Noll, *America's God*.

16. A short introduction: Dale Brown, *Understanding Pietism* (Grand Rapids, MI: William B. Eerdmans, 1978).

17. Stoeffler, *Evangelical Pietism*, 9–12.

18. Quote is from Stoeffler, *Evangelical Pietism*, 13. Stoeffler's shorthand for these characteristics is experientialism, perfectionism, biblicism, and protest (13–23). Frederick Rapp (chapters 1–3) used very similar phrases—"true imitation on Jesus" and "model picture of Jesus"—in a letter to his family in Germany. FR to family, May 17, 1813, HSR, 2335.

19. Ted Campbell, *The Religion of the Heart: A Study of European Religious Life in the Seventeenth and Eighteenth Centuries* (Eugene, OR: Wipf and Stock Publishers, 2000), 44–57, 71–75, 99–124; F. Ernest Stoeffler, ed., *Continental Pietism and Early American Christianity* (Grand Rapids, MI: William B. Eerdmans, 1976).

20. Max Weber, *The Protestant Ethic and the "Spirit" of Capitalism and other Writings* (New York: Penguin, 2002). An example of a scholar weaving Weber into the narrative of early American capitalism and religion is Stephen Innes, *Creating the Commonwealth: The Economic Culture of Puritan New England* (New York: Norton, 1995).

21. For example, Sean Wilentz's influential history of postrevolutionary New York City argues that new modes of manufacturing destabilized the city, while its newly emergent working-class culture attracted the attention of reform-minded evangelical businessmen. Wilentz, *Chants Democratic: New York City and the Rise of the American Working Class, 1788–1850* (New York: Oxford University Press, 1986).

22. The Social Control School includes foundational works such as Charles I. Foster, "The Urban Missionary Movement, 1814–1837," *Pennsylvania Magazine of History and Biography* 75, no. 1 (January 1951): 47–65; Charles C. Cole Jr., *The Social Ideas of the Northern Evangelists, 1820–1860* (New York: Columbia University Press, 1954); Clifford Griffin, *Their Brother's Keepers: Moral Stewardship in the United States, 1800–1865* (New Brunswick, NJ: Rutgers University Press, 1960); Paul E. Johnson, *Shopkeepers' Millennium: Society and Revivals in Rochester, New York, 1815–1837* (New York: Hill and Wang, 1978); Wilentz, *Chants Democratic*; Christine Stansell, *City of Women: Sex and Class in New York, 1789–1860* (Urbana-Champaign: University of Illinois Press, 1987); Sellers, *The Market Revolution*.

23. Marianne Perciaccante, *Calling Down Fire: Charles Finney and Revivalism in Jefferson County, New York* (New York: State University of New York Press, 2003).

24. Important works in the Democratization School include Terry Bilhartz, *Urban Religion and the Second Great Awakening: Church and Society in Early National Baltimore* (Madison, NJ: Fairleigh Dickinson University Press, 1986); Hatch, *The Democratization of American Christianity*; Curtis Johnson, *Islands of Holiness: Rural Religion in Upstate New York, 1790–1860* (Ithaca, NY: Cornell University Press, 1989); Peter Wosh, *Spreading the Word: The Bible Business in Nineteenth-Century America* (Ithaca, NY: Cornell University Press, 1994); Jama Lazerow, *Religion and the Working Class in Antebellum America* (Washington, DC: Smithsonian Institution, 1995); William R. Sutton, *Journeymen for Jesus: Evangelical Artisans Confront Capitalism in Jacksonian Baltimore* (University Park: Penn State University Press, 1998); Perciaccante, *Calling Down Fire*; David Paul Nord, *Faith in Reading: Religious Publishing and the Birth of Mass Media in America* (New York: Oxford University Press, 2007).

25. See "The First Charter of Virginia; April 10, 1606," Avalon Project, Yale Law School, https://avalon.law.yale.edu/17th_century/va01.asp, and "The Charter of Massachusetts Bay: 1629," Avalon Project, Yale Law School, https://avalon.law.yale.edu/17th_century/mass03.asp (both accessed April 12, 2023).

26. A study in the *Journal of Business Ethics* attempted to answer the question of what defines a CBE. The authors examined how 275 companies interacted with their employees, customers, suppliers, and communities, concluding that evangelistic Christian activity was a consistently common characteristic—whether through employee Bible studies, playing Christian music in stores, including Bible verses on checks or packaging, or donating money to local Christian charities. See Nabil A. Ibrahim, Leslie W. Rue, Patricia P. McDougall, and G. Robert Greene, "Characteristics and Practices of 'Christian-Based' Companies," *Journal of Business Ethics* 10, no. 2 (February 1991): 123–132.

27. "Pioneerism," *The Craftsman*, April 21, 1829.

28. The most prominent example of the latter was the firing/sanctioning of Pioneer stage drivers who drank or treated women in rude and vulgar ways. "Pioneerism," *The Craftsman*, April 21, 1829.

29. "The Christian Sabbath," *New York Observer*, September 17, 1831.

PART ONE. CHRISTIAN COMMUNAL CAPITALISM

1. Richard Kreitner, "Paterson: Alexander Hamilton's Trickle-Down City," *The Nation*, March 13, 2017, 18–24.

2. Barbara M. Tucker, *Samuel Slater and the Origins of the American Textile Industry, 1790–1860* (Ithaca, NY: Cornell University Press, 1984).

3. Robert F. Dalzell, *Enterprising Elite: The Boston Associates and the World They Made* (Cambridge, MA: Harvard University Press, 1987), and "The Rise of the Waltham-Lowell System and Some Thoughts on the Political Economy of Modernization in Ante-Bellum Massachusetts," *Perspectives in American History* 9 (1975): 229–268.

4. Anthony F. C. Wallace, *Rockdale: The Growth of an American Village in the Early Industrial Revolution* (New York: Knopf, 1978). Wallace uses the terms "Christian industrialism" and "communal industrialism" (esp. 293, 394–397) to describe separate and exclusive approaches to creating rational, equitable, efficient, successful, and sustainable textile manufacturing. Harmony blended elements of both approaches, undermining some of Wallace's core arguments.

5. John F. Kasson, *Civilizing the Machine: Technology and Republican Values in America, 1776–1900* (1976; repr., New York: Hill and Wang, 1999), 55–106.

6. Winnifred Barr Rothenberg, *From Market-Places to a Market Economy: The Transformation of Rural Massachusetts, 1750–1850* (Chicago: University of Chicago Press, 1992), 28–33. The prolific historian of the Harmony Society, Karl J. R. Arndt, used the term "communist-capitalist" to describe the society. "Communal capitalism" is a more accurate description of the kind of utopias that sprung up in the early nineteenth century. *DHID1*, xvii–xviii.

7. Overview of communal societies: Donald Pitzer, ed., *America's Communal Utopias* (Chapel Hill: University of North Carolina Press, 1997). For Mormon communalism, specifically: Amanda Porterfield, Darren E. Grem, and John Corrigan, eds., *The Business Turn in American Religious History* (New York: Oxford University Press, 2017); Leonard J. Arrington, Feramorz Y. Fox, and Dean L. May, *Building the City of God: Community and Cooperation Among the Mormons*, 2nd ed. (Urbana: University of Illinois Press, 1992), 15–40.

8. Prominent works on early national-period industrialization/republican factory towns that omit Harmony: Kasson, *Civilizing the Machine*; Thomas Cochran, *Frontiers of Change: Early Industrialism in America* (New York: Oxford University Press, 1981); Walter Licht, *Industrializing America: The Nineteenth Century* (Baltimore: Johns Hopkins University Press, 1995); David R. Meyer, *The Roots of American Industrialization* (Baltimore: Johns Hopkins University Press, 2003); Daniel Walker Howe, *What Hath God Wrought: The Transformation of America, 1815–1848* (New York: Oxford University Press, 2007).

9. The Shakers hoped to form a business collaboration with Harmony: GR to RF, June 22, 1816, *DHID1*, 228–229; A. Meacham to RLB, August 13, 1839, *GRYG*, 399–402; RLB to A. Meacham, November 14, 1839, *GRYG*, 409–411. However, Harmony and the Shakers held too many theological differences to form a

236   *Part One. Christian Communal Capitalism*

lasting collaboration, although the Shakers appreciated how the Harmonists "hate the lusts & ways of the world." Joseph Lockwood to JLB, January 1, 1817, *DHID1*, 290. Differences over theology did not stop the Harmonists from forming cordial relationships with other communal societies, and even extending financial aid to many communal utopian groups over the years, including their fellow separatists at Zoar. Kathleen Fernandez, *Zoar: The Story of an Intentional Community* (Kent, OH: Kent State University Press, 2019), 93–102.

10. J. S. Buckingham, *The Eastern and Western States of America*, vol. 2 (London: Fisher, Son, & Co., 1843), 233–234.

11. Mathew Carey, *The New Olive Branch* (Philadelphia: M. Carey & Son, 1820), 179.

12. Karl Arndt wrote the most complete account of the society, *George Rapp's Harmony Society, 1785–1847* (Philadelphia: University of Pennsylvania Press, 1965), while the sole recent monograph on the Harmonists, Alice Ott's *The Sunwoman in the Wilderness: The Religious Beliefs and Practices of George Rapp's Harmony Society* (Lexington, KY: Emeth Press, 2014), focuses on the society's theology. A lack of citations limits Arndt's account, although he is primarily responsible (not without some controversy) for assembling much of the massive archival and documentary collections of the Harmony Society. Older works on Harmony include Aaron Williams, *The Harmony Society at Economy* (Pittsburgh: W. S. Haven, 1866); George Browning Lockwood, *The New Harmony Communities* (Marion, IN: Chronicle Company, 1902), and *The New Harmony Movement* (New York: Augustus M. Kelley, 1905); John Archibald Bole, *The Harmony Society: A Chapter in German American Culture History* (Philadelphia: Americana Germanica Press, 1904); John S. Duss, *The Harmonists: A Personal History* (Harrisburg, PA: Telegraph Press, 1943); Christiana F. Knoedler, *The Harmony Society: A 19th-Century American Utopia* (New York: Vantage Press, 1954); Hilda Adam Kring, *The Harmonists: A Folk-Cultural Approach* (Metuchen, NJ: Scarecrow Press and American Theological Library Association, 1973). Chris Jennings's *Paradise Now: The Story of American Utopianism* (New York: Random House, 2016), is an example of a recently published popular history that omits Harmony from its "five representative movements." Another recent work that focuses on critiques of capitalism in the early nineteenth century, but which neglects Harmony, is Philip Gura, *Man's Better Angels: Romantic Reformers and the Coming of the Civil War* (Cambridge, MA: Belknap Press of Harvard University Press, 2017). Two recent works that demonstrate Harmony's place as a model to other aspiring utopians, while neglecting the story of Harmony itself, are Alex Krieger, *City on a Hill: Urban Idealism in America from the Puritans to the Present* (Cambridge, MA: Belknap Press of Harvard University Press, 2019), 257–259, and Adam Morris, *American Messiahs: False Prophets of a Damned Nation* (New York: Norton, 2019), 142–148.

Part One. Christian Communal Capitalism 237

13. Dotan Leshem argues we can find the roots of such intermingling between the spiritual and economic in the fourth-century Roman Empire, and his discussion of Saint Paul's writings about the Christian *oikonomos* (Greek for "who's in charge") is particularly relevant. Leshem, *The Origins of Neoliberalism: Modeling the Economy from Jesus to Foucault* (New York: Columbia University Press, 2016), 25–53.

14. The society's business operations also used the name "George Rapp and Company" for a brief time: Account, November 24, 1804, *HOTC*, 40–41.

15. Donald Pitzer, "How the Harmonists Suffered Disharmony: Schism in Communal Utopias," *American Communal Societies Quarterly* 5, no. 2 (April 2011): 58.

16. William Herbert, *A Visit to the Colony of Harmony, in Indiana, in the United States of America . . .* (London: George Mann, 1825), 8.

17. Richard Flower, *Letters from Lexington and the Illinois . . .* (London: J. Ridgway, 1819), 16.

18. For the concept of an "economist-philosopher," see Leshem, *Origins*, 101.

19. George Rapp, *Thoughts on the Destiny of Man, Particularly with Reference to the Present Times* (New Harmony, IN: Harmonie Society Press, 1824), 65.

20. Rapp, 65. Emphasis in original.

21. Rapp, 44. Emphasis in original.

22. Two works that emphasize Pietism's influence in early America are F. Ernest Stoeffler, *Continental Pietism and Early American Christianity* (Grand Rapids, MI: William B. Eerdmans, 1976), and Jonathan Strom, Hartmut Lehmann, and James Van Horn Melton, eds., *Pietism in Germany and North America, 1680–1820* (Burlington, VT: Ashgate, 2009).

23. Franklin H. Littell, "Radical Pietism in American History," in Stoeffler, *Continental Pietism*, 165; Strom, Lehmann, and Melton, *Pietism*, 23–32.

1. COMMUNAL INDUSTRY

1. Economy was the third of Rapp's communal villages. To avoid confusion, when referencing the society I will use "Harmony" and when referring to the first two settlements I will use the older spelling, "Harmonie."

2. William Herbert, *A Visit to the Colony of Harmony, in Indiana, in the United States of America . . .* (London: George Mann, 1825), 4.

3. "Mr. Owen's Address to the Citizens of the United States," *Norwich Courier*, November 23, 1825. A contrast of Rapp's adopted son explaining their religious foundation: FR to Edward Page, March 7, 1822, *DHID2*, 363–364.

4. This embrace of technology and industry bears similarity with the Pietistic Amana communities of Iowa. Franklin H. Littell, "Radical Pietism in

American History," in *Continental Pietism and Early American Christianity*, ed. F. Ernest Stoeffler (Grand Rapids, MI: William B. Eerdmans, 1976), 173–179.

5. Howard Bodenhorn, *A History of Banking in Antebellum America: Financial Markets and Economic Development in an Era of Nation-Building* (New York: Cambridge University Press, 2000), 1–6.

6. RLB to Israel Rupp, July 24, 1847, *GRYG*, 1067. Little is known about George's wife, Christina. She arrived at Harmony with George and died in 1830. Eileen English, *Demographic Directory of The Harmony Society*, 2nd ed. (Clinton, NY: Richard W. Couper Press, 2016), 107.

7. Alexander Boloni Farkas, *Journey in North America*, trans. and ed. Theodore and Helen Benedek Schoenman (1834; repr., Philadelphia: American Philosophical Society, 1977), 158; John Finch, "Notes of Travel in the United States: Letters VI–XI," *New Moral World: Gazette of the Rational Society* 5, nos. 34–39 (February 17–March 23, 1844).

8. The Thirty Years War was especially cruel to Württemberg. Aaron Fogleman, *Hopeful Journeys: German Immigration, Settlement, and Political Culture in Colonial America, 1717–1775* (Philadelphia: University of Pennsylvania Press, 1996), 15–35.

9. Shannon Dawdy, *Building the Devil's Empire: French Colonial New Orleans* (Chicago: University of Chicago Press, 2008), 43.

10. For Law: Dawdy, 14–15, 42–47, 101; *GRS*, xxi–xxii.

11. *GRS*, 18–19.

12. Farkas, *Journey*, 158; Finch, "Notes of Travel, VII."

13. Warning decrees: January 16, 1700, *GRS*, 5–6; June 25, 1709, *GRS*, 11–12; January 27, 1764, *GRS*, 59–60; March 25, 1766, *GRS*, 60–61.

14. Emigration enticements: 1751, *GRS*, 43–44; December 25, 1751, *GRS*, 45–49; March 23 and 25, 1753, *GRS*, 50–58.

15. Warning decrees: September 8, 1717, *GRS*, 14–16; February 28, 1750, *GRS*, 35–42; January 16, 1790, *GRS*, 152; May 20, 1805, *GRS*, 458–461.

16. "Separatism" can refer to either the act of separating from an established church or separating from society. Although the Harmonists exemplify both, here the focus is primarily on the latter. Harmony's theology: Alice T. Ott, *The Sunwoman in the Wilderness: The Religious Beliefs and Practices of George Rapp's Harmony Society* (Lexington, KY: Emeth Press, 2104), 3–11.

17. I follow Alice Ott in using a "narrow" definition of Pietism, referring to a specific renewal movement within German Lutheranism. Ott, *Sunwoman*, 11–14. One may consider Rapp a "radical Pietist" due to the role mysticism played in forming his theology and eschatology and the extremes to which he and his followers went to find purity: F. Ernest Stoeffler, *German Pietism During the*

Eighteenth Century (Leiden: E. J. Brill, 1973), 168–216; Fogleman, *Hopeful Journeys*, 100–107. The roots of the broader Pietist movement are much older, dating to sixteenth-century England and Netherlands: F. Ernest Stoeffler, *The Rise of Evangelical Pietism* (Leiden: E. J. Brill, 1965), 24–108, 109–179. Emergence of Lutheran Pietism: Stoeffler, *Rise of Evangelical Pietism*, 180–246, and *German Pietism*, 39–87.

18. Spener's influence on Württemberg: Stoeffler, *German Pietism*, 88–130. Influence on the Wesleys: Stoeffler, *Continental Pietism*, 184–221. GR letter, *GRS*, 70–74.

19. Unaddressed FR letter, May 17, 1813, *HOTC*, 657.

20. George Marsden, *The Evangelical Mind and the New School Presbyterian Experience: A Case Study of Thought and Theology in Nineteenth-Century America* (New Haven, CT: Yale University Press, 1970), 31–32.

21. Ott, *Sunwoman*, 13–14.

22. Reports, minutes, correspondence, and decrees, April 1787–December 1803, *GRS*, 96–226, 238–242, 368–412.

23. [FR] to Edward Page, March 7, 1822, *DHID2*, 363; [FR] to Samuel Worchester, December 19, 1822, HSR, 2335. Bible passages are King James Version (the most popular early nineteenth-century translation).

24. Declarations: March 1, 1798, *GRS*, 272–279; November 1799, *GRS*, 294–300.

25. Ott, *Sunwoman*, 51–52.

26. Undated letter, *GRS*, 281–284; emigration songs, spring 1804, *GRS*, 441–449; decree, November 1, 1805, *GRS*, 461–462; GR to Jacob Neff, March 3, 1807, *HOTC*, 215–218; Ott, *Sunwoman*, 33–35.

27. Amillennialism denies a specific period of peace (millennium) before the final judgment. (Instead, the church's present work in the world comprises a symbolic millennium.) When the early church began to fuse with the Roman state in the fourth century, Augustine articulated an eschatology that equated the church's "reign" on earth to Christ's millennial epoch. Consequently, the church's official eschatological position shifted toward what came to be known as amillennialism, the official doctrine of the church for more than a thousand years, despite periodic bursts of premillennialism (and excepting the first three hundred years of Christianity, when premillennialism predominated).

28. Finding synergy with the Enlightenment's philosophies of human and societal improvement, postmillennialism came to dominate Protestant eschatology in America, although premillennialism did enjoy a reemergence in the nineteenth century, particularly among separatists and Pietist German sects such as the Harmonists. Jonathan Edwards and the revivals of the eighteenth and nineteenth centuries popularized postmillennialism. In the late eighteenth and

early nineteenth centuries, "millenarian" was equivalent to "premillennialism," while postmillennialism was so hegemonic in the early national period that it did not have a specific term. (The terms "premillennialism" and "postmillennialism" did not emerge until the mid-nineteenth century.) See Robert G. Clouse, "Introduction," 7–13; George Eldon Ladd, "Historic Premillennialism," 17–40; and Loraine Boettner, "Postmillennialism," 117–141, all in *The Meaning of the Millennium: Four Views*, ed. Robert Clouse (Downers Grove, IL: InterVarsity Press, 1977); Fred Hood, "Presbyterianism and the New American Nation, 1783–1826: A Case Study of Religion and National Life" (PhD diss., Princeton University, 1968), 133–134; George Marsden, *Jonathan Edwards: A Life* (New Haven, CT: Yale University Press, 2003), 263–265, 335–337. More recently, scholars have minimized the significance of millennialism during the American Revolution: James P. Byrd, *Sacred Scripture, Sacred War: The Bible and the American Revolution* (New York: Oxford University Press, 2013), 143–163.

29. Ruth Bloch, *Visionary Republic: Millennial Themes in American Thought, 1756–1800* (New York: Cambridge University Press, 1985), 187–201.

30. George Rapp, *Thoughts on the Destiny of Man, Particularly with Reference to the Present Times* (New Harmony, IN: Harmonie Society Press, 1824), 20, 53–56, 73, 80; Ott, *Sunwoman*, 303–333.

31. "Woman in the Wilderness" was also the name of another group of all-male Pietist separatists from Württemberg that settled in Pennsylvania in 1694 near Germantown: Delburn Carpenter, *The Radical Pietists: Celibate Communal Societies Establishing in the United States Before 1820* (New York: AMS Press, 1975), 37–60. Emigration songs, spring 1804, *GRS*, 441–448; *GRS*, 357–358; GR to J. G. Mayer, January 31, 1842, *GRYG*, 580–582; Ott, *Sunwoman*, 106–127; Karl J. R. Arndt, *George Rapp's Harmony Society, 1785–1847* (Philadelphia: University of Pennsylvania Press, 1965), 56.

32. Passenger list, *HOTC*, 103–107.

33. Commission, October 7, 1803, *HOTC*, 1. Approximately ninety families founded Rapp's first commune. Fortescue Cuming, *Sketches of a Tour to the Western Country Through the States of Ohio and Kentucky* (Pittsburgh: Cramer, Spear & Eichbaum, 1810), 493.

34. GR to FR, October 12, 1803, and February 3–11, 1804, *HOTC*, 1–8; Farkas, *Journey*, 158.

35. Henry Adams, ed., *The Writings of Albert Gallatin*, vol. 1 (Philadelphia: J. B. Lippincott and Company, 1879), 199–200; memorial, January 6, 1806, *HOTC*, 137–141.

36. *Annals of Congress*, 9th Cong., 1st sess., Senate: 45, 52–53, 68–69, 72, 74, 78; House: 409, 414, 463–465, 468–470, 473–477.

1. Communal Industry 241

37. *Poulson's American Daily Advertiser,* July 10, 1804; *Maryland Gazette,* July 12, 1804; Heinrich Muntz to Friedrich Wilhelm, August 1804, *HOTC,* 28–30; Arndt, *Harmony Society,* 65.

38. Passenger lists: September 15, 19, 1804, *HOTC,* 30–38; *Poulson's American Daily Advertiser,* September 17, 1804. For other Ohio settlements, including Zoar: Catherine Rokicky, *Creating a Perfect World: Religious and Secular Utopias in Nineteenth-Century Ohio* (Athens: Ohio University Press, 2002); R. Douglas Hurt, *The Ohio Frontier: Crucible of the Old Northwest, 1720–1830* (Bloomington: Indiana University Press, 1996), 302–308; Elwin C. Robinson, "Heavenly Aspirations and Earthly Realities: Four Northeast Ohio Religious Utopias," *Timeline* 17, no. 6 (November–December 2000): 15–19; Carpenter, *The Radical Pietists,* 198–213.

39. Articles of Agreement, D. B. Muller and GR, October 17, 1804, *HOTC,* 46–49, 52–54; Cuming, *Sketches,* 493. Rapp made numerous subsequent purchases. HSR, 2321 deeds: Henry Pratt to GRA, November 7, 1805; D. B. Muller to GRA, November 8,1805; Bank of North America to GRA, November 8, 1805; John/Anne Purviance to GR, November 14, 1809; Stephen/Catherine Stone to GR, January 5, 1810; Hugh Nesbit to GR, March 8, April 6, 26, 1811; D. B. Muller to GR, March 16, April 1, 1811.

40. The down payment was equivalent to over $80,000 in 2021 (% increase in Consumer Price Index, or CPI) or $2.6 million (per-capita Gross Domestic Product, or GDP). All estimates: MeasuringWorth.com, as of 2021. Settlement of accounts, December 31, 1804–January 14, 1805, *HOTC,* 60–77.

41. Pastoral Letter of GR, January 28, 1800, *GRS,* 308–310; Ott, *Sunwoman,* 72–94.

42. Articles of Agreement, February 15, 1805, HSR, 2313.

43. Articles of Agreement, February 15, 1805, HSR, 2313. There is uncertainty over the articles' dating. The articles of 1805 were probably modified at some later date to include a provision for the return of personal property if one were to leave the society. This element was missing from the articles submitted to the Pennsylvania Legislature on December 15, 1807, in the society's quest for incorporation (they were subsequently annulled by the society in 1836). The legal basis of the 1805 articles was established by their use in court in 1822 as the covenant of the society and its founding principles. *HOTC,* 80–82; memorial, December 15, 1807–January 23, 1808, *HOTC,* 253–256; annulment of article 6, 1827 Articles of Association, October 31, 1836, *GRYG,* 220–233; record of the annulment proceedings, October 31, 1836, *GRYG,* 233–234; Karl J. R. Arndt, "A Pious Fraud: Rapp's 1805 Harmony Society Articles of Association," *Western Pennsylvania Historical Magazine* 68, no. 3 (July 1985): 277–286. I side with Alice Ott's conclusion that communalism was intrinsic to Harmony's theology, not merely a late evolution in response to material needs: *Sunwoman,* 132–143.

44. GR to Jacob Neff, April 10, 1806, *HOTC*, 182.

45. Deed, Peter Shriver to GRA, August 26, 1826, HSR, 2322.

46. "Stinks" (German *stinckt*): Michael Hagmann to the Harmony Society, undated, *HOTC*, 288.

47. GR to FR, August, *HOTC*, 96–103; FR receipt, June 7, 1808, *HOTC*, 283–284; Johannes Rapp to FR, December 5, 1808, *HOTC*, 310–311; J. Georg Munz to FR, December 27, 1808, *HOTC*, 312–313; John Melish, *Travels in the United States of America . . .* , vol. 2 (Philadelphia: Thomas & George Palmer, 1812), 79–80.

48. Inventory, deceased member, January 1, 1806, *HOTC*, 131–132; GH to FR, undated, *HOTC*, 313–316.

49. Correspondence between FR and Conrad/Nicara Thorwarth, July 18–August 12, 1832, *EOTO*, 796–803.

50. Memorial, January 23, 1808, *HOTC*, 255. Frederick believed the lack of incorporation provided protection from lawsuits. [FR] to DS, February 22, 1822, *DHID2*, 357.

51. [FR] to Samuel Worchester, December 19, 1822, HSR, 2335; GR to Jacob Neff, April 10, 1806, HSR, 2335.

52. Schaalen, Rapp, and Muntz v. GR, December 1806, *HOTC*, 210–211; summons, March 7, 1807, *HOTC*, 218–219; Johannes Rapp to FR, December 5, 1808, *HOTC*, 310–311. For wages, see George Miller suit correspondence: January 1822–June 1823, *DHID2*, 348–351, 358–359, 397–398, 407–410, 599–612.

53. FR to Chester Chadwick, September 28, 1822, HSR, 2329.

54. GR to FR, September 4, 1805, *HOTC*, 113–115; member accounts, December 31, 1804–January 14, 1805, *HOTC*, 60–77; fragmentary record of original contributions, December 1, 1805, *HOTC*, 126–127; annulment of article 6, 1827 Articles of Association, October 31, 1836, *GRYG*, 220–233.

55. Biography of John Reif, June 3, 1836, *GRYG*, 193–195.

56. Marriages, 1808, *HOTC*, 270–271; [FR] to Edward Page, March 7, 1822, *DHID2*, 363; Aaron Williams, *The Harmony Society at Economy* (Pittsburgh: W. S. Haven, 1866), 56–59; Jacob Boehme, *The Way to Christ*, trans. Peter Erb (New York: Paulist Press, 1978), 149–155; Andrew Weeks, *Boehme: An Intellectual Biography of the Seventeenth-Century Philosopher and Mystic* (Albany: State University of New York Press, 1991), 114–121; Ott, *Sunwoman*, 143–154, 275–279; Willi Temme, "From Jakob Böhme via Jane Leade to Eva von Buttlar—Transmigrations and Transformations of Religious Ideas," in *Pietism in Germany and North America, 1680–1820*, ed. Jonathan Strom, Hartmut Lehmann, and James Van Horn Melton (Burlington, VT: Ashgate, 2009), 101–106; Donald F. Durnbaugh, "Work and Hope: The Spirituality of the Radical Pietist Communitarians," *Church History* 39, no. 1 (March 1970): 85–87.

1. Communal Industry 243

57. Data on marriages is not as precise as one would like. Many marriages do not list exact dates, or any dates at all. However, it provides a helpful pattern of Harmony's marriages and along with the birthing data undermines the idea that celibacy reigned in the society. English, *Demographic Directory of the Harmony Society*, 257–268. Discussion of voluntary celibacy: Christian Mertz to Baker and Henrici, February 27, 1864, *GRRH*, 697–698.

58. Ott, *Sunwoman*, 148, 150–154. Ott asserts some men and women lived on different floors of their houses, but I have not been able to corroborate this in the archives.

59. Lord Byron, *Don Juan: Cantos VII–XVI*, vol. 2 (London: Thomas White, 1826), 322–323.

60. Arndt, *George Rapp's Harmony Society*, 418. Unlike Harmony, the Shakers, Mormons, and Oneida communities have attracted a great deal of attention over their teachings on sexuality. A small sampling: Stephen C. Taysom, *Shakers, Mormons, and Religious Worlds: Conflicting Visions, Contested Boundaries* (Bloomington: Indiana University Press, 2010); Lawrence Foster, *Religion and Sexuality: Three American Communal Experiments of the Nineteenth Century* (New York: Oxford University Press, 1981); Louis J. Kern, *An Ordered Love: Sex Roles and Sexuality in Victorian Utopias—the Shakers, the Mormons, and the Oneida Community* (Chapel Hill: University of North Carolina Press, 1981).

61. Chapter 3's conclusion briefly addresses this transition in a bit more detail.

62. Land Sale, Henry Pratt to GRA, November 7, 1805, HSR, 2321.

63. FR to family, May 17, 1813, HSR, 2335; GR sermon, February 11, 1838, *GRYG*, 320–323; J. S. Buckingham, *The Eastern and Western States of America*, vol. 2 (London: Fisher, Son, & Co., 1843), 229–230; Arndt, *George Rapp's Harmony Society*, 308–309.

64. Donald Pitzer claims the Harmonists used the Golden Rose on their manufactured goods, citing Harmony records and John W. Larner Jr., "'Nails and Sundrie Medicines': Town Planning and Public Health in the Harmony Society, 1805–1840," *Western Pennsylvania Historical Magazine* 45 (June 1962): 119; Donald Pitzer and Josephine Elliott, "New Harmony's First Utopians, 1814–1824," *Indiana Magazine of History* 75 (September 1979): 235. I have not found the "survey of trade records" Pitzer cites as evidence, but the University of Southern Indiana also makes this claim: "New Harmony Is the site of Many Historic Firsts, from Science and Industry to Arts and Culture," University of Southern Indiana, accessed April 20, 2023, https://www.usi.edu/hnh/student-and-faculty-engagement-opportunities/univ101-new-harmony-experience/first-facts.

65. Ott, *Sunwoman*, 207–214.

66. Jacob Eckensperger to Friedrich Eckensperger, March 5, 1808, *HOTC*, 282.

67. Criticism of Rapp's character and personality: Gerhard K. Friesen, "An Additional Source on the Harmony Society of Economy, Pennsylvania," *Western Pennsylvania Historical Magazine* 61, no. 4 (October 1978): 308, 309, 311. Anti-Semitism: D. B. Muller to FR, December 24, 1805, *HOTC*, 128–130.

68. Jacob Eckensperger to Friedrich Eckensperger, March 5, 1808, *HOTC*, 282; English, *Demographic Directory*, 48. Sample of Rapp's conflicts (just five months in 1809): FR to Peter Eyster, May 15, 1809, *HOTC*, 327–329; Peter Eyster to GR, May 27, 1809, *HOTC*, 330–332; Jacob Schaal to Christopher Muller, May 31, 1809, *HOTC*, 334–336; Butler County inquest, June, 1809, *HOTC*, 336–340; Harmony statements, September 25, 1809, *HOTC*, 348–350.

69. Lewis David von Schweinitz, *The Journey of Lewis David von Schweinitz to Goshen, Bartholomew County*, trans. Adolf Gerber (Indianapolis: Indiana Historical Society Publications, 1927), 279. Von Schweinitz was also the great-grandson of the founder of the Moravian church, Count Nikolaus Ludwig von Zinzendorf.

70. Warrant, April 13, 1807, *HOTC*, 221–222; Butler County inquest, June 1807, *HOTC*, 232–233; Butler County verdict, June 1807, *HOTC*, 233–234.

71. GR to FR, September 30, 1805, *HOTC*, 115–118.

72. Jacob Schieck to family, June 14, 1816, *DHID1*, 224–225. The Schaal family breakup is the one of the most documented cases: Jacob Schaal Renunciation, June 27, 1808, *HOTC*, 284–286; Jacob Schaal to Margarethe Schaal, August 5, 1808, *HOTC*, 293–296; Johann and Gottfried Schaal to Margarethe Schaal, August 18, 1808, *HOTC*, 299–302; Schaal family indenture, April 10, 1809, *HOTC*, 322–323; William Ayres to FR, April 13, 1809, *HOTC*, 324; Jacob Schaal to Christopher Muller, May 31, 1809, *HOTC*, 334–336; Magdalena Schieck to Judith Schieck, June 14, 1823, *DHID2*, 622–623. Other examples: AWC to FR, August 9, 1823, *DHID2*, 656; Wolfangel v. Rapp et al., [September 24, 1823], *DHID2*, 678–681; divorce petition, August 2, 1824, *HOTW*, 103–104.

73. English, *Demographic Directory*, 120; Jacob Schieck to GR, July 4, 1814, *HOTC*, 858–860. Two examples of Rapp's court activity (from a single month in 1807): George Mutschler v. GRA, June 1807, *HOTC*, 234–235; Esterle, Wilhelm, and Heckenlaible v. FR, June 1807, *HOTC*, 235–238.

74. Buckingham, *The Eastern and Western States of America*, 2:222.

75. Resignation of citizenship, July 9, 1798, *GRS*, 280–281; English, *Demographic Directory*, 107.

76. For FR's role from earliest years, see FR account book (1804–1805), KAC, 5159.

77. Power of Attorney (GRA to FR), [May 21–22, 1824], *DHID2*, 893–902.

78. Cotton factory: undated entry, memorandum book, 1835, HSR, 2480. Textile machinery: undated entry, memorandum book, 1838, HSR, 2480. Competitors: memorandum book, RLB, 1836–1838, HSR, 2480.

1. Communal Industry 245

79. In one letter, Rapp is described as wanting to have a local businessman "in his power." P. Neville to Joseph St. Leger d'Happart, October 26, 1810, *HOTC*, 410–411. Hard bargaining: FR to Franz Hilveti, April 5, 1811, *HOTC*, 432 and Franz Hilveti to FR, April 17, 1811, *HOTC*, 433–434; Franz Hilveti to FR, February 17, 1812, *HOTC*, 508–509. Lawsuits: [FR] to DS, July 9, 1819, *DHID1*, 739–740; John Law to FR, July 1, 1822, *DHID2*, 421–422; *"Frederick Rapp v. Bank of Vincennes," Western Sun*, July 13, 1822, *DHID2*, 429.

80. FR Statement, July 20, 1825, *HOTW*, 597–600. See note 43 for controversy over the articles.

81. [FR] to Edward P. Page, March 7, 1822, *DHID2*, 363. Several historians have misidentified the existence of "companies" at Harmony as work units. Ott has demonstrated they were spiritual and cultural groupings of families instead: Jonathan Strom, *Pietism and Community in Europe and North America, 1650–1850* (Boston: Brill, 2010), 249–277.

82. One visitor claimed GR also signed off on store disbursements: William Blane, [December 1812], *DHID2*, 524; For one year's worth of member disbursements: Harmony accounts, 1824, HSR, 2528. Also, see HSR, 2528; Record of footwear issued, 1838–1860 and the book for women's clothing, 1821–1827; HSR, 2528.

83. Finch, "Notes of Travel, VI."

84. GR to John Reichert and RLB, [May 11, 1822], *DHID2*, 396; Caroline Dale Snedeker, ed., *The Diaries of Donald MacDonald, 1824–1826* (Indianapolis: Indiana Historical Society, 1942), 247; Victor Colin Duclos diary, in Harlow Lindley, ed., *Indiana as Seen by Early Travelers: A Collection of Reprints from Books of Travel, Letters and Diaries Prior to 1830* (Indianapolis: Indiana Historical Commission, 1916), 540; Pitzer and Elliott, "New Harmony's First Utopians," 277, 279; Arndt, *George Rapp's Harmony Society*, 242–243; Donald Pitzer and Darryl Jones, *New Harmony Then & Now* (Bloomington: Indiana University Press, 2012), 20.

85. Sworn testimony, Shreiber v. Rapp, December 1835, *GRYG*, 155–156.

86. Cuming, *Sketches*, 494–496; Stubbs report, 1809, *HOTC*, 357–359. Morality of distilling: DS to FR, January 24, 1813, *HOTC*, 620.

87. $5,841.27 equates to $115,000 (CPI) or $4.1 million (per-capita GDP): 1808 account, *HOTC*, 316–318; 1809 account, *HOTC*, 354–357. List of occupations: Cuming, *Sketches*, 494–496. For comparison, see 1811 account, *HOTC*, 500–501.

88. J. Boyd to FR, June 3, 1811, *HOTC*, 440.

89. GH to FR, December 20, 1810, *HOTC*, 417. Praise for Harmony's spirits: Simon Snyder to GR, September 1813, *HOTC*, 716; Caspar Beyrer to GR/FR, February 14, 1814, *HOTC*, 796.

90. John Boyd to FR, October 19, 1811, *HOTC*, 483–484.

91. Factory: Stephen Stone and J. Hull to Edward A Gibbs, March 15, 1810, *HOTC*, 374; contract, March 22, 1810, *HOTC*, 378–379; John Whatmough to FR, August 10, 1810, *HOTC*, 403; Melish, *Travels*, 2:70. Sheep: Francis Hilveti to FR, September 24, 1811, *HOTC*, 474–476; Francis Hilveti to FR, October 23, 1811, *HOTC*, 484–485; David Ruff to FR, January 1, 1812, *HOTC*, 502; Francis Hilveti to FR, February 17, 1812, *HOTC*, 508–510.

92. William Rayen to J. Langenbacher, February 5, 1812, *HOTC*, 507; Increase Mathews to FR, June 11, 1812, *HOTC*, 526; John Walwork to Miller, July 27, 1812, *HOTC*, 538; John Baker for FR to John Walwork, August 6, 1812, *HOTC*, 544; Seth Adams to FR, August 15, 1812, *HOTC*, 548–549.

93. FR to Thomas Rotch, September 1, 1812, *HOTC*, 551–552. The carding machine was a source of frustration. FR spent most of 1812 trying to acquire a carding machine—it was finally shipped to Harmony in November of 1812, although they struggled to get it operational until June 1813. FR to Daniel Norton, August 12, 1812, *HOTC*, 546–547; Daniel Norton to FR, September 3, 1812, *HOTC*, 552–553; Daniel Norton to FR, September 19, 1812, *HOTC*, 554; FR to Daniel Norton, September 25, 1812, *HOTC*, 560; Daniel Norton and Abram Baldwin to FR, November 8, 1812, *HOTC*, 577; Norton and Baldwin Account, January 30, 1813, *HOTC*, 618–619; FR to James Mosher, April 14, 1813, *HOTC*, 646; FR to Daniel Norton, May 24, 1813, *HOTC*, 657; FR to Daniel Norton, June 18, 1813, *HOTC*, 662; FR to Increase Mathews, November 16, 1813, *HOTC*, 742.

94. Quote: FR to Seth Adams, February 6, 1813, *HOTC*, 623. M. Murray to John Mason, February 9, 1813, *HOTC*, 623; contract, April 1, 1813, *HOTC*, 637–638.

95. Memorial to postmaster general, undated, *HOTC*, 213–214; Isaac Burneston to Alexander McKim, February 17, 1813, *HOTC*, 625. The Rapps also petitioned for the removal of their regional postmaster: Samuel Smith to postmaster general, February 16, 1811, *HOTC*, 427–428; Samuel Smith to FR, February 19, 1811, *HOTC*, 428.

96. For example, Robert Owen first learned of the society through this report in 1815. For context, $220,000 equates to $4 million (CPI) or $137 million (per-capita GDP). Melish, *Travels*, 2:77–80.

97. Contract, June 17, 1813, *HOTC*, 660–661; GH to FR, August 7, 1813, *HOTC*, 689–690; C. Orth to FR, August 19, 1813, *HOTC*, 699; C. Orth to FR, August 23, 1813, *HOTC*, 705; Isaac Bean to FR, December 13, 1813, *HOTC*, 761. Envy: Charles Brearley to FR, August 31, 1814, *HOTC*, 884–885.

98. Fire engine: GH to FR, October 19, 1812, *HOTC*, 573; FR to Lyon, October 13, 1813, *HOTC*, 729–730; GH to FR, December 27, 1813, *HOTC*, 765–767; John Jordan to Isaac Bean, January 5, 1814, *HOTC*, 781; FR to John Jordan, February 14, 1814, *HOTC*, 798. Furnace: agreement, December 23, 1813, *HOTC*, 764;

1. Communal Industry 247

John Glasser to FR, January 24, 1814, *HOTC*, 789–791; John Baker to FR, March 10, 1814, *HOTC*, 805; Harold White, "Bassenheim Furnace," *Journal of Beaver County History* 26, no. 3 (Summer 2001), https://www.bcpahistory .org/beavercounty/BeaverCountyTopical/SteelandIron/BassenheimFurnace /BassenheimFurnace.html.

99. Simon Snyder to GR, September 21, 1813, *HOTC*, 716.

100. Quote: du Pont Bauduy & Co. to William McKinsie, February 26, 1813, *HOTC*, 630; FR to E.I. du Pont, May 5, 1813, *HOTC*, 652–654; FR to B. Burneston, March 6, 1813, *HOTC*, 634–635.

101. Purchasing: William Hoge to FR, September 19, 1812, *HOTC*, 553–554; Judah Colt to FR, September 19, 1812, *HOTC*, 554–555; John Street to FR, June 4, 1813, *HOTC*, 659. Processing: FR to George Parsons, June 10, 1813, *HOTC*, 559–560; Increase Mathews to FR, June 23, 1813, *HOTC*, 665; William Barr to Frederick, June 29, 1813, *HOTC*, 667; John Baker to FR, November 21, 1813, *HOTC*, 744; FR to William Barr, August 16, 1813, *HOTC*, 697–698. Kentucky: William Chambers to FR, March 2, 1814, *HOTC*, 800–802.

102. FR to George Heide, undated, *HOTC*, 476–478; Georg Heide to FR, September 27, 1811, *HOTC*, 478–480; John Bedford to FR, June 11, 1820, *DHID2*, 63–64.

103. Memorandum of goods, August 6, 1828, HSR, 2499: account volumes. For example, in 1812, bright green was not in style, so Rapp's agent, GH, recommended darker green as being more "fashionable": GH to FR, January 4, 1813, *HOTC*, 590.

104. FR to Finley & Son, May 14, 1812, *HOTC*, 522; Isaac Bean to FR, June 18, 1812, *HOTC*, 528; agreement, April 1, 1813, *HOTC*, 639–640. Iron: FR to Clendinen & Co., July 20, 1812, *HOTC*, 534.

105. Quote: FR to Isaac Burneston, June 29, 1812, *HOTC*, 531. FR to Finley & Son, November 4, 1811, *HOTC*, 491–492; Welsch and Sterrett to FR, February 14, 1812, *HOTC*, 507–508; FR to Welsh and Sterrett, March 10, 1812, *HOTC*, 513–514; A. Welsh to FR, March 24, 1812, *HOTC*, 516–517.

106. Harmony memorandum books include clippings of economic news, snippets of presidential elections, and census data: memorandum book, April 14, 1831–December 20, 1841, HSR, 2499: account volumes.

2. INDUSTRY ON THE FRONTIER

1. GR to FR, April 20, 1814, *DHID1*, 1–3; JLB/GR to FR, April 26, 1814, *DHID1* 3–5.

2. [FR] to Joseph Leobold, July 20, 1816, *DHID1*, 235. RLB affirmed these factors as causing the move: RLB and John Reichert to the Royal District Office, Schorndorf, [November 1, 1822], *DHID2*, 490.

3. George Browning Lockwood, *The New Harmony Communities* (Marion, IN: Chronicle Company, 1902), 24. Visitor Henry Schoolcraft mentioned climate: Henry R. Schoolcraft, *Travels in the Central Portions of the Mississippi Valley...* (New York: Collins and Hannay, 1825), 165. Arndt mentions only crowding and increasingly expensive land: *DHID1*, xi–xii; Karl J. R. Arndt, *George Rapp's Harmony Society, 1785–1847* (Philadelphia: University of Pennsylvania Press, 1965), 133.

4. Edouard de Montulé, *Travels in America, 1816–1817*, trans. Edward D. Seeber (Bloomington: Indiana University Press, 1951), 146–147; Jeremiah Warder to George Flower, August 28, 1817, *DHID1*, 382–383.

5. George Rogers Taylor, *The Transportation Revolution, 1815–1860* (New York: Rineheart, 1951), 207–249; Walter Licht, *Industrializing America: The Nineteenth Century* (Baltimore: Johns Hopkins University Press, 1995), 21–35; Adam Rothman, *Slave Country: American Expansion and the Origins of the Deep South* (Cambridge, MA: Harvard University Press, 2005); Johnathan Levy, *Ages of American Capitalism: A History of the United States* (New York: Random House, 2021), 150–164.

6. *DHID1*, 147n; "Appendix: America's Communal Utopias Founded by 1965," in *America's Communal Utopias*, ed. Donald Pitzer (Chapel Hill: University of North Carolina Press, 1997), 457.

7. The new site was approximately twenty-five miles northwest of Evansville, in the southwest corner of Indiana. GR to FR, May 10, 1814, *DHID1*, 7; Thomas Rogers to GR, May 9, 1814, *HOTC*, 834; undated memorandum, *DHID1*, 5–6. GRA purchased an additional 5,370 acres in June: unsigned/undated to Nathaniel Ewing and John Badollet, *DHID1*, 9–10. Initially, the purchase was for 2,435 acres, but within one year, Harmonie encompassed 17,000 acres: *Niles' Weekly Register*, October 28, 1815, *DHID1*, 146. By 1816, FR claimed over 20,000 acres. [FR] to Joseph Leobold, July 20, 1816, *DHID1*, 236. For details of subsequent land purchases: Legal File/Deeds (1796–1822), HSR, 2321.

8. [FR] to Joseph Leobold, July 20, 1816, *DHID1*, 235–236.

9. Although George realized the waterworks would be located more than a mile from the settlement, and a steam engine would be required to make up for the river's inadequacies: GR to FR, May 10, 1814, *DHID1*, 7–8.

10. JLB to GR, July 20, 1814, *DHID1*, 17–20; [FR] to JLB, August 11, 1814, *DHID1*, 27. JLB was a founding member of the original settlement in western Pennsylvania and one of three advance agents (including GR) sent to find new land for the society. His younger brother Romelius, also a founding member, would become one of Frederick's most important business agents, an elder, and head of finances after Frederick's death. Arndt, *George Rapp's Harmony Society,*

2. Industry on the Frontier 249

133–134; Eileen English, *Demographic Directory of The Harmony Society*, 2nd ed. (Clinton, NY: Richard W. Couper Press, 2016), 86–87.

11. FR to Ewing and Badollet, August 8, 1814, *DHID1*, 25; [FR] to JLB, August 11, 1814, *DHID1*, 27.

12. Oliver Wolcott to Caleb Lownes, October 10, 1814, *DHID1*, 56–57. Religion and the market facilitated this process in the Northwest Territory in complex ways. For example, some Native peoples remained in the Ohio Country and participated in the emerging regional economic marketplace: Lori Daggar, *Cultivating Empire: Capitalism, Philanthropy, and the Negotiation of American Imperialism in Indian Country* (Philadelphia: University of Pennsylvania Press, 2023), esp. 123–145.

13. This sum equates to $2.1 million (CPI) or $70 million (per capita GDP). GH to FR, December 16, 1814, *DHID1*, 87–88n1; Christopher Miller to GR, December 17, 1814, *DHID1*, 89.

14. Purchase: FR power of attorney, June 14, 1814, *HOTC*, 842–847; John Heckewelder to FR, November 27, 1814, *HOTC*, 915–917; contract, May 6, 1815, *HOTC*, 970–974; FR to GR, May 8, 1815, *DHID1*, 124–128; financial distress: FR to DS, May 14, 1816, *DHID1*, 219–220; FR to DS, July 8, 1816, *DHID1*, 233–234; [FR] to DS, November 9, 1816, *DHID1*, 266–268; [FR] to DS, February 1, 1817, *DHID1*, 304–306; FR to DS, April 18, 1818, *DHID1*, 499–500; FR to AWC, November 14, 1818, *DHID1*, 603; FR to DS, May 3, 1819, *DHID1*, 696–700; AWC to FR, May 10, 1819, *DHID1*, 702–703; loss of credit in Philadelphia: FR to AWC, June 19, 1819, *DHID1*, 727–729.

15. [FR] to DS, February 22, 1822, *DHID2*, 355–356; [FR] to AWC, February 22, 1822, *DHID2*, 358–359; DS to FR, September 9, 1822, *DHID2*, 455–459.

16. For the extreme shortage of money: FR to GR, July 23, 1817, *DHID1*, 365–368; Abraham Ziegler to GR/FR, May 12, 1818, *DHID1*, 522; [FR] to DS, December 19, 1818, *DHID1*, 621; AWC to FR, February 8, 1819, *DHID1*, 642–643; [RLB] to AWC, March 6, 1819, *DHID1*, 663–664.

17. DS to FR, June 18, 1819, *DHID1*, 725.

18. [FR] to DS, July 9, 1819, *DHID1*, 739–741; [FR] to AWC, July 31, 1819, *DHID1*, 752–753. Ziegler dispute: correspondence, November 22, 1815–August 30, 1819, *DHID1*, 155, 193–195, 210–211, 298–304, 309–311, 338–339, 350–352, 365–368, 400–401, 426–429, 458–459, 500–503, 522–524, 533, 546–547, 555–559, 582–583, 590–592, 619–620, 631–632, 756–757, 766–767.

19. December 14, 1814, licenses: HSR, 2326. Survey of items stocked in the Harmonie store: April 11, 1825, Harmonie store, account volumes: HSR, 2499.

20. Nathaniel Ewing to GR, November 6, 1814, *DHID1*, 66–67; FR to John Woods, December 23, 1815, *DHID1*, 170–171; Nathaniel Ewing to FR, May 8, 1816, *DHID1*,

214–215; [FR] to Jonathan Meigs, June 4, 1816, *DHID1*, 220–221; [FR] to DS, September 14, 1816, *DHID1*, 250; water: GR to FR, November 8, 1814, *DHID1*, 68–69.

21. William Chambers to GR, January 28, 1815, *DHID1*, 103–104. For the sickness, see letters of DHID1, September 1814–January 1815, DHID1, 34–99; esp. [FR] to A & J Wilson, July 3, [1815], *DHID1*, 131.

22. Consequently, an order for two hundred pounds of coarse wool went unfulfilled. It was a rare example of GR making a business decision and not deferring to FR. Additionally, GR did not seem to know Great Britain and the United States had signed the Treaty of Ghent in December, which had driven down the price of wool in American markets. As a result, he agreed to terms FR found completely unacceptable. GR to FR, March 10, 1815, *DHID1*, 106–109; William Chambers to GR, March 11, 1815, *DHID1*, 110; William Chambers to GR, April 23, 1815, *DHID1*, 120–122. FR to Allan Thom, February 1, 1816, *DHID1*, 185. Dogs: Joel W. Hiatt, ed., *Diary of William Owen, from November 10, 1824 to April 20, 1825* (Indianapolis: Bobbs-Merrill Company, 1906; repr., New York: Augustus M. Kelley, 1973), 75.

23. Taking delivery of the engine and getting it working was another matter—it was a struggle, and the delay caused financial loss. GR to FR, November 29, 1814, *DHID1*, 77; DS to FR, December 6, 1815, *DHID1*, 164–165; John Arthurs to [FR], December 12, 1815, *DHID1*, 166; FR to Bean & Butler, January 5, 1816, *DHID1*, 176–177.

24. Harmonie might not have been impacted by the hot summers until after 1818, due to the volcanic eruption of Tambora, which led to abnormally colder years from 1816 to 1818. Andrew H. Browning, *The Panic of 1819: The First Great Depression* (Columbia: University of Missouri Press, 2019), 75–86; William Herbert, *A Visit to the Colony of Harmony, in Indiana, in the United States of America . . .* (London: George Mann, 1825), 8; Donald E. Pitzer and Darryl D. Jones, *New Harmony Then & Now* (Bloomington: Indiana University Press, 2012), 26–27.

25. Counterfeit currency was a problem in Pennsylvania too: bank notes at Harmonie store (1810–1814), account volumes: HSR, 2499. Ambiguity of credit/currency in early United States: Joshua R. Greenberg, "The Era of Shinplasters: Making Sense of Unregulated Paper Money," in *Capitalism by Gaslight: Illuminating the Economy of Nineteenth-Century America*, ed. Brian P. Luskey and Wendy A. Woloson (Philadelphia: University of Pennsylvania Press, 2015), 53–75; Andrew M. Schocket, *Founding Corporate Power in Early National Philadelphia* (DeKalb: Northern Illinois University Press, 2007), 77–108; Stephen Mihm, *A Nation of Counterfeiters: Capitalists, Con Men, and the Making of the United States* (Cambridge, MA: Harvard University Press, 2007).

2. Industry on the Frontier 251

26. Jane Ellen Knodell, *The Second Bank of the U.S.: "Central" Banker in an Era of Nation-Building, 1816–1836* (New York: Routledge, 2017), 69–70, 138–140. In comparison, by 1850, currency in the United States was valued at over $285,000: U.S. Department of Commerce, *Historical Statistics of the United States, Colonial Times to 1957* (Washington, DC: Government Printing Office, 1960), Series X:281–284, 647.

27. Howard Bodenhorn, *State Banking in Early America: A New Economic History* (New York: Oxford University Press, 2003), 141–145. By 1830, Pennsylvania possessed nine times the bank money per capita and fourteen times the bank credit as Indiana. (Bank money equals circulation plus deposits and minus the notes of other banks. Bank credit equals loans and discounts plus bills of exchange.) The situation was worse in Illinois and Ohio, although it was better in Illinois by 1830: Howard Bodenhorn, *A History of Banking in Antebellum America: Financial Markets and Economic Development in an Era of Nation-Building* (New York: Cambridge University Press, 2000), 63–64. Banking in the early national-period West: Bodenhorn, *State Banking*, 219–248.

28. Sharon Murphy, *Other People's Money: How Banking Worked in the Early American Republic* (Baltimore: Johns Hopkins University Press, 2017), 79.

29. Murphy, 57, 67.

30. Logan Esarey, "State Banking in Indiana, 1814–1873," *Indiana University Bulletin* 10, no. 2 (1912): 219–305. Wildcatting: Murphy, *Other People's Money*, 117–119; Bodenhorn, *State Banking*, 202–204.

31. Abraham Ziegler blamed Schnee, among other things, for his inability to pay the Rapps. After its failure, Ziegler and others started their own bank, the Harmony Farmers Company. Jacob Schnee to FR, January 25, 1815, *HOTC*, 944–945; Abraham Ziegler to FR, January 20, 1817, *DHID1*, 298–300; DS to FR, January 22, 1817, *DHID1*, 301–302; DS to FR, February 28, 1817, *DHID1*, 309–311; DS to FR, June 30, 1817, *DHID1*, 350–352; FR to GR, July 23, 1817, *DHID1*, 365. Institute: Abraham Ziegler to GR/FR, May 12, 1818, *DHID1*, 522–524; FR to DS, July 25, [1818], *DHID1*, 555–557. "Monstrously": AWC to FR, July 21, 1818, *DHID1*, 554–555. Jacob's brother John moved into the New Harmony society of Robert Owen after the Harmonists moved back to Pennsylvania, and rented land from Harmony in 1820, before the Rapps sold out to Owen: John Schnee to FR, July 31, 1819, *DHID1*, 753–754; lease, FR and John Schnee, February 14, 1820, HSR, 2325. Private bankers were common in the early national period: Richard Sylla, "Forgotten Men of Money: Private Bankers in Early U. S. History," *Journal of Economic History* 36, no. 1 (March 1976): 173–188; Bodenhorn, *A History of Banking*, 177–185.

32. A rumor circulated in 1817 that Frederick was involved in counterfeiting: David Robb to JLB, October 22, 1817, *DHID1*, 412. Currency troubles (including

252   *2. Industry on the Frontier*

counterfeiting): John Caldwell to FR, July 22, 1815, *DHID1*, 133; JLB to FR June 26, 1816, *DHID1*, 230; DS to FR, April 18, 1818, *DHID1*, 502; AWC to FR, December 18, 1818, *DHID1*, 619–620; FR to JLB, January 19, 1819, *DHID1*, 629; FR to GR, January 22, 1819, *DHID1*, 631; [JLB] to Dent & Rearick, February 4, 1819, *DHID1*, 637; JLB to FR, February 4, 1819, *DHID1*, 640; AWC to FR, February 8, 1819, *DHID1*, 643; Samuel Campbell to FR, October 15, 1820, *DHID2*, 120–121; John Caldwell to FR, September 9, 1824, *HOTW*, 153–154; Daniel Grass to FR, October 8, 1824, *HOTW*, 202–203. Bank of Vincennes: Nathaniel Ewing to FR, November 24, 1815, *DHID1*, 159; FR to DS, March 1, 1816, *DHID1*, 194–195; Nathaniel Ewing to commissioners, March 17, 1817, *DHID1*, 315–316.

33. The branch banks at Posey and Gibson Counties (with which Harmonie overlapped) were both authorized $10,000 of capital stock. Frederick was named director of the Posey branch. Logan Esarey, "The First Indiana Banks," *Indiana Magazine of History* 6 (December 1910): 147, and *State Banking in Indiana*, 227; Arndt, *George Rapp's Harmony Society*, 178–179.

34. Murphy, *Other People's Money*, 81–83.

35. FR to Ferdinand Ernst, December 3, 1821, *DHID2*, 332.

36. The terms of the loan were ultimately beneficial to Harmony because it allowed Frederick to recoup $4,000 worth of worthless bank stock in exchange for a loan to the State of Indiana, while erasing some of the society's debt. This loan was more about recovering Harmony's losses from the failure of the disastrous Bank of Vincennes than it was an act of altruism. [FR] to Charles Battell, November 30, 1821, *DHID2*, 330–331. Other examples of institutional lending: Samuel Merrill to FR, October 4, 1823, *DHID2*, 691; [FR] to Samuel Merrill, October 25, 1823, *DHID2*, 701; William Hendricks to FR, December 19, 1823, *DHID2*, 754; Samuel Merrill to Jesse Merrill, January 25, 1824, *DHID2*, 783. The loan to the governor was for $1,000 at 10 percent interest: Jonathan Jennings to FR, August 12, 1822, *DHID2*, 439–440; [FR] to Jonathan Jennings, August 24, 1822, *DHID2*, 449–450.

37. The terms for this loan were not explicitly stated, but the loan was $5,000 and Indiana paid $734 interest on the loan, a sum that equates to just shy of 14.7 percent: Samuel Merrill to FR, October 4, 1823, *DHID2*, 691; [FR] to Samuel Merrill, October 25, 1823, *DHID2*, 701; *Journal of the Senate of the State of Indiana*, 9th session, 29, 34, 49, and 11th session, 40, 44; William Hendricks to FR, December 19, 1823, *DHID2*, 754; FR to Samuel Merrill, November 20, 1824, *HOTW*, 284; Samuel Merrill to FR, December 6, 1824, *HOTW*, 333; FR to Samuel Merrill, October 24, 1825, *HOTW*, 669; Samuel Merrill to FR, March 21, 1826, *EOTO*, 21–22.

38. The one exception seems to be a loan to the society's lead lawyer, Walter Forward. The fact that it occurred after Frederick was gone is probably not an

accident. After Frederick died, RLB recorded a loan of $1,000 during the Panic of 1837. He later refused a large loan to longtime society merchant/banker J. Solms. Walter Forward to GR, September 30, 1837, *GRYG*, 287–288; JS to GR, May 7, 1840, *GRYG*, 493–494; RLB to JS, February 18, 1846, *GRYG*, 911–912; JH to David Benzinger, July 13, 1846, *GRYG*, 984–985.

39. FR to Frederick Dent, November 4, 1824, *HOTW*, 250.

40. $20,000 equates to more than $580,000 (CPI) or $17.5 million (per capita GDP). Pittsburgh: John Snowden to FR, March 11, 1826, *EOTO*, 18. Wheeling requested $20,000 in 1826, and then $10,000 and $2,000 in 1830: John M. Snowden to [FR], March 11, 1826, *EOTO*, 18; correspondence between John McLure and FR, August–November 1830, *EOTO*, 524–525, 547; RLB to J. List, January 15, 1835, *GRYG*, 62.

41. Karl Arndt is convinced this policy derived from religious belief, particularly the Old Testament prohibitions on usury. While this explanation probably contains some truth, the Rapp correspondence does not support this as the sole, or primary, explanation: FR to Henry Jones, February 24, 1821, *DHID2*, 196–197; FR to Ferdinand Ernst, December 3, 1821, *DHID2*, 332.

42. Indiana made little progress during the years Harmony was located there. John Lauritz Larson, *Internal Improvement: National Public Works and the Promise of Popular Government in the Early United States* (Chapel Hill: University of North Carolina Press, 2001), 39–107, 204–217; Taylor, *The Transportation Revolution*, 34–36, 43–45, 63–67; Joseph Austin Durrenberger, *Turnpikes: A Study of Toll Road Movement in the Middle Atlantic States and Maryland* (Cos Cob, CT: John E. Edwards, 1968), 28–44, 144–152; J. L. Ringwalt, *Development of Transportation Systems in the United States* (Philadelphia: J. L. Ringwalt, 1888; repr., New York: Johnson Reprint Corporation, 1966), 23–27, 40–41.

43. The steam engine continued to plague Frederick well into fall 1816. GR to FR, November 29, 1814, *DHID1*, 77; DS to FR, December 6, 1815, *DHID1*, 164–165; John Arthurs to [FR], December 12, 1815, *DHID1*, 166; FR to Bean & Butler, January 5, 1816, *DHID1*, 176–177; FR to DS, February 1, 1816, *DHID1*, 182–185; [FR] to James Douglas, February 2, 1816, *DHID1*, 186–187; FR to William Chambers, February 3, 1816, *DHID1*, 188; FR to George Sutton, March 28, 1816, *DHID1*, 203–204; [FR] to DS, March 29, 1816, *DHID1*, 206–207; [FR] to John Arthurs, May 14, 1816, *DHID1*, 218; FR to DS, May 14, 1816, *DHID1*, 219–220; GR to FR, June 22, 1816, *DHID1*, 227; [FR] to DS, September 14, 1816, *DHID1*, 249; Robert Hamilton to FR, September 1816, *DHID1*, 253–254.

44. Bean & Butler to FR, February 9, 1816, *DHID1*, 189.

45. Detmar Basse to FR, April 22, 1816, *DHID1*, 211. Four to five weeks seems to have been standard for a letter from Harmonie to points in Pennsylvania: GH to FR, May 4, 1816, *DHID1*, 213; [JLB for FR] to John Bedford, July 3, [1817],

254   *2. Industry on the Frontier*

DHID1, 353; [FR] to DS, February 8, 1818, *DHID1*, 458–459; John Solms to FR, October 30, 1822, *DHID2*, 485–486.

46. [FR] to DS, June 9, 1817, *DHID1*, 338–339; William Smith to John Gray, undated, *DHID1*, 495; William Smith to Jonathan Meigs, April 17, 1818, *DHID1*, 498. Two postal carriers on the route between Harmonie and Corydon were fired for incompetence: William Smith to Johnathan Meigs Jr., undated, *DHID1*, 462. Frederick also complained about the St. Louis postmaster: [FR] to Tracy & Wahrendorff, April 12, 1822, *DHID2*, 382.

47. [FR] to Jonathan Jennings, December 14, 1822, *DHID2*, 510.

48. [FR] to Jonathan Jennings, December 14, 1822, *DHID2*, 511.

49. There was a total of forty-one delegates. Harmonie overlapped two counties (one of them Gibson) and was officially part of neighboring Posey County. Tuesday morning, June 11, 1816, *Journal of the Convention of the Indiana Territory*; Alexander Devin to GR, May 11, 1816, *DHID1*, 216–217. Constitutional conventions of the Old Northwest: Silvana R. Siddali, *Frontier Democracy: Constitutional Conventions in the Old Northwest* (New York: Cambridge University Press, 2016).

50. Wednesday morning, June 12, 1816, *Journal of the Convention of the Indiana Territory*. Receipt for exemption taxes: March 25, 1815, *DHID1*, 116; September 1, 1815, *DHID1*, 143–144; April 4, 1816, *DHID1*, 208.

51. Commissioners appointed, [June 7, 1820], *DHID2*, 62–63; FR to David Robb, December 9, 1820, *DHID2*, 159–160.

52. Donald Pitzer and Josephine Elliott, "New Harmony's First Utopians, 1814–1824," *Indiana Magazine of History* 75 (September 1979): 231, 242. Details of formerly enslaved persons are scarce in Harmony records, but Alexander Farkas testified to one family still living in Economy during his visit in 1831: Alexander Boloni Farkas, *Journey in North America*, trans. and ed. Theodore and Helen Benedek Schoenman (1834; repr., Philadelphia: American Philosophical Society, 1977), 161. A free family that almost came to Harmony under indenture but did not want to leave Kentucky: William Chambers to GR, January 15, 1816, *DHID1*, 179–180; FR to William Chambers, February 3, 1816, *DHID1*, 188; William Chambers to GR, January 25, 1817, *DHID1*, 302–303.

53. George Muller to FR, March 20, 1819, *DHID1*, 673.

54. Wednesday morning, June 19, 1816, *Journal of the Convention of the Indiana Territory*; Arndt, *George Rapp's Harmony Society*, 168–169.

55. As Andrew Shankman points out, some Whigs like Mathew Carey advocated for slavery's expansion: Andrew Shankman, "Capitalism, Slavery, and the New Epoch: Mathew Carey's 1819," in *Slavery's Capitalism: A New History of American Economic Development*, ed. Sven Beckert and Seth Rockman (Philadelphia: University of Pennsylvania Press, 2016), 244.

2. Industry on the Frontier 255

56. Mathew Carey, *The New Olive Branch* (Philadelphia: M. Carey & Son, 1820), 176. The most noteworthy description of Harmony, referenced by numerous publications, is John Melish, *Travels in the United States of America . . .* (Philadelphia: Thomas & George Palmer, 1812), 2:64–83, who relied in part on Fortescue Cuming, *Sketches of a Tour to the Western Country Through the States of Ohio and Kentucky* (Pittsburgh: Cramer, Spear & Eichbaum, 1810), 491–495. Melish visit: [FR] to Samuel Worchester, December 19, 1822, HSR, 2335. Other prominent accounts include those of Bernhard, Buckingham, Duclos, Farkas, Featherstonhaugh, Finch, Flower, Follen, Fordham, Herbert, Martineau, de Montulé, Maximilian, Passavant, Russell, Schoolcraft, von Schweinitz, Woods, and von Wrede (listed in the bibliography). The *Evangelical Magazine* and *Philanthropist* were two periodicals that were especially important in raising Harmony's profile in England.

57. Bodenhorn, *A History of Banking*, 88–90.

58. Pennsylvania itself grew in population from 602,365 (1800) to 2,311,786 (1850). U.S. Department of Commerce, *Historical Statistics of the United States*, Series A:1–3, 7; Series A:123–180, 13; Taylor, *The Transportation Revolution*, 250–300; Licht, *Industrializing America*, 46–73.

59. John Bedford to Christian Rapp, November 28, 1816, *DHID1*, 272. Bedford entered into business with Harmony the following year: [JLB for FR] to John Bedford, July 3, [1817], *DHID1*, 353.

60. "Harmony, Ind.," *Niles' Weekly Register*, September 7, 1822. Written queries: Constantine S. Rafinesque to Christopher Miller, January 16, 1818, *DHID1*, 450–454; Edward Page to Harmony, January 5, 1822, *DHID2*, 338–339; Cornelius C. Blatchly to FR, April 22, 1822, *DHID2*, 388–390; Samuel Worchester to FR, May 23, 1822, *DHID2*, 401–403; H. R. Parck to GR, January 8, 1827, *EOTO*, 92–93. Harmony's neighbors were also curious about the society, as more than two hundred of them visited the commune on July 4, 1817: GR to FR, July 5, 1817, *DHID1*, 356. The governor of the new state also visited Harmonie at least twice: JLB to FR, July 6, 1817, *DHID1*, 358; William Smith to FR, August 14, 1817, *DHID1*, 373.

61. Samuel Worcester to FR, 23, May 1822, *DHID2*, 402.

62. [FR] to Edward P. Page, March 7, 1822, *DHID2*, 363–364.

63. [FR] to Samuel Worchester, December 19, 1822, HSR, 2335.

64. [FR] to Samuel Worchester, December 19, 1822, HSR, 2335.

65. "Chief object": FR to Chester Chadwick, September 21, 1822, HSR, 2329. See also: [FR] to Samuel Worchester, December 19, 1822, HSR, 2335; RLB and John Reichert to the Royal District Office, Schorndorf, [November 1, 1822], *DHID2*, 491.

66. Outsiders commented that laborers worked long and hard at Harmony: Caroline Dale Snedeker, ed., *The Diaries of Donald MacDonald, 1824–1826*

(Indianapolis: Indiana Historical Society, 1942), 230; Herbert, *A Visit to the Colony of Harmony*, 3, 9.

67. [FR] to AWC, July 6, 1822, *DHID2*, 423.

68. Schoolcraft, *Travels*, 167; Snedeker, *The Diaries of Donald MacDonald*, 291. Also see William Blane, undated report, *DHID2*, 524.

69. Schoolcraft, *Travels*, 167–168.

70. Hiatt, *Diary of William Owen*, 76, 78; Snedeker, *The Diaries of Donald MacDonald*, 248; Bernhard, Duke of Saxe-Weimar-Eisenach, *Travels Through North America, During the Years 1825 and 1826*, vol. 2 (Philadelphia: Carey, Lea & Carey, 1828), 164; FR to Gertrude Rapp, January 11, 1825, *HOTW*, 404; Richard Wetzel, "J. C. Muller and W. C. Peters at Economy: A Reappraisal," *Communal Societies* 3 (1983): 158–174.

71. Melchizedek is one of the most mysterious characters in the Bible—referred to in Genesis 14:18, Psalm 110:4, and Hebrew 5:6 as a king/priest of Salem (in Canaan). Some Christians consider him a theophany—an incarnation of Christ prior to his New Testament ministry. [FR] to Samuel Worchester, December 19, 1822, *DHID2*, 513. Englishman William Blane called George a "Governor and Priest": William Blane, [December 1812], *DHID2*, 526; Snedeker, *The Diaries of Donald MacDonald*, 230.

72. Rüdiger Glaser, Iso Himmelsbach, and Annette Bösmeier, "Climate of Migration? How Climate Triggered Migration from Southwest Germany to North America During the 19th Century," *Climate of the Past* 13 (2017): 1573–1592.

73. Georg Friedrich Krimmel to the King of Württemberg, May 12 and 25, 1817, *DHID1*, 330–337. For more on emigration problems: Lord Bathurst to the Württemberg ambassador, June 21, 1817, *DHID1*, 340–341; Casimir Kurtz to [FR], July 25, 1817, *DHID1*, 369; Jacob Hofmann et al. to GH, February 12, 1818, *DHID1*, 463–464; Friedrich Schnabel to GH, February 24, 1818, *DHID1*, 473–474; Conrad Lamppert to Matheus Rein, [April 19, 1818], *DHID1*, 505–506; Casimir Kurtz to FR, April 20, 1818, *DHID1*, 506–507; Ann Reed to FR, April 25, 1818, *DHID1*, 508–509; Leonhard Worner to cousin in Harmony, undated, *DHID1*, 519–520; GH to FR, May 29, 1818, *DHID1*, 531–532; Boller & Solms to FR, May 30, 1818, *DHID1*, 532; Christian Schnabel et al. to FR, undated, *DHID1*, 588–589; Jacob Boller to FR, November 4, 1818, *DHID1*, 600–602.

74. More than two hundred died (including children) in one trip alone: Christian Friedrich Schnabel et al. to Johannes Schnabel, February 24, 1818, *DHID1*, 474–475; Jakob Weyhing to Matheus Rein, June 15, 1818, *DHID1*, 539–540; [FR to Ann Reed], June 25, 1818, *DHID1*, 541–542. Not all merchants were nefarious. For example, the prominent Philadelphia merchant Henry Pratt shows up in the Harmony emigration indenture records, as does Philip Mowry, a well-known "old light" Presbyterian. Bond, George Lohrer, and Henry Pratt, May 24, 1806,

2. Industry on the Frontier 257

HSR, 2318. The bond was $94, or $2,150 (CPI) or $67,000 (per capita GDP). Bond, William Nesbit and Hugh Nesbit, and Philip Mowry, July 29, 1805, HSR, 2318 (for $103.12). Pratt and Mowry: John W. Jordan, ed., *Colonial and Revolutionary Families of Pennsylvania* (New York: Lewis Publishing Company, 1911), 3:1185, 1533.

75. Georg Friedrich Krimmel to the King of Württemberg, May 12, 1817, *DHID1*, 333.

76. New members lived in Harmony under a probationary status for several months to one year before earning permission to sign the Articles of Agreement, while children were included in their membership until age twenty-one (when they signed for themselves). Arndt, *George Rapp's Harmony Society*, 198. English, *Demographic Directory*, 195–210.

77. J. S. Buckingham, *The Eastern and Western States of America* (London: Fisher, Son, & Co., 1843), 2:218. Also see John Woods, *Two Years' Residence in the Settlement on the English Prairie in the Illinois Country, United States* (London: A. & R. Spottiswoode, 1829), 238, 242; Herbert, *A Visit to the Colony of Harmony*, 9. Frederick confirms that German (Swabian) is the only spoken language: FR to Chester Chadwick, September 28, 1822, HSR, 2329.

78. "Best": Elias Pym Fordham, *Personal Narrative of Travels in Virginia, Maryland, Pennsylvania, Ohio, Indiana, Kentucky...*, ed. Frederic Austin Ogg (Cleveland, OH: Arthur H. Clark Company, 1906), 207. Textiles: Jos. & R. Woods to FR, July 7, 1819, *DHID1*, 737.

79. William Blane, undated report, *DHID2*, 523–528. Aesthetics: Tamara Plakins Thornton, "Capitalist Aesthetics: Americans Look at the London and Liverpool Docks," in *Capitalism Takes Command: The Social Transformation of Nineteenth-Century America*, ed. Michael Zakim and Gary J. Kornblith (Chicago: University of Chicago Press, 2012), 169–198. This is one crack in the society's communalism: inequality of dwelling places. Frederick and some of the previously wealthy members of Harmony lived in nicer homes than those of the ordinary members: FR 1824 list, *HOTW*, 372–373. How this dynamic played out within Harmony is not clear. Perhaps the hierarchical nature of early nineteenth-century Württemberg conditioned Harmonists to accept the discrepancy. Old Economy Village explains this discrepancy by comparing the Rapps to other leaders of their era, concluding they were living simply in comparison and that the other inhabitants of Harmonie/Economy expected their leaders to have a higher standard of living. Tour of Old Economy Village, June 8, 2017.

80. Hiatt, *Diary of William Owen*, 72–73. The village was estimated at six hundred yards long and four to five hundred yards wide in 1824: Snedeker, *The Diaries of Donald MacDonald*, 245–246.

81. Hiatt, *Diary of William Owen,* 77.

82. Snedeker, *The Diaries of Donald MacDonald,* 245.

83. The lone exception is the testimony of Donald MacDonald, a companion of Robert Owen. He did not think the Harmony machines were very up-to-date. He visited in 1824, after much of the society left for Economy and Frederick stopped seeking upgrades to the Harmonie operations. It is also possible that he was comparing the society's technology to that available in Britain. In general, he was the most critical visitor to write an account of Harmonie. Snedeker, *The Diaries of Donald MacDonald,* 247.

84. Ferdinand Ernst, "Visit to Harmonie on the Wabash," July 18, 1819, *DHID1,* 744. The society also operated a horse-powered cotton gin: Hiatt, *Diary of William Owen,* 88.

85. A. W. Sorgenfrey to FR, March 17, 1822, *DHID2,* 372–373.

86. The looms were damaged during shipping and erroneously sent first to Lexington, Kentucky: Boller & Solms to FR, July 16, 1818, *DHID1,* 550–551; Jacob Boller to FR, September 28, 1818, *DHID1,* 575–576; [JLB] to Vernon & Blake, February 13, 1819, *DHID1,* 646; James Berthoud & Son to FR, March 19, 1819, *DHID1,* 670; [FR] to Jacob Boller, May 14, 1819, *DHID1,* 707–708. Steamboat: [FR] to DS, August 22, 1818, *DHID1,* 561–562; AWC to FR, October 10, 1818, *DHID1,* 580–581; AWC to FR, October 22, 1818, *DHID1,* 582; [FR] to Fetter & Hughes, October 31, 1818, *DHID1,* 597; Thomas Boggs to FR, June 11, 1819, *DHID1,* 718–719.

87. Ferdinand Ernst, "Visit to Harmonie on the Wabash," July 18, 1819, *DHID1,* 745. FR to George Muller, May 14, 1819, *DHID1,* 708–709.

88. Jonathan Jennings to FR, October 4, 1821, *DHID2,* 298. For an overview of manufacturing during the society's stint in Indiana: Memorandum of Orders, 1812–1823, HSR, 2538.

89. Historians have demonstrated that the Panic of 1819 was far too complex to simply scapegoat the Second Bank of the United States. See essays in the *Journal of the Early Republic* 40, no. 4 (Winter 2020): 665–739; Andrew Browning, *The Panic of 1819: the First Great Depression* (Columbia: University of Missouri Press, 2019); Scott Reynolds Nelson, *A Nation of Deadbeats: An Uncommon History of America's Financial Disasters* (New York: Alfred A Knopf, 2012), 61–78; Murphy, *Other People's Money,* 85–88; Charles Sellers, *The Market Revolution: Jacksonian America, 1815–1846* (New York: Oxford University Press, 1991), 131–139; Daniel Walker Howe, *What Hath God Wrought: The Transformation of America, 1815–1848* (New York: Oxford University Press, 2007), 142–147; John Lauritz Larson, *The Market Revolution in America* (New York: Cambridge University Press, 2010), 39–45.

90. The bank closed in 1821. Joseph Lockwood to RLB, 28 May 28, 1820, *DHID2,* 59; [FR] to JDH, June 17, [1820], *DHID2,* 66; JDH to FR, June 20, 1820, *DHID2,*

2. Industry on the Frontier 259

67–68; Abijah Bayless to FR, January 24, 1821, *DHID2*, 183. Karl J. R. Arndt deserves the credit for first discovering Frederick's role in the recovery of debts to the bank: correspondence, May–July 1821, *DHID1*, 225–226, 236–237, 239–241, 245–246; E. nos. 5–7, April 5, May 4, 22, 1821, *American State Papers: Finance* 3:738–739.

91. The next year, Harmony faced the opposite problem as two days of "incessant hard rain" and flooding submerged the society's fields, destroyed bridges, and made roads unpassable: [FR] to DS, October 24, 1822, HSR, 2329. Low water levels: [FR] to DS, November 30, 1820, *DHID2*, 154; RLB to FR, January 27, 1821, *DHID2*, 185–186. Currency issues: FR to Henry Jones, February 24, 1821, *DHID2*, 196–197; FR to DS, June 2, 1821, *DHID2*, 230–231.

92. Murphy, *Other People's Money*, 85.

93. Taylor, *The Transportation Revolution*, 10–14. Jonathan Levy calls this the emergence of an "industrial society": Levy, *Ages of American Capitalism*, 164–175.

94. Taylor, *The Transportation Revolution*, 132–144, 158–160; Ringwalt, *Development of Transportation Systems in the United States*, 27–34.

95. Taylor, *The Transportation Revolution*, 149–152; Ringwalt, *Development of Transportation Systems in the United States*, 45–48.

96. Murphy, *Other People's Money*, 90–91. Banknotes had to be redeemed at the bank of issue, thus Rapp & Associates had agents redeem notes and ship the specie back to Harmonie. Obviously, this was unwieldly and inefficient, to say nothing of the difficulty of redeeming the notes of rural banks. Specie transport cost/distance: Knodell, *The Second Bank of the U.S.*, 70, 78–79.

97. Bartering became common as a response to the currency freeze: [FR] to Abraham Ziegler, October 27, 1821, *DHID2*, 311–312. Low prices: William Barber & Co. to FR, May 4, 1818, *DHID1*, 511–512; William Barber & Co. to FR, May 21, 1818, *DHID1*, 526–527; Kummer & Dietsch to FR, April 28, 1819, *DHID1*, 689–690; [FR] to Jacob Boller, May 14, 1819, *DHID1*, 707–708; FR to George Muller, May 14, 1819, *DHID1*, 708–709; [FR] to James Old & Co., July 1, 1819, *DHID1*, 732–733. Currency problems: Chillion Lichtenberger to FR, November 2, 1818, *DHID1*, 598; AWC to FR, December 18, 1818, *DHID1*, 620; [FR] to DS, December 19, 1818, *DHID1*, 621–622; [FR] to Christopher Hobson, December 30, 1818, *DHID1*, 625–626; Abraham Ziegler and John Ziegler to FR et al., January 25, 1819, *DHID1*, 631–632; [JLB] to Dent & Rearick, February 4, 1819, *DHID1*, 636–637; JLB to FR, February 4, 1819, *DHID1*, 639–640; AWC to FR, February 8, 1819, *DHID1*, 642–643; [RLB] to AWC, March 6, 1819, *DHID1*, 663–664; FR to JDH, June 7, 1819, *DHID1*, 716–717; [FR] to James Old & Co., August 12, 1819, *DHID1*, 761; AWC to FR, August 30, 1819, *DHID1*, 766; John Jacob Hutt to FR, undated, *DHID1*, 776–777; JLB to FR, September 20, 1820, *DHID2*, 105–106; [FR] to James Old & Co., October 4, 1820, *DHID2*, 112.

98. By January 1823, Rapp & Associates boasted three cotton-spinning machines (360 spindles total), with a fourth machine under construction. FR to RLB and John Reichert, January 10, 1823, *DHID2*, 531. Despite all the technology and efficiency, it still took two to three months to manufacture wool textiles. [FR] to Benjamin Blythe, January 25, 1822, *DHID2*, 347; 1820 report, [October 24, 1820], *DHID2*, 130–136.

99. Frederick wrote, "every one has Grain to spare"—this despite the miserable economic climate of the West in 1821: [FR] to DS, October 20, 1821, *DHID2*, 306.

100. [FR] to AWC, March 30, 1820, *DHID2*, 43.

101. Dexter: Jane Kamensky, *The Exchange Artist: A Tale of High-Flying Speculation and America's First Banking Collapse* (New York: Viking Press, 2008). See also Mihm, *A Nation of Counterfeiters*; Edward Balleisen, *Navigating Failure: Bankruptcy and Commercial Society in Antebellum America* (Chapel Hill: University of North Carolina Press, 2001); Scott A. Sandage, *Born Losers: A History of Failure in America* (Cambridge, MA: Harvard University Press, 2005); Jonathan Levy, *Freaks of Fortune: The Emerging World of Capitalism and Risk in America* (Cambridge, MA: Harvard University Press, 2012).

102. W. Maddox to JDH, November 5, 1817, *DHID1*, 413–414. Harmony's block voting was a consistent complaint, even after the society moved back to western Pennsylvania. Petition, [January 1818], *DHID1*, 440–442; FR to JDH, November 10, 1825, *HOTW*, 701–702; "George Rapp's Economy," *Western Journal*, October 13, 1827, *EOTO*, 181–182; FR to Isaac Blackford, January 8, 1828, HSR, 2329; *Beaver Republican*, November 19 and 29, 1829, *EOTO*, 457–458, 459–460. JS to FR, July 16, 1830, *EOTO*, 519–520; *Beaver Argus*, October 28, 1831, *EOTO*, 630–631.

103. Charles Battell to FR, January 23, 1820, *DHID2*, 9–10; Charles Battell to FR, January 24, 1820, *DHID2*, 11–12; John Dunbar to FR, January 25, 1820, *DHID2*, 12–13; Charles Battell to FR, February 8, 1820, *DHID2*, 19–20.

104. Posey County Circuit Court indictment, March 1820, *DHID2*, 44. Appeal of indictment: Friedrich Eckensperger, [June 1820], *DHID2*, 75–76; Posey County Grand Jury, [June 1820], *DHID2*, 77–78; FR to JLB, [October] 14, 1820, *DHID2*, 118–119.

105. Lockwood, *The New Harmony Communities*, 32; RLB to JLB, October 22, 1820, *DHID2*, 125. For the prevalence of indenture: HSR, 2318 (Legal File, Bonds).

106. Commentary, *DHID2*, 11.

107. Appeals indictment, June 1820, *DHID2*, 75–76.

108. FR to JLB, September [October] 14, 1820, *DHID2*, 118–119.

109. William Blane, undated report, *DHID2*, 527. Also, Lockwood, *The New Harmony Communities*, 38.

2. *Industry on the Frontier* 261

110. Mills: [FR] to Frederick Haymaker, March 24, (no year), *DHID1*, 319–320; *Niles' Weekly Register*, September 6, 1817, *DHID1*, 386; GR to FR, [September 30, 1817], *DHID1*, 398. Stores: account of the store at Vincennes, IN (August 1823–September 1831), and store at Shawneetown, IL (October– May 1828), HSR, 2499; FR and JDH, agreement, undated, *DHID2*, 662–663; John Day to FR, August 26, 1823, *DHID2*, 663–664; JLB to FR, October 24, 1823, *DHID2*, 699–700; JLB to FR, October 31, 1823, *DHID2*, 705–708. Success of Vincennes store: FR to JDH, November 1, 1823, *DHID2*, 708–709; JDH to FR, November 4, 1823, *DHID2*, 712; FR and John Caldwell, agreement, undated, *DHID2*, 763–765.

111. John Woolverton to FR, January 9, 1824, *DHID2*, 775–776; JDH to FR, January 12, 1824, *DHID2*, 776–777; FR to JLB, January 18, 1824, *DHID2*, 779–780; Robert Payne to FR, undated, *DHID2*, 876; Wilson Lagow to FR, October 4, 1825, *HOTW*, 650–651.

112. Tavern: Elisha Harrison to FR, December 24, 1816, *DHID1*, 276. Distillery: Peter Moseley to JLB, July 6, 1817, *DHID1*, 358–359. The patent holder also visited Harmonie in 1817, but the Rapps ignored him: William Smith to FR, July 7, 1817, *DHID1*, 363; Peter Mosely to JLB, August 18, 1817, *DHID1*, 378–379.

113. Hiatt, *The Diary of William Owen*, 106.

114. Some individuals had multiple leases with Rapp. Lease, GRA and Robert Cartwright, January 13, 1816, Legal File, Leases, 1816–1904, HSR, 2324. Only one lease is listed here, but for hundreds more, see Legal File, Leases (1816–1904), HSR, 2324–2325. Income from agricultural leasing was not an important part of income after the move to Economy, reflective of an increased emphasis on manufacturing. General details on leasing: Snedeker, *The Diaries of MacDonald*, 244–245; FR to Thomas Miller, July 20, 1824, *HOTW*, 81; Hiatt, *Diary of William Owen*, 107–108. Farms during the Indiana years (including diagrams of individual plots): Income and Outlay Book for Farms, 1815–1825, and Householder Book, 1821–1854, HSR, 2538 (contains information on export of horses, cattle, sheep, and pigs).

115. Charles Graze to FR, December 29, 1823, *DHID2*, 761–762.

116. Lockwood, *The New Harmony Communities*, 27–32, 38; Cannon: George Rapp's 1823 diary, excerpted in Arndt, *George Rapp's Harmony Society*, 248.

117. Liverpool: William Barber to FR, September 8, 1817, *DHID1*, 388–390; William Barber to FR, December 15, 1817, *DHID1*, 424–426. New Orleans: James Old to FR, December 9, 1817, *DHID1*, 421–423; James Stewart and John Trusdell, December 17, 1817, *DHID1*, 430–431; George Muller to FR, January 16, 1820, *DHID2*, 7–8; FR to JLB, [October 14], 1820, *DHID2*, 118–119.

118. GR to FR, September 23, 1824, *HOTW*, 181.

119. J. D. Hay to JLB, June 1, 1824, *HOTW*, 26; Scoby Stewart to RLB, July 13, 1824, *HOTW*, 74–75; *Gazette* (Indianapolis), May 4, 1825, *HOTW*, 558.

3. REPUBLICAN INDUSTRY

1. Robert Owen to GR, August 4, 1820, *DHID2*, 89–90; J. F. C. Harrison, *Robert Owen and the Owenites in Britain and America: The Quest for the New Moral World* (New York: Charles Scribner's Sons, 1969).
2. FR to RLB and John Reichert, January 10, 1823, *DHID2*, 532.
3. Robert Owen to GR, August 4, 1820, *DHID2*, 89.
4. Robert Owen, "A Declaration of Mental Independence," *The New Harmony Gazette* 1, no. 42 (July 12, 1826): 330.
5. Robert Dale Owen, *Threading My Way* (New York: G. W. Carleton & Co., 1874), 240.
6. Elizabeth Johnson, "A Welcome Attack on American Values: How the Doctrines of Robert Owen Attracted American Society," *Constructing the Past* 8, no. 1 (2007): 87–106. Meanwhile, one of Frederick's agents, J. Solms, mused that Harmonie would instead make a good location for Mordecai Noah's plan to gather all Jews and establish a new Zion: JS to FR, 28 June 28, 1824, *HOTW*, 57–58.
7. Heat: Alexander Boloni Farkas, *Journey in North America*, trans. and ed. Theodore and Helen Benedek Schoenman (1834; repr., Philadelphia: American Philosophical Society, 1977), 159. Frederick did not think the second site was any better for viniculture: FR to Gottlieb Reichert, August 2, 1821, *DHID2*, 264. Nearly twenty years later, RLB claimed antagonistic neighbors were also part of the decision to move again: John Finch, "Notes of Travel in the United States: Letters VI–XI," *New Moral World: Gazette of the Rational Society* 5, nos. 34–39 (February 17–March 23, 1844): 273.
8. GR to FR, April 8, 1824, *DHID2*, 837–838.
9. Quote: GR to FR, December 6, 1824, *HOTW*, 331. As the Owen party journeyed to Harmonie, two of Robert's party recorded that the public's general suspicion was that the society was moving back east because Harmonie was "unhealthy" land: Caroline Dale Snedeker, ed., *The Diaries of Donald MacDonald, 1824–1826* (Indianapolis: Indiana Historical Society, 1942), 231; Joel W. Hiatt, ed., *Diary of William Owen, from November 10, 1824 to April 20, 1825* (Indianapolis: Bobbs-Merrill Company, 1906; repr., New York: Augustus M. Kelley, 1973), 56.
10. A site near Wheeling, Ohio, was the first site Frederick pursued. [FR] to Noah Zane, January 3, 1824, *DHID2*, 769–770; Noah Zane to FR, January 28, 1828, *DHID2*, 786; DS to FR, February 16, 1824, *DHID2*, 793–794; RLB journal,

[February to June 1824], *DHID2*, 802–805; GR to FR, March 6, 1824, *DHID2*, 812–813; FR to Gertrude Rapp, March 15, 1824, *DHID2*, 817–819; DS to FR, March 27, 1824, *DHID2*, 826–828; DS to FR, April 7, 1824, *DHID2*, 834–836; Archibald Woods to FR, [May 6, 1824], *DHID2*, 869–870; John McClure to FR, May 8, 1824, *DHID2*, 870.

11. Journal of RLB, [February to June, 1824], *DHID2*, 802–805; GR to FR, March 6, 1824, *DHID2*, 812–813; FR and James Blaine, agreement, May 4, 1824, *HOTW*, 5–7; deed, N. Biddle to FR, July 9, 1824, HSR, 2322. As he did at the previous two sites, Frederick continued purchasing additional land: Legal File, Deeds (1823–1949) HSR, 2322.

12. Sale of Harmonie: FR to Richard Flower, April 15, 1824, *DHID2*, 856–857; Richard Flower to FR, April 19, 1824, *DHID2*, 857–858; [FR] to Richard Flower, April 28, 1824, *DHID2*, 865–866; Richard Flower to FR, May 10, 1824, *DHID2*, 870–871; FR draft advertisement, undated, *DHID2*, 871–872; FR to JS, May 11, 1824, *DHID2*, 872–874.

13. Howard Bodenhorn, *State Banking in Early America: A New Economic History* (New York: Oxford University Press, 2003), 147; John Lauritz Larson, *Internal Improvement: National Public Works and the Promise of Popular Government in the Early United States* (Chapel Hill: University of North Carolina Press, 2001), 80–87, 195–224.

14. Bodenhorn, *State Banking*, 227–228; Larson, *Internal Improvement*, 225–255; George Rogers Taylor, *The Transportation Revolution, 1815–1860* (New York: Rineheart, 1951), 52.

15. Donald C. Jackson, "Roads Most Traveled: Turnpikes in Southeastern Pennsylvania in the Early Republic," in *Early American Technology: Making and Doing Things from the Colonial Era to 1850*, ed. Judith A. McGraw (Chapel Hill: University of North Carolina Press, 1994), 199; Taylor, *The Transportation Revolution*, 15–31; Joseph Austin Durrenberger, *Turnpikes: A Study of Toll Road Movement in the Middle Atlantic States and Maryland* (Cos Cob, CT: John E. Edwards, 1968), 45–58.

16. *Plough Boy* log, [May–June 1824], *DHID2*, 906–915; *Niles Weekly Register*, October 8, 1825.

17. Contract with *Bolivar*, May 8, 1825, *HOTW*, 548–550.

18. Quote: GR to FR, October 17, 1824, *HOTW*, 229. AWC to FR, December 2, 1824, *HOTW*, 305–307. Frederick was intimately involved with nearly every detail of the steamboat's construction: A. Way to FR, June 16, 1824, *HOTW*, 39–40; H. M. Shreve to FR, June 21, 1824, *HOTW*, 44–45; Stephen Phillips to FR, June 23, 1824, *HOTW*, 46–47; A. Way to FR, July 29, 1824, *HOTW*, 89–91; JLB to FR, August 1, 1824, *HOTW*, 96; FR to AWC, September 11, 1824, *HOTW*, 157; JLB to FR, September 12, 1824, *HOTW*, 166; FR to JLB, September 25, 1824, *HOTW*,

188–189; P. Anderson to JLB, October 2, 1824, *HOTW*, 201; JLB to FR, October 10, 1824, *HOTW*, 213–215; FR to AWC, October 16, 1824, *HOTW*, 216; AWC to FR, October 18, 1824, *HOTW*, 230–231; AWC to FR, November 10, 1824, *HOTW*, 266–268; GR to FR, November 28, 1824, *HOTW*, 286–292; I. & W. Stewart to FR, February 23, 1825, *HOTW*, 449–451.

19. James Way to FR, June 15, 1825, *HOTW*, 567. The "Lower Waters" are usually defined as the Mississippi River's junction with the Ohio River to the Gulf of Mexico. Francis Erwin [Irwin] to FR, March 8, 1825, *HOTW*, 468–469. *William Penn* and *Pittsburgh & Wheeling Packet* ledgers (1825–1828), HSR, 2499.

20. GR to FR, February 1, 1825, *HOTW*, 434; GR to FR, March 18, 1825, *HOTW*, 480. Interestingly, Captain Henry Shreve (legendary steamboat captain—for whom Shreveport, Louisiana, is named) disapproved of the *William Penn*'s engineer: Paul Anderson to FR, February 25, 1825, *HOTW*, 452.

21. I. & W. Stewart to FR, March 9, 1825, *HOTW*, 469–470; FR to John Caldwell, March 10, 1825, *HOTW*, 472–473; FR to I. & W. Stewart, March 18, 1825, *HOTW*, 484–485; Jacob Beckwith to FR, March 19, 1825, *HOTW*, 486; Conrad Feucht to FR, March 24, 1825, *HOTW*, 489–491; GR to FR, March 7–31, 1825, *HOTW*, 505; contract with *Velocipede*, May 2, 1825, *HOTW*, 539–540.

22. I. & W. Stewart to FR, September 6, 1825, *HOTW*, 635; FR to I. & W. Stewart, October 10, 1825, *HOTW*, 653–654.

23. George Rapp, *Thoughts on the Destiny of Man, Particularly with Reference to the Present Times* (New Harmony, IN: Harmonie Society Press, 1824), 63–64. Emphasis in the original.

24. Rapp, 63–64.

25. FR to Richard Flower, November 4, 1824, *HOTW*, 252.

26. GR to FR, December 5, 1824, *HOTW*, 322. Upon further reflection, George would express severe criticism to Frederick regarding Owen's atheistic socialist project and philosophies: GR to FR, 18 January 1825, *HOTW*, 418.

27. Hiatt, *Diary of William Owen*, 53.

28. The $150,000 figure equates to $4.2 million (CPI) or $4.2 billion (GDP). Agreements: Robert Owen and FR, January 3, April 21 and 26, 1825, *HOTW*, 377–379, 529–532, 535–537. Deed to New Harmony, December 10, 1825, *HOTW*, 749–754; Hiatt, *Diary of William Owen*, 70–93; Snedeker, *The Diaries of Donald MacDonald*, 244–265; Owen, *Threading My Way*, 241. The Rapps subsequently sold off smaller tracts over the next few years: deeds, February 21, November 17, 1830, April 10, 1837, HSR, 2322. One tract that New Harmony sold back to GR was a burial ground, which they returned to Harmony for $600 in 1846: deed, Vaux Rector, Lyman Stickery, Michael Braddock et. al. to GRA, August 20, 1846, HSR, 2322.

29. Agreement, Robert Owen and FR, January 3, 1825, *HOTW*, 378.

3. Republican Industry

30. Snedeker, *The Diaries of Donald MacDonald*, 293. The sinking of the steamboat *Mechanic*, carrying General Lafayette on his grand American tour, delayed this final trip of Harmonists to Economy: "Loss of the Mechanic," *Richmond Enquirer*, May 31, 1825, 4; Isaac & Willis Stewart to FR, May 14, 1825, *HOTW*, 553–554. More humorously, the Harmonists' music and singing brought people to the riverbank expecting to witness Lafayette's passing, only to disappointedly learn it was the German society: *Gazette* (Indianapolis), May 24, 1825, *HOTW*, 558.

31. Editorial commentary, *HOTW*, xiii.

32. FR to Isaac & Willis Stewart, July 8, 1824, *HOTW*, 72–73; Conrad Feucht to FR, July 11, 1824, *HOTW*, 73; FR to Isaac & Willis Stewart, July 15, 1824, *HOTW*, 75–76; Isaac & Willis Stewart to FR, July 30, 1824, *HOTW*, 92–93; FR to AWC, July 30, 1824, *HOTW*, 93; FR to E. L. Blaine, August 13, 1824, *HOTW*, 110; FR to I. & W. Stewart, August 20, 1824, *HOTW*, 129–130; JLB to FR, September 25, 1824, *HOTW*, 184; FR to JLB, September 25, 1824, *HOTW*, 189; FR to Isaac & Willis Stewart, September 26, 1824, *HOTW*, 190–191; FR to AWC, September 26, 1824, *HOTW*, 194–195; FR to I. & W. Stewart, October 9, 1824, *HOTW*, 205; AWC to FR, April 8, 1825, *HOTW*, 516–517. Arndt's commentary in the documentary record first brought this currency issue to my attention: *HOTW*, 60, 106. In 2021 figures, $2,000 is equivalent to over $56,000 (CPI), so these were large sums. Frederick was also aggressive in trying to secure inheritances (of current Harmony members) in Württemberg to cover building expenses: FR to J. M. Scheidler, August 13, 1824, *HOTW*, 106–107.

33. Arndt speculates that George was annoyed at preaching to a smaller community and that those remaining behind in Harmonie enjoyed their freedom from autocratic George. I do not have reason to doubt Arndt's judgment, but have not found any concrete evidence to support this: *HOTW*, 366–367.

34. Robert Owen's son William described JLB's role as interpreter since his command of English was very good—especially compared to GR. Hiatt, *Diary of William Owen*, 52; Snedeker, *The Diaries of Donald MacDonald*, 230–231; *HOTW*, 315.

35. Quote: GR to FR, October 29, 1824, *HOTW*, 236 (Arndt theorizes that no replies to this letter exist because George censored the mail and routinely destroyed letters: *HOTW*, 233); GR to FR, November 15, 1824, *HOTW*, 281–282; GR to FR, December 31, 1824, *HOTW*, 365.

36. Editorial commentary, *HOTW*, 239–240. Again, $2,000 was roughly equal to over $56,000. GR to FR, November 4, 1824, *HOTW*, 247–249; GR to FR, November 8, 1824, *HOTW*, 258–263; GR to FR, December 1, 1824, *HOTW*, 299.

37. Karl J. R. Arndt, "The Pittsburgh Meeting of General Lafayette, GR, and Frances Wright: Prelude to Frances Wright's Nashoba," *Western Pennsylvania Historical Magazine* 62, no. 3 (July 1979): 281–300, http://journals.psu.edu/wph/article/view/3608/3439. Sean Wilentz stresses the important impact freethinkers such as Owen and Wright had on the burgeoning labor movement in America: Sean Wilentz, *Chants Democratic: New York City and the Rise of the American Working Class, 1788–1850* (New York: Oxford University Press, 1986). For Wright and her ideology: Christopher Grasso, *Skepticism and American Faith: From the Revolution to the Civil War* (New York: Oxford University Press, 2018), 279–293.

38. Gertrude Rapp to Rosina Rapp, March 23, 1825, *HOTW*, 488–489; Hiatt, *Diary of William Owen*, 128; Snedeker, *The Diaries of Donald MacDonald*, 289; Karl J. R. Arndt, *George Rapp's Harmony Society, 1785–1847* (Philadelphia: University of Pennsylvania Press, 1965), 298.

39. Frances Wright to JLB, May 31, 1825, *HOTW*, 560–561; JLB to Frances Wright, [June 1], 1825, *HOTW*, 561; Frances Wright to FR, June 7, 1825, *HOTW*, 562; Frances Wright to FR, August 16, 1825, *HOTW*, 618; FR to George Flower, December 15, 1825, *HOTW*, 58; RLB to FR, December 15, 1825, *HOTW*, 759–762; George Flower to FR, March 4, 1826, *EOTO*, 17–18; FR to J. Richardson, January 20, 1827, *EOTO*, 95; Frances Wright, *Biography, Notes and Political Letters of Frances Wright D'Arusmont*, no. 1 (New York: J. Windt, 1844), 25–28; Arndt, "The Pittsburgh Meeting of General Lafayette, GR, and Frances Wright"; J. D. Hay to FR, September 27, 1825, *HOTW*, 648; George Flower to FR, October 24, 1825, *HOTW*, 669–671; FR to Frances Wright, February 15, 1827, *EOTO*, 120–121; Frances Wright receipt, May 8, 1828, *EOTO*, 322. See also: Cheryl Coulthard, "Frances Wright's Nashoba: Seeking a Utopian Solution to the Problem of Slavery," *Communal Societies* 39, no. 2 (2019): 58–74.

40. For example, the subject of chapter 4, Josiah Bissell Jr., loathed outspoken freethinkers and secularists such as Wright (particularly in light of her gender and liberal sexuality).

41. This was contrary to the official line that the "society never . . . engaged in speculation, for the object of making money." RLB to Israel Rupp, July 24, 1847, *GRYG*, 1069.

42. Directories refer to Solms as "John" until 1828, then as "Joseph." In the early 1830s he was director of Mechanic's Bank; by 1835, president of Moyamensing Bank. Robert Desilver, *The Philadelphia Index, or Directory, for 1823* (Philadelphia: Desilver, 1823); *Desilver's Philadelphia Directory and Stranger's Guide, for 1828* (Philadelphia: Desilver, 1828); *Desilver's Philadelphia Directory and Stranger's Guide, for 1835 & 36* (Philadelphia: Desilver, 1835).

43. This equates to more than $560,000 (CPI). JS to FR, August 22, 1825, *HOTW*, 619–621; JS to FR, September 2, 4, and 5, 1825, *HOTW*, 633–635; JS to FR, September 12, 1825, *HOTW*, 637–640; JS to FR, September 20, 1825, *HOTW*, 645–647; JS to FR, October 15, 1825, *HOTW*, 656–657; JS to FR, October 27, 1825, *HOTW*, 674–677; JS to FR, November 5, 1825, *HOTW*, 693–694; FR to RLB, November 10, 1825, *HOTW*, 697–700; FR to RLB, November 21, 1825, *HOTW*, 719–722; FR to RLB, November 29, 1825, *HOTW*, 728–729.

44. In 1831, Alexander Farkas claimed Harmony was worth $2 million, although this seems a wild exaggeration, and it is unclear where the estimate came from. Farkas, *Journey*, 161. By 1833, the society's net worth was more accurately self-assessed at $209,734, which equates to $7 million (CPI): Harmony assessment, 1833, *EOTO*, 835–837. By 1840, the society's net worth was estimated at $500,000, which equates to more than $13 million (CPI): J. S. Buckingham, *The Eastern and Western States of America* (London: Fisher, Son, & Co., 1843), 2:213.

45. GR to FR, December 13, 1824, *HOTW*, 338–339.

46. Frederick arrived at Economy on May 17, 1825. Unfortunately, although many Economy buildings have survived to the present day, none of the factories remain. Contract between FR and Mark Stackhouse, May 24,1825, *HOTW*, 556; RLB to JDH and John Caldwell, May 25, 1825, *HOTW*, 559.

47. C. H. Orth to FR, June 19, 1825, *HOTW*, 571; contract between FR and March Stackhouse, October 28, 1825, *HOTW*, 677; Bernhard, Duke of Saxe-Weimar-Eisenach, *Travels Through North America, During the Years 1825 and 1826* (Philadelphia: Carey, Lea & Carey, 1828), 2:162.

48. FR to JDH, December 2, 1825, *HOTW*, 734; FR to John Caldwell, December 16, 1825, *HOTW*, 762–763.

49. One hundred fifty persons/2,500 spindles: FR to Carl Basse, October 1, 1827, *EOTO*, 178. Seven hundred fifty persons: "The Harmonists," *National Gazette*, October 9, 1827, *EOTO*, 180–181. Profit: Farkas, *Journey*, 159. Women were the primary operators of the cotton factory: Ludwig Braun report, May 2, 1830, *EOTO*, 501–502.

50. Farkas, *Journey*, 160–161; JH/GR to RLB, March 18, 1839, *GRYG*, 390–391.

51. "Culture of Silk," *Niles' Weekly Register* 39 (August 14, 1830): 441.

52. FR to John Gilmore, March 26, 1830, *EOTO*, 489; Gideon Smith to FR, May 29, 1830, *EOTO*, 509–510; Daniel Rose to FR, August 19, 1830, *EOTO*, 523; FR to Gertrude Rapp, September 19, 1830, *EOTO*, 532–534; FR to Guilford Coleman, October 21, 1830, *EOTO*, 541; Levi Price to FR, December 23, 1830, *EOTO*, 554–555; RLB to John Clarke, January 22, 1836, *GRYG*, 178–179; G. Smith to RLB, December 14, 1837, *GRYG*, 305–306; Harmony Society to N. E. Chaffee, October 18, 1838, *GRYG*, 367; Gideon Smith to RLB, December 14, 1839, *GRYG*,

413–414; GR to L. Y. Atkins, January 21, 1840, *GRYG*, 439; H. A. Redfield to GR, February 10, 1841, *GRYG*, 536.

53. Friedrich List visit, November 1825, *HOTW*, 684–689; Snedeker, *The Diaries of Donald MacDonald*, 332; Bernhard, *Travels*, 2:160–161; Josephine M. Elliott, ed., *To Holland and to New Harmony: Robert Dale Owen's Travel Journal, 1825–1826* (Indianapolis: Indiana Historical Society, 1969), 239–241; William A. Passavant, "A Visit to Economy in the Spring of 1840," *Western Pennsylvania Historical Magazine* 4, no. 3 (July 1921): 145; Farkas, *Journey*, 159; J. A. Roebling, autumn 1831, *EOTO*, 626–627.

54. Bernhard, *Travels*, 2:162–163. Bernhard fought in the Battle of Waterloo and eventually commanded the Dutch East Indies Army.

55. Buckingham, *The Eastern and Western States*, 2:232.

56. Bernhard, *Travels*, 2:163.

57. Buckingham, *The Eastern and Western States*, 2:214–216, 232.

58. Bernhard, *Travels*, 2:163; Economy's steam-heated factories were novel enough that a factory owner from Philadelphia inquired of them: W. Young to FR, August 30, 1827, *EOTO*, 172–173.

59. "Appendix: America's Communal Utopias Founded by 1965," in *America's Communal Utopias*, ed. Donald Pitzer (Chapel Hill: University of North Carolina Press, 1997), 459. Like Harmony, the Teutonians' constitution justified the abolition of private property (modeled after the first-century church). Peter Kaufmann to FR, November 12, 1827, *EOTC*, 201–206; Constitution of Teutonia, *EOTO*, 206–211.

60. GR to FR, February 1, 1827, *EOTO*, 108–112. Columbiana started as a rival to Harmony in 1803, and continued to attract former members of Rapp's commune, including the father of the aforementioned children: P. Kaufmann to Charles V. Bonnhorst, November 16, 1827, *EOTO*, 212–213.

61. GR to FR, January 26, 1826, *EOTO*, 99–103.

62. Frederick worked hard to counter negative press. One example among many: Salomon Sala to FR, July 12, 1830, *EOTO*, 516–517.

63. *Beaver Republican*, November 19 and 29, 1829, *EOTO*, 457–458, 459–460.

64. John Clark to FR, October 23, 1828, *EOTO*, 354–355.

65. *Pittsburgh Gazette*, February 26, 1830, *EOTO*, 485–486.

66. Wilhelm Schmidt to FR, February 10, 1827, *EOTO*, 116–119; FR to GR, September 2, 1829, *EOTO*, 400–407. Rapp and Mutschler were intimate enough that Bernhard assumed they were related: Bernhard, *Travels*, 2:163.

67. Alice T. Ott, *The Sunwoman in the Wilderness: The Religious Beliefs and Practices of George Rapp's Harmony Society* (Lexington, KY: Emeth Press, 2014), 280–293. For Paracelsus and Pietist medicine, see Renate Wilson, *Pious Traders*

3. Republican Industry 269

in Medicine: A German Pharmaceutical Network in Eighteenth-Century North America (University Park: Pennsylvania State University Press, 2000), 49–66.

68. John Hopkins to FR, September 1826, *EOTO*, 60–61; Articles of Association, [March 9, 1827], *EOTO*, 122–141; sworn testimony, *Schreiber v. Rapp*, December 1835, *GRYG*, 151–152.

69. Hopkins was a lawyer turned clergyman who became the first Episcopal bishop of Vermont and a national figure in the reunion of the Episcopal Church following the Civil War. "John Henry Hopkins," in *Dictionary of American Biography*, vol. 5, ed. Dumas Malone (New York: Charles Scribner's Sons, 1933), 212–213.

70. Baker v. Nachtrieb, 60 U.S. 126 (1856); Speidel v. Henrici, 120 U.S. 377 (1887). A third Supreme Court case involved heirs to the Harmony fortune: Schwartz v. Duss, 187 U.S. 8 (1902). Zoar also had an important case that provided precedent for Baker: Goesele v. Bimeler 55 U.S. 14 (1852); Kathleen Fernandez, *Zoar: The Story of an Intentional Community* (Kent, OH: Kent State University Press, 2019), 137–147.

71. The actual petition is missing—the documentary record contains a copy dated November 22, 1827: Jacob Schreiber et al. to the governor and legislature of Pennsylvania, November 22, 1827, *EOTO*, 214–225; Charles von Bonnhorst to FR, November 22 and December 14, 1827, *EOTO*, 226–231, 243–248.

72. Charles von Bonnhorst to FR, December 3, 11, 14, 17, 18, 1827, *EOTO*, 235–236, 238–241, 243–248, 252–254, 264–265; Moses Sullivan to FR, December 12, 1827, *EOTO*, 241–242; JS to Peter Hay, December 15, 1827, *EOTO*, 249–251; Peter Hay to JS, December 17, 1827, *EOTO*, 251; W. B. Foster to FR, December 17, 1827, *EOTO*, 254–255; Ross Wilkins to FR, December 17, 1827, EOTO, 255; report, *Journal of the Senate*, December 17, 1827, *EOTO*, 255–260; JS to FR, December 20, 1827, *EOTO*, 266; JS to FR, December 27, 1827, *EOTO*, 269–270; FR to Hare Powell, January 4, 1828, *EOTO*, 285.

73. Schreiber v. Rapp, October 1835, *EOTO*, 270–275; Walter Forward to RLB, October 22, 1836, *GRYG*, 218; GR to J. Bredin, October 25, 1836, *GRYG*, 219; James Allison to GR, October 31, 1836, *GRYG*, 219–220; *Schreiber v. Rapp*, Frederick Watts, ed., *Reports of Cases Argued and Determined in the Supreme Court of Pennsylvania*, Vol. 5 (Philadelphia: James Kay Jun. and Brother, 1837), 351–364.

74. Articles of Agreement, February 15, 1805, *HOTC*, 80, 89; Harmony Society memorial containing the early Articles of Association and incorporation request, December 15, 1807–January 23, 1808, *HOTC*, 253–256; annulment of article 6, 1827 Articles of Association, October 31, 1836, *GRYG*, 220–233; record of the annulment proceedings, October 31, 1836, *GRYG*, 233–234. In contrast, Ohio did grant communal Zoar a corporate charter in 1832: Fernandez, *Zoar*, 137–138, 239.

75. Manifestoes, March 21, 1829, *EOTO*, 377–380; meeting record, September 27, 1829, *EOTO*, 408–434; J. G. Gontgen to GR, September 11, 1831, *EOTO*, 591–600;

Count de Leon to GR, September 29, 1831, *EOTO*, 615–616. For Leon: Eileen Aiken English, "The Life and Legacy of Count Leon: The Man Who Cleft the Harmonie," *Communal Societies* 33, no. 1 (June 2013): 45–82.

76. Passenger list, *Isabella*, September 5, 1831, *EOTO*, 585–586; Count de Leon to Andrew Jackson, September 7, 1831, *EOTO*, 587–591 (quote from 590); Andrew Jackson to Count de Leon, September 14, 1831, *EOTO*, 602; U.S. Department of State to Count de Leon, September 16, 1831, *EOTO*, 602–603.

77. GR to J. G. Gontgen, October 29, 1829, *EOTO*, 445; GR to FR, September 17, 1831, *EOTO*, 603–604; Ott, *Sunwoman*, 309–311; *EOTO*, 365.

78. Economy Report, May 13, 1832, *EOTO*, 781–782.

79. FR to J. G. Gontgen, January 17, 1832, *EOTO*, 654–657; G. W. Featherstonhaugh, *A Canoe Voyage of the Minnay Sotor*, vol. 1 (London: Richard Bentley, 1847), 73.

80. There are 166 names on the first declaration, but Arndt believes there were unregistered additions and deletions, and a later declaration published in various newspapers claimed 240 dissenters. The greater body of evidence suggests approximately a third of the members joined the dissenters, which would suggest the 240 number is probably accurate—bolstered by Frederick's count of 500 supporters and 250 dissenters. Declaration, January 25, 1832, *EOTO*, 658–667; J. G. Gontgen to Anti-Rappites, January 27, 1832, *EOTO*, 669–675; declaration, January 28, 1832, *EOTO*, 675–683; "Harmony Society," *Salem Gazette*, February 24, 1832, 2; A. Way to H. Denny, March 1, 1832, *EOTO*, 721–722; FR to Walter Forward, March 3–5, 1832, *EOTO*, 743.

81. Declaration, January 25, 1832, *EOTO*, 663–667 ("disappointment" and "Christian obligations": 663); "contradict": Declaration, January 28, 1832, *EOTO*, 680.

82. Appeal, February 25, 1832, *EOTO*, 712–715. Bylaws, February 20, 1832, *EOTO*, 705–708; election of elders, February 21, 1832, *EOTO*, 708–709. "To the American Public," *Pennsylvania Reporter*, May 3, 1833, *EOTO*, 869–870. "Rubber stamp": minutes of Council of Elders, April 5, 1832, *EOTO*, 761.

83. More than four hundred members signed a resolution pledging support for the Rapps. Declaration, February 4, 1832, *EOTO*, 694–697; "Affray at Economy," *Eastern Argus*, April 17, 1833, 3; Cobb Wyman & Co., February 24, 1832, *EOTO*, 710–711; Brown & Lewis to FR, February 27, 1832, *EOTO*, 716; von Bonnhorst to Walter Forward, March 1, 1832, *EOTO*, 720–721.

84. FR to Walter Forward, March 3–5, 1832, *EOTO*, 743; agreement, March 6, 1832, *EOTO*, 744–749; GR to Ernst Ludwig Brauns, February 1, 1844, *GRYG*, 714.

85. "To the American Public," *Pennsylvania Reporter*, May 3, 1833, *EOTO*, 869–880; "Affray at Economy," *Eastern Argus*, April 17, 1833, 3; RLB to F. Graff, April 9, 1833, *EOTO*, 884–885; RLB to von Bonnhorst, April 9, 1833, *EOTO*, 885–887; "To the American Public," *Harrisburger Morgenrothe*, April 19, 1833, *EOTO*,

916–918; Zelie Passavant to Detmar Basse, April 20, 1833, *EOTO*, 918–920; RLB to Walter Forward, March 26, 1847, *GRYG*, 1050–1051.

86. FR to W. Wilkins, May 27, 1833, *EOTO*, 926; RLB to Walter Forward, May 27, 1833, *EOTO*, 926–927; Commonwealth of Pennsylvania to New Sewickley Constable, May 31, 1833, *EOTO*, 927–928; RLB to A. Way, June 6, 1833, *EOTO*, 929; John George Wagner et al. v. George Rapp et al., June 1833, *EOTO*, 930–933; FR to Joseph Maddox, June 12, 1833, *EOTO*, 933; FR to John Marshall, October 12, 1833, *EOTO*, 956; Christoph Muller to GR/FR, October 18, 1833, *EOTO*, 960–961; Walter Forward to FR, November 20, 1833, *EOTO*, 974–975; *EOTO*, 977–978; Willis Stewart to FR, January 2, 1834, *EOTO*, 997; James Allison correspondence, June 1833–May 1836, *EOTO*, 929–930, 933–934; *GYRG*, 45–46, 109, 191, 237–238; RLB to JS, February 7, 1837, *GRYG*, 254.

87. Jacob Zundel to RLB, July 3, 1846, *GRYG*, 975–984; Jacob Zundel to RLB, September 1847, *GRYG*, 1106–114; "Abraham Zundel," OrsonPrattBrown.org, accessed April 25, 2023, http://www.orsonprattbrown.net/CJB/05Abigail-Smith-Abbott/abraham-zundel.html.

88. Harmony usually did not provide departing members with anything of material value. Even those who spent years working for the financial benefit of the society still left with essentially empty pockets. For one of the more detailed examples of how this created conflict, see correspondence between Conrad and Nicara Thorwarth and FR/GR, July 8, 18, 27, and August 12, 1832, *EOTO*, 794–803.

89. The town is today called Monaca. FR to JDH, March 31, 1832, *EOTO*, 757–759; unsigned report, Easter, 1832, *EOTO*, 759–761; Joseph H. Bausman, *History of Beaver County, Pennsylvania and Its Centennial Celebration*, vol. 2 (New York: Knickerbocker Press, 1904), 796–798; Arndt, *George Rapp's Harmony Society*, 496–497.

90. FR to JDH, December 15, 1832, *EOTO*, 825–826; FR to William Burtch, December 15, 1832, *EOTO*, 826. Economy also suffered a fire during the winter of 1832 that caused between $10,000 and $12,000 in property damage: FR to Jeremiah Warder, December 19, 1832, *EOTO*, 827.

91. Fire: RLB to A. Way, November 26, 1833, *EOTO*, 979–980; J. Allison to RLB, December 14, 1833, *EOTO*, 988–989; RLB to James Patterson, December 18, 1833, *EOTO*, 992; J. Allison to FR, December 30, 1833, *EOTO*, 993; J. W. Kirk to RLB, February 15, 1837, *GRYG*, 258. Frederick's health: Conrad Feucht to Constantin Hering, November 19, 1833, *EOTO*, 973–974; Constantin Hering to FR, November 25, 1833, *EOTO*, 978–979; FR to Constantin Hering, December 5, 1833, *EOTO*, 983; Conrad Feucht to Constantin Hering, December 5, 1833, *EOTO*, 983–984; RLB to John Clark, December 14, 1833, *EOTO*, 991; FR to Constantin Hering, December 17, 1833, *EOTO*, 991–992; Conrad Feucht

account, January 13, 1834, *EOTO*, 1002–1004; Gertrude Rapp to GR, May 8, 1834, *EOTO*, 1015–1017; Constantin Hering to FR, June 17, 1834, *EOTO*, 1023–1026.

92. By 1833, an evaluation of the society's net worth pegged the total valuation of real estate and industrial equipment at $209,734, which equates to more than $6.4 million (CPI) or $177 million (per capita GDP). Harmony 1833 assessment, *EOTO*, 835–837. For the manufacturing of GRA at Economy in years before the death of GR: Orders Sent (1823–1842, 1844) and Received (1824–1842, 1845), Business File, Domestic and Handicraft Industries, HSR, 2538.

93. Contract between FR and Stephen Phillips, June 23, 1827, *EOTO*, 158–159; Stephen Phillips to FR, June 26, 1827, *EOTO*, 159–160.

94. Praise: W. D. Jones to FR, November 21, 1827, *EOTO*, 214; *American Advertiser*, March 4, 1828, *EOTO*, 304–305; FR to Tracy & Wahrendorf, December 26, 1827, *EOTO*, 268–269. For sale: "For Sale," *Louisville Public Advertiser*, May 3, 1828. Frederick sold the *Pittsburgh and Wheeling Packet* on August 25, 1828, for $8,250: R. Wilson to FR, August 29, 1828, *EOTO*, 347–348.

95. Accounts, *Pittsburgh* and *Wheeling Packet* (1827–1828), Account Volumes, HSR, 2499; Ledger, *William Penn, Pittsburgh,* and *Wheeling Packet* (1825–1828), Account Volumes, HSR, 2499; GR to FR, March 17, 1828, *EOTO*, 309.

96. R. C. Mallary to FR, January 2, 1828, *EOTO*, 282–283; FR to J. S. Stevenson and FR to R. C. Mallery, January 10, 1828, *EOTO*, 291–293; FR to W. A. Docker, September 5, 1833, *EOTO*, 955; A. Beelen to GR, May 18, 1846, *GRYG*, 951. For a list of visitors, see chapter 2, note 56.

97. Harmony 1833 assessment, *EOTO*, 836. Cotton textile production: Cotton and Silk Book (1826–1844) and Memorandum of Yarn Spun in the Cotton Factory (1826–1830), HSR, 2539.

98. Entry dated June 12, 1835, Memorandum Book (1835–1836), HSR, 2480. Record of wool production: Woolen Book (1826–1848), HSR, 2539.

99. H. Denny to FR, January 16, 1832, *EOTO*, 652; FR to H. Denny, January 27, 1832, *EOTO*, 668.

100. Quote in FR to W. B. Clarke, July 1, 1828, *EOTO*, 337. Support for the American System: FR to Isaac Blackford, January 8, 1828, and Samuel Patterson, February 12, 1824, HSR, 2329; FR to J. C. Marthens, July 25, 1827, *EOTO*, 162–163; JS to FR, October 22, 1827, *EOTO*, 184–186; J. S. Stevenson to FR, January 2, 1828, *EOTO*, 281–282; FR to J. S. Stevenson, January 10, 1828, *EOTO*, 291–292; Frederick List to FR, February 2, 1828, *EOTO*, 300; Arndt, *George Rapp's Harmony Society*, 379–399; FR to A. Reed, February 26, 1828, *EOTO*, 304; Alexander Reed to FR, May 21, 1828, *EOTO*, 327–328; *Beaver Argus*, October 28, 1831, *EOTO*, 630–631; GR to John Clark, February 3, 1836, *GRYG*, 180; GR to John Dicky, February 16, 1836, *GRYG*, 186.

3. Republican Industry 273

101. GR to FR, December 13, 1824, *HOTW,* 339. GR darkly wondered if God was using Jackson and Van Buren to bring about the end times: GR to JS, November 6, 1837, *GRYG,* 293–294.

102. Charles Shaler to FR, June 2, 1827, *EOTO,* 154–155; Peter Kaufmann account, *EOTO,* 191–192; *EOTO,* 380; Henry Clay to the Rapps, April 14, 1829, *EOTO,* 384; FR to Henry Clay, January 21, 1833, *EOTO,* 843–844; Henry Clay to FR, January 27, 1833, *EOTO,* 845–846.

103. [FR] to Samuel Worchester, December 19, 1822, HSR, 2335.

104. A threatening letter sent to the society referred to the violence visited upon Joseph Smith and his followers for a similar practice. Society concern with Locofoco began sometime in 1838–1839. GR to John Davis, February 23, 1839, *GRYG,* 380–381; GR to Thomas Henry, February 25, 1839, *GRYG,* 382–383; unsigned letter to Harmony Society, October 7, 1844, *GRYG,* 775–776; RLB record, October 7, 1844, *GRYG,* 776; various correspondence, October 1844, *GRYG,* 779–785; "Infamous Outrage," *Courant* (Hartford, CT), October 26, 1844, *GRYG,* 785–787; "A Friend of Peace to Harmony Society," October 28, 1844, *GRYG,* 792; "The Economy Outrage," *Beaver Argus* (Beaver Falls, PA), October 30, 1844, *GRYG,* 793–795.

105. Thomas Henry to RLB, May 11, 1835, *GRYG,* 103; Thomas Henry to RLB, May 13, 1835, *GRYG,* 107–108; GR to Thomas Henry, May 14, 1835, *GRYG,* 108–109. GR to Thomas Henry, February 22, 1841, *GRYG,* 537–538. The lobbying included a silk garment for President Tyler: JS to John Tyler, July 1, 1841, *GRYG,* 551–552; John Tyler to JS, July 16, 1841, *GRYG,* 555–556.

106. Leicester King to RLB, May 14, 1846, *GRYG,* 950. Many early American corporations used such direct public offerings to sell shares of stock, but unlike modern initial public offerings, this practice did not utilize banks or other third parties. Robert E. Wright, *Corporation Nation* (Philadelphia: University of Pennsylvania Press, 2015), 87, 119–121; Andrew M. Schocket, *Founding Corporate Power in Early National Philadelphia* (DeKalb: Northern Illinois University Press, 2007), 25–27.

107. Thomas Henry to GR, January 19, 1842, *GRYG,* 575–576; Harmony Society to Thomas Henry, January 24, 1842, *GRYG,* 576–578.

108. Friederich List to FR, February 2, 1828, *EOTO,* 300.

109. Richard Owen to RLB, September 8, 1842, *GRYG,* 626–627. Harmony records contain fascinating items, such as the anonymous (the handwriting resembles FR) "Principles of Dyeing," undated, KAC, 5159.

110. E. A. Brown & Brothers to RLB, May 24, 1843, *GRYG,* 665. For details on silk manufacturing: Cotton and Silk Book (1826–1844), Silk Goods Book (1844–1845), Record of Silk Production (1847), HSR, 2539; Silk Account Book (1843), KAC, 5159.

111. Agent Jacob Henrici wrote that Frederick died of "dropsy of the chest." JH to W. Pietsch, March 14, 1835, *GRYG*, 93. The society designated George as financial head in a memorandum signed by all men and women of Harmony: Memorandum, July 5, 1834, KAC, 5153; RLB to J. D. Hay, July 3, 1834, *GRYG*, 9. George decided that he alone would sign the society's checks. RLB to cashier of U.S. Bank of Louisville, August 26 and September 19, 1834, *GRYG*, 29; power of attorney to GR, July 5, 1834, *GRYG*, 10–14; Death of Frederick: RLB funeral address, June 25, 1834, *EOTO*, 1026–1027; remarks, June 25, 1834, *EOTO*, 1028–1030; "Death of Mr. Rapp," *New-London Gazette, and General Advertiser*, August 6, 1834, 3; Gertrude Rapp to Nanette Ritter, 1834, *EOTO*, 1034.

112. RLB, Samuel Hall, July 14, 1834, *GRYG*, 18–19; RLB to J. B. Anthony, August 4, 1834, *GRYG*, 23; Finch, "Notes of Travel, VI."

113. Deposition of RLB v. Jacob Wagner, December 15, 1845, *GRYG*, 878–885; RLB to JH, December 16, 1845, *GRYG*, 887–891; JS to RLB, February 12, 1846, *GRYG*, 907–909; RLB to JS, February 18, 1846, *GRYG*, 911–912. The spying targeted dissidents in Philippsburg who left the society with Count de Leon. Karl Arndt first discovered that RLB used the pseudonym of "Bohm" by comparing handwriting of various letters in his archives. H. Frank to J. Lentz, May 10, 1846, *GRYG*, 946–947; H. Frank to J. Lentz, June 14, 1846, *GRYG*, 957–963. The spy, A. Bimber, also slipped up and referred to RLB by name in the body of a letter dated August 14, 1846: A. Bimber correspondence, June–October 1846, *GRYG*, 971–974, 989–994, 1006–1011. RLB initiated more than sixty legal proceedings; see Index, Legal File, Court Cases and Legal Proceedings, HSR, 2319.

114. JS to RLB, July 1, 1834, *GRYG*, 7–9. This number is an estimate achieved by combining the 1833 assessment of the society's valuation of real estate and industrial equipment ($209,734), the 1835 inventory of debts owed to Harmony, bank accounts, cash, and paper notes on hand ($310,274.46), and a secret account known only to Frederick and J. Solms ($14,866.65). J. S. Buckingham repeated this number in 1840. This sum equates to over $15 million (CPI) or $411 million (per capita GDP). Harmony 1833 assessment, *EOTO*, 835–837; RLB financial reports, January 1, 1835, *GRYG*, 54–58; JS to GR, May 28, 1835, *GRYG*, 110–111. The woolen factory was operational again too. RLB to William C. Peters, January 21, 1835, *GRYG*, 63.

115. JS to RLB, July 12, 1834, *GRYG*, 15–16.

116. JS to GR, September 2, 1834, *GRYG*, 32. T. P. Cope & A. Ferguson, "City Exchange," *Hazard's Register of Pennsylvania* 8 (July 23, 1831): 64.

117. "Sovereign" is a term for British gold coins. JS to GR, January 29, *GRYG*, 66; GR to JS, February 4, 1835, *GRYG*, 72–74; JS to GR, February 12, 1835, *GRYG*, 74; GR to JS, August 5, 1835, *GRYG*, 133–134; GR to JS, February 3, 1838, *GRYG*, 318–319; GR to JS, March 22, [1838], *GRYG*, 330; RLB to GR, April 16, 1840, *GRYG*,

3. Republican Industry   275

481–483. A concise explanation of Jackson's bank war: Sharon Murphy, *Other People's Money: How Banking Worked in the Early American Republic* (Baltimore: Johns Hopkins University Press, 2017), 1–7.

118. RLB to N. Biddle, December 26, 1837, *GRYG*, 306–307; RLB to GR, April 25, 1838, *GRYG*, 340; GR to J. Cowperthwait, May 14, 1838, *GRYG*, 341–342; RLB to GR, October 30, 1838, *GRYG*, 371; GR to J. Cowperthwait, May 2, 1839, *GRYG*, 392.

119. RLB to GR, May 10, 1841, *GRYG*, 548.

120. Jane Ellen Knodell, *The Second Bank of the U.S.: "Central" Banker in an Era of Nation-Building, 1816–1836* (New York: Routledge, 2017), 39. Post office stats: Richard R. John, *Spreading the News: The American Postal System from Franklin to Morse* (Cambridge, MA: Harvard University Press, 1995), 3, 51.

121. Development was uneven and slow, as the commercial banking system only barely outpaced population growth while bank capital per capita fell throughout the decade. Pennsylvania's banking sector stagnated in the 1830s and 1840s as the state stopped chartering new banks. Indiana's per capita bank capital was $1.19 in 1820, $1.47 in 1830, and $4.94 by 1850. Bodenhorn, *State Banking*, 4, 252; Knodell, *The Second Bank of the U.S.*, 40–44, 127–128, 170–173.

122. Testimony, Schreiber v. Rapp, December 1835, *GRYG*, 146–158.

123. "The best": testimony, Schreiber v. Rapp, December 1835, *GRYG*, 149; "those who originally": Passavant, "A Visit to Economy in the Spring of 1840," 145.

124. Friedrich List, May 1835, *GRYG*, 60; Harmony 1833 assessment, *EOTO*, 837.

125. Testimony, Schreiber v. Rapp, December 1835, *GRYG*, 147–148.

126. Featherstonhaugh, *A Canoe Voyage*, 79–80.

127. Teasels are a dried plant flower with thin spindles used to clean or disentangle fibers, a vital step in textile production. JH to RLB, September 10, 1834, *GRYG*, 35–36; RLB to JS, March 14, 1835, *GRYG*, 90.

128. Closed to membership: GR to Johann Ulrich Klein, September 6, 1835, *GRYG*, 33; JH to W. Pietsch, March 14, 1835, *GRYG*, 91–94; Arndt, *George Rapp's Harmony Society*, 545–555.

129. FR to C. A. Morris, February 25, 1831, *EOTO*, 565–566; Gideon B. Smith to FR, March 8, 1831, *EOTO*, 566; Gideon Smith to FR, May 9, 1831, *EOTO*, 573; GR to John Clarke, January 16, 1836, *GRYG*, 176–178.

130. Buckingham, *The Eastern and Western States*, 2:231–232.

131. RLB to J. Fox, May 21, 1838, *GRYG*, 342; GR to J. Ritner, August 18, 1838, *GRYG*, 357–359.

132. Gerhard K. Friesen, "An Additional Source on the Harmony Society of Economy, Pennsylvania," *Western Pennsylvania Historical Magazine* 61, no. 4 (October 1978): 308.

133. Featherstonhaugh, *A Canoe Voyage*, 62. Featherstonhaugh served as a commissioner for Great Britain in negotiations over the Ashburton Treaty and British consul for Calvados and Seine, France: *GRYG*, 53.

134. Featherstonhaugh, *A Canoe Voyage*, 68.

135. Featherstonhaugh, 63.

136. GR to JS, September 2, 1835, *GRYG*, 137–138; GR to JDH, September 25, 1835, *GRYG*, 139–140; GR to JS, November 3, 1835, *GRYG*, 140–142; unsigned diary entry, April 26, 1841, *GRYG*, 545–546.

137. Lenor Lemox to Isaac Pitman, 25 February 1840, *GRYG*, 446.

138. GR to Davidson & Parks, December 20, 1836, *GRYG*, 243.

139. GR to Gideon Smith, April 28, 1840, *GRYG*, 483; GR to Joseph Ritner, December 26, 1840, *GRYG*, 531–532; Buckingham, *The Eastern and Western States*, 2:231–232.

140. GR to Ernst Ludwig Brauns, February 1, 1844, *GRYG*, 713.

141. GR to Ernst Ludwig Brauns, February 1, 1844, *GRYG*, 713.

142. RLB to T. B. Wakeman, September 4, 1839, *GRYG*, 403; T. B. Wakeman to RLB, November 25, 1839, *GRYG*, 411–412; RLB to T. B. Wakeman, December 3, 1839, *GRYG*, 412; RLB to Gideon Smith, December 4, 1839, *GRYG*, 412–413; T. Passavant to RLB, July 29, 1844, *GRYG*, 762; E. Beelen to RLB, September 30, 1844, *GRYG*, 775; Charles Wells to RLB, November 27, 1844, *GRYG*, 801; Gideon Smith to Gertrude Rapp, October 4, 1845, *GRYG*, 860–861.

143. George had one biological son, John, who died in 1812. Gertrude was John's lone child. "Harmony Society," *Indiana Farmer*, November 26, 1836, *GRYG*, 240–241; RLB to R. B. Wakeman, September 4, 1839, *GRYG*, 403; Gideon Smith to GR, June 2, 1840, *GRYG*, 499; David Maclean to RLB, April 5, 1842, *GRYG*, 596; Harmony Society to Samuel Hall, January 10, 1843, *GRYG*, 644–645; Gideon Smith to Gertrude Rapp, October 4, 1845, *GRYG*, 860–861; A. C. Van Epps to Gertrude Rapp, May 12, 1846, *GRYG*, 948; Featherstonhaugh, *A Canoe Voyage*, 81–82; Eileen English, *Demographic Directory of The Harmony Society*, 2nd ed. (Clinton, NY: Richard W. Couper Press, 2016), 109.

144. Buckingham, *The Eastern and Western States*, 2:212–213.

145. Panic of 1837: see Jessica M. Lepler, *The Many Panics of 1837: People, Politics, and the Creation of a Transatlantic Financial Crisis* (New York: Cambridge University Press, 2013); Alasdair Roberts, *America's First Great Depression: Economic Crisis and Political Disorder After the Panic of 1837* (Ithaca, NY: Cornell University Press, 2012), 13–47; Scott Reynolds Nelson, *A Nation of Deadbeats: An Uncommon History of America's Financial Disasters* (New York: Alfred A Knopf, 2012), 95–125; Edward E. Baptist, "Toxic Debt, Liar Loans, Collateralized and Secularized Human Beings, and the Panic of 1837," in *Capitalism Takes*

3. Republican Industry   277

Command: The Social Transformation of Nineteenth-Century America, ed. Michael Zakim and Gary J. Kornblith (Chicago: University of Chicago Press, 2012), 69–92; Murphy, *Other People's Money*, 99–102; Charles Sellers, *The Market Revolution: Jacksonian America, 1815–1846* (New York: Oxford University Press, 1991), 343–355; John Lauritz Larson, *The Market Revolution in America* (New York: Cambridge University Press, 2010), 92–97; Peter Temin, *The Jacksonian Economy* (New York: W. W. Norton & Company, 1969), 113–171.

146. Buckingham, *The Eastern and Western States*, 2:219.

147. Buckingham, 2:219–220.

148. Correspondence, May–June 1837, *GRYG*, 266–275; JS to GR, October 25, 1837, *GRYG*, 291–293. Absence of want: RLB and Paul Anderson to Irwin Whiteman, May 29, 1837, *GRYG*, 273; GR to J. W. Maddox, August 19, 1837, *GRYG*, 279–280.

149. GR to JS, March 2, 1840, *GRYG*, 449; Description of the panic: RLB to J. F. Fink, June 12, 1838, *GRYG*, 345–347.

150. Nelson Felch to GR, October 20, 1837, *GRYG*, 290–291.

151. GR to JS, November 6, 1837, *GRYG*, 293–294.

152. Many area papers got the date of George's death wrong. "A Patriarch Gone," *Pittsburgh Daily Morning Post*, August 11, 1847, 2; "Death of GR," *Pittsburgh Gazette*, August 11, 1847, 2. His granddaughter wrote in September that her dad died at 1:00 p.m., August 7, 1847: Gertrude Rapp to Maria Wilson, September 2, 1847, *GRYG*, 1099.

153. The article was published in English for the first time in Karl Marx and Friedrich Engels, *Collected Works*, vol. 4 (New York: International Publishers, 1975), 218–228.

154. Marx and Engels, *Collected Works*, 4:222.

155. F. List, *Amerikanisches Magazin*, May 1, 1835, *GRYG*, 58–61. See also *EOTO*, 804.

156. The estimates of Economy's currency reserve vary widely, from $110,000 (RLB to GR, October 30, 1838, *GRYG*, 371) to $30,000 (JS to GR, July 9, 1841, *GRYG*, 554; GR to John Snyder, August 2, 1841, *GRYG*, 562–563).

157. Articles of Agreement, August 12, 1847, *GRYG*, 1077–1081.

158. Official notice of GR's death, August 14, 1847, *GRYG*, 1081; RLB to Nannette Ritter Ott, September 2, 1847, *GRYG*, 1098; Gertrude Rapp to Maria Wilson, September 2, 1847, *GRYG*, 1100.

159. "RLB," Pennsylvania Vol. 17 Beaver County, 1845–1890, 159, RGD / Dun & Bradstreet Collections, Baker Library, Harvard Business School, Boston, MA.

160. RLB to Nannette Ritter Ott, September 2, 1847, *GRYG*, 1098; Articles of Agreement, August 12, 1847, *GRYG*, 1077–1079.

161. Coal works: JH to RLB, May 7, 1858, *GRRH*, 458; Baker & Henrici to T. D. Eells, September 10, 1859, *GRRH*, 512–513; JH to John White, June 25, 1860, *GRRH*,

278   *3. Republican Industry*

533; JH to Wilmington Gas Light Company, July 7, 1860, *GRRH*, 536–537; RLB to JH, September 29, 1861, *GRRH*, 602–603; Baker & Henrici to I. H. Moore, March 6, 1862, *GRRH*, 625–626. Economy Oil Company: Michael Merkle to RLB, August 11, 1860, *GRRH*, 543–544; JH to RLB, October 2, 1860, *GRRH*, 551; JH to Jonathan Lenz, March 11, 1861, *GRRH*, 575–576; JH to RLB, April 8, 1861, *GRRH*, 581–582; Van Scoter & Co. to Baker & Henrici, December 20, 1862, *GRRH*, 650; J. L Cowgill to JH, June 29, 1867, *GRRH*, 850–851. Darlington Railroad: JH to Cyrus Prentiss, April 18, 1854, *GRRH*, 269–270; F. Andriessen to RLB, March 3, 1862, *GRRH*, 625; JH to RLB, June 23, 1864, *GRRH*, 712–713; Old Economy Village Archives, MG-185, Maps 73 and 75 ("Economy tract" of oil and gas wells).

162. This is equivalent to $154 million (CPI) or $2.2 billion (per capita GDP). "RLB," Pennsylvania Vol. 17 Beaver County, 1845–1890, 159, RGD.

163. *Niles Weekly Register*, May 28, 1814, *HOTC*, 840–841.

164. Marx and Engels, *Collected Works*, 4:222–223. Although similar to the theological foundations of Shaker communalism, Harmony's conception of private property was different from the motivating force behind Mormon communalism, in which all property was regarded as the Lord's and was to be for the "benefit of all the people of the Order." Quoted in Dean May, "One Heart and Mind: Communal Life and Values among the Mormons," in Pitzer, *America's Communal*, 135, see also 139, 148–149. Mormon "consecration ceremonies" committed property to the church through deeds, but the property was leased back to the individual for life. Smith argued his system provided more autonomy for members than that of Harmony and other communal societies: Leonard J. Arrington, Feramorz Y. Fox, and Dean L. May, *Building the City of God: Community and Cooperation Among the Mormons*, 2nd ed. (Urbana: University of Illinois Press, 1992), 4–12, 15–40.

165. Stock purchase was the Pittsburgh Manufacturing Company. Receipt, January 13, 1812, *HOTC*, 504; FR to Isaac Bean, June 15, 1812, *HOTC*, 526–527.

166. Lease, GRA to James Anderson, April 1, 1823, *HSR*, 2324.

167. Steam gig: Memorandum, Calvin Cook and GR, September 22, 1836, Patents, *HSR*, 2326. Competitive innovation: Anthony F. C. Wallace, *Rockdale: The Growth of an American Village in the Early Industrial Revolution* (New York: Knopf, 1978), 188–189.

168. For patents and contracts for cotton spinning, threshing, thrashing, kitting, rolling, boring and washing machines, cloth soap, whitening agent, bee house, and oil/gas lamp substitute, see Legal File—Licenses, Commissions, and Appointments (1811–1913), Patents, *HSR*, 2326.

169. John Field to GR, March 31, 1837, *GRYG*, 264.

170. Farkas, *Journey*, 155.

3. Republican Industry 279

171. Robert Owen, "Address Delivered by Robert Owen, of New-Lanark," *New Harmony Gazette* 1, no. 1 (October 1, 1825): 1. See also Robert Owen to William Allen, April 21, 1825, *HOTW*, 533–534; Robert Owen, "A Declaration of Mental Independence," *New Harmony Gazette* 1, no. 42 (July 12, 1826): 329–333; Robert Owen, "New Harmony Sunday Meeting for Instruction in the New-System," *New Harmony Gazette* 1, no. 42 (July 12, 1826): 334–335.

172. RLB to FR, May 8, 1828, *EOTO*, 322–324.

PART TWO. CHRISTIAN REFORM CAPITALISM

1. Daniel Walker Howe, *Victorian America* (Philadelphia: University of Pennsylvania Press, 1976), 47–58; Paul E. Johnson, *A Shopkeeper's Millennium: Society and Revivals in Rochester, New York, 1815–1837* (New York: Hill and Wang, 1978); Fred Hood, *Reformed America: The Middle and Southern States, 1783–1837* (Tuscaloosa: University of Alabama Press, 1980), 113–197; Mary P. Ryan, *Cradle of the Middle Class: The Family in Oneida County, New York, 1790–1865* (New York: Cambridge University Press, 1981); Charles I. Foster, *An Errand of Mercy: The Evangelical United Front, 1790–1837* (Chapel Hill: University of North Carolina Press, 1960).

2. Richard Carwardine, *Evangelicals and Politics in Antebellum America* (New Haven, CT: Yale University Press, 1993).

3. Teresa A. Goddu, *Selling Antislavery: Abolition and Mass Media in Antebellum America* (Philadelphia: University of Pennsylvania Press, 2020); Bronwen Everill, *Not Made by Slaves: Ethical Capitalism in the Age of Abolition* (Cambridge, MA: Harvard University Press, 2020).

4. Goddu, *Selling Antislavery*, 10.

5. Julie L. Holcomb, *Moral Commerce: Quakers and the Transatlantic Boycott of the Slave Labor Economy* (Ithaca, NY: Cornell University Press, 2016); Mary Ann Yannessa, *Levi Coffin, Quaker: Breaking the Bonds of Slavery in Ohio and Indiana* (Richmond, IN: Friends United Press, 2001), 13–18, 25–28; *Constitution of the Free Produce Society of Pennsylvania* (Philadelphia: D. & S. Neall, 1827).

6. Everill, *Not Made by Slaves*, 11. Emphasis in the original.

7. Josh Lauer's *Creditworthy: A History of Consumer Surveillance and Financial Identity in America* (New York: Columbia University Press, 2017) is an excellent work, but neglects the religious dimension of Tappan's Mercantile Agency.

8. Partly, this is because stagecoaches and canal boats became less relevant with the advent of railroads. Tappan's Mercantile Agency became R. G. Dun & Company, and then Dun & Bradstreet, a company based out of New Jersey, and still listed on the New York Stock Exchange. Lauer, *Creditworthy*, 26–77; James D. Norris, *R. G. Dun & Co., 1841–1900: The Development of Credit-Reporting in*

the Nineteenth Century (Westport, CT: Greenwood Press, 1978); Scott A. Sandage, *Born Losers: A History of Failure in America* (Cambridge, MA: Harvard University Press, 2005), 99–188; Edward Balleisen, *Navigating Failure: Bankruptcy and Commercial Society in Antebellum America* (Chapel Hill: University of North Carolina Press, 2001), 146–151. The Pioneer receives the briefest of mentions in two classic works: Whitney Cross, *The Burned-Over District: The Social and Intellectual History of Enthusiastic Religion in Western New York, 1800–1850* (Ithaca, NY: Cornell University Press, 1950), 132–134, and Johnson, *A Shopkeeper's Millennium*, 85–88. There is also a chapter in a nonacademic work, Richard F. Palmer, *The "Old Line Mail": Stagecoach Days in Upstate New York* (Lakemont, NY: North Country Books, 1977), 112–128, which contains several unacknowledged verbatim passages/phrases from works such as *Collections of Cayuga County Historical Society*, no. 7 (Auburn, NY: Jas. W. Burroughs, 1889), 95–100 (located in the Office of the Cayuga County Historian, Auburn), and Israel Parsons, *The Centennial History of the Town of Marcellus, Delivered in the Presbyterian Church, of Marcellus, Onondaga County, N.Y., July 4, 1876* (Marcellus, NY: Reed's Printing House, 1878), 27. Richard John takes the Pioneer Line more seriously, devoting a handful of pages to it in *Spreading the News: The American Postal System from Franklin to Morse* (Cambridge, MA: Harvard University Press, 1995), 180–185, and "Taking Sabbatarianism Seriously: The Postal System, the Sabbath, and the Transformation of American Political Culture," *Journal of the Early Republic* 10, no. 4 (Winter 1990): 536–537, 549. But that is the entirety of the historiography of the Pioneer Line. Another article that takes an evenhanded approach to Sabbatarianism is James R. Rohrer, "Sunday Mails and the Church-State Theme in Jacksonian America," *Journal of the Early Republic* 7, no. 1 (Spring 1987): 53–74.

9. "Pioneerism," *The Craftsman*, April 21, 1829, 82.

10. "Freemen Stand, or Freemen Fall!," *The Craftsman*, March 10, 1829, 33. Emphasis in the original.

11. John, "Taking Sabbatarianism Seriously," 541. Richard John goes so far as to argue that the General Union was Bissell's "brainchild": "Taking Sabbatarianism Seriously, 537–538. "Cause-and-effect": Johnson, *A Shopkeeper's Millennium*; Charles Sellers, *The Market Revolution: Jacksonian America, 1815–1846* (New York: Oxford University Press, 1991); and Ryan, *The Cradle of the Middle Class*.

12. "Religious Liberty," *Rochester Observer*, January 1, 1830. Emphasis in the original.

13. An introduction: Heman Humphrey, *Essays upon the Origin, Perpetuity, Change, and Proper Observance, of the Sabbath* (New York: Jonathan Leavitt, 1829).

Part Two. Christian Reform Capitalism 281

14. Daniel Walker Howe, *What Hath God Wrought: The Transformation of America, 1815–1848* (New York: Oxford University Press, 2007), 230.

15. For an overview of how reforming Protestants of the 1820s and 1830s viewed the state as a covenantal, "moral being": Carwardine, *Evangelicals and Politics in Antebellum America*, 17–30.

16. This contrasts with the dispensational premillennialism so influential in late twentieth-century American fundamentalism and evangelicalism, which emphasizes a declension narrative.

4. THE SABBATARIANS

1. In 1819, the state changed the title of the village corporation from "Rochesterville" to "Rochester": Elisha Ely, *Directory for the Village of Rochester* (Rochester, NY: Everard Peck, 1827), 94.

2. Based on an account by Bissell's son Josiah W. Bissell, most likely occurring in 1823, when Josiah W. was five years old. Since Bissell purchased the property for $300, his sale price represented a tidy profit in one year's time, demonstrating the influence of the Erie Canal on Rochester's property values. Josiah W.'s account: Josiah W. Bissell, "Reminiscences of Early Rochester," in Foreman, *RHPF*, 6:237; indenture, JBJ and Charles and Ann Carroll, January 25, 1822, MCLR, Deed Book 2:284–285; indenture, Josiah and Henrietta Bissell Jr. and Harvey Ely, October 1, 1823, MCLR, Deed Book 2:101.

3. Histories claim that Bissell moved to Rochester in 1813, 1815, or 1817. Pittsfield/1813: William E. Peck, *Semi-Centennial History of the City of Rochester with Illustrations and Biographical Sketches of Some of Its Prominent Men and Pioneers* (Syracuse, NY: D. Mason & Co., 1884), 159. Red Mill: Ely, *Directory for the Village of Rochester*, 90. Store: "Cheap Goods! Good Goods!," *Rochester Telegraph*, July 7, 14, 21, 1818. Among the goods listed are wine, whiskey, and other spirits—interesting, given Bissell's leading role ten years later in Protestant reform movements. Additional stores/newly married: Bissell, "Reminiscences of Early Rochester," 238–240. West Springfield/mill/1817: Edward R. Foreman, ed., *Centennial History of Rochester, New York*, vol. 1, *1931* (Rochester, NY: Rochester Historical Society, 1931–1933), 174–177. For 1815: Blake McKelvey, "Civic Medals Awarded Posthumously," *Rochester History* 22, no. 2 (April 1960): 7. Mill in 1815: Henry O'Reilly, *Sketches of Rochester: With Incidental Notices of Western New York* (Rochester: William Alling, 1838), 257.

4. Speculating: "Lands for Sale," *Rochester Telegraph*, May 27, 1823; "Village Lots," *Rochester Observer*, October 13, 1827; "200 Village Lots for Sale," *Rochester Observer*, December 15, 1827; Index of Mortgages, MCLR, 156–157. Skids/potash: Bissell, "Reminiscences of Early Rochester," 238–240.

282 *Part Two. Christian Reform Capitalism*

5. Third Presbyterian: McKelvey, "Civic Medals Awarded Posthumously," 7. Observer: "Freemen Stand, or Freemen Fall!" *The Craftsman*, March 10, 1829, 33. Tract Society: Ely, *Directory for the Village of Rochester*, 109. Sabbath school: O'Reilly, *Sketches of Rochester*, 295. American Board of Commissioners for Foreign Missions: *Rochester Observer*, September 29, 1827. There is a brief reference to Bissell donating to the American Colonization Society, but nothing else in the archive regarding his abolitionist activity: "Josiah Bissell, Jun.," *The Craftsman*, March 17, 1829, 42.

6. Henrietta: Mary B. Allen King, *Looking Backward: Memories of the Past* (New York: Anson D. F. Randolph and Company, 1870), 119; Ely, *Directory for the Village of Rochester*, 105, 107. Multiple sources claim that Josiah Bissell was the first to have the idea of putting a Bible in the home of every American family. If this is an exaggeration, it was certainly his goal for Monroe County: "Obituary," *Rochester Observer*, April 21, 1831; Peck, *Semi-Centennial History of the City of Rochester*, 246; Foreman, *Centennial History of Rochester*, 3:264.

7. Gerrit Smith was an ardent abolitionist, supporter of the temperance movement, Free Soil congressman, and leader of the Liberty Party. JBJ to GS, April 28, 1830, GSP.

8. Josiah Bissell to Charles Finney, September 15, 1829, in McKelvey, *The Rochester Historical Society Publication Series*, 21:33–35.

9. Foreman, *RHPF*, 6:333.

10. Ely, *Directory for the Village of Rochester*, 92, 106; McKelvey, *RHPF*, 21:22.

11. Notice, *Rochester Daily Advertiser*, March 4, 1828.

12. F. De W. Ward, *Churches of Rochester: Ecclesiastical History of Rochester, N.Y.* (Rochester, NY: Erastus Darrow, 1871), 92–93; "Valuable Lots," *Rochester Observer*, November 10, 1827, and January 25, 1828; Deed, Elisha Johnson and William Atkinson to State of New York, December 15, 1828, B0691, Monroe County Clerk's Office Records of Awards, Deeds, Claims for Canal Lands, 1822–1884, CRNY.

13. J. M. Schermerhorn to Louisa Schermerhorn, September 22, 1832, Schermerhorn Letters, Monroe County Public Library, Rochester, NY.

14. Ward, *Churches of Rochester*, 92; Paul E. Johnson, *A Shopkeeper's Millennium: Society and Revivals in Rochester, New York, 1815–1837* (New York: Hill and Wang, 1978), 91–92.

15. Ely, *Directory for the Village of Rochester*, 106, 109.

16. C. and M. Morse, *Charter and Directory of the City of Rochester* (New York: Marshall & Dean, 1834), 7; James L. Elwood and Dellon M. Dewey, *A Directory and Gazetteer of the City of Rochester* (Rochester, NY: Canfield & Warren, 1844), 19.

17. McKelvey, *RHPF*, 21:69.

18. Son: "Bissell, Josiah, Jr.," Rochester Historical Society Pioneer File 3346, 2; WikiTree, accessed April 25, 2023, https://www.wikitree.com/wiki/Bissell-617.

4. The Sabbatarians 283

19. Notice, *Rochester Observer*, April 11, 1828.

20. "Editorial Notices," *The Craftsman*, July 14, 1829, 185. The $300,000 figure is equivalent to nearly $10 million (CPI) or $252 million (per capita GDP). The title of "richest man in America" in the 1830s typically is given to Stephen Girard, who is estimated to have been worth $7.6 million when he died in 1831: George Wilson, *Stephen Girard: America's First Tycoon* (Conshohocken, PA: Combined Publishing, 2000), 330. Aristarchus Champion Papers, Monroe County Public Library Local History Division contains records of Champion's Ohio land deals.

21. The $1,000,000 figure is equivalent to more than $28 million (CPI) or $390 million (per capita GDP). "A. Champion," New York 162, Monroe County (1841–1872), 316, R. G. Dun & Co. / Dun & Bradstreet Collections, Baker Library, Harvard Business School, Boston, MA.

22. October 31, 1784, Original Covenant and Church Records (1729–1804), 113, WCCR. Aristarchus's twin brother died two years later: February 13, 1786, Records (1729–1804), 158, WCCR. Deacons: April 7, 1775, Records (1729–1804), 138; May 14, 1813, Records (1812–1864), 17, WCCR.

23. May 21, 1809, Records (1759–1889), 142, WCCR; Francis Bacon Trowbridge, *The Champion Genealogy: History of the Descendants of Henry Champion of Saybrook and Lyme, Connecticut*, vol. 2 (New Haven, CT: n.p., 1891), 282n.

24. "Death of Aristarchus Champion," *Rochester Evening Express*, September 19, 1871; Aristarchus Champion obituary, *Rochester Democrat and Chronicle*, September 18, 1871; "Death of Aristarchus Champion," *Union and Advertiser*, September 19, 1872; "The Late Aristarchus Champion," *Rochester Democrat and Chronicle*, September 21, 1871. The *Rochester Daily Union and Advertiser* obituary viciously attacked his personality, character, and discernment, prompting a letter to the *Democrat and Chronicle* editor defending him. *Democrat and Chronicle* transcribed in Champion, Aristarchus file, Container 4, Western Reserve Manuscripts 5362, Western Reserve Historical Society, Cleveland, OH.

25. Aristarchus Champion Last Will and Testament, ACP. Samuel Chipman, *Report of an Examination of Poor-Houses, Jails, &c . . . Addressed to Aristarchus Champion, Esq., of Rochester, N.Y.* (Albany: New York State Temperance Society, 1836), 2. Champion funded eighty thousand copies of this New York State Temperance Society report.

26. Charles Bush, in McKelvey, *The Rochester Historical Society Publication Fund Series* 6:332.

27. Ely, *Directory for the Village of Rochester*, 114; William Swift Jr., *Directory of the City of Rochester for 1838* (Rochester, NY: C. S. Underwood, 1838), 15.

28. JBJ to GS, August 12, 1828, GSP.

29. "Address of the Sabbath Convention," *Western Recorder*, June 3, 1828, 2.

30. George Marsden, *Fundamentalism and American Culture*, 2nd ed. (New York: Oxford University Press, 2005), 13; Alexis McCrossen, *Holy Day, Holiday: The American Sunday* (Ithaca, NY: Cornell University Press, 2018), 10–15; John Duncan, *Travels Through Part of the United States and Canada in 1818 and 1819* (Glasgow: University Press, 1823), 117; Francis J. Grund, *The Americans in Their Moral, Social, and Political Relations*, vol. 1 (London: Longman, Rees, Orme, Brown, Green, and Longman, 1838), 64.

31. "An Act Regulating the Post Office Establishment," *Annals of Congress*, 11th Cong., 2nd sess., appendix, 2570.

32. Alfred Creigh, ed., *History of Washington County from Its First Settlement to the Present Time...* (Harrisburg, PA: B. Singerly, 1871), 487.

33. By the end of 1815, Congress had received more than a hundred petitions (see National Archives, RG 46 and 233). Most seem to be the product of a joint Presbyterian-Congregationalist organizing effort. Richard R. John, "Taking Sabbatarianism Seriously: The Postal System, the Sabbath, and the Transformation of American Political Culture," *Journal of the Early Republic* 10, no. 4 (Winter 1990): 525.

34. David Sehat, *The Myth of American Religious Freedom* (New York: Oxford University Press, 2011), 57–62.

35. Supporters of seven-day service also understandably cited the War of 1812 as necessitating daily service. No. 26: "Remonstrance Against the Delivery of Letters, Papers, and Packets, at the Post Offices, on the Sabbath," January 30, 1811, and No. 29: "Sunday Mails," January 16, 1815, *American State Papers: Post Office Department*, 7:44–46. Richard John argues economic concerns triumphed as Postmaster General Return J. Meigs Jr. lobbied Congress that halting the mail on Sundays would undermine the nation's transportation system by increasing the shipping cost per mile: John, "Taking Sabbatarianism Seriously," 523–534. Wayne Fuller argues that Republicans, who moved to declare the petitions invalid (on the grounds they violated the establishment clause of the Constitution), feared an issue that could revive the Federalist Party: Fuller, *Morality and the Mail in Nineteenth Century America* (Urbana: University of Illinois Press, 2003), 1–2, 14–17.

36. Daniel Walker Howe, *What Hath God Wrought: The Transformation of America, 1815–1848* (New York: Oxford University Press, 2007), 229–230; Richard R. John, *Spreading the News: The American Postal System from Franklin to Morse* (Cambridge, MA: Harvard University Press, 1995), 162–166.

37. "Sabbath on the Canal," *Rochester Observer*, March 17, 1827.

38. "Sanctification of the Sabbath," *Rochester Observer*, April 3, 1827.

39. Roger E. Carp, "The Limits of Reform: Labor and Discipline on the Erie Canal," *Journal of the Early Republic* 10, no. 2 (Summer 1990): 195–219; Peter Way,

Common Labor: Workers and the Digging of North American Canals, 1780–1860 (New York: Cambridge University Press, 1993), 96–98.

40. Way, *Common Labor*, 172–187.

41. "The Western Waters," *New York Evangelist*, May 12, 1838.

42. Blake McKelvey, *The Rochester Historical Society Publication Series*, vol. 21 (Rochester, NY: Rochester Historical Society, 1943), 136–137.

43. Paul E. Johnson, *Sam Patch, the Famous Jumper* (New York: Hill and Wang, 2004), 133.

44. "Chief" and "debasing": "Theatrical Amusements," *Rochester Observer*, November 13, 1829. "Third tier": "Effects of the Theatre," *Rochester Observer*, April 25, 1828. "Noise": quoted in McKelvey, *Rochester*, 145. Also: "The Circus Again," *Rochester Observer*, July 24, 1829; "The Theatre," *New York Observer*, October 16, 1830; *RHPF*, 1:17–28.

45. "Rochester Circus" and "Corporation," *Rochester Daily Advertiser*, April 12 and 17, 1828.

46. Rochester news, *Rochester Observer*, November 13, 1829; "Sam Patch Has Taken His Last Jump!," *Utica Sentinel & Gazette*, November 17, 1829; "Sam Patch's Last Jump," *Rochester Observer*, November 20, 1829. Bissell "murder" quote attested to by Mary B. King in *Looking Backward*, 117–118, and Charles P. Bush, "Historettes: The Bissells, Father and Son," in *Rochester Historical Society Publication Fund Series*, vol. 6, ed. Edward Foreman (Rochester, NY: Rochester Historical Society, 1927), 333. See also Johnson, *Sam Patch*.

47. "Touched off": McKelvey, *Rochester*, 188.

48. "Sam Patch's Last Jump," *Rochester Observer*, November 20, 1829.

49. Memorial to the Senate and House of Representatives from the Village of Rochester, NY, January 15, 1827, RG 233: Petitions to House Committee on Postal Service, National Archives; "The Sabbath Memorials," *New York Observer*, January 3, 1829.

50. *AGUS*, 9–10.

51. Mark Hopkins, "Sermon CCCCL: The Sabbath and Free Institutions," *American National Preacher* 21, no. 6 (June 1847): 136–137.

52. Drunkenness was the most common complaint, but foul language and gambling were often mentioned: "Sabbath Breaking," *Rochester Observer*, April 11, 1928; and even death: "Another Warning to Drunkards and Sabbath Breakers," *Rochester Observer*, November 21, 1928.

53. "Religious," *Onondaga Register*, September 24, 1828.

54. "The Sabbath," *Onondaga Register*, July 5, 1830. Francis J. Grund, *The Americans in their Moral, Social, and Political Relations*, vol. 1 (London: Longman, Rees, Orme, Brown, Green, and Longman, 1838), 64–65.

55. *AGUS*, 14–15.

286   *4. The Sabbatarians*

56. David Magie, "Sermon CLXXXI: The Sabbath a National Blessing," *American National Preacher* 9, no. 8 (January 1835): 122. "riots"/"playing cards": Rochester news, *Rochester Observer*, February 22, 1828.

57. *AGUS*, 12–13 (quote on 13).

58. *AGUS*, 13.

59. Magie, "Sermon CLXXXI," 120–121.

60. *AGUS*, 10.

61. *AGUS*, 10.

62. *AGUS*, 14.

63. Lyman Beecher, "Sermon LVI: Pre-eminent Importance of the Christian Sabbath," *American National Preacher* 3, no. 10 (March 1829): 160. Emphasis in the original.

64. For example, see the drafts of Washington's Farwell Address, which are rife with these themes. Fred Hood, *Reformed America: The Middle and Southern States, 1783–1837* (Tuscaloosa: University of Alabama Press, 1980), 7–26, 48–67.

65. Albert Barnes, "Sermon CCCCXIV: The Value of the Sabbath to Young Men," *American National Preacher* 20, no. 6 (June 1846): 137–140; Nathan O. Hatch, *The Sacred Cause of Liberty: Republican Thought and the Millennium in Revolutionary New England* (New Haven, CT: Yale University Press, 1977), 139–175.

66. Noah Porter, "Sermon CCLXIII: Profanation of the Sabbath," *American National Preacher* 23, no. 4 (April 1839): 53–57; Hopkins, "Sermon CCCCL," 126–136, 138–141; Barnes, "Sermon CCCCXIV," 140–141.

67. *AGUS*, 13–14.

68. Porter, "Sermon CCLXIII," 59; Hopkins, "Sermon CCCCL," 125–141.

69. *AGUS*, 9–10.

5. THE PIONEERS

1. Richard R. John, "Taking Sabbatarianism Seriously: The Postal System, the Sabbath, and the Transformation of American Political Culture," *Journal of the Early Republic* 10, no. 4 (Winter 1990): 525.

2. George Marsden, *Fundamentalism and American Culture*, new ed. (New York: Oxford University Press, 2005), 86, 88. Joseph Moore brought the Covenanters to my attention at a conference in 2016 and is probably correct that the Covenanters are "the most important religious sect in American history that no one remembers today." The Covenanters were fervent nationalists who longed to make America an explicitly Christian nation. If forgotten today, early Americans knew them well—John Adams blamed them for his defeat in the election of 1800. Joseph S. Moore, *Founding Sins: How a Group of Antislavery Radicals Fought to Put Christ into the Constitution* (New York: Oxford University, 2016).

Despite Christopher Grasso's criticism that the "ghost" of Puritan covenantal theology is still "haunting" the scholarship of U.S. historians, the archival record supports the argument of this chapter that a residual covenantal mentality was one of the most important foundations of Sabbatarian ideology and the proponents of Christian reform capitalism. Christopher Grasso, *Skepticism and American Faith: From the Revolution to the Civil War* (New York: Oxford University Press, 2018), 583n9. My arguments about Sabbatarian covenantal thinking are a blend of Nicholas Guyatt's "judicial" and "historical" providentialism: Guyatt, *Providence and the Invention of the United States, 1607–1876* (New York: Cambridge University Press, 2007), 6.

3. Israel's covenant: Exodus 20–24; covenant renewed: Joshua 24 and Ezra 8–10.

4. George Marsden, *The Evangelical Mind and the New School Presbyterian Experience: A Case Study of Thought and Theology in Nineteenth-Century America* (New Haven, CT: Yale University Press, 1970), 22–23, and *Fundamentalism and American Culture,* 86, 88; Andrew R. Murphy, *Prodigal Nation: Moral Decline and Divine Punishment from New England to 9/11* (New York: Oxford University Press, 2009), 10–14; 17–43. The classic discussion of the covenant in early America is Perry Miller, *The New England Mind: The Seventeenth Century* (Cambridge, MA: Harvard University Press, 1954). See also Perry Miller, *Errand Into the Wilderness* (Cambridge, MA: Belknap Press of Harvard University Press, 1956); Francis T. Butts, "The Myth of Perry Miller," *American Historical Review* 87, no. 3 (June 1982): 665–694. A relevant, provocative work on moral reform, legislation, and the U.S. Constitution: John W. Compton, *The Evangelical Origins of the Living Constitution* (Cambridge, MA: Harvard University Press, 2014). See also Ernest Lee Tuveson, *Redeemer Nation: The Idea of America's Millennial Role* (Chicago: University of Chicago Press, 1968); Robert N. Bellah, *The Broken Covenant: American Civil Religion in Time of Trial* (New York: Seabury Press, 1975), 13–18, 36–60; Nathan O. Hatch, *The Sacred Cause of Liberty: Republican Thought and the Millennium in Revolutionary New England* (New Haven, CT: Yale University Press, 1977), 16–17; and Philip Gorski, *American Covenant: A History of Civil Religion from the Puritans to the Present* (Princeton, NJ: Princeton University Press, 2017), 37–59.

5. David Magie, "Sermon CLXXXI: The Sabbath a National Blessing," *American National Preacher* 9, no. 8 (January 1835): 128. Emphasis in the original.

6. *Minutes of the General Assembly of the Presbyterian Church in the United States of America, From Its Organization A. D. 1789 to A. D. 1820 Inclusive* (Philadelphia: Presbyterian Board of Publication, n.d.), 152.

7. Charles I. Foster, *An Errand of Mercy: The Evangelical United Front, 1790–1837* (Chapel Hill: University of North Carolina Press, 1960), 217–218.

8. *Extracts from the Minutes of the General Assembly of the Presbyterian Church in the United States of America, A.D. 1812*, vol. 3 (Philadelphia: Jane Aitken, 1812), 27.

9. Fred Hood, *Reformed America: The Middle and Southern States, 1783–1837* (Tuscaloosa: University of Alabama Press, 1980), 27–47.

10. John, "Taking Sabbatarianism Seriously," 529; James R. Rohrer, "Sunday Mails and the Church-State Theme in Jacksonian America," *Journal of the Early Republic* 7, no. 1 (Spring 1987): 71.

11. JBJ to Charles Finney, September 15, 1829, *RHPF*, 21:34; Carol Sheriff, *The Artificial River: The Erie Canal and the Paradox of Progress, 1817–1862* (New York: Hill and Wang, 1996), 150.

12. "Sunday Mails-Church and State," *Rochester Observer*, July 30, 1830.

13. Richard John is one of the few historians who even mentions covenant theology as a possible factor in the emergence of mass religious movements in the early nineteenth century. John, "Taking Sabbatarianism Seriously," 529–530.

14. "The Sabbath," *Rochester Observer*, June 27, 1828.

15. *AGUS*, 14.

16. Champion's church was in a small community, Westchester, which never received official town status. Consequently, the church is often identified with the nearest town, Colchester.

17. Covenant dated December 17, 1728, Church Records, 1729–1804, 1–3, WCCR; *Celebrating 275 Years of Service to God and Community, 1728–2003* (Colchester, CT: Westchester Congregational Church, 2003), 3–4.

18. Baptism of "Sybyl Negro Child belonging to Henry Champion," May 2, 1773, baptism of "Negro Child of Col. Henry Champion," July 21, 1776, Church Records, 1729–1804, 110–111, WCCR; "baptism of Roderick Drinkwater a servant boy in the household of Henry Champion," April 26, 1807, Church Records, 1759–1889, 116, WCCR. "Fornication" was one of the most common violations: see Church Records, 1729–1804, 83, WCCR.

19. Zebulon Ely, *A Gospel Minister, Though Young, Should Be Respectable by His Example: A Sermon, Delivered at the Ordination of the Rev. Ezra Stiles Ely, to the Pastoral Care of the Church in West-Chester, in Colchester, October 1, 1806* (Hartford, CT: Lincoln & Gleason, 1806), 6.

20. Ezra Stiles Ely, *A Sermon, Delivered by Ezra Stiles Ely, on the First Sabbath After His Ordination* (Hartford, CT: Lincoln & Gleason, 1806), 6.

21. Coincidentally, J. Seymour published the sermon cited here at almost the exact moment a young James Harper (chapter 7) came to work at Seymour's print shop: Ezra Stiles Ely, *A Sermon for the Rich to Buy: That They May Benefit Themselves and the Poor* (New York: J. Seymour, 1810).

22. Ezra Stiles Ely, *A Discourse, Delivered at the Opening of the General Assembly of the Presbyterian Church in the United States of America, on the 21st of May, A.D. 1829* (Princeton University Libraries, Princeton, NJ).

23. Ezra Stiles Ely, *The Duty of Christian Freemen to Elect Christian Rulers* (Philadelphia: W. F. Geddes, 1828), 1–13 (quotes 11, 12). Ely's divisive approach to social reform: Grasso, *Skepticism and American Faith*, 195–215, 227–249.

24. Ely, *The Duty of Christian Freemen to Elect Christian Rulers*, 15; "Freemen Stand, or Freemen Fall!," *The Craftsman*, March 10 1829, 33. Champion continued in the Congregational tradition. In 1853, he helped lead the founding of a new Congregational church in Rochester, Plymouth Church, where he served as a trustee: J. O. Bloss to A. Champion, December 28, 1859, *RHPF*, 21:116.

25. Grasso, *Skepticism and American Faith*, 206.

26. F. De W. Ward, *Churches of Rochester: Ecclesiastical History of Rochester, N.Y.* (Rochester, NY: Erastus Darrow, 1871), 32–33, 35–36; Mary B. Allen King, *Looking Backward: Memories of the Past* (New York: Anson D. F. Randolph and Company, 1870), 117.

27. Parker moved to New York City in June 1830 to pastor First Free Presbyterian Church, a revivalist church focused on evangelism. He left Third Presbyterian on good terms. "Rev. Joel Parker," *Rochester Observer*, June 18, 1830; Yates, "First Church Chronicles," RHFP, 1:213–214.

28. "New Church," *Rochester Observer*, March 3, 1827; William E. Peck, *Semi-Centennial History of the City of Rochester with Illustrations and Biographical Sketches of Some of Its Prominent Men and Pioneers* (Syracuse, NY: D. Mason & Co., 1884), 246. Some of the secondary sources list nineteen founding members, while the oldest source (the *Rochester Observer*) claims twenty-two. As it contains much more detailed membership information, I place more faith in its accounting and use the number twenty-two: "Rev. Joel Parker," *Rochester Observer*, June 18, 1830. Aristarchus Champion's involvement at Second Presbyterian led to his being labeled a "Brick Church man": Edward R. Foreman, ed., *Centennial History of Rochester, New York*, vol. 3 (Rochester, NY: Rochester Historical Society, 1933), 248–250; "Brick Church Man," in Foreman, *Centennial History of Rochester*, 3:292; name change: Ward, *Churches of Rochester*, 25; Bissell, "Reminisces of Early Rochester," 239; 22/date: Henry O'Reilly, *Sketches of Rochester: With Incidental Notices of Western New York* (Rochester: William Alling, 1838), 285.

29. McKelvey also argues the 1801 Plan of Union added to this crisis by combining Congregationalists and Presbyterians into one organization: Blake McKelvey, *The Rochester Historical Society Publication Series*, vol. 21 (Rochester, NY: Rochester Historical Society, 1943), 126–127.

30. Marsden, *The Evangelical Mind*, 75–82.

31. "Church Difficulties," *The Craftsman*, March 9, 1830, 30–31. Penny: Ward, *Churches of Rochester*, 17–18.

32. General Assembly is the highest governance body in the Presbyterian organizational structure, so his nomination to it was significant for Bissell. *Minutes of the General Assembly of the Presbyterian Church in the United States of America*, 6:6, 23, 28.

33. Rochester also experienced a recession and the cratering of real estate prices in the early 1830s. This would have contributed to Third Presbyterian's financial difficulties, along with the death of Bissell in 1831. O'Reilly, *Sketches of Rochester*, 285–286.

34. St. Luke's original building is still standing and is the oldest public building still standing in Rochester. Peck, *Semi-Centennial History of the City of Rochester*, 256; O'Reilly, *Sketches of Rochester*, 279–280; "A Short History of the Church of St. Luke & St. Simon Cyrene," Episcopal Church of St. Luke & St. Simon Cyrene, accessed April 14, 2017, http://www.twosaints.org/about-us/our-history.

35. Ward, *Churches of Rochester*, 79–80; 92–93, 184; "Vestryman" is a member of a church "vestry," or congregational leadership body. Wardens are elected to positions of liaison between the rector and parish. It seems that Atkinson was the senior warden, thus serving as a lay leader who could run vestry meetings when the rector was absent.

36. The church went through a second foreclosure in 1842 and went to auction. Foreman, *Centennial History of Rochester*, 3:251; O'Reilly, *Sketches of Rochester*, 280, 286–287.

37. Charles P. McIlvaine, *Rev. Mr. McIlvaine in Answer to the Rev. Henry U. Onderdonk* (Philadelphia: William Stavely, 1827), 25–30.

38. Ironically, the two men crossed paths a few years later, serving together as vice presidents of the American Society for the Diffusion of Useful Knowledge, a group that factors into the Harper & Brothers story. American Society for the Diffusion of Useful Knowledge, *Prospectus of the American Library for Schools and Families* (New York: American Society for the Diffusion of Useful Knowledge, 1837), i. McIlvaine, *Rev. Mr. McIlvaine in Answer to the Rev. Henry O. Onderdonk*, 4, 12–15, 34–36; Ward, *Churches of Rochester*, 79, 92–93.

39. William Atkinson to Henry U. Onderdonk, July 21, 1827, in McIlvaine, *Rev. Mr. McIlvaine in Answer to the Rev. Henry O. Onderdonk*, 4–5.

40. William Atkinson to Charles McIlvaine, March 30, 1827, and William Atkinson and Giles Boulton to Charles McIlvaine, June 1, 1827, in McIlvaine, *Rev. Mr. McIlvaine in Answer to the Rev. Henry O. Onderdonk*, 7, 8; also 9–11; Paul E. Johnson, *A Shopkeeper's Millennium: Society and Revivals in Rochester, New York, 1815–1837* (New York: Hill and Wang, 1978), 92.

5. The Pioneers 291

41. William died on July 17, 1843, probably of dysentery. Elizabeth was wife two of three for Finney and was intimately involved in planning and executing his revivals. Leonard I. Sweet, "The Female Seminary Movement and Woman's Mission in Antebellum America," *Church History* 54, no. 1 (March 1985): 41–55; Helen Lefkowitz Horowitz, *Alma Mater: Design and Experience in Women's Colleges from Their Nineteenth Century Beginnings to the 1930s*, 2nd ed. (Amherst: University of Massachusetts Press, 1984), 11; "Charles Grandison Finney: A Gallery of Critics, Friends, Sweethearts, and Acquaintances," *Christianity Today*, 1988, http://www.christianitytoday.com/history/issues/issue-20/charles-grandison-finney-gallery-of-critics-friends.html.

42. "The Sabbath," *Rochester Observer*, May 16, 1828. Emphasis in the original.

43. "General Sabbath Union," *New York Observer*, May 16, 1829; John, "Taking Sabbatarianism Seriously," 537–538, 540.

44. John, "Taking Sabbatarianism Seriously," 537–538; "Constitution," *AGUS*, 7–8.

45. Ronald E. Shaw, *Canals for a Nation: The Canal Era in the United States, 1790–1860* (Lexington: University Press of Kentucky, 1990), 195; "A Prospectus," *Rochester Observer*, February 17, 1827; advertisement for the *Christian Spectator*, *Rochester Observer*, July 21, 1827; "Journal of Commerce," *Rochester Observer*, October 24, 1828; Bertram Wyatt-Brown, *Lewis Tappan and the Evangelical War Against Slavery* (Cleveland, OH: Press of Case Western Reserve, 1969), 54–55. Vermont: "Stages on the Sabbath," *New York Observer*, August 23, 1828; "Stages on the Sabbath," *Rochester Observer*, September 5, 1828. New York: "Moscow Stage," *New York Observer*, August 30, 1828; "To Stage Proprietors," *Rochester Observer*, May 16, 1828.

46. "Prospectus," *Rochester Observer*, February 17, 1827.

47. "New Arrangement," *Rochester Observer*, November 3, 1827; notice to subscribers, *Rochester Observer*, December 29, 1827; "Agents for the Observer," *Rochester Observer*, January 28, 1828.

48. Ecumenicalism (Sabbatarianism at Baptist prayer meetings): entries dated May 29, May 30, and July 18, 1828, Journal of Lewis Tappan, 32, 38, Lewis Tappan Papers, LOC. Suspicions that Sabbatarianism was a Presbyterian plot: "Sunday Line of Stages," July 5, 1828, "The Pioneer," September 13, 1828, *Gospel Advocate and Impartial Investigator* (Auburn, NY), 223, 303. Twentieth-century historians such as Paul Johnson (*A Shopkeeper's Millennium*) internalized the charge of sectarianism, and by narrowly focusing on Rochester's reformed churches, erroneously concludes that the second Sabbath movement was Presbyterian-led.

49. "Pioneer Stages," *Rochester Observer*, October 3, 1828.

50. Lois W. Banner, "Religious Benevolence as Social Control: A Critique of an Interpretation," *Journal of American History* 60, no. 1 (June 1973): 27.

51. "Sanctification of the Sabbath," *Rochester Observer,* June 13, 1828.

52. "Things that Will Be Done," *Rochester Observer,* May 26, 1827. Emphasis in the original.

53. "Sabbaths on the Canal," *Rochester Observer,* March 17, 1827; "Sanctification of the Sabbath," *Western Recorder,* October 2, 1827; "The Sabbath," *Western Recorder,* October 9, 1827; Chapin sold out to four of his friends and business associates (Allen, Tibbets, & Co.) in April 1829: "New Arrangement," advertisement, *Rochester Daily Advertiser and Telegraph,* April 14, 1829. Efficiency boast: "Sabbath on the Canal," *Rochester Observer,* September 29, 1827; Chapin judge: Elisha Ely, *Directory for the Village of Rochester* (Rochester, NY: Everard Peck, 1827), 11.

54. Passenger list of canal boat *Herald,* April 24–May 24, 1828 (Box 1, Folder 2), and May 27–July 2, 1828 (Box 1, Folder 4); passenger list of canal boat *Waterloo,* July 1–August 1, 1828 (Box 4); October 4–November 1, 1828, and November 1–December 1, 1828 (Box 1, Folder 7), CRNY, A1057–78; 1829 statement of tolls paid (Box 1, Folder 3), CRNY, A1438.

55. Certificate of clearance for canal boat *Herald,* January 15, 1845, A1139: Bills of Lading and Clearances for Cargoes, Box 1, CRNY.

56. JBJ, "Old Line Circular," *Rochester Observer,* May 2, 1828; "At a Meeting of a Few of the Friends to the Observance of the FOURTH COMMANDMENT," *Rochester Observer,* February 1, 1828; "Remember the Sabbath Day, to Keep It Holy!!," handbill, n.d., RPF.

57. The $25,000 figure equates to over $725,000 (CPI) or $23.5 million. "The Sabbath," *Rochester Observer,* February 8, 1828; "Sabbath Convention," *Onondaga Register,* February 2, 1828; John E. Becker, *A History of the Village of Waterloo, New York and Thesaurus of Related Facts* (Waterloo, NY: Waterloo Library and Historical Society, 1949), 111.

58. "In Pursuance of the Circular," *Rochester Observer,* February 22, 1828; "Sabbath Convention," February 27, 1828, and "To the Public," April 16, 1828, *Onondaga Register;* "The Sabbath," *Rochester Daily Advertiser,* March 8, 1828; Henry Hall, *The History of Auburn* (Auburn, NY: Dennis Brothers, 1860), 169; Becker, *The Village of Waterloo,* 111.

59. "To the Public," *Onondaga Register,* February 27, 1828.

60. "Meeting at Newark," "Meeting at Batavia," "Meeting in Utica," and untitled announcement, *Rochester Observer,* February 29, 1828; "Observance of the Sabbath," *Rochester Observer,* March 14, 1828; "Observance of the Sabbath," *Rochester Observer,* March 28, 1828; "The Sabbath," *Rochester Observer,* April 18, 1828; "The Sabbath," *Rochester Observer,* May 9, 1828; "The Sabbath Cause," *Rochester Observer,* May 23, 1828; "Sunday Stages," *New York Observer,* July 5, 1828; "The Sabbath," *Rochester Observer,* July 25, 1828; "Sabbath Association

5. The Pioneers 293

at Saratoga Springs," *New York Observer*, July 26, 1828; "The Sabbath Cause," *Rochester Observer*, August 1, 1828; "Travelling on the Sabbath," *New York Observer*, May 30, 1829.

61. "From the *Connecticut Observer*" and "The Erie Canal Alive," *Rochester Observer*, March 7, 1828; "Profanation of the Sabbath," *Rochester Observer*, March 21, 1828; "The Sabbath," *New York Observer*, June 28, 1828; "Presbytery of Philadelphia," *Rochester Observer*, May 9, 1828; "The Sabbath," *Rochester Observer*, June 27, 1828; "The Sabbath," *Rochester Observer*, July 4, 1828; "The Sabbath in Philadelphia," *New York Observer*, July 26, 1828.

62. "Respect for the Sabbath," *Rochester Observer*, May 9, 1828.

63. To Stage Proprietors," *Rochester Observer*, May 16, 1828.

64. "Moscow Stage," *New York Observer*, August 30, 1828; "Stages on the Sabbath," *Rochester Observer*, September 5, 1828.

65. "In Pursuance of the Circular," *Rochester Observer*, February 22, 1828; "Sabbath Convention," *Onondaga Register*, February 27, 1828; "To the Public," *Onondaga Register*, April 16, 1828; Hall, *The History of Auburn*, 169; Becker, *The Village of Waterloo*, 111.

66. *Cayuga Free Press*, March 19, 1828. Emphasis in the original.

67. "New Line of Stages," *Rochester Observer*, March 14, 1828; Rochester news, *Rochester Observer*, March 28, 1828; "Observance of the Sabbath," *Rochester Observer*, April 25, 1828.

68. "Pioneer Stages," *Rochester Observer*, October 3, 1828.

69. Becker, *The Village of Waterloo*, 111–112.

70. "Arrangements for the Pioneer Stages," *Rochester Observer*, April 11, 1828; "Arrangements for the 'Pioneer Stages,'" *Western Recorder*, April 29, 1828.

71. "Pioneer Stages," *Rochester Observer*, June 6, 1828.

72. "'Pioneer' Stages," advertisement, *Rochester Daily Advertiser*, June 18, 1828; "Pioneer," *Rochester Observer*, June 17, 1828; "Pioneer," advertisement, *Rochester Daily Advertiser*, June 28, 1828; "Pioneer," *Rochester Observer*, July 11, 1828; "Pioneer Stages," advertisement, *Rochester Observer*, July 21, 1828; "Pioneer Stages," advertisement, *New York Observer*, September 13, 1828. There is no evidence the Pioneer Line was incorporated. The state discontinued awarding stagecoach franchises in 1817 and never passed a general incorporation statute for stagecoach companies. (An omnibus general incorporation statute was passed for New York City in 1854.) Ronald E. Seavoy, *The Origins of the American Business Corporation, 1784–1855: Broadening the Concept of Public Service During Industrialization* (Westport, CT: Greenwood Press, 1982), 45.

73. "Pioneer Stages," *New York Observer*, June 14, 1828.

74. JBJ to GS, October 25, 1827, and "Subscriptions for Augmenting the Funds of the American Board of Commissioners for Foreign Missions," Box 3, GSP;

Ralph V. Harlow, *Gerrit Smith: Philanthropist and Reformer* (New York: Henry Holt and Company, 1939), 58–59.

75. Peterboro also became an important stop on the Underground Railroad. Harlow, *Gerrit Smith*, 70–71.

76. "M" meant "thousand": JBJ to GS, March 4, 1828, Box 3, GSP. Emphasis in the original. The $25,000 amount is over $725 (CPI) or $23.5 million (per capita GDP).

77. almost "full toned": JBJ to GS, August 12, 1828, Box 3, GSP; "ready"/"your brother": JBJ to GS, July 10, 1828, Box 3, GSP; Harlow, *Gerrit Smith*, 56.

78. JBJ to GS, August 12, 1828, Box 3, GSP (emphasis in the original); Harlow, *Gerrit Smith*, 56–57.

79. Entries dated May 20, 29, and 30, and July 20, 1828, February 13 and 14, 1829, Journal of Lewis Tappan, 29, 32, 39, 76–77, LTP. (Pages 76–77 are missing from the microfilm copy—see complete original journal at LOC.)

80. Sources sometimes use the word "stock" to describe the $60,000, equivalent to $1.8 million (CPI) or $53 million (per capita GDP), although there is no evidence that stock certificates were issued. If stock was issued, it was contrary to the founders' original principles. Henry O'Reilly claims one of the principal figures of the Pioneer movement wrote the summary of the Pioneer Line reprinted in his 1838 history of Rochester. Since Bissell died in 1831, that leaves William Atkinson or Aristarchus Champion as the likely authors. The best guess is Champion, since the author does not reveal the names of the $10,000 donors, and in general, Champion was modest and kept a relatively low profile regarding his immense wealth: O'Reilly, *Sketches of Rochester*, 303.

81. Articles of association and agreement constituting the Connecticut Land Company, September 5, 1795, Early American Imprints, Series 1, no. 28475, *America's Historical Imprints*; Deed to Henry Champion, October 9, 1798, Box 79, Folder 1, HCP. Claude L. Shepard, *The Connecticut Land Company and Accompanying Papers* (Cleveland, OH: Western Reserve Historical Society, 1916), 71–73, 119–124, 135–136, 145–157. The $85,675 figure equals almost $2 million (CPI) or $70 million (per capita GDP). Champion's obituary claimed he lost "considerable" money in the Pioneer: "Death of Aristarchus Champion," *Rochester Evening Express*, September 19, 1871.

82. Shepard, *The Connecticut Land Company and Accompanying Papers*, 89–90; R. Douglas Hurt, *The Ohio Frontier: Crucible of the Old Northwest, 1720–1830* (Bloomington: Indiana University Press, 1996), 164–166.

83. Shepard, *The Connecticut Land Company and Accompanying Papers* 85–91; Hurt, *The Ohio Frontier*, 315–344, 388–396.

84. For Connecticut land deals: Box 81, Folder 1 and Folder 2, HCP. For Massachusetts land deals: Box 81 Folder 3, HCP. For New York land deals: Box 81, Folder

5. The Pioneers 295

3 and Folder 4, HCP. For Vermont: Box 81, Folder 4, HCP. For Ohio land deals: ACP.

85. Loan between the directors of the Wayne and Cuyahoga Turnpike Company and Aristarchus Champion, January 31, 1826, ACP; Rufus Ferril to Aristarchus Champion, February 16, 1826, ACP; Aristarchus Champion to Rufus Ferril, May 12, 1826, ACP. The $5,000 figure equals more than $140,000 (CPI) and $4.5 million (per capita GDP).

86. Rochester and Penfield border one another within Monroe County, New York (originally Ontario County). Some of the Champion land was also in what was then called Carthage, about one mile north of the Lower Falls of the Genesee River (in present-day Rochester). For land deals between Daniel and Mary Penfield and Champion (1809–1828), Box 81, Folders 3 and 4, HCP.

6. CONFLICT, DEFEAT, AND VICTORY

1. Samuel Murdock, "To the Editor of the *Rochester Observer*," *Rochester Observer*, July 11, 1828.
2. J. B. Pitt, "Mr. Editor," *Rochester Observer*, August 15, 1828.
3. "Pioneer Stages," *Rochester Observer*, August 8, 1828.
4. "Beware of impositions!," *Rochester Observer*, February 6, 1829.
5. Richard S. Merchant, "Pioneer Management," *Utica Sentinel & Gazette*, March 10, 1828.
6. "Pioneer Stages," *Rochester Observer*, July 31, 1829.
7. A charge that was vigorously refuted a week later. "A Card," *Rochester Observer*, August 8, 1828; J. B. Pitt, "Mr. Editor," *Rochester Observer*, August 15, 1828.
8. "Six Day Line of Stages," *Rochester Observer*, August 22, 1828.
9. Statement by the passengers of the canal packet boat *Citizen of the Citizens*, *Utica Sentinel & Gazette*, September 1, 1829; A. R. Moen in a letter to the editor refuted the charges: *Utica Sentinel & Gazette*, September 15, 1829.
10. Ira Merrill, "To the Public," *Rochester Observer*, July 11, 1828.
11. "Pioneer," *Rochester Observer*, November 28, 1828.
12. "Stones and Brick Bats from 'Glass Houses,'" *Utica Sentinel & Gazette*, July 15, 1828; Rochester news, *Rochester Observer*, August 29, 1828; "Pioneer Stages," *Rochester Observer*, April 24, 1829.
13. "Pioneer," *Rochester Observer*, November 28, 1828.
14. Quotes: "Stage Drivers," *Rochester Observer*, January 29, 1830; emphasis in the original. "Stage Drivers' Dialogue," *Rochester Observer*, February 5, 1830.
15. "Pioneer Stages," *Rochester Observer*, July 31, 1829; note on Pioneer Line, *Rochester Observer*, December 25, 1829.
16. "The Pioneer Line," *New York Observer*, September 6, 1828.

17. "Anti-Sabbath Meeting," *New York Observer*, December 20, 1828; "Anti-Sabbath Meetings," *Rochester Observer*, December 26, 1828; "Meeting at Rochester," *Utica Sentinel & Gazette*, December 23, 1828; "Sanctification of the Sabbath," *Onondaga Register*, August 13, 1828. Anti-Sabbath meetings also popped up in places such as Lowell, Massachusetts: "Sabbath Regulations," *Utica Sentinel & Gazette*, October 21, 1828.

18. "Orthodox Line of Stages," *Gospel Advocate and Impartial Investigator*, March 1, 1828, 73–75.

19. "Josiah Bissell, Jun.," *The Craftsman*, March 17, 1829, 41.

20. Bissell detailed the sale price in "Old Line Circular," *Rochester Observer*, May 2, 1828. The figure of $175,000 was a huge sum, equivalent to over $5 million (CPI) or $164 million (per capita GDP). Colonel Sherwood was known not only for his stagecoach line, but also for his size, estimated at 410 pounds. (He succeeded his father, Isaac Sherwood, who was also a large man.) Nineteenth-century sources compare the Sherwoods to the Vanderbilt family—if not for size of wealth, for their power as transportation magnates. Colonel Sherwood also served as the president of the New York Agricultural Society in 1846 and was a founding member of Second Presbyterian of Auburn—something that surely infuriated Josiah Bissell Jr. "The Genesee Pike," *Syracuse Herald*, September 1, 1886, RPF; "Death of John M. Sherwood," *Auburn Daily Bulletin*, May 22, 1871, RPF; *Transactions of the New York State Agricultural Society* (Albany, NY: Argus Company, 1873), 32:vi; *Transactions of the New York State Agricultural Society*, 31:36. Vanderbilt reference: Israel Parsons, *The Centennial History of the Town of Marcellus, Delivered in the Presbyterian Church, of Marcellus, Onondaga County, N.Y., July 4, 1876* (Marcellus, NY: Reed's Printing House, 1878), 29–30; E. Norman Leslie, *History of Skaneateles and Vicinity, 1781–1881* (Auburn, NY: Chas. P. Cornell, 1882), 75. Isaac Sherwood: "Died," *Cayuga Patriot*, April 29, 1840, RPF.

21. The offer appeared in numerous papers: "To the Public," *Cayuga Republican* (Auburn, NY), April 9, 1828; "To the Public," *Rochester Daily Advertiser*, April 14, 1828; "To the Public," *Onondaga Register*, April 16, 1828.

22. "To the Public," *Cayuga Republican* (Auburn, NY), April 9, 1828.

23. "Moral Crusades Recalled," November 15, 1899, *Post Standard* (Syracuse, NY).

24. "To the Proprietors of the Old Line of Stages," *Rochester Observer*, May 9, 1828.

25. Richard R. John, "Taking Sabbatarianism Seriously: The Postal System, the Sabbath, and the Transformation of American Political Culture," *Journal of the Early Republic* 10, no. 4 (Winter 1990): 536–537.

26. John McLean to JBJ, November 26, 1828, Records of the Post Office Department, Records of the Postmaster General, Letters Sent, National Archives,

6. Conflict, Defeat, and Victory 297

Washington DC, RG 28; "Pioneer Stages," *Gospel Advocate and Impartial Investigator* (Auburn, NY), December 20, 1828, 4:411.

27. "Six Passengers Only," advertisement, *New York Spectator*, November 25, 1828, RPF; "New Line of Stages," *Onondaga Register*, June 11, 1828; "Rapid Traveling," *Onondaga Register*, September 10, 1828; "Old Line Forever!" *Utica Sentinel & Gazette*, February 9, 1830; "We the Undersigned," advertisement, *Utica Sentinel & Gazette*, February 9, 1830; Elisha Harrington, *The Utica Directory, 1828* (Utica, NY: C.N. Gaffney, 1828), 59.

28. Parsons, *The Centennial History of the Town of Marcellus*, 28–29; Leslie, *History of Skaneateles and Vicinity*, 72–73; Robert Barclay, *Agricultural Tour in the United States and Canada* (London: William Blackwood & Sons, 1842), 30–31.

29. In one case, a judge fined the Old Line twenty dollars for "speeding" in the village of Geddes (Syracuse), New York. "A Good Example," *Onondaga Register and Syracuse Gazette*, July 22, 1829. Twenty dollars equates to $526 (CPI).

30. "Stage Accident," *Rochester Daily Advertiser and Telegraph*, April 18, 1829; Leslie, *History of Skaneateles and Vicinity*, 73; Parsons, *The Centennial History of the Town of Marcellus*, 27–28; James O. Lyford, *History of Concord, New Hampshire, from the Original Grant in 1725 to the Opening of the Twentieth Century* (Concord, NH: Mumford Press, 1903), 850–851.

31. Lyford, *History of Concord*, 852; Ron Vineyard, *Stage Waggons and Coaches* (Williamsburg, VA: Colonial Williamsburg Foundation Library, 2002), 33–34.

32. Parsons, *The Centennial History of the Town of Marcellus*, 28–29; Leslie, *History of Skaneateles and Vicinity*, 73–74; Foreman, *RHPF*, 4:244–245.

33. On August 28, 1828, supposedly more than a thousand people attended an anti-Sabbatarian rally in Auburn. Henry Hall, *The History of Auburn* (Auburn, NY: Dennis Brothers, 1860), 169–170; "Moral Crusades Recalled," *Post Standard*, November 15, 1899. Auburn's role as a locus of reformers: Dorothy Wickenden, *The Agitators: Three Friends Who Fought for Abolition and Women's Rights* (New York: Scribner, 2021).

34. Eliot G. Storke, *The History of Cayuga County, New York* (Syracuse, NY: D. Mason & Co., 1879), 45.

35. John's father Isaac, of nearby Skaneateles, cofounded the Old Line in 1809, partnering with Jason Parker of Utica and Thomas Powell of Geneva, while John Sherwood was a student at Hamilton College. In addition to securing the lucrative federal mail contract in 1823, the Old Line enjoyed a monopoly on the passenger traffic between Albany and Buffalo. It was at this time of competition with the Pioneer Line that the Old Line officially became J. M. Sherwood & Company, even though it remained a partnership. *Transactions of the New York State Agricultural Society*, 31:34–36; John E. Becker, *A History of the Village of*

298   6. *Conflict, Defeat, and Victory*

Waterloo, New York and Thesaurus of Related Facts (Waterloo, NY: Waterloo Library and Historical Society, 1949), 110; Parsons, *The Centennial History of the Town of Marcellus*, 29–30; Storke, *The History of Cayuga County*, 44; "Death of John M. Sherwood," *Auburn Daily Bulletin*, May 22, 1871, RPF.

36. "Moral Crusades Recalled," November 15, 1899, *Post Standard*; Hall, *The History of Auburn*, 170; Storke, *The History of Cayuga County*, 45.

37. JBJ, "Mr. Editor," *Utica Sentinel & Gazette*, March 24, 1829.

38. "To all Editors of papers in the U. States," *Rochester Observer*, May 28, 1828. Emphasis in the original. See also: *Gospel Advocate and Impartial Investigator*, May 31, 1828; *Utica Evangelical Magazine*, August 23, 1828, 85; *Utica Sentinel & Gazette*, June 10, 1828.

39. This passage is often cited by twenty-first-century evangelicals (for example, it is commonly framed and displayed in homes). "From the Rochester Observer," *Utica Sentinel & Gazette*, June 10, 1828. Emphasis in the original.

40. "From the Rochester Observer of May 23," *Gospel Advocate and Impartial Investigator* (Auburn, NY), June 21, 1828. Emphasis in the original.

41. "From the Same as Above," *Gospel Advocate and Impartial Investigator* (Auburn, NY), June 21, 1828. Emphasis in the original.

42. "From the Same as Above," *Gospel Advocate and Impartial Investigator*, June 21, 1828. Emphasis in the original.

43. "Pioneer Stages," *Gospel Advocate and Impartial Investigator*, December 20, 1828, 411.

44. "Pioneerism," *The Craftsman* (Rochester, NY), April 21, 1829, 82.

45. "Written for the Craftsman," *The Craftsman*, December 22, 1829, 365.

46. *The Craftsman* was primarily a pro-Masonry paper. Joel Parker, *The Signs of the Times: A Sermon, Delivered in Rochester, December 4, 1828* (Rochester, NY: E. Peck & Co., 1828), 13–16.

47. The "molasses affair" could refer to Bissell's operation of his store. As for the double mortgage, evidence suggests Bissell's real estate holdings were highly leveraged. "Lockport Journal," *The Craftsman*, December 22, 1829, 365.

48. Patrick Carey and Joseph Lienhard, *Biographical Dictionary of Christian Theologians* (Westport, CT: Greenwood Publishing, 2000), 95; Christopher Grasso, *Skepticism and American Faith: From the Revolution to the Civil War* (New York: Oxford University Press, 2018), 324–327, 332–334; "Sunday Line of Stages," *Gospel Advocate and Impartial Investigator*, July 5, 1828, 223.

49. "Sunday Line of Stages," *Gospel Advocate and Impartial Investigator*, July 5, 1828, 223.

50. "New Line of Stages," *Gospel Advocate and Impartial Investigator*, March 15, 1828, 95; "The Pioneer," *Gospel Advocate and Impartial Investigator*, September 13, 1828, 303; "Presbyterianism," *The Craftsman*, March 31, 1829, 59.

6. Conflict, Defeat, and Victory

51. "Great Meeting at Auburn," *Gospel Advocate and Impartial Investigator*, September 13, 1828, 303.

52. Ezra Stiles Ely, *The Duty of Christian Freemen to Elect Christian Rulers (Philadelphia: W. F. Geddes, 1828)*, 1–13.

53. "Church and State," *Rochester Observer*, April 24, 1829; "Union of Church and State," *New York Observer*, April 18, 1829.

54. Hall records the population of Auburn as 2,982 in 1825 and 4,486 in 1830. Hall, *The History of Auburn*, 170, 172–173; Storke, *The History of Cayuga County*, 45.

55. Rochester news, *Rochester Observer*, December 12, 1828.

56. "Remonstrance," *Rochester Daily Advertiser*, December 13, 1828. Also: "Public Opinion," *Rochester Daily Advertiser*, December 16, 1828.

57. "Public Meeting," *Rochester Daily Advertiser*, December 11, 1828.

58. "Rochester and Buffalo Stage," advertisement, *Rochester Daily Advertiser*, December 27, 1828.

59. "To Our Patrons," *Rochester Observer*, December 26, 1828; "New Editorial Arrangement," *Rochester Observer*, January 2, 1829.

60. "Freemen Stand or Freemen Fall!," *The Craftsman*, March 10, 1829, 33.

61. Thomas Paine, *Common Sense* (Philadelphia: W. and T. Bradford, 1776), 9.

62. Massachusetts was the final state to disestablish an official church, in 1833. John D. Cushing, "Notes on Disestablishment in Massachusetts, 1780–1833," *William and Mary Quarterly* 26, no. 2 (April 1969): 169–190; Steven K. Green, *The Second Disestablishment: Church and State in Nineteenth-Century America* (New York: Oxford University Press, 2010).

63. Sabbatarian petitions: "The Sabbath Memorial," *Rochester Observer*, December 26, 1828; petition update, *Rochester Observer*, February 6, 1829; "Sunday Mails," *New York Observer*, November 7, 1829; letter from New York, *Rochester Observer*, November 13, 1829; "Sunday Mail Meeting at Rochester," *New York Observer*, December 5, 1829; "Sabbath Memorial," *New York Observer*, December 19, 1829; "Sabbath Memorials," *New York Observer*, December 26, 1829; "Sunday Mails—New-York Memorial," *New York Observer*, March 20, 1830. Anti-Sabbatarian petitions: "The Sabbath," *Rochester Observer*, February 6, 1829; "Spirit of the Sabbath Memorials," *New York Observer*, December 12, 1829; "Public Meeting at Salina," *Onondaga Register and Syracuse Gazette*, January 20, 1830; "Public Meeting," *Onondaga Register and Syracuse Gazette*, February 3, 1830; "Public Meeting in Lysander," *Onondaga Register and Syracuse Gazette*, March 3, 1830. See also Wayne E. Fuller, *Morality and the Mail in Nineteenth Century America* (Urbana: University of Illinois Press, 2003), 22–48; Richard R. John, *Spreading the News: The American Postal System from Franklin to Morse* (Cambridge, MA: Harvard University Press, 1995), 179–200.

64. "President Adams and the Sabbath Day," *New York Observer*, August 30, 1828; "Violation of the Sabbath," *Rochester Observer*, September 19, 1828; "Travelling on the Sabbath," *Onondaga Register*, February 18, 1829.

65. "Stopping the Mail," *The Watch-Tower* (Cooperstown, NY), May 4, 1829; "Stopping the Mail at Princeton," *Republican Star and General Advertiser*, June 9, 1829; "Stopping the Mail," *Onondaga Register and Syracuse Gazette*, June 24, 1829.

66. "Sabbath-Keeping Stages," *Rochester Observer*, January 2, 1829; "Consistency," *Rochester Observer*, January 9, 1829; "Pioneer Stages," *Rochester Observer*, April 24, 1829; "Pioneer Stages," *Rochester Observer*, July 31, 1829.

67. The Cayuga Lake Bridge was located just west of Auburn, New York. Aaron Burr's lieutenant, John Swartwout, was a driving force behind the construction of the bridge. Cayuga Bridge Company Ledger, Buffalo and Erie County Historical Society, Buffalo, New York, 3–43; Brian Murphy, *Building the Empire State: Political Economy in the Early Republic* (Philadelphia: University of Pennsylvania Press, 2015), 103.

68. "Pioneer Stages," advertisement, *New York Observer*, December 12, 1829; "Anti-Pioneer Ball," *Rochester Observer*, January 22, 1830.

69. The segment of the Pioneer Line from Rochester to Canandaigua only ran one stage per day for a few months, but was back to twice-a-day service by June 1830. Pioneer Line advertisement, *Rochester Advertiser and Telegraph*, April 1, 1829; Pioneer Line advertisement, *Rochester Observer*, December 25, 1829; notice, *Rochester Observer*, June 11, 1830; "Six Days Only Pioneer Stages," advertisement, *Rochester Observer*, June 11, 1830.

70. Advertisement, *Rochester Advertiser and Telegraph*, January 20, 1829; "Village Lots," advertisement, *Rochester Observer*, April 9, 1830.

71. Senate and House reports, William Addison Blakely, *American State Papers Bearing on Freedom in Religion* (Tacoma Park, WA: Review and Herald, 1911), 190–205.

72. There are too many examples to list comprehensively. Sabbatarian: Methodist address on Sabbath, *Rochester Observer*, March 20, 1829; "Sabbath Mails," *Rochester Observer*, January 1, 1830; Alexander Leighton, letter to the editor, *Rochester Observer*, January 8, 1830; "Respect in Congress for the Sabbath," *Rochester Observer*, January 15, 1830; "Sabbatarians," *Rochester Observer*, March 12, 1830; "Johnson's Report," *Rochester Observer*, April 2, 1830; "Sunday Mails-Church and State," *Rochester Observer*, July 30, 1830; Rochester news, *Rochester Observer*, December 17, 1830. Anti-Sabbatarian: "Religious Liberty," *Rochester Observer*, January 22, 1830; "Acadia Sabbath Meeting," *Rochester Observer*, January 29, 1830; "Pembroke Meeting in Favor of Saturday Mails," *Rochester Observer*, February 12, 1830; "Public Meeting in Philadelphia, in Favor of Sunday Mail," *Rochester Observer*, March 5, 1830.

73. "Public Meeting," *Rochester Observer*, March 20, 1829.

74. Rochester began appointing mayors after reincorporation as a city in 1834. Jacob Gould, letter, *Rochester Observer*, March 20, 1829; Blake McKelvey, "Rochester Mayors Before the Civil War," *Rochester History* 26, no. 1 (January 1964): 3–5.

75. Records for the Cayuga Bridge Company show the Pioneer Line still paying tolls up through March 1831, and then record no tolls for the Pioneer Line thereafter. Cayuga Bridge Company Ledger, 46.

76. "Stages," *Utica Sentinel & Gazette*, June 15, 1830.

77. The $20,000 figure is equivalent to $600,000 (CPI) or $17.5 million (per capita GDP). "Editorial Notices," *The Craftsman*, July 14, 1829, 185.

78. Paul E. Johnson, *A Shopkeeper's Millennium: Society and Revivals in Rochester, New York, 1815–1837* (New York: Hill and Wang, 1978), 88. This judgment echoes the conclusion of the upstate New York village histories, such as Storke, *The History of Cayuga County*, 45.

79. Parsons, *The Centennial History of the Town of Marcellus*, 28–29; Leslie, *History of Skaneateles and Vicinity*, 73–74; Hatch, "Memories of Village Days, 1822–1830," *RHPF*, 4:244–245.

80. Richard Palmer, Blake McKelvey, and Paul Johnson all overlook this timing, instead solely blaming the unpopularity of the Pioneer Line for its failure. "Obituary," *Rochester Observer*, April 21, 1831.

81. Henrietta Bissell to Charles Finney, April 16, 1831, *RHPF*, 21:35–39; "Obituary," *Rochester Observer*, April 21, 1831. Flour mill: "Died," *New York Observer*, April 16, 1831.

82. Quote: William E. Peck, *Semi-Centennial History of the City of Rochester with Illustrations and Biographical Sketches of Some of Its Prominent Men and Pioneers* (Syracuse, NY: D. Mason & Co., 1884), 668. A. W. Riley: "The Sabbath," *Rochester Observer*, February 8, 1828; "To the Public," *Rochester Observer*, April 2, 1830.

83. Monroe County Land Records indicate that Josiah W. Bissell retained some manner of control over much of the Bissell real estate holdings. Will of JBJ, April 26, 1831, *Monroe County Record of Wills*, No. 1, 85–92, New York Probate Records, 1629–1971, Monroe County; New York Probate Records, 1629–1971, Family Search, accessed April 12, 2023, https://www.familysearch.org/search/collection/1920234; Index of Deeds, Monroe County Land Records, 156–157, Office of the Monroe County Clerk, Rochester, NY; Elizabeth S. S. Eaton to Amos B. Eaton, December 2, 1839, *RHPF*, 66–67; announcement of Rochester chapter of ABCFM, *Rochester Observer*, September 29, 1827; "insolvency": Henry O'Reilly, *Sketches of Rochester: With Incidental Notices of Western New York* (Rochester: William Alling, 1838), 303.

84. Quote: "J. W. Bissell," New York Vol. 162, Monroe County, 1841–1872, 288, RGD; Index of Deeds, Monroe County Land Records, 156–157, Office of the Monroe County Clerk, Rochester, NY; index of Mortgages, Monroe County Land Records, 156–157.

85. By 1838, Josiah W. had entered the banking world, working as a clerk and exchange agent at the Rochester City Bank, where vocal Pioneer critic Jacob Gould was the bank's first president. Later, for five years, he sold fire and life insurance, and by 1851 had started his own private banking firm, Bissell & Amsden. *King's Rochester City Directory and Register, 1841*, 39; James L. Elwood and Dellon M. Dewey, *A Directory and Gazetteer of the City of Rochester* (Rochester, NY: Canfield & Warren, 1844), 103; *Cranfield & Warren's Director of the City of Rochester, for 1845–1846* (Rochester, NY: Canfield & Warren, 1845), 37.

86. *Daily American Directory of the City of Rochester, for 1847–8* (Rochester, NY: Jerome & Brothers, 1847), 65; "J. W. Bissell," New York Vol. 162, Monroe County, 1841–1872, 288, 290, 291 ("embarrassed"), RGD; Donovan A. Shilling "The Great Water Bridges: The Story of the Magnificent Genesee River Aqueducts," *Crooked Lake Review*, no. 75 (June 1994), http://www. crookedlakereview.com /articles/67_100/75june1994/75shilling.html.

87. Joseph W. Barnes, "Bridging the Lower Falls," *Rochester History* 36, no. 1 (January 1974): 13–20; *RHPF*, 6:335–336; Foreman, *Centennial History of Rochester*, 3:179.

88. "Pioneerism," *The Craftsman*, April 21, 1829, 82. Emphasis in the original.

89. Certificate of refund for *Herald*, January 21, 1845, A1139: Bills of Lading and Clearances for Cargoes, Box 1, CRNY.

90. "Sundays Excepted," *Rochester Observer*, June 12, 1829. Pioneerism influenced taverns along the turnpikes in a similar manner: "Traveling on the Sabbath," *Rochester Observer*, June 5, 1829; "From the *Connecticut Observer*," *Rochester Observer*, July 17, 1829.

91. Certificate of Registry of *Temperance*, April 25, 1833, A1137–77: Certificates of Registry of Canal Boats, 1837–1888, Box 1, CRNY; Consent and Agreement for Line of Boats, Clinton Line, April 24, 1834, and Commercial Line, 1834, A1178: Agreements for Commutation of Passenger Tolls on Freight Boats Carrying Passengers, CRNY; Express Stage Ticket, RPF; Merchant's and Millers' Line: Elwood and Dewey, *A Directory and Gazetteer of the City of Rochester*, 72.

92. "Opposition Stages," in Foreman, *Centennial History of Rochester*, 2:153. This is consistent with Alexis McCrossen, who argues that by 1840s and 1850s, Sabbatarianism had succeeded in spreading throughout the western regions of Pennsylvania and New York, as well as Ohio and Indiana: *Holy Day, Holiday: The American Sunday* (Ithaca, NY: Cornell University Press, 2018), 28. See also McCrossen's chapter in David K. Adams and Cornelius van Minnen, *Religious*

6. Conflict, Defeat, and Victory 303

and Secular Reform in America (New York: New York University Press, 1999), 133–158.

93. However, even then, the purpose for Sunday travel was not commercial, but recreational in nature. McCrossen, *Holy Day, Holiday*, 79–92.

94. John, *Spreading the News*, 200–201.

PART THREE. CHRISTIAN VIRTUE CAPITALISM

1. "Culture," as Wendy Griswold notes, "is one of those words that people use all the time but have trouble defining," ranging from narrow definitions such as "high art" to expansive definitions such as "the totality of humanity's material and nonmaterial products." The next two chapters examine how Harper produced specific "cultural objects" that expressed specific "cultural ideas" in the hopes they would in turn shape "cultural behavior." Griswold, *Cultures and Societies in a Changing World* (Thousand Oaks, CA: Pine Forge Press, 1994), 1, 11–15.

2. David Paul Nord, *Faith in Reading: Religious Publishing and the Birth of Mass Media in America* (New York: Oxford University Press, 2007); Peter Wosh, *Spreading the Word: The Bible Business in Nineteenth-Century America* (Ithaca, NY: Cornell University Press, 1994); Sam Haselby, *The Origins of American Religious Nationalism* (New York: Oxford University Press, 2015), 234–281; John Fea, *The Bible Cause: A History of the American Bible Society* (New York: Oxford University Press, 2016).

3. The lone exception is Candy Gunther Brown, *The Word in the World: Evangelical Writing, Publishing, and Reading in America, 1789–1880* (Chapel Hill: University of North Carolina Press, 2004), which briefly covers the Harpers. The introduction of Matthew Hedstrom's *The Rise of Liberal Religion: Book Culture and American Spirituality in the Twentieth Century* (New York: Oxford University Press, 2013), 11–15, is typical in emphasizing the ABS, while arguing that nineteenth-century conservative Protestants were generally hostile to the popular press. Although this was often the stance of religious publishers such as the American Bible Society or the American Tract Society, it certainly never reflected the views of conservative Protestant publishers such as the Harpers and their competitors. Nord, *Faith in Reading*, 115–118.

4. Hedstrom, *The Rise of Liberal Religion*, 3–21, 54–61, 80–114. Daniel Vaca's *Evangelicals Incorporated: Books and the Business of Religion in America* (Cambridge, MA: Harvard University Press, 2019) is another example of a focus on twentieth-century Protestant publishing and culture.

5. William Charvat, *Literary Publishing in America, 1790–1850* (Philadelphia: University of Pennsylvania Press, 1959), 60.

304   *6. Conflict, Defeat, and Victory*

6. The original name (listed in the Harper contract) was *The Whale*. Agreement between H&B and Herman Melville, September 12, 1851, AHB: 53; Eugene Exman, *The Brothers Harper* (New York: Harper & Row, 1965), 282–302.

7. Hedstrom, *The Rise of Liberal Religion*, 6.

8. Brown, *The Word in the World*, 75.

9. Brown, 113.

10. Additionally, some publishers, such as Riverside Press of Hurd & Houghton and Lockwood & Books, partnered with nondenominational groups, such as the American Tract Society. Brown, *The Word in the World*, 66.

11. John W. Francis, *Old New York: Or, Reminiscences of the Past Sixty Years* (New York: Charles Roe, 1858), 50.

12. Brown, *The Word in the World*, 50.

13. Cathy N. Davidson, *Revolution and the Word: The Rise of the Novel in America*, expanded ed. (New York: Oxford University Press, 2004); Maria Carla Sanchez, *Reforming the World: Social Activism and the Problem of Fiction in Nineteenth Century America* (Iowa City: University of Iowa Press, 2008). Opposition: H&B to ELB, January 15, 1835, HBR, Series II, Box 16, Folder 4. Even though Bulwer is often referred to as Edward Bulwer-Lytton today, the Harpers addressed him as E. L. Bulwer, so the abbreviation follows their convention.

14. John Wigger, *Taking Heaven by Storm: Methodism and the Rise of Popular Christianity in America* (New York: Oxford University Press, 1998), 180.

15. George Marsden, *Fundamentalism and American Culture*, new ed. (New York: Oxford University Press, 2005), 21.

16. Ronald Zboray estimates that a book in the antebellum period would cost approximately $50–$150 in today's purchasing power (even though it sold for a rough equivalent of $12), making even $0.50 titles too expensive for many Americans: Ronald Zboray, *A Fictive People: Antebellum Economic Development and the American Reading Public* (New York: Oxford University Press, 1993), 11–12. His estimate is conservative, as $0.50 equates to $15 (CPI) and over $400 (per capita GDP). Lawrence W. Levine, *Highbrow/Lowbrow: The Emergence of Cultural Hierarchy in America* (Cambridge, MA: Harvard University Press, 1988).

17. Marsden, *Fundamentalism and American Culture*, 17.

18. A. D. F. Randolph, "Fletcher Harper," *Publishers' Weekly*, June 9, 1877, 604.

19. "James and Wesley Harper," *Trade Circular Annual for 1871, Including the American Catalogue of Books Published in the United States During the Year 1870* (New York: Office of the Trade Circular and Literary Bulletin, 1871), 114; R. R. Bowker, "The Harper Brothers," *The Publishers' Trade List Annual, 1877* (New York: Office of the Publishers' Weekly, 1877), xiii; Exman, *The Brothers Harper*, xiv.

Part Three. Christian Virtue Capitalism　305

20. Russell, *A History of Modern Europe, with a View of the Progress of Society from the Rise of the Modern Kingdoms to the Peace of Paris, 1763*, vol. 3 (New York: J. & J. Harper, 1833), back matter, SL.

21. Charvat, *Literary Publishing in America*, 42.

22. John Tebbel, *A History of Book Publishing in the United States*, vol. 1, *The Creation of an Industry, 1640–1865* (New York: R. R. Bowker, 1972), 263.

23. Exman wrote two books with a fair amount of overlap, *The Brothers Harper* (1965) and Eugene Exman, *The House of Harper* (1967), on the publishing output of the Harpers (and less on their character and business operation), in part due to the limitations of the firm's surviving archival record. Exman's history at Harper & Brothers: Matthew S. Hedstrom, "The Commodification of William James: The Book Business and the Rise of Liberal Spirituality in the Twentieth-Century United States," in *Religion and the Marketplace in the United States*, ed. Jan Stievermann, Philip Goff, and Detlef Junker (New York: Oxford University Press, 2015), 134–140, and Hedstrom, *The Rise of Liberal Religion*, 88–114; Stephen Prothero, *God the Bestseller: How One Editor Transformed American Religion a Book at a Time* (New York: HarperOne, 2023).

24. "A Word of Apology," *Harper's New Monthly Magazine*, January 1854, 147.

25. Brown, *The Word in the World*, 174.

26. "Allison's History of Europe," *Southern Literary Messenger* 9, no. 3 (March 1843): 136. The next chapter discusses how Americans of more modest means would have had access to the Harpers' books through schools and libraries.

27. Nathan O. Hatch, "The Puzzle of American Methodism," in *Methodism and the Shaping of American Culture*, ed. Nathan O. Hatch and John Wigger (Nashville, TN: Kingswood Books, 2001), 25–27, 31–36. Recent works that are starting to address this: Dee E. Andrews, *The Methodists and Revolutionary America, 1760–1800* (Princeton, NJ: Princeton University Press, 2000); Kyle T. Bulthuis, *Four Steeples Over the City Streets: Religion and Society in New York's Early Republic Congregations* (New York: New York University Press, 2014); Kyle B. Roberts, *Evangelical Gotham: Religion and the Making of New York City, 1783–1860* (Chicago: University of Chicago Press, 2016).

28. Hatch, "The Puzzle of American Methodism," 38.

29. Charles Sellers, *The Market Revolution: Jacksonian America, 1815–1846* (New York: Oxford University Press, 1991), 28–33, 157–161, 299–300; Max Weber, *The Protestant Ethic and the "Spirit" of Capitalism and Other Writings* (New York: Penguin, 2002), 95–98; Robert H. Nelson, "Max Weber Revisited," in *Religion, Economy, and Cooperation*, ed. Ilkka Pyysiainen (New York: Walter de Gruyter, 2010), 157–217. Mark Valeri dissects Weber's negative view of the contribution of Methodism to capitalist development in "Weber and

306   *Part Three. Christian Virtue Capitalism*

Eighteenth-Century Religious Developments in America," in Stievermann, Goff, and Junker, *Religion and the Marketplace in the United States*, 63–78.

30. This egalitarianism enforced limits on racial equality in the early decades of the nineteenth century. Richard Carwardine, "Charles Seller's 'Antinomians' and 'Arminians': Methodists and the Market Revolution," in *God and Mammon: Protestants, Money, and the Market, 1790–1860*, ed. Mark Noll (New York: Oxford University Press, 2002), 80. David Hempton and John Walsh also challenge the Sellers Methodist narrative: see "E. P. Thompson and Methodism," in Noll, *God and Mammon*, 99–115.

31. Nicole C. Kirk, *Wanamaker's Temple: The Business of Religion in an Iconic Department Store* (New York: New York University Press, 2018), 60.

32. Kirk, 60.

33. Kirk, 75.

34. Kirk, 77, 126, 127, 129, 197–200.

35. Kirk, 202.

7. METHODIST PRINTER-PUBLISHERS

1. The brothers also all died within eight years of one another. James was eldest, born April 13, 1795, John, January 22, 1797, Joseph Wesley (who went by Wesley), December 25, 1801, and Fletcher, January 31, 1806. R. R. Bowker, "The Harper Brothers," in *The Publishers' Trade List Annual, 1877* (New York: Office of the *Publishers' Weekly*, 1877), vi.

2. J. C. Derby, *Fifty Years Among Authors, Books, and Publishers* (New York: Carleton, 1884), 89. "James C. Derby-OBIT," *Publisher's Weekly*, October 1, 1892, 559–560.

3. The Methodism of the Harpers' father almost prevented his marriage to the boys' mother, as her father was prejudicial against the sect. Derby, *Fifty Years*, 88; "James and Wesley Harper," in *The Trade Circular Annual for 1871, Including the American Catalogue of Books Published in the United States during the Year 1870* (New York: Office of the Trade Circular and Literary Bulletin, 1871), 114; "Fletcher Harper," *Harper's Weekly*, June 16, 1877; Bowker, "The Harper Brothers," vi.

4. J. Henry Harper, *The House of Harper: A Century of Publishing in Franklin Square* (New York: Harper & Brothers, 1912), 33.

5. John and Charles Wesley were Arminians who emphasized the role of free will in salvation and striving for "Christian perfection," with an emphasis on the work of the Holy Spirit. The more well-known Wesley sermons on money: "The Use of Money," in Albert C. Outler and Richard P. Heitzenrater, *John Wesley's Sermons: An Anthology (Nashville, TN: Abingdon Press, 1991)*,

7. Methodist Printer-Publishers 307

348–357; and the following from *The Works of the Reverend John Wesley*, vol. 7 (New York: J. & J. Harper, 1826): "The Danger of Riches," 55–65; "On Wealth," 224–230; "Causes of the Inefficacy of Christianity," 262–263; "On the Danger of Increasing Riches," 316–322.

6. Wesley, "The Use of Money," 350–353. Emphasis in the original.

7. The archives of Harper & Brothers do not include account books from the antebellum period. A huge 1853 fire at their establishment probably destroyed some of them, but many contracts still survive from this period. Along with these contracts, the archives include many scratch pieces of financial records, which are typically messy and hard to interpret, such as those relating to their edition of the *Webster's Dictionary*: AHB, 58 (Miscellaneous Correspondence and Documents Relating to Authors). The brothers' dispute with Theodore Sedgwick Fay over payment and loans in the mid-1840s is a good example of the brothers' less than precise record keeping. Eugene Exman, *The Brothers Harper* (New York: Harper & Row, 1965), 211–229.

8. Wesley, "The Use of Money," 353. Emphasis in the original.

9. As his biographer John Wigger points out, Asbury's austere posture was often not shared by his laity: Wigger, *American Saint: Francis Asbury and the Methodists* (New York: Oxford University Press, 2009), 176.

10. Francis Asbury, May 27, 1787, in *The Journal and Letters of Francis Asbury*, vol. 1, 540, Wesley Center Online, accessed April 12, 2023, http://wesley.nnu.edu/other-theologians/francis-asbury/the-journal-and-letters-of-francis-asbury-volume-i/francis-asbury-the-journal-vol-1-chapter-16/. Asbury visited some ten thousand homes: John Wigger, *Taking Heaven by Storm: Methodism and the Rise of Popular Christianity in America* (New York: Oxford University Press, 1998), 43.

11. Wigger, *Taking Heaven by Storm*, 12.

12. These are my summaries, as the brothers never left behind any such list. Bowker, "The Harper Brothers," v; Harper, *The House of Harper*, 22–23.

13. John Wesley, *The Nature, Design, and General Rules of the United Societies*, 5th ed. (Bristol, GB: Felix Farley, 1747); Dee E. Andrews, *The Methodists and Revolutionary America, 1760–1800* (Princeton, NJ: Princeton University Press, 2000), 166.

14. Wesley, "Causes of the Inefficacy of Christianity," 262.

15. Wesley, "On the Danger of Increasing Riches," 316.

16. Wesley, "Causes of the Inefficacy of Christianity," 263. Emphasis in the original.

17. "Harper & Brothers," *New Yorker*, November 10, 1838, 126; Karen Halttunen, *Confidence Men and Painted Ladies: A Study of Middle-Class Culture in America, 1830–1870* (New Haven, CT: Yale University Press, 1982); Edward Balleisen, *Navigating Failure: Bankruptcy and Commercial Society in Antebellum*

America (Chapel Hill: University of North Carolina Press, 2001); Scott A. Sandage, *Born Losers: A History of Failure in America* (Cambridge, MA: Harvard University Press, 2005); Stephen Mihm, *A Nation of Counterfeiters: Capitalists, Con Men, and the Making of the United States* (Cambridge, MA: Harvard University Press, 2007); Jane Kamensky, *The Exchange Artist: A Tale of High-Flying Speculation and America's First Banking Collapse* (New York: Viking Press, 2008); Jonathan Levy, *Freaks of Fortune: The Emerging World of Capitalism and Risk in America* (Cambridge, MA: Harvard University Press, 2012).

18. H&B to ELB, January 15, 1835, HBR, Series II, Box 16, Folder 4.

19. H&B to ELB, April 7, 1835, HBR, Series II, Box 16, Folder 4.

20. "Harper & Co.," New York Vol. 201 New York City, 456, RGD.

21. "Fletcher Harper," *Harper's Weekly*, June 16, 1877; Bowker, "The Harper Brothers, viii.

22. Derby, *Fifty Years*, 107; "Contributions to Trade History, no. XI," *American Bookseller*, July 1, 1885, 7.

23. "Harper & Brothers," *New Yorker*, November 10, 1838, 126. Another account likened their collective strength to a "bundle of rods": Probus, "Letters from New York, Number II," *Southern Literary Messenger* 5, no. 9 (September 1839), 629.

24. Harper, *The House of Harper*, 28.

25. "James and Wesley Harper," *The Trade Circular Annual for 1871*, 114–115; "Contributions to Trade History," *American Bookseller*, 1 June 1885, 301; Derby, *Fifty Years*, 90–92; Bowker, "The Harper Brothers," xii. Sean Wilentz turns James's penchant for merriment into a parody (*Chants Democratic*, 318–319), dismissing him as an objectionable simpleton, an assertion that is not supported by any contemporary accounts. If anything, all the nineteenth-century sources, while acknowledging his penchant for jokes, assert that James was capably in charge of overseeing the entire operations of Harper & Brothers and that he was regarded a keen businessman by his rivals, critics, and admirers. For example: Davis W. Clark, "A Visit to the Publishing House of the Messrs. Harper & Brothers," *Ladies' Repository*, November 1853, 512–513.

26. "James and Wesley Harper," *The Trade Circular Annual for 1871*, 114–115; Clark, "A Visit to the House of the Messrs. Harper & Brothers," 512. All the earliest secondary accounts assert the church attendance as fact, but James does not show up in any New York City Methodist records until 1813.

27. S. G. Goodrich, *Recollections of a Lifetime, Men and Things I Have Seen: In a Series of Familiar Letters to a Friend, Historical, Biographical, Anecdotical, and Descriptive*, vol. 2 (New York: Miller, Orton and Mulligan, 1856), 254; "Destructive Fire," *New-York Daily Times*, December 12, 1853; Clark, "A Visit to the House of the Messrs. Harper & Brothers," 512; "Contributions to Trade History," *American Bookseller*, June 1, 1885, 301; John Tebbel, *A History of Book*

Publishing in the United States, vol. 1, *The Creation of an Industry, 1640–1865* (New York: R. R. Bowker, 1972), 271.

28. "John Street Church," in *Encyclopedia of World Methodism*, vol. 1, ed. Nolan B. Harmon (Nashville, TN: United Methodist Publishing House, 1974), 1269. Although there is some debate on the matter of primacy, John Street called itself the "Mother Church of American Methodism" in 1932: see the foreword to Francis Bourne Upham, *The Story of Old John Street Methodist Episcopal Church* (New York: John Street Methodist Church, 1932). One of the leading scholars of Methodism, Russell Richey, called it a "White House of Methodism for a while" in an email exchange (Russell Richey to author, June 15, 2016). See also J. B. Wakeley, *Lost Chapters Recovered from the Early History of Methodism* (New York: Carlton & Porter, 1858), 178–189; Samuel Seaman, *Annals of New York Methodism, Being a History of the Methodist Episcopal Church in the City of New York* (New York: Hunt & Eaton, 1892), 36–37. Bookseller William Gowans told of meeting James at an early age, at the beginning of his long career. Desperately in need of a loan, James extended one unsolicited, an act that Gowans stated was "stamped upon my memory," and which he never forgot. Harper, *House of Harper*, 48–49

29. Methodist "classes" functioned as vehicles of sanctification or holiness within the Methodist system. Although like "accountability groups" of late twentieth- and early twenty-first-century evangelicalism, Methodist classes were much more institutional and important to early Methodism's theology. Wigger, *Taking Heaven by Storm*, 80–87; Philip F. Hardt, *The Soul of Methodism: The Class Meeting in Early New York City Methodism* (Lanham, MD: University Press of America, 2000), 50–61.

30. "James Harper," *Harper's Weekly*, April 17, 1869.

31. Williams was either the third or the fourth sexton of John Street (in charge of the building's maintenance), and he purchased his freedom outright within two years of his purchase by John Street Church and was officially manumitted after fifteen years of "official" slavery to John Street Church. His son Peter Williams Jr. became an important figure in the city's all-Black churches, rising to rector of St. Philips Episcopal. Kyle T. Bulthuis, *Four Steeples Over the City Streets: Religion and Society in New York's Early Republic Congregations* (New York: New York University Press, 2014), 63–74, 98–105, 110–113, 118–119, 133–143, 147–148, 153–154, 172–178. Wakeley, *Lost Chapters*, 438–471. John Street Church's 1932 history claims Williams was free upon his reimbursement to the church's trustees: "Peter Williams, The Slave," in Upham, *The Story of Old John Street Methodist Episcopal Church*, n.p.; Will Gravely, "'. . . Many of the Poor Affricans Are Obedient to the Faith': Reassessing the African American Presence in Early Methodism in the United States, 1769–1809," in *Methodism*

310 *7. Methodist Printer-Publishers*

and the Shaping of American Culture, ed. Nathan O. Hatch and John Wigger (Nashville, TN: Kingswood Books, 2001), 175–195; Wigger, *Taking Heaven by Storm,* 125–150.

32. Class Lists, 1813, Vol. 80, MECR; Wigger, *Taking Heaven by Storm,* 82–86; Hardt, *The Soul of Methodism,* 14–18, 24–30.

33. In the early nineteenth century, New York City's Methodist churches did not have assigned clergy, but instead shared them. Wigger, *Taking Heaven by Storm,* 189–190; Abel Stevens, *The Life and Times of Nathan Bangs* (New York: Carlton & Porter, 1863), 182–183.

34. MECR Vols. 66–96.

35. Building Subscription List, 1817, Vol. 250, MECR.

36. Interestingly, Thurlow Weed moved a short time later to Rochester, New York, in 1822, where he worked for a short time on the *Rochester Telegraph* and most likely would have run into Josiah Bissell. Weed, *Life of Thurlow Weed Including His Autobiography and a Memoir,* vol. 1 (Boston: Houghton, Mifflin and Company, 1884), 57; Harper, *The House of Harper,* 15–16.

37. Weed, *Life of Thurlow Weed,* 2:5.

38. Bulthuis, *Four Steeples,* 59–62; Wigger, *Taking Heaven by Storm,* 48–62; John H. Wigger, "Fighting Bees: Methodist Itinerants and the Dynamics of Methodist Growth, 1770–1820," in Hatch and Wigger, *Methodism and the Shaping of American Culture,* 88–95.

39. Producerists saw themselves as occupying the middle between the "rough" and "fashionable" Methodists. They advocated for a traditional artisanal ethic of business and exchange. William R. Sutton, " 'To Extract Poison from the Blessings of God's Providence': Producerist Respectability and Methodist Suspicions of Capitalist Change in the Early Republic," in Hatch and Wigger, *Methodism and the Shaping of American Culture,* 223–255.

40. Nathan Hatch argues Methodism fostered social mobility: see Hatch, "The Puzzle of American Methodism," in Hatch and Wigger, *Methodism and the Shaping of American Culture,* 29–31. Bulthuis, *Four Steeples,* 50, 56–62, 76, 128.

41. Max Weber, *The Protestant Ethic and the "Spirit" of Capitalism and other Writings (New York: Penguin, 2002),* 95–98; Richard Carwardine, "Charles Seller's 'Antinomians' and 'Arminians': Methodists and the Market Revolution," in *God and Mammon: Protestants, Money, and the Market, 1790–1860,* ed. Mark Noll (New York: Oxford University Press, 2002), 84–86.

42. Wigger, *Taking Heaven by Storm,* 16–17.

43. July 25, 1802, *The Journal of the Rev. Francis Asbury, Bishop of the Methodist Episcopal Church, from August 7, 1771, to December 7, 1815,* vol. 3 (New York: N. Bangs and T. Mason, 1821), 72.

44. Laodicea was a Greek city in present-day southwestern Turkey. Revelation 3:17.

7. Methodist Printer-Publishers   311

45. May 22, 1083, *The Journal of the Rev. Francis Asbury,* 3:103. Emphasis in the original.

46. August 5, 1804, *The Journal of the Rev. Francis Asbury,* 3:143. Emphasis in the original. "Valley of dry bones" is a reference to Ezekiel 37.

47. 1 Timothy 6:7.

48. *The Journal of the Rev. Francis Asbury,* vol. 3 (numbers following colons refer to pages): June 6, 1802: 64; July 25, 1802: 72; June 11, 1804: 138; May 27, 1811: 309.

49. Treasurer Records, Vol. 92, MECR. Vocational demographics of eighteenth-century Methodism: Andrews, *The Methodists and Revolutionary America,* 252–254. For the early nineteenth century, see Bulthuis, *Four Steeples,* 59–62.

50. Some accounts claim they moved because of rapid growth, others because of fire. "Fletcher Harper," *Harper's Weekly,* June 16, 1877; Bowker, "The Harper Brothers," vi-viii, xv; Tebbel, *A History of Book Publishing,* 1:271.

51. Wesley: "James and Wesley Harper," *The Trade Circular Annual for 1871,* 115; "Contributions to Trade History," *American Bookseller,* June 15, 1885, 324; Derby, *Fifty Years,* 98, 104; "Fletcher Harper," *Harper's Weekly,* June 16, 1877; Fletcher: "Fletcher Harper," *Publishers' Weekly,* June 2, 1877; Both: Bowker, "The Harper Brothers," xiv–xv; Tebbel, *A History of Book Publishing,* 1:272.

52. January 5, 1843, *Diaries of Evert A. Duyckinck,* Duyckinck Collection, New York Public Library. Duyckinck: Steven Carl Smith, *An Empire of Print: The New York Publishing Trade in the Early American Republic* (University Park, PA: Penn State University Press, 2017), 138–174. In New York City, members of the Young America movement were writer-intellectuals that "shared a generational distaste for the clique of conservative critics, publishers, and magazine editors whose mutual backscratching made it difficult for newcomers to penetrate the market." Edwin G. Burrows and Mike Wallace, *Gotham: A History of New York to 1898* (New York: Oxford University Press, 1999), 686.

53. "Noss": Bowker, "The Harper Brothers," xii; "temperance man": "James Harper," *Harper's Weekly,* April 17, 1869.

54. Derby, *Fifty Years,* 95–96; Harper, *The House of Harper,* 53. The historian of publisher Carey & Lea, the brothers' main competition in the 1830s, contradicts the rest of the historical record by claiming the brothers did print on Sundays. His evidence for the claim the Harpers worked seven days a week was a fear expressed in a letter composed by Carey & Lea that the Harpers would beat them to the market with a new reprint (by printing on Sunday). The earliest primary source (Derby's first-hand account) to address the Harpers' work habits dates to 1884, and claims that at the time, the current policy of Harper & Brothers was to not work on Sunday. This is an easily refuted claim if false, so I side with the overwhelming historiographical judgment over solitary speculation to the contrary. Several secondary sources from the 1850s also mention the Sabbath as a

non-workday at Harper & Brothers. David Kaser, *Messrs. Carey & Lea of Philadelphia: A Study in the History of the Booktrade* (Philadelphia: University of Pennsylvania Press, 1957), 107, 167–168. Kyle Bulthuis doubts the Sabbath firing story, but confuses James with John, a key detail. Bulthuis, *Four Steeples*, 188.

55. I consider these stories apocryphal and to be taken with a grain of salt. However, the important point regarding the Harpers is that their religiosity was testified to by all who knew them. Derby, *Fifty Years*, 96.

56. Derby, *Fifty Years*, 99–100.

57. "Fletcher Harper," *Publishers' Weekly*, June 2, 1877, 585.

58. Davis W. Clark, "A Visit to the House of the Messrs. Harper & Brothers," *Ladies' Repository*, November 1853, 512. Emphasis in the original.

59. Harper, *The House of Harper*, 6.

60. Harper, 34; Derby, *Fifty Years*, 108.

61. Harper, *The House of Harper*, 34–35.

62. "John Harper," *Harper's Weekly*, May 8, 1875, 374. Wesley was known as "The Captain" from his time as an artillery officer, while Fletcher was called "The Major." "John Harper," *Harper's Weekly*, May 8, 1875; Bowker, "The Harper Brothers," xii, xiv; *The Publishers' Trade List Annual, 1877*, xii, xiv, xv.

63. "It is so much easier": "James Harper," *Harper's Weekly*, April 17, 1869, 242.

64. James and reform: Benson John Lossing, *History of New York City, Embracing an Outline of Events from 1609 to 1830, and a Full Account of Its Development from 1830 to 1884*, vol. 2 (New York: George E. Perine, 1885), 494n; Ecumenicalism: Harper, *The House of Harper*, 59.

65. Derby, *Fifty Years*, 107.

66. Seaman, *Annals of New York Methodism*, 495.

67. Nathan Bangs, *A History of the Methodist Church*, vol. 4 (New York: G. Lane and P. P. Sandford, 1841), 70. Bangs: Nathan O. Hatch, *The Democratization of American Christianity* (New Haven, CT: Yale University Press, 1989), 202–204; Richard J. Carwardine, "Methodists, Politics, and the Coming of the American Civil War," in Hatch and Wigger, *Methodism and the Shaping of American Culture*, 236.

68. Tebbel, *A History of Book Publishing*, 1:203; Bowker, "The Harper Brothers," vii.

69. H&B to ELB, September 12, 1836, HBR, Series II, Box 16, Folder 4; Tebbel, *A History of Book Publishing*, 1:208; Meredith McGill, *American Literature and the Culture of Reprinting, 1834–1853* (Philadelphia: University of Pennsylvania Press, 2003), 105; Exman, *The Brothers Harper*, 23.

70. J. & J. Harper to ELB, July 31, 1830, and February 24, 1832, HBR, Series II, Box 16, Folder 4; Tebbel, *A History of Book Publishing*, 1:208–209.

71. "Rough Notes of Thirty Years in the Trade," *American Publishers' Circular* 10 (July 15, 1863): 243–244.

7. Methodist Printer-Publishers   313

72. H&B to ELB, n.d. (probably spring/summer 1836), HBR, Box 16, Folder 4; Derby, *Fifty Years*, 551. Exman maintains that Carey & Hart printed *Rienzi* as a reprisal against the Harpers: *The Brothers Harper*, 52–55.

73. Printing is distinguished from publishing—the former being done for clients who place an order, whereas the latter is produced, marketed, and sold by the printer. The Harpers printed some other works before *An Essay Concerning Human Understanding*, but sources differ on how many. "James Harper," *Harper's Weekly*, April 17, 1869; Bowker, "The Harper Brothers," vii; William H. Demarest, *The Harper's Catalogue*, 1817–1879, AHB, 24.

74. "Decalogue" is a term for the Ten Commandments. Seneca, *Seneca's Morals* (New York: Evert Duyckinck, 1817), iv.

75. Seneca, *Seneca's Morals*, vii–viii; Mark A. Noll, *America's God: From Jonathan Edwards to Abraham Lincoln* (New York: Oxford University Press, 2002), 73–113, 330–364.

76. William Russell, *A History of Modern Europe, with a View of the Progress of Society from the Rise of the Modern Kingdoms to the Peace of Paris, 1763*, vol. 3 (New York: J. & J. Harper, 1833), back matter, SL.

77. Wakeley, *Lost Chapters*, 581–582.

78. Seaman, *Annals of New York Methodism*, 40.

79. May 11, 1810, *The Journal of the Rev. Francis Asbury*, 3:288.

80. The second John Street building cost approximately $30,000, which is equivalent to over $600,000 (CPI) or $23.7 million (per capita GDP). Stevens, *The Life and Times of Nathan Bangs*, 225–226; Seaman, *Annals of New York Methodism*, 205–206, 219; Bulthuis, *Four Steeples*, 128–130; William R. Sutton, *Journeymen for Jesus: Evangelical Artisans Confront Capitalism in Jacksonian Baltimore* (University Park, PA: Penn State University Press, 1998), 75–78.

81. Seaman, *Annals of New York Methodism*, 137; Bulthuis, *Four Steeples*, 129.

82. Samuel Stilwell was the leader of the splinter group. Samuel Stilwell, *Historical Sketches of the Rise and Progress of the Methodist Society, in the City of New-York* (New York: William Bates, 1821), 15–16; Seaman, *Annals of New York Methodism*, 215–231; Bulthuis, *Four Steeples*, 127–133

83. The $50 figure in 1818 equates to more than $1,000 (CPI) or $42,500 (per capita GDP). Building Subscription, 1817–1818, Vol. 250, MECR.

8. CREATING A MORAL REPUBLIC

1. "A Word of Apology," *Harper's New Monthly Magazine*, January 1854, 146; "James Harper," *Harper's Weekly*, April 17, 1869.

2. "A Word of Apology," *Harper's New Monthly Magazine*, January 1854, 146; John Tebbel, *A History of Book Publishing in the United States*, vol. 1, *The Creation*

of an Industry, 1640–1865 (New York: R. R. Bowker, 1972), 272; Hellmut Lehmann-Haupt, *The Book in America: A History of the Making and Selling of Books in the United States* (New York: R. R. Bowker Company, 1952), 80–81.

3. Probus, "Letters from New York, Number II," *Southern Literary Messenger* 5, no. 9 (September 1839): 632.

4. *United States Literary Gazette*: "List of Works in Press," June 15, 1824, 1:79; April 1, 1825, 2:40; May 15, 1825, 160; July 15, 1825, 320; "List of New Publications," October 15, 1824, 1:206; February 15, 1826, 3:399; "American Editions of Foreign Works," April 15, 1826, 4:80; "Literary and Philosophical Intelligence, &c. and New Publications," *Literary and Evangelical Magazine*, August 1827, 434; *The Critic*: "Reviews of New Books," November 8, 1828, 25–30; January 10, 1829, 177–182; February 7, 1829, 229–232, 243–247; February 21, 1829, 260–262; April 4, 1829, 341–346; March 7, 1829, 273–275; March 21, 1829, 309–316; April 4, 1829, 350; April 11, 1829, 371–376; April 18, 1829, 373–376; "Varieties," November 15, 1828, 44–45; Tebbel, *A History of Book Publishing in the United States*, 1:271–272; Eugene Exman, *The Brothers Harper* (New York: Harper & Row, 1965), 14–15.

5. "Sermons LIV, LV, VLI," *National Preacher*, March 1829, 1087, 145–160; Exman, *The Brothers Harper*, 16–17.

6. H&B was only spending $4,000 per year on advertising, even at mid-century, when observers labeled them the largest (or second-largest) publishing firm in the world: F. S., "The Publishing Business," *Literary World*, January 5, 1850, 12.

7. Kyle T. Bulthuis, *Four Steeples Over the City Streets: Religion and Society in New York's Early Republic Congregations* (New York: New York University Press, 2014), 158–159; Edwin G. Burrows and Mike Wallace, *Gotham: A History of New York to 1898* (New York: Oxford University Press, 1999), 456–457. It is worth noting that the capitalized use of the name "Downtown" would not become common in New York City until the 1830s. I retain lowercase here to indicate more of a generic, directional usage.

8. Marriage Certificate, James Harper and Maria Arcularius, October 15, 1823, JHP-BL, Box 5, Folder 1, Series III; J. B. Wakeley, *Lost Chapters Recovered from the Early History of Methodism* (New York: Carlton & Porter, 1858), 544–546.

9. Philip F. Hardt, *The Soul of Methodism: The Class Meeting in Early New York City Methodism* (Lanham, MD: University Press of America, 2000), 65–67, 69–74.

10. Mark A. Noll, *America's God: From Jonathan Edwards to Abraham Lincoln* (New York: Oxford University Press, 2002), 354.

11. Samuel Seaman, *Annals of New York Methodism, Being a History of the Methodist Episcopal Church in the City of New York* (New York: Hunt & Eaton, 1892), 268–269, 276–277; Bulthuis, *Four Steeples*, 164.

8. Creating a Moral Republic   315

12. MECR: John Street Class Lists, Vol. 238: 1831, 1832, 1840; Vol. 240: 1842, 1843, 1844, 1848(?); Bulthuis, *Four Steeples*, 189–190.

13. B. B. Thatcher, *Indian Biography: Or, an Historical Account of Those Individuals Who Have Been Distinguished Among the North American Natives as Orators, Warriors, Statesmen, and Their Remarkable Characters*, vol. 2 (New York: Harper & Brothers, 1832), back matter: "Family Library."

14. "James Harper," *Harper's Weekly*, April 17, 1869.

15. H&B to ELB, July 31, 1830, HBR, Series II, Box 16, Folder 4; "Harper's Family Library," *HINPB* 37, inside front cover, HLHU; "Literature for the People," *Littell's Living Age*, October 21, 1854, 119; Thatcher, *Indian Biography*, 2: back matter: "Family Library."

16. Some titles have multiple volumes. *Harper's Illustrated Catalogue of Valuable Standard Works* (1847), 140, HBR, Series V, Box 226.

17. Thatcher, *Indian Biography*, 2: back matter: "Family Library." Emphasis in the original.

18. "Harper's Family Library," *HINPB* 37, inside front cover, HLHU.

19. H&B to ELB, April 7, 1835, HBR, Series II, Box 16, Folder 4. Family Library on the *United States*: Jay Leyda, ed., *The Melville Log: A Documentary Life of Herman Melville, 1819–1891*, vol. 1 (New York: Gordian Press, 1969), 180; Hershel Parker, *Herman Melville: A Biography*, vol. 1, *1819–1851* (Baltimore: Johns Hopkins Press, 1996), 267–268; Exman, *The Brothers Harper*, 179–180.

20. "Notices of New Works," *Southern Literary Messenger* 9, no. 5 (May 1843): 320.

21. H&B, *Catalogue of Books* (1845), HBR, Series II, Box 14, Folder 1, 15.

22. *Harper's Illustrated Catalogue of Valuable Standard Works* (1847), 140, HBR, Series V, Box 226.

23. The Family Library was the only specific item Adams listed besides the Bible. "Mr. Adam's Letter to Certain Young Men in Baltimore," *Southern Literary Messenger* 5, no. 1 (January 1839): 81.

24. *New York Observer*, April 9, 1831, contains this quote from the *New York Mercantile Advertiser* and numerous similar blurbs from other publications.

25. "Letters from New York, Number II," *Southern Literary Messenger* 5, no. 9 (September 1839): 630.

26. "Notices of New Works," *Southern Literary Messenger* 9, no. 5 (May 1843): 320. Exman points out this move was part of a plan to combat the competition of cheap weekly magazines: *The Brothers Harper*, 160–161.

27. "Moderate" is an accurate description of the reduced price, as $0.25 is equivalent to $8 (CPI). These quotes all come from "Harper's Family Library," *New York Observer*, April 9, 1831.

28. H&B to RDJ, August 20, 1840, DFP, Box 7.

29. "Contributions to Trade History," *American Bookseller*, July 15, 1885, 35. The collection ultimately grew to 295 volumes in six series: Exman, *The House of Harper*, 109.

30. American Society for the Diffusion of Useful Knowledge, *Prospectus*, 3.

31. American Society for the Diffusion of Useful Knowledge, *Prospectus*, 4.

32. American Society for the Diffusion of Useful Knowledge, *Prospectus*, 24–25, 37; American Society for the Diffusion of Useful Knowledge, *Prospectus of the American Library for Schools and Families* (New York: American Society for the Diffusion of Useful Knowledge, 1837), 8–12. It is unclear what happened to the partnership between Harper and ASDUK. Marilyn Haas believes Harper stole the District Library idea and strong-armed ASDUK, taking over sole control of the library series, depriving the ASDUK of its sole purpose of existence. Marilyn Haas, "New York's School District Library Movement and Harper's School District Library Books, 1839–1846," paper presented at Reading in America, 1840–1940, a Symposium, Strong Museum, Rochester, New York, November 22, 1986, 10–11. The reality is that ASDUK was part of a larger movement. It modeled itself on a similar organization in the United Kingdom (the Society for the Diffusion of Useful Knowledge), while domestic societies, such as the Boston Society for the Diffusion of Useful Knowledge, had suggested such programs nearly ten years prior: Boston Society for the Diffusion of Useful Knowledge, *A Number of Gentlemen Who Feel Interested in the Promotion and Diffusion of Useful Knowledge . . .* (Boston: Society for the Diffusion of Useful Knowledge, 1829).

33. "An Act to appropriate the income of the United States deposite [*sic*] fund to the purposes of education and the diffusion of knowledge," Chapter 237, 61st Session, April 17, 1838, *Laws of New York*, 220–221. This act followed an act in 1835 that allowed school districts to levy a tax to support the establishment of public libraries: "An Act relating to public instruction," Chapter 80, 58th Session, April 13, 1835, *Laws of New York*, 65–66.

34. Literary Notices," *The Knickerbocker*, February 1840, 155.

35. Haas, "New York's School District Library Movement," 2.

36. "Literary Notices," *The Knickerbocker*, February 1840, 156; "Common School Libraries," *The Jeffersonian*, July 7, 1838, 162. Volumes 91–95 retailed for $0.76 a volume because they were twice as large: "Harper's School District Library," *District School Journal, for the State of New York*, July 1, 1841, 24. The Harpers seemed to have coordinated the $0.38 figure with the state of New York. Marilyn Haas claims the price was even lower, $0.30–$0.33 per volume, but she does not explain how she arrived at that amount. Haas, "New York's School District Library Movement," 3.

8. Creating a Moral Republic   317

37. John C. Spencer, *Circular by the Superintendent of Common Schools of the State of New York: To Trustees of School Districts, Librarians of District Libraries, Commissioners of Common Schools and Clerks of Counties, Containing "An Act Respecting School District Libraries" and Regulations for the Preservation of the Libraries . . .* (Albany, NY: Hoffman & White, 1839), 5, 12.

38. J. C. Derby, *Fifty Years Among Authors, Books, and Publishers* (New York: Carleton, 1884), 102–104; Glyndon G. Van Deusen, *Thurlow Weed: Wizard of the Lobby* (Boston: Little, Brown and Company, 1947), 53–113.

39. "Harper's School District Library," *District School Journal, for the State of New York,* June 1, 1840, 16.

40. *The Knickerbocker* was a prominent New York literary magazine published monthly from 1833 to 1865 and included William Cullen Bryant, Henry Wadsworth Longfellow, and Oliver Wendell Holmes among its many prominent contributors. Quote: "Literary Notices," *The Knickerbocker,* February 1840, 156. *The Jeffersonian* was a short-lived weekly published in Albany, New York. "Common School Libraries," *The Jeffersonian,* July 7, 1838, 161–162, and "School Libraries," *The Jeffersonian,* January 19, 1839, 386.

41. Haas, "New York's School District Library Movement," 3.

42. Spencer, *Circular by the Superintendent,* 12–13.

43. "School District Library," *District School Journal,* September 1, 1841, 19.

44. H&B, *Catalogue of Books,* 15, HBR, Box 14, Folder 1, Series II.

45. "Literary Notices," *The Knickerbocker,* February 1840, 157.

46. Spencer, *Circular by the Superintendent,* 11–12.

47. Probus, "Letters from New York, Number II," *Southern Literary Messenger* 5, no. 9 (September 1839): 631.

48. In the latter half of the nineteenth century the following states established school district libraries: Missouri, 1853; California and Oregon, 1854; Illinois, 1855; Kansas and Virginia, 1870; New Jersey, 1871; Kentucky and Minnesota, 1873; and Colorado, 1876: Herbert Baxter Adams and Frederick William Ashley, *Public Libraries and Popular Education* (Albany: University of the State of New York, 1900), 100.

49. Zboray is adamant that the antebellum period was not a literary democracy as most publications were out of the reach of rural and poorer Americans. But he does not account for how people could access books without purchasing them through collections such as Harper's library series: Ronald Zboray, *A Fictive People: Antebellum Economic Development and the American Reading Public* (New York: Oxford University Press, 1993), 3–16.

50. Harper & Brothers, *Catalogue of Books* (1945), 15, HBR, Box 14, Folder 1, Series II; J. Henry Harper, *The House of Harper: A Century of Publishing in Franklin Square* (New York: Harper & Brothers, 1912), 122; Exman, *The Brothers Harper,*

318   *8. Creating a Moral Republic*

111. Milman regarded the authors of these texts as premoderns who described their world with wonderment and awe. Consequently, even though he believed in God's omnipotence, he argued one had to take their descriptions of the supernatural with a grain of salt. For example, he concluded that the parting of the Red Sea in Exodus was probably due to predictable phenomena that Moses knew well and expected. Milner also argued Exodus wildly exaggerated the number of Hebrews living in Egypt during Moses's lifetime: H. H. Milman, *The History of the Jews, from the Earliest Period Down to Modern Times*, vol. 1, 4th ed. (London: John Murray, 1866), iii–xxxiv. Backlash: T. E., *Milman's History of the Jews, Published in the Family Library, Examined and Refuted on the Evidence of the Scriptures* (London: James Ridgway, 1830).

51. Chambers, *Vestiges of the Natural History of Creation*, 7–38. Backlash: "Spirit of the Age," *New Yorker*, November 10, 1838, 125.

52. *Harper's Illustrated Catalogue of Valuable Standard Works* (1847), 140, 146, HBR, Box 226, Series V.

53. Dana entered Harvard Law School upon his return to Cambridge, Massachusetts. Jeffrey Amestoy, *Slavish Shore: The Odyssey of Richard Henry Dana, Jr.* (Cambridge, MA: Harvard University Press, 2015), 21–51.

54. RDS to RDJ, 2 March 1840, DFP, Box 7.

55. H&B to RDJ, June 9, 1840, DFP, Box 7. Emphasis in the original.

56. RDS to RDJ, March 14, 1840, DFP, Box 7.

57. RDJ to RDS, June 16, 1840, DFP, Box 7.

58. RDS to RDJ, June 19, 1840, DFP, Box 7

59. *Two Years Before the Mast, A Personal Narrative of Life at Sea* (New York: Harper & Brothers, 1840), 247.

60. "Harper's Family Library," *New York Observer*, April 9, 1831.

61. "Family Library," *Boston Masonic Mirror*, May 14, 1831, 367.

62. Bulthuis, *Four Steeples*, 62.

63. "Co-Partnerships," *New York Commercial Advertiser*, October 29, 1833. Within twenty years, the brothers installed more than thirty steam-driven Adams presses before a catastrophic fire destroyed the company's entire operations. Clark, "A Visit to the Publishing House of the Messrs. Harper & Brothers," *Ladies' Repository*, November 1853, 514; "A Word of Apology," *Harper's New Monthly Magazine*, January 1854, 146. Presses: "A Printed Book," *Harper's New Monthly Magazine*, July 1887, 174–175; Bowker, "Daniel Treadwell, Inventor," *Atlantic Monthly*, October 1873, 473–474; Lehmann-Haupt, *The Book in America*, 77.

64. Asa Greene, *A Glance at New York: Embracing the City Government, Theatres, Hotels, Churches, Mobs, Monopolies, Learned Professions, Newspapers, Rogues, Dandies, Fires and Firemen, Water and Other Liquids, & C., & C.* (New York:

A. Greene, 1837), 151. Exman cites the same number/source (although he mistakenly lists 20,000 original American works, vice the 200,000 Greene cites). It seems reliable since many estimates pegged their output by 1850 at 2 million: Exman, *The Brothers Harper*, 92.

65. "Publisher's Notice," *Southern Literary Messenger* 2, no. 1 (December 1835): 1. Examples of Poe's work for *Southern Literary Messenger*: "Berenice—A Tale," *Southern Literary Messenger* 1, no. 7 (March 1835): 333–336; "Morella—A Tale," *Southern Literary Messenger* 1, no. 8 (April 1835): 448–450; "Lion-izing—A Tale," *Southern Literary Messenger* 1, no. 9 (May 1835): 515–516; "Critical Notices," *Southern Literary Messenger* 2, no. 1 (December 1835): 41–68.

66. H&B to Edgar Allen Poe, June 2, 1836, AHB, 58 (Miscellaneous Correspondence and Documents Relating to Authors).

67. H&B to Edgar Allen Poe, June 2, 1836, AHB, 58 (Miscellaneous Correspondence and Documents Relating to Authors)

68. Poe's "Tales of the Folio Club" appeared in the *Philadelphia Saturday Courier* and the *Southern Literary Messenger* from 1832 to 1836. It was never published as a stand-alone volume. "Tales of the Folio Club," Edgar Allan Poe Society of Baltimore, last modified February 21, 2022, http://www.eapoe.org/works/editions/folio.htm.

69. Greene, *A Glance at New York*, 152–153.

70. J. & J. Harper to ELB, July 31, 1830, HBR, Series II, Box 16, Folder 4.

71. J. & J. Harper to ELB, July 31, 1830, HBR, Series II, Box 16, Folder 4.

72. They suggested men such as Oliver Cromwell, Peter the Great, Richard III, or George IV. J. & J. Harper to ELB, July 31, 1830, HBR, Series II, Box 16, Folder 4.

73. Exman, *The Brothers Harper*, 96.

74. H&B to ELB, May 25, 1837, HBR, Series II, Box 16, Folder 4. The brothers had to get creative, using an agent in Calcutta, India, to transmit funds: H&B to ELB, July 31, 1837, H&B to ELB, August 1, 1837, H&B to ELB, August 16, 1837, HBR, Series II, Box 16, Folder 4.

75. Subscription Book, 1838–1839, Record Group 2, Subgroup 1, John Street Church Archive. John and Wesley had moved uptown and were attending elsewhere.

76. H&B to Henry Wadsworth Longfellow, June 25, 1838, Letters to Henry Wadsworth Longfellow, Folder 2545, HLHU.

77. "Critical Notices," no. 22, *New-York Review*, October 1838, III:489.

78. John Street Class List, 1832, Vol. 238, MECR.

79. James disappears from the class leader lists in 1850. His name appears on a record that dates to either 1848 or 1849. Unfortunately, John Street records are not complete for every year. John Street Class List, 1839, 1840, Vol. 239, 1842, 1843, 1844, 1848(?), Vol. 240, MECR.

80. Hardt, *The Soul of Methodism*, 50–55.

81. F. S., "The Publishing Business," *Literary World*, January 5, 1850, 12.
82. Quote: RDS to WCB, July 9, 1839, DFP, Box 7. RDS to WCB, May 13, 17, 1839, DFP, Box 7.
83. RDS to WCB, June 12, 1839, DFP, Box 7.
84. Example contract: Articles of Agreement between James and John Harper, Booksellers and Publishers, and Theodore Sedgwick, Junior, February 2, 1833, AHB, Reel 1, Contract Books Volume 1, 1823–1867, 2–3.
85. Indenture between Harper & Brothers and Sidney E. Morse and Samuel Breese, April 7, 1844, AHB, Reel 1, Contract Books Volume 1, 1823–1867, 102–104.
86. Articles of Agreement between Herman Melville and Harper & Brothers, November 15, 1848, July 2, September 13, 1849, September 12, 1851, AHB, Reel 53, Correspondence Relating to Contracts; G. Thomas Tanselle, "The Sales of Melville's Books," *Harvard Library Bulletin* 18 (April 1969): 195–215; William Charvat, *Literary Publishing in America, 1790–1850* (Philadelphia: University of Pennsylvania Press, 1959), 43–44.
87. Articles of Agreement between James K. Paulding and Harper & Brothers, November 19, 1833, AHB, Reel 1, Contract Books Volume 1, 1823–1867, 5–8; Articles of Agreement between Benjamin Morell J & J Harper, March 7, 1832, AHB, Reel 1, Contract Books Volume 1, 1823–1867, 1–2; Charvat, *Literary Publishing in America*, 43–44.
88. Quote: RDS to RDJ, January 29, 1840, DFP, Box 7. RDS to RDJ, February 4, 13, 20, 1840, DFP, Box 7.
89. RDS to RDJ, March 14, 1840, DFP, Box 7.
90. RDS to WCB, October 14, 1840, DFP, Box 7.
91. Articles of Agreement, 1834–1850 AHB, Reel 1, Contract Books Volume 1, 1823–1867, 8–350.
92. RDS to WCB, October 14, 1840, DFP, Box 7.
93. RDS to WCB, November 30, 1840, DFP, Box 7.
94. RDS to WCB, November 30, 1840, DFP, Box 7.
95. Harper claimed the book was only selling well in New England and a few Atlantic cities. H&B to RDJ, March 5, 1841, DFP, Box 8.
96. RDS to RDJ, April 5, 1841, DFP, Box 8; Little & Brown to RDJ, March 29, 1841, DFP, Box 8.
97. H&B to RDJ, June 14, 1841, DFP, Box 8.
98. H&B to RDJ, June 16, 1841, DFP, Box 8.
99. Little & Brown to RDJ, June 28, 1841, DFP, Box 8; D. Appleton to RDJ, July 1, 1841, DFP, Box 8.
100. The firm did not use double-entry bookkeeping until 1857. Exman, *The Brothers Harper*, 211–229.

8. Creating a Moral Republic 321

101. William H. Prescott to Francis Lieber, August 6, 1845, Francis Lieber Papers, 1815–1888, Box 59, Huntington Library, San Marino, CA. Agreement between William H. Prescott and Harper & Brothers, April 25, 1843, November 16, 1844, December 18, 1846, AHB, Reel 54, Correspondence Relating to Contracts; Exman, *The Brothers Harper*, 225–226.

102. William H. Prescott to Francis Lieber, August 6, 1845, Francis Lieber Papers.

103. William H. Prescott to Francis Lieber, August 6, 1845, Francis Lieber Papers. Emphasis in the original.

104. William H. Prescott to Francis Lieber, August 6, 1845, Francis Lieber Papers.

9. FOSTERING AN AMERICAN PROTESTANT IDENTITY

1. Probus, "Letters from New York, Number II," *Southern Literary Messenger* 5, no. 9 (September 1839): 629.

2. Probus, 632.

3. Quote: Probus, 629. William Charvat, *Literary Publishing in America, 1790–1850* (Philadelphia: University of Pennsylvania Press, 1959), 19, 26–27.

4. "done more": "Miscellaneous Notices," *American Monthly Magazine* 4 (December 1834): 214. "revolution": "Miscellaneous Notices," *American Monthly Magazine* 4 (February 1835): 354.

5. "Harper & Brothers," *New Yorker*, November 10, 1838, 126.

6. "Miscellaneous Notices," *American Monthly Magazine* 4 (November 1834): 143.

7. James was elected in 1838. Minutes of the Board of Trustees, 1838–1858, 1, Record Group 2, Subgroup 1, John Street Church Archives; Samuel Seaman, *Annals of New York Methodism, Being a History of the Methodist Episcopal Church in the City of New York* (New York: Hunt & Eaton, 1892), 279–280.

8. John Street Class List, 1848(?), 1851, 1852, 1853(?) Vol. 240, MECR.

9. Nolan B. Harmon, ed., *The Encyclopedia of World Methodism*, vol. 2 (Nashville, TN: United Methodist Publishing House, 1974), 2248–2249, 2370–2371.

10. Bulthuis is one such example but does not present evidence to support this claim. Instead, the records of John Street Church reveal consistent involvement in church affairs by James and Fletcher all through the 1840s. Kyle T. Bulthuis, *Four Steeples Over the City Streets: Religion and Society in New York's Early Republic Congregations* (New York: New York University Press, 2014), 186.

11. Thomas Longworth, *Longworth's American almanac, New-York Register and City Directory* (New York: Thomas Longworth, 1829), 274; *Longworth's American Almanac* (1835), 309; *Longworth's American Almanac* (1841), 332; Tappan: Eugene Exman, *The Brothers Harper* (New York: Harper & Row, 1965), 189.

12. Seaman, *Annals of New York Methodism*, 281–283; Edwin G. Burrows and Mike Wallace, *Gotham: A History of New York to 1898* (New York: Oxford University

Press, 1999), 459; Bulthuis, *Four Steeples*, 190–191. The third building was smaller due to decreased attendance and the city's desire to widen John Street, necessitating the second church building's demolition or significant alteration. Raynor Rogers, *The Story of Old John Street Church* (New York: Raynor R. Rogers, 1984), 30–33.

13. Contract between White & Sheffield and H&B, May 26, 1843, AHB, 56 (Correspondence Related to Contracts). The parties agreed to revisit the contract every three years. Examples (1847–1856): Agreement between White & Sheffield and H&B, June 21, 1847, November 20, 1850, December 12, 1853, February 20, 1856, AHB, 56 (Correspondence Related to Contracts).

14. Royal-octavo is a specific publishing technique yielding pages of ten by six and one-quarter inches.

15. Quarto refers to the original 1828 edition of Webster's dictionary. The name refers to a publishing technique whereby sheets are printed with eight pages of text (four to a side) on each sheet. These are then folded twice to produce eight book pages. Underlined in the original. H&B to White & Sheffield, August 21, 1849, *AHB*, 58 (Miscellaneous Correspondence and Documents Related to Authors).

16. Quoted in *Recommendations of Worcester's Dictionaries; to Which Is Prefixed a Review of Webster's System of Orthography, from the United States Democratic Review, for March 1856* (Boston: Hickling, Swan and Brown, 1856), 2; Noah Webster, *An American Dictionary of the English Language; Exhibiting the Origin, Orthography, Pronunciation, and Definitions of Words* (New York: Harper & Brothers, 1845), Preface, Preface of the Revised Edition, Synopsis; Tim Cassedy, "'A Dictionary Which We Do Not Want': Defining America Against Noah Webster, 1783–1810," *William and Mary Quarterly* 71, no. 2 (April 2014): 229–254; Jill Lepore, *A Is for American: Letters and Other Characters in the Newly United States* (New York: Vintage Books, 2002), 3–7, 15–60; Joshua Kendall, *The Forgotten Founding Father: Noah Webster's Obsession and the Creation of an American Culture* (New York: G. P. Putnam's Sons, 2010).

17. "Review of Webster's System," *United States Democratic Review*, March 1856, 198–199. The article is unsigned, but a subsequent promotional text for a rival dictionary that reprinted the review identified Gould as the author: *Recommendations of Worcester's Dictionaries*, 2. Gould's correspondence supports his authorship: Edward Gould to Evert Duyckinck, numerous undated letters, Duyckinck Family Papers, Manuscripts and Archives Division, New York Public Library Digital Collections, http://digitalcollections.nypl.org/items/358f3fb0 -5a5a-0133-5a13-00505686a51c. Gould suspected Wesley's decision was part of the Harper contract with Webster, although archival evidence does not support this assertion.

9. Fostering an American Protestant Identity 323

18. "pernicious 'system' ": "Propensity to Gothicism," *New Hampshire Sentinel*, May 26, 1804, 2; "educated" and "have repudiated": "Review of Webster's System," 198.

19. Edward Gould to Evert Duyckinck, undated, image 5383288, Duyckinck Family Papers, Manuscripts and Archives Division, New York Public Library Digital Collections.

20. Oliver Wendell Holmes, *The Poetical Works of Oliver Wendell Holmes* (London: G. Routledge, and Co., 1852), 112.

21. Davis W. Clark, "A Visit to the Publishing House of the Messrs. Harper & Brothers," *Ladies' Repository*, November 1853, 515.

22. Lepore, *A Is for American*, 3–7, 15–60; Ronald Zboray, *A Fictive People: Antebellum Economic Development and the American Reading Public* (New York: Oxford University Press, 1993), 101–103.

23. Morse ran in 1836 under the banner of the ironically named Native American Democratic Association, winning a mere 6 percent of the vote. The American Republican Party, founded in 1843, changed its name to the Native American Party in 1845 after a national convention. Richardson calls James a "militantly anti-foreign, anti-Catholic crusader," but does not provide evidence: Darcy G. Richardson, *Others: Third-Party Politics from the Nation's Founding to the Rise and Fall of the Greenback-Labor Party* (New York: iUniverse, 2004), 164–170; Sean Wilentz, *Chants Democratic: New York City and the Rise of the American Working Class, 1788–1850* (New York: Oxford University Press, 1986), 267–271, 316–324; Burrows and Wallace, *Gotham*, 544–546.

24. Bulthuis, *Four Steeples*, 159–160.

25. Draft speeches, Folder 15, JHP-NYHS. Bulthuis, *Four Steeples*, 158–160.

26. Wilentz describes James as a caricature of an unintelligent artisan, even ridiculing his physical appearance: *Chants Democratic*, 318–322. Carwardine also lumps James into the larger nativist movement of the 1840s: Richard Carwardine, *Evangelicals and Politics in Antebellum America* (New Haven, CT: Yale University Press, 1993), 84, 119. Burrows and Wallace label all the brothers as nativists, on the assumption they published *Maria Monk: Gotham*, 546, 632.

27. Daniel Walker Howe, *The Political Culture of the American Whigs* (Chicago: University of Chicago Press, 1979), 32.

28. Undated draft speech, Folder 15, JHP-NYHS. Underlined in the original. None of Harper's speeches in the NYHS collection contains nativist elements. These include a series of undated draft speeches in Folder 15, JHP-NYHS, as well as delivered orations like an "Address to the People of New York," February 24, 1845, Folder 1, JHP-NYHS.

29. Independent Order of Rechabites to James Harper, July 29, 1844, Folder 5, JHP-NYHS; Initiation to the United Brothers of Temperance, n.d., Folder 12,

324   *9. Fostering an American Protestant Identity*

JHP-NYHS; Henry A. Fay to James Harper, May 15, 1844, Folder 4, JHP-NYHS; Wilentz, *Chants Democratic*, 318.

30. "A Proclamation," June 1844, Folder 14, JHP-NYHS; Augustine E. Costello, *Our Police Protectors: History of the New York Police from the Earliest Period to the Present Time* (New York: Augustine E. Costello, 1885), 100–107; Wilentz, *Chants Democratic*, 322. Burrows and Wallace also claim (without evidence) that James purged foreigners from municipal jobs: *Gotham*, 632–634, 638.

31. American Republican Party principles, n.d., Folder 1, JHP-NYHS. James's letter to Weed discusses his willingness to run as the Whig nominee for governor of New York: James Harper to Thurlow Weed, September 16, 1854, Folder 8, JHP-NYHS.

32. When the national leadership of Harper's party began gravitating toward Henry Clay, Whigs abandoned him along with his party: Charles H. Haswell, *Reminiscences of an Octogenarian of the City of New York* (New York: Harper & Brothers, 1896), 409, 420.

33. I have not come across any mention of this anywhere in the Harper histories, including Exman, *The Brothers Harper*. James Harper to Thurlow Weed, September 16, 1854, Folder 8, JHP-NYHS.

34. Bill for Stereotyping, H&B to William Emerson, March 7, 1836, AHB, 53 (Correspondence Relating to Contracts).

35. Maria Monk was a real person (even if these stories were not), although there is some question as to her mental acuity, and her ultimate motivations were most likely manipulated by other actors. The Harper records contain several pieces of correspondence containing her signature: "Affidavit," January 9, 1836, Maria Monk to P. Gordon, February 10, 1836, Maria Monk to H&B, August 18, 1837, AHB, 53 (Correspondence Relating to Contracts).

36. Susan M. Griffin, *Anti-Catholicism and Nineteenth-Century Fiction* (New York: Cambridge University Press, 2004), 27–61.

37. "Awful Disclosures," *New York Observer*, January 23, 1836. Ray Allen Billington, *The Protestant Crusade, 1800–1860: A Study of the Origins of American Nativism* (New York: Macmillan Company, 1938), 101–102. Billington cites the following source as verifying the "dummy" company theory (which makes no mention of any such thing): Charles Edwards, ed., *Reports of Chancery Cases, Decided in the First Circuit of the State of New York, by the Honorable William T. McCoun, Vice-Chancellor*, vol. 3 (New York: Gould, Banks, and Company, 1843), 109–110. As Exman first discovered, the document does not mention any such arrangement, and to the contrary, significant evidence suggests the publishers were legitimate: *The Brothers Harper*, 186–187. Billington's narrative persisting: Wikipedia, s.v. "James Harper (Publisher)," last modified April 30, 2023, 06:32, https://en.wikipedia.org/wiki/James_Harper_(publisher); Burrows and

9. Fostering an American Protestant Identity 325

Wallace, *Gotham*, 545–546, 632; Cassandra L. Yacovazzi, *Escaped Nuns: True Womanhood and the Campaign Against Convents in Antebellum America* (New York: Oxford University Press, 2018), 6; Cara M. French, "Prejudice for Profit: Escaped Nun Stories and American Catholic Print Culture," *Journal of the Early Republic* 39, no. 3 (Fall 2019): 511–512.

38. Exman, *The Brothers Harper*, 186–187.

39. [Unreadable] to James Harper, April 24, 1844, Folder 3, JHP-NYHS.

40. Steven K. Green, *The Second Disestablishment: Church and State in Nineteenth-Century America* (New York: Oxford University Press, 2010), 266–271, and *The Bible, the School, and the Constitution: The Clash that Shaped Modern Church-State Doctrine* (New York: Oxford University Press, 2012), 33–36.

41. "Authorized version" is another term for the King James Version. In reality, Catholics would have preferred the Douay-Rheims Version. *HINPB* 33, inside front cover, HLHU. Emphasis in the original.

42. "Literary Bulletin," *United States Magazine and Democratic Review*, July 1843, 111.

43. Beach's lists of the wealthy citizens of New York City are unreliable, as are his estimates of wealth. His many versions are also confusing. For example, there are two versions of his 3rd edition (1842). One contains a profile of H&B (valuing it at $200,000) that includes this quote, while the other one omits them entirely: Moses Y. Beach, *Wealth and Pedigree of the Wealthy Citizens of New York City*, 3rd ed. (New York: Sun Office, 1842), 12; Edward Pessen, "Moses Beach Revisited: A Critical Examination of His Wealthy Citizens Pamphlets," *Journal of American History* 58, no. 2 (September 1971): 415–426.

44. Moses Y. Beach, *Wealth and Biography of the Wealthy Citizens of New York City*, 6th ed. (New York: Sun Office, 1845), 15.

45. By 1844, Harper & Brothers averaged fifty-five new titles per year; the next year they released eighty-seven: Exman, *The Brothers Harper*, 230–231.

46. "Notices of New Works, and Literary Intelligence," *Southern Literary Messenger* 7, no. 11 (November 1841): 807.

47. S. G. Goodrich, *Recollections of a Lifetime, Men and Things I Have Seen: In a Series of Familiar Letters to a Friend, Historical, Biographical, Anecdotical, and Descriptive*, vol. 2 (New York: Miller, Orton and Mulligan: 1856), 382–383.

48. Karen Halttunen, *Confidence Men and Painted Ladies: A Study of Middle-Class Culture in America, 1830–1870* (New Haven, CT: Yale University Press, 1982); John F. Kasson, *Rudeness and Civility: Manners in Nineteenth-Century Urban America* (New York: Hill & Wang, 1990); Richard L. Bushman, *The Refinement of America: Persons, Houses, Cities* (New York: Knopf, 1992).

49. Frank Weitenkampf, *The Illustrated Book* (Cambridge, MA: Harvard University Press, 1938), 179. For a detailed treatment of Harper's *Illuminated Bible*:

Joseph P. Slaughter, "A 'True Commentary': The Gendered Imagery of Harper's Illuminated and New Pictorial Bible," *Journal of the Early Republic* 41, no. 4 (Winter 2021): 587–619. Parts of this chapter derive from this article.

50. "Harper's Illuminated Pictorial Bible," *Daily Atlas*, January 1, 1844.

51. "Original designs": Contact between Joseph Alexander Adams and H&B, April 4, 1843, Box 1, AHB, 48 (Correspondence Relating to Contracts). "The most splendid": "Literary Record," *The Knickerbocker*, July 1843, 96. Chapman: "Notices of New Works," *Southern Literary Messenger* 10, no. 2 (February 1844): 126.

52. Harper claimed over 1,600 (*HINPB* 36, back cover HLHU), but the contract was for 1,565 (my count is 1,558). Many scholars have just repeated the Harper claim: Paul C. Gutjahr, *An American Bible: A History of the Good Book in the United States, 1777–1880* (Stanford, CA: Stanford University Press, 1999), 70.

53. "Critical notices," *Auburn Journal, HINPB* 33, inside front cover, HLHU.

54. Electrotyping: Jacob Abbott, *The Harper Establishment, or How the Story Books Are Made* (New York: Harper & Brothers, 1855), 96–102; "Making the Magazine," *Harper's New Monthly Magazine*, December 1865, 12–13; "Electrotyping," *American Dictionary of Printing and Bookmaking*, 157–166; Edward S. Pilsworth, *Electrotyping in Its Relation to the Graphic Arts* (New York: Macmillan, 1923). Wood engraving: Abbot, *The Harper Establishment*, 103–108, W. J. Linton, "The History of Wood-Engraving in America," *American Art Review* 1, no. 6 (April 1880): 236–242. Technically, "engraving" refers to the intaglio process: Jane R. Pomeroy, "Alexander Anderson's Life and Engravings Before 1800, with a Checklist of Publications Drawn from His Diary," *Proceedings of the American Antiquarian Society* 100, no. 1 (April 1990): 137–230, esp. 171–172.

55. Peter Wosh, *Spreading the Word: The Bible Business in Nineteenth-Century America* (Ithaca, NY: Cornell University Press, 1994), 20–24.

56. This price is equivalent to more than $800 (CPI). Memorandum of agreement between Joseph A. Adams and H&B, August 13, 1856, 329–331, and J. A. Adams to Harpers, March 16, 1867, 531, AHB, 1 (Contract Books Volume 1, 1823–1867), 329–331; *HINPB* 53–54 HLHU; Candy Gunther Brown, *The Word in the World: Evangelical Writing, Publishing, and Reading in America, 1789–1880* (Chapel Hill: University of North Carolina Press, 2004), 76–77.

57. "Perfection": *HINPB* 1–50, back page, HLHU; numbered in error as follows: volume 45 (1), 46 (2), 47 (17), 48 (9), 29 (29) of HLHU collection. Harper also republished numerous illustrations without attribution in the *Illuminated Bible*, see Slaughter, "A 'True Commentary,'" 596–597.

58. Seth Perry, "'What the Public Expect': Consumer Authority and the Marketing of Bibles, 1770–1850," *American Periodicals* 24, no. 2 (2014): 128–144, and *Bible Culture and Authority in the Early United States* (Princeton, NJ: Princeton University Press, 2018), 40–62.

9. Fostering an American Protestant Identity   327

59. *HINPB*, 33, inside front cover, HLHU.

60. *HINPB*, 669–671, HLHU.

61. *HINPB*, 36, back cover, HLHU.

62. Michaela Giebelhausen, *Painting the Bible: Representation and Belief in Mid-Victorian Britain* (Burlington, VT: Ashgate, 2006), 128–34; David Morgan, *Protestants and Pictures: Religion, Visual Culture, and the Age of American Mass Production* (New York: Oxford University Press, 1999), 283–292.

63. Richard Bushman's description of "refined Christians" informs my definition of "refinement": *The Refinement of America*, 182–86, 319–352; Coleen McDannell, *The Christian Home in Victorian America, 1840–1900* (Bloomington: Indiana University Press, 1986), 25–28, 38–49, 128–136, and *Material Christianity: Religion and Popular Culture in America* (New Haven, CT: Yale University Press, 1995), 67–98; Lori Merish, *Sentimental Materialism: Gender, Commodity Culture and Nineteenth-Century American Literature* (Durham, NC: Duke University Press, 2000). I am relying on Shirley Samuels's definition of sentimentality: "a set of cultural practices designed to evoke a certain form of emotional response, usually empathy, in the reader or viewer": *The Culture of Sentiment: Race, Gender, and Sentimentality in Nineteenth-Century America* (New York: Oxford University Press, 1992), 4. Richard Jenkyns stresses the contradictory natures of Victorianism, including the portrayal of women, expressed through its art, in *Dignity and Decadence: Victorian Art and the Classical Inheritance* (Cambridge, MA: Harvard University Press, 1992), 17, 284–289. Romanticism was not solely the purview of liberal Protestants or Transcendentalists: Brett Grainger, *Church in the Wild: Evangelicals in Antebellum America* (Cambridge, MA: Harvard University Press, 2019).

64. The *Illuminated Bible* includes far more female images (350) than any Bible of its era. However, the percentage of images including women (22.5 percent) is lower than its competitors, a factor of the inclusion of the *Illuminated Bible*'s small images in the total count. The proportion of large images (31.9 percent) is similar to other early national-period Bibles. Slaughter, "A 'True Commentary,'" 603–604.

65. The term "aesthetic entrepreneurs" comes from Catherine E. Kelly, *Republic of Taste: Art, Politics, and Everyday Life in Early America* (Philadelphia: University of Pennsylvania Press, 2016), 11, 56–91.

66. Kathryn T. Long, "Consecrated Respectability: Phoebe Palmer and the Refinement of American Methodism," in *Methodism and the Shaping of American Culture*, ed. Nathan O. Hatch and John Wigger (Nashville, TN: Kingswood Books, 2001), 281–307; Bushman, *The Refinement of America*, 256–267, 273–279; McDannell, *Material Christianity*, 87–98, and *The Christian Home in Victorian America, 1840–1900*, 25–28, 38–49, 79, 98

328   *9. Fostering an American Protestant Identity*

67. Anne C. Loveland, "Domesticity and Religion in the Antebellum Period: The Career of Phoebe Palmer," *The Historian* 39, no. 3 (May 1977): 455–471; Long, "Consecrated Respectability," 281–307; Kyle B. Roberts, *Evangelical Gotham: Religion and the Making of New York City, 1783–1860* (Chicago: University of Chicago Press, 2016), 181–218; Bulthuis, *Four Steeples*, 75–96; McDannell, *The Christian Home in Victorian America*, 77–85, 99–103, 143–45; Kathryn Long, *Revival of 1857–58: Interpreting an American Religious Awakening* (New York: Oxford University Press, 1998), 68–92.

68. Gutjahr, *An American Bible*, 71.

69. *HINPB* dedication page, HLHU; *HINPB*, volume 33, inside front cover, HLHU; R. Laurence Moore, *Selling God: American Religion in the Marketplace of Culture* (New York: Oxford University Press, 1994), 34–35.

70. McDannell, *The Christian Home in Victorian America*, 25–28, 38–49, 79, 97–98.

71. "Literary Notices," *The Knickerbocker*, July 1846. Emphasis in the original.

72. *HINPB*, dedication page, HLHU; Stephen Nissenbaum first noted the nature of *HINPB* as gift book: *The Battle for Christmas: A Cultural History of America's Most Cherished Holiday* (New York: Vintage, 1996), 153; Slaughter, "A 'True Commentary,'" 616.

73. "Literary Bulletin," *United States Magazine and Democratic Review*, July 1843, 111.

74. "Extracts from New Books," *American Publishers' Circular and Literary Gazette* 4, no. 33 (August 14, 1858): 391.

75. "Publishers: Their Past, Present, and Future in the U.S.: The Present," *American Publishers' Circular and Literary Gazette*, Vol. 1 (November 17, 1855), 166.

76. "Notices of New Books," *United States Magazine and Democratic Review*, July 1846, 78.

77. "American Illustrated Book," *Broadway Journal*, February 8, 1845, 83.

78. Morgan, *Protestants and Pictures*, 61–62; Michael Leja, "Issues in Early Mass Visual Culture," in *A Companion to American Art*, ed. John David, Jennifer Greenhill, and Jason LaFountain (Malden, MA: Wiley-Blackwell, 2015), 1313–1315; Wosh, *Spreading the Word*, 19. Gutjahr, *An American Bible*, 70.

79. Hatch and Wigger, *Methodism and the Shaping of American Culture*, 30; Bushman, *The Refinement of America*, 335–348.

80. The pastor of John Street Church, Rev. Jason P. Radmacher, raised the question of why Maria has a plaque and James does not, wondering what it says about the attitude of the congregation toward James. My sense is that James pushed for the plaque to celebrate a woman who otherwise did not garner much attention or praise in comparison to himself. Additionally, James was still head of trustees at the time of his wife's death. Since he (and his brothers) had long since

9. Fostering an American Protestant Identity   329

moved to another church by the time of James's death in 1869, it might have been awkward to honor a member who departed years earlier (or perhaps the departure itself was a sore subject), and besides, it was not really in the brothers' disposition to celebrate themselves in such a manner anyway. Conversation with Rev. Jason P. Radmacher, John Street Church, June 24, 2016.

81. Even though James and Fletcher had moved uptown and were no longer active in the congregation, they were still listed in the 1850s as eligible to vote in John Street trustee elections. John Street Class List, 1852, Vol. 240, MECR; Minutes of the Board of Trustees, 1838–1858, 4–138, 156–157, Record Group 2, Subgroup 1, John Street Church Archives.

82. The figure is calculated as a percentage increase of CPI (per capita GDP equals nearly $4 million). The 2 percent rate of interest was much lower than the era standard of 7 percent. John Street Class List, 1852, Vol. 240, MECR; Minutes of the Board of Trustees, 1838–1858, 132, 138–157, Record Group 2, Subgroup 1, John Street Church Archives.

83. Accounts differ on the number of Adams presses—thirty or thirty-three. "The Publishing Business," *Literary World*, January 5, 1850; "A Visit to the Publishing House of Messrs. Harper & Brothers," *Ladies' Repository*, November 1853, 513–514; "A Word of Apology," *Harper's New Monthly Magazine*, January 1854, 146.

84. Quote: "The Publishing Business," *Literary World*, January 5, 1850. No other publisher had more than five in the 1840s. The number of Harper bestsellers in the 1840s compares with only two Harper titles of seventeen total bestsellers in the 1830s. This categorization is based on Frank Luther Mott's statistics in *Golden Multitudes: The Story of the Best Sellers in the United States* (New York: R. R. Bowker, Co., 1947), 303, 306–307. Mott bestowed "bestseller" status on a work that sold 1 percent of the American population (175,000 copies in the 1840s). The Harper bestsellers were *Home Influence, Wuthering Heights, Vanity Fair,* and *History of England.* Exman first pointed this out, but made an error, claiming five: *The Brothers Harper,* 281.

85. "Word at the Start," *Harper's New Monthly Magazine*, vol. 1, *June to November 1850* (New York: Harper & Brothers Publishers, 1850), 1.

86. "Word at the Start," 2.

87. Henry Mills Alden, "Fifty Years of Harper's Magazine," *Harper's Magazine*, May 1900, 94.

88. "Advertisement," *Harper's New Monthly Magazine*, 1:ii; Lorman A. Ratner, Paula T. Kaufman, and Dwight L. Teeter Jr., *Paradoxes of Prosperity: Wealth-Seeking Versus Christian Values in Pre-Civil War America* (Urbana: University of Illinois Press, 2009), 48–51.

330   *9. Fostering an American Protestant Identity*

89. Alden, "Fifty Years of Harper's Magazine," 948; Barbara M. Perkins, *"Harper's Monthly Magazine,"* in *American Literary Magazines: The Eighteenth and Nineteenth Centuries*, ed. Edward E. Chielens (Westport, CT: Greenwood Press, 1986), 168.

90. Frederick Lewis Allen, "One Hundred Years of Harper's," *Harper's Magazine*, October 1950, 28–29.

91. "Contributions to Trade History," *American Bookseller*, July 15, 1885, 36; Alden, "Fifty Years of Harper's Magazine," 948; Exman, *The Brothers Harper*, 305–308.

92. Quotes: "Periodical Literature," *National Magazine*, July 1852, 1. Brown, *The Word in the World*, 164.

93. "Periodical Literature," *National Magazine*, July 1852, 2.

94. Accounts claim more than 20,000 spectators gathered to watch the immense blaze. The *Daily Times* included a detailed accounting of Harper's property to arrive at its $1.2 million estimate (equivalent to $43 million [CPI] or $650 million [per capita GDP]). The company's stereotype plates were safe belowground in a special vault, allowing the brothers to start up production soon after the fire. "Destructive Fire," *New-York Daily Times*, December 12, 1853; Allan Nevins and Milton Halsey Thomas, *The Diary of George Templeton Strong: The Turbulent Fifties, 1850–1859* (New York: Macmillan Company, 1952), 139; "Contributions to Trade History," *American Bookseller*, June 1, 1885, 302–303.

95. The buildings were seven stories, if one counted their two subterranean floors. Abbott, *The Harper Establishment*, 13–23, 41–54. Brockhaus in (Leipzig) is mentioned as potentially larger in some accounts, others cite Harper: "Publishers and Publishing in New York," *Norton's Literary Gazette*, April 1, 1854, 166; "A Word of Apology," *Harper's New Monthly Magazine*, January 1854, 145; F. S. "The Publishing Business," *Literary World*, January 5, 1850.

96. Zboray, *A Fictive People*, 6–9.

97. Clark, "A Visit to the Publishing House of the Messrs. Harper & Brothers," 516.

98. Clark, 514–515.

99. "Publishers' Association Banquet at the Crystal Palace," *New-York Daily Tribune*, September 28, 1855, 5. Two million: "The Publishing Business," *Literary World*, January 5, 1850. The 4.5 million figure comes from an average of 25 volumes/minute, ten hours/day, six days a week: "Destructive Fire," *New-York Daily Times*, December 12, 1853. Exman uses the *Daily Times* estimate: *The Brothers Harper*, 349.

100. The postage law of March 3, 1851, allowed books to be mailed for one cent per ounce for 500 miles, plus an additional cent for each additional 1,000 miles, up

9. Fostering an American Protestant Identity 331

to five cents for 3,500 miles. Arthur H. Bissell and Thomas B. Kirby, eds., *The Postal Laws and Regulations of the United States of America* (Washington, DC: Government Printing Office, 1879), 446; Exman, *The Brothers Harper*, 325; Zboray, *A Fictive People*, 59–68. National advertising, see Perry, "'What the Public Expect,'" 139.

101. Roger Finke and Rodney Starke, "How Upstart Sects Won America: 1776–1850," *Journal for the Scientific Study of Religion* 28 (1989): 31; Hatch and Wigger, *Methodism and the Shaping of American Culture*, 27.

102. Hardt, *The Soul of Methodism*, 36–40, 65–66, 148.

103. Exman, *The Brothers Harper*, 9–10.

104. Ratner, Kaufman, and Teeter Jr., *Paradoxes of Prosperity*, 50.

105. "Reviews of New Books," *The Critic*, November 29, 1828, 68–69.

106. H&B to ELB, January 15, 1835, HBR, Series II, Box 16, Folder 4.

107. H&B to ELB, April 7, 1835, HBR, Series II, Box 16, Folder 4.

108. Goodrich, *Recollections of a Lifetime*, 2:254n.

109. Fellow transcendentalist Ralph Waldo Emerson was no fan of Harper & Brothers, either. Henry David Thoreau, *Walden* (New York: Houghton Mifflin, 1995), 106.

110. "A Word of Apology," *Harper's New Monthly Magazine*, January 1854, 147.

CONCLUSION

1. Meloon: Joseph P. Slaughter, "The Virginia Company to Chick-fil-A: Christian Business in America, 1600–2000," *Seattle University Law Review* 44, no. 2 (Winter 2021): 447–449.

2. Fred Hood argues that by the early nineteenth century the millennial issue was largely settled among Reformed Americans and consequently was not a frequent topic of conversation: *Reformed America: The Middle and Southern States, 1783–1837* (Tuscaloosa: University of Alabama Press, 1980), 68–87.

3. Ian A. Mitroff, *A Spiritual Audit of Corporate America: A Hard Look at Spirituality, Religion, and Values in the Workplace* (San Francisco: Jossey-Bass Publishers, 1999).

4. Liz Moyer, "Funds Invoke Bible Values in Choosing Investments," *New York Times*, March 1, 2017, BU1; Jeff Haanen, "Investing in the Kingdom," *Christianity Today*, December 2016, 50–53. There are similar funds for other religions: Tom Verde, "Investing Along Religious Guidelines," *New York Times*, July 2, 2017, BU3. Religion does not have a monopoly in this field: Tim Gray, "Aiming to Do Good, Not Just Well," *New York Times*, July 16, 2017, BU12.

5. Joshua Clark Davis, *From Head Shops to Whole Foods: The Rise and Fall of Activist Entrepreneurs* (New York: Columbia University Press, 2020).

6. "About Us," A Christian Plumber, accessed May 8, 2023, http://achristianplumber .com/about-us/; "A Christian Plumber," Dun & Bradstreet, accessed May 8, 2023, https://www.dnb.com/business-directory/company-profiles.a_christian _plumber.d2bfafa3d13cef72afd01898fd65ed3b.html.

7. "Why Do We Do It?," Whey Station(ary), accessed May 8, 2023, https://www .wheystationary.com/outreach.

8. Mary-Jane Rubenstein made this clear to me during a presentation of her research associated with her book *Astrotopia*: Faculty lecture, October 21, 2021, Wesleyan University, Middletown, CT. Also: Rubenstein, "A Tale of Two Utopias: Musk and Bezos in Outer Space," Metapolis, March 2022, https://metapolis .net/project/a-tale-of-two-utopias-musk-and-bezos-in-outer-space/.

9. David Gelles, "Benefiting Earth Through 'Hedonistic Altruism,'" *New York Times*, August 29, 2021, BU6.

10. Henry Ford lost a court battle with shareholders over what to do with excess profits—reinvest or pay dividends: Richard Snow, *I Invented the Modern Age: The Rise of Henry Ford* (New York: Scribner, 2013), 255–256.

11. David Gelles and David Yaffe-Bellany, "Shareholder Value Is No Longer Everything, Top C.E.O.s Say," *New York Times*, August 19, 2020, https://www.nytimes .com/2019/08/19/business/business-roundtable-ceos-corporations.html; "Business Roundtable Statement on the Purpose of a Corporation," Business Roundtable, accessed May 8, 2023, https://www.businessroundtable.org/purpose anniversary.

12. "Board of Directors," Business Roundtable, accessed May 8, 2023, https://www .businessroundtable.org/about-us/board-of-directors.

13. Peter S. Goodman, "Stakeholder Capitalism Gets a Report Card. It's Not Good," *New York Times*, September 22, 2020, https://www.nytimes.com/2020/09/22 /business/business-roudtable-stakeholder-capitalism.html; Lucien A. Bebchuk and Roberto Tallarita, "'Stakeholder' Talk Proves Empty Again," *Wall Street Journal*, August 18, 2021, https://www.wsj.com/articles/stakeholder-capitalism -esg-business-roundtable-diversity-and-inclusion-green-washing-11629313759.

14. Public discussions of morality and ethics in the marketplace are legion, for example: Andrew Ross Sorkin, "A Free Market Manifesto that Changed the World, Reconsidered," *New York Times*, September 11, 2020, https://www .nytimes.com/2020/09/11/business/dealbook/milton-friedman-doctrine -social-responsibility-of-business.html.

15. It is not just conservative Protestants who hold this view, either. William G. McLoughlin is an example of a mainstream academic who argued conservative Christianity expanded and endorsed free market ideology in the nineteenth century: William G. McLoughlin, "Introduction," in *The American Evangelicals, 1800–1900: An Anthology* (Gloucester, MA: Peter Smith, 1976), 1–27.

Conclusion 333

16. An example of such a critique by an evangelical: Skye Jethani, *The Divine Commodity: Discovering a Faith Beyond Consumer Christianity* (Grand Rapids, MI: Zondervan, 2013). An example of a critique from someone outside the evangelical tent (by a self-described "nontheist"): William E. Connolly, *Capitalism and Christianity, American Style* (Durham, NC: Duke University Press, 2008).

334 *Conclusion*

Bibliography

ARCHIVAL COLLECTIONS

Archives of Harper & Brothers, 1817–1914. Somerset House, Teaneck, NJ.

Aristarchus Champion Papers, 1806–1892. Monroe County Public Library, Rochester, NY.

Canal Records. New York State Archives, Albany, NY.

Cayuga Bridge Company Ledger. Buffalo and Erie County Historical Society, Buffalo, NY.

City of Rochester Village Trustee Proceedings, March 1828–May 1832. http://www.cityofrochester.gov/historiccouncilproceedings.aspx.

Dana Family Papers. Massachusetts Historical Society, Boston, MA.

Duyckinck Family Papers. New York Public Library, New York City.

Harmony Society Papers. Manuscript Group 185. Pennsylvania State Archives, Harrisburg.

Harper Brothers Records. Butler Library, Columbia University, New York City.

Henry Champion Papers, 1719–1862. Connecticut Historical Society, Hartford.

Gerrit Smith Papers. Bird Library, Syracuse University, Syracuse, New York.

James Harper Papers. Butler Library, Columbia University, New York City.

James Harper Papers. New York Historical Society, New York City.

John Street Church Archives. John Street Church, New York City.

Karl Arndt Collection of Harmony Society Materials. Manuscript Group 437. Pennsylvania State Archives, Harrisburg.

Lewis Tappan Papers. Library of Congress, Washington, DC.

Letters to Henry Wadsworth Longfellow, 1761–1904. Houghton Library, Harvard University, Cambridge, MA.

Methodist Episcopal Church Records. New York Public Library, Manuscripts and Archives Division, New York City.

Monroe County Index of Deeds, Monroe County Land Records, 156–157. Office of the Monroe County Clerk, Rochester, NY.

Monroe County Land Records. Office of the Monroe County Clerk, Rochester, NY.

Records of the Post Office Department. RG 28. National Archives, Washington, DC.

Records of the United States House of Representatives. RG 233. National Archives, Washington, DC.

Records of the United States Senate. RG 46. National Archives, Washington, DC.

R. G. Dun & Co. / Dun & Bradstreet Collections. Baker Library, Harvard Business School, Boston, MA.

Richard Palmer Files. Seymour Public Library, Auburn, NY.

Rochester Public Library Local History Division Map Collection. Monroe County Public Library, Rochester, NY.

Westchester Congregational Church Records. Westchester Congregational Church, Colchester, CT.

Western Reserve Manuscripts. Western Reserve Historical Society, Cleveland, OH.

PUBLISHED PRIMARY SOURCES

Abbott, Jacob. *The Harper Establishment, or How the Story Books Are Made.* New York: Harper & Brothers, 1855.

Adams, Henry, ed. *The Writings of Albert Gallatin.* Philadelphia: J. B. Lippincott and Company, 1879.

American Society for the Diffusion of Useful Knowledge. *Prospectus.* New York: American Society for the Diffusion of Useful Knowledge, 1837.

——. *Prospectus of the American Library for Schools and Families.* New York: American Society for the Diffusion of Useful Knowledge, 1837.

American State Papers. Buffalo, NY: W. S. Hein, 1998.

Arndt, Karl J. R., ed. *A Documentary History of the Indiana Decade of the Harmony Society, 1814–1819.* Indianapolis: Indiana Historical Society, 1975.

——. *A Documentary History of the Indiana Decade of the Harmony Society, 1820–1824.* Indianapolis: Indiana Historical Society, 1978.

——. *Economy on the Ohio, 1826–1834. George Rapp's Third Harmony. A Documentary History.* Worchester, MA: Harmony Society Press, 1984.

——. *George Rapp's Re-established Harmony Society: Letters and Documents of the Baker-Henrici Trusteeship, 1848–1868. A Documentary History.* New York: Peter Lang, 1993.

——. *George Rapp's Separatists, 1700–1803. A Documentary History.* Worchester, MA: Harmony Society Press, 1980.

——. *George Rapp's Years of Glory. Economy on the Ohio, 1834–1847. George Rapp's Third Harmony Society. A Documentary History.* New York: Peter Lang, 1987.

——. *Harmony on the Connoquenessing, 1803–1815. A Documentary History.* Worchester, MA: Harmony Society Press, 1980.

——. *Harmony on the Wabash in Transition, 1824–1826. A Documentary History.* Worcester, MA: Harmony Society Press, 1982.

Asbury, Francis. *The Journal and Letters of Francis Asbury.* Vol. 1. Wesley Center Online. http://media.sabda.org/alkitab-6/wh3-ref/aj-v1.pdf.

——. *The Journal of the Rev. Francis Asbury, Bishop of the Methodist Episcopal Church, from August 7, 1771, to December 7, 1815, Vol. I–III.* New York: N. Bangs and T. Mason, 1821.

Barclay, Robert. *Agricultural Tour in the United States and Canada.* London: William Blackwood & Sons, 1842.

Beach, Moses Y. *Wealth and Biography of the Wealthy Citizens of New York City.* 6th ed. New York: Sun Office, 1845.

——. *Wealth and Pedigree of the Wealthy Citizens of New York City.* 3rd ed. New York: Sun Office, 1842.

Bernhard, Duke of Saxe-Weimar-Eisenach. *Travels Through North America, During the Years 1825 and 1826.* 2 vols. Philadelphia: Carey, Lea & Carey, 1828.

Bissell, Arthur H., and Thomas B. Kirby, eds. *The Postal Laws and Regulations of the United States of America.* Washington, DC: Government Printing Office, 1879.

Blakely, William Addison, compiler. *American State Papers Bearing on Freedom in Religion.* Tacoma Park, WA: Review and Herald, 1911.

Boehme, Jacob. *The Way to Christ.* Trans. Peter Erb. New York: Paulist Press, 1978.

Boston Society for the Diffusion of Useful Knowledge. *Constitution.* Boston: Boston Society for the Diffusion of Useful Knowledge, 1829.

Bowker, R. R. *The Publishers' Trade List Annual, 1877.* New York: Office of the Publishers' Weekly, 1877.

Buckingham, J. S. *The Eastern and Western States of America.* Vol. 2. London: Fisher, Son, & Co., 1843.

Byron, Lord. *Don Juan: Cantos VII–XVI.* 2 vols. London: Thomas White, 1826.

Carey, Mathew. *The New Olive Branch.* Philadelphia: M. Carey & Son, 1820.

Chambers, Robert. *Vestiges of the Natural History of Creation.* London: John Churchill, 1844. Reprinted with an introduction by Gavin de Beer. New York: Humanities Press, 1969.

Chipman, Samuel. *Report of an Examination of Poor-Houses, Jails, &c . . . Addressed to Aristarchus Champion, Esq., of Rochester, N.Y.* Albany: New York State Temperance Society, 1836.

Bibliography 337

Clark, Davis W. "A Visit to the Publishing House of the Messrs. Harper & Brothers." *Ladies' Repository*, November 1853, 512–513.

Constitution of the Free Produce Society of Pennsylvania. Philadelphia: D & S Neall, 1827.

Cope, T. P., and A. Ferguson. "City Exchange." *Hazard's Register of Pennsylvania* 8 (July 23, 1831): 64.

Cranfield & Warren's Directory of the City of Rochester, for 1845–1846. Rochester, NY: Canfield & Warren, 1845.

Cuming, Fortescue. *Sketches of a Tour to the Western Country Through the States of Ohio and Kentucky*. Pittsburgh: Cramer, Spear & Eichbaum, 1810.

Daily American Directory of the City of Rochester, for 1847–8. Rochester, NY: Jerome & Brothers, 1847.

D'Arusmont, Frances Wright. *Life, Letters, and Lectures, 1834/1844*. New York: Arno Press, 1972.

DeBow, J. D. B. *Statistical View of the United States*. Washington, DC: Beverly Tucker, 1854.

Desilver, Robert. *The Philadelphia Index, or Directory, for 1823*. Philadelphia: Desilver, 1823.

——. *Desilver's Philadelphia Directory and Stranger's Guide, for 1828*. Philadelphia: Desilver, 1828.

——. *Desilver's Philadelphia Directory and Stranger's Guide, for 1835 & 36*. Philadelphia: Desilver, 1835.

Derby, J. C. *Fifty Years Among Authors, Books, and Publishers*. New York: Carleton, 1884.

Duncan, John. *Travels Through Part of the United States and Canada in 1818 and 1819*. Glasgow: University Press, 1823.

E., T. *Milman's History of the Jews, Published in the Family Library, Examined and Refuted on the Evidence of the Scriptures*. London: James Ridgway, 1830.

Edwards, Charles, ed. *Reports of Chancery Cases, Decided in the First Circuit of the State of New York, by the Honorable William T. McCoun, Vice-Chancellor, Volume III*. New York: Gould, Banks, and Company, 1843.

Elliott, Josephine M., ed. *To Holland and to New Harmony: Robert Dale Owen's Travel Journal, 1825–1826*. Indianapolis: Indiana Historical Society, 1969.

Elwood, James L., and Dellon M. Dewey. *A Directory and Gazetteer of the City of Rochester*. Rochester, NY: Canfield & Warren, 1844.

Ely, Elisha. *Directory for the Village of Rochester*. Rochester, NY: Everard Peck, 1827.

Ely, Ezra Stiles. *A Discourse, Delivered at the Opening of the General Assembly of the Presbyterian Church in the United States of America, on the 21st of May, A.D. 1829*. Princeton University Libraries, Princeton, NJ.

——. *The Duty of Christian Freemen to Elect Christian Rulers*. Philadelphia: W. F. Geddes, 1828.

——. *A Sermon, Delivered by Ezra Stiles Ely, on the First Sabbath After His Ordination*. Hartford, CT: Lincoln & Gleason, 1806.

——. *A Sermon for the Rich to Buy: That They May Benefit Themselves and the Poor*. New York: J. Seymour, 1810.

Ely, Zebulon. *A Gospel Minister, Though Young, Should Be Respectable by His Example: A Sermon, Delivered at the Ordination of the Rev. Ezra Stiles Ely, to the Pastoral Care of the Church in West-Chester, in Colchester, October 1, 1806*. Hartford, CT: Lincoln & Gleason, 1806.

Extracts from the Minutes of the General Assembly of the Presbyterian Church in the United States of America, A.D. 1812, Vol. III. Philadelphia: Jane Aitken, 1812.

Farkas, Alexander Boloni. *Journey in North America*. 1834. Trans. and ed. Theodore and Helen Benedek Schoenman. Philadelphia: American Philosophical Society, 1977.

Featherstonhaugh, G. W. *A Canoe Voyage of the Minnay Sotor*. Vol. 1. London: Richard Bentley, 1847.

Finch, John. "Notes of Travel in the United States: Letters VI–XI." *New Moral World: Gazette of the Rational Society* 5, nos. 34–39 (February 17–March 23, 1844).

First Annual Report of the General Union for the Promoting the Observance of the Christian Sabbath. New York: J. Collord, 1829.

Flower, Richard. *Letters from Lexington and the Illinois . . .* London: J. Ridgway, 1819.

Follen, E. L. *The Life of Charles Follen*. Boston: Thomas Webb and Company, 1844.

Fordham, Elias Pym. *Personal Narrative of Travels in Virginia, Maryland, Pennsylvania, Ohio, Indiana, Kentucky . . .* Ed. Frederic Austin Ogg. Cleveland: Arthur H. Clark Company, 1906.

Francis, John W. *Old New York: Or, Reminiscences of the Past Sixty Years*. New York: Charles Roe, 1858.

Friesen, Gerhard K. "An Additional Source on the Harmony Society of Economy, Pennsylvania." *Western Pennsylvania Historical Magazine* 61, no. 4 (October 1978): 301–314.

Goodrich, S. G. *Recollections of a Lifetime, Men and Things I Have Seen: In a Series of Familiar Letters to a Friend, Historical, Biographical, Anecdotical, and Descriptive*. Vol 2. New York: Miller, Orton and Mulligan, 1856.

Greene, Asa. *A Glance at New York: Embracing the City Government, Theatres, Hotels, Churches, Mobs, Monopolies, Learned Professions, Newspapers, Rogues, Dandies, Fires and Firemen, Water and Other Liquids, & C., & C.* New York: A. Greene, 1837.

Grund, Francis J. *The Americans in Their Moral, Social, and Political Relations*. Vol. 1. London: Longman, Rees, Orme, Brown, Green, and Longman, 1838.

Bibliography 339

Hall, Basil. *Forty Etchings: From Sketches Made with the Camera Lucida, in North America, in 1827 and 1828.* Edinburgh: Cadell & Co., 1829.

Harper's Illustrated Catalogue of Valuable Standard Works, in the Several Departments of General Literature. New York: Harper & Brothers, 1847.

Harper's New Monthly Magazine. Vol. 1, June to November 1850. New York: Harper & Brothers, 1850.

Harrington, Elisha. *The Utica Directory, 1828.* Utica, NY: C. N. Gaffney, 1828.

Haswell, Charles H. *Reminiscences of an Octogenarian of the City of New York.* New York: Harper & Brothers, 1896.

Herbert, William. *A Visit to the Colony of Harmony, in Indiana, in the United States of America* . . . London: George Mann, 1825.

Hiatt, Joel W., ed. *Diary of William Owen, from November 10, 1824 to April 20, 1825.* Indianapolis: Bobbs-Merrill Company, 1906. Reprint, New York: Augustus M. Kelley, 1973.

Holmes, Oliver Wendell. *The Poetical Works of Oliver Wendell Holmes.* London: G. Routledge, and Co., 1852.

Humphrey, Heman. *Essays Upon the Origin, Perpetuity, Change, and Proper Observance, of the Sabbath.* New York: Jonathan Leavitt, 1829.

The Illuminated Bible: Containing the Old and New Testaments; with Marginal Readings, References, and Chronological Dates: Also, the Apocrypha. New York: Harper & Brothers, 1843. 54 vols.

The Illuminated Bible: Containing the Old and New Testaments; with Marginal Readings, References, and Chronological Dates: Also, the Apocrypha. New York: Harper & Brothers, 1846.

Journal of the Convention of the Indiana Territory. Indiana Historical Bureau, https://www.in.gov/history/about-indiana-history-and-trivia/explore-indiana-history-by-topic/indiana-documents-leading-to-statehood/journal-of-the-convention-of-the-indiana-territory/.

King, Mary B. Allen. *Looking Backward: Memories of the Past.* New York: Anson D. F. Randolph and Company, 1870.

King's Rochester City Directory and Register, 1841. Rochester, NY: Welles and Hayes, 1840.

Laws of New York. Albany, NY: E. Croswell, 1835.

Laws of New York. Albany, NY: E. Croswell, 1838.

Leyda, Jay, ed. *The Melville Log: A Documentary Life of Herman Melville, 1819–1891.* New York: Gordian Press, 1969.

Lindley, Harlow, ed. *Indiana as Seen by Early Travelers: A Collection of Reprints from Books of Travel, Letters and Diaries Prior to 1830.* Indianapolis: Indiana Historical Commission, 1916.

Longworth, Thomas. *Longworth's American Almanac, New-York Register and City Directory*. New York: Thomas Longworth, 1823, 1825, 1829, 1835, 1836, 1841, 1844.

Marx, Karl, and Frederick Engels. *Collected Works*. Vol. 4. New York: International Publishers, 1975.

McIlvaine, Charles P. *Rev. Mr. McIlvaine in Answer to the Rev. Henry U. Onderdonk*. Philadelphia: William Stavely, 1827.

McKelvey, Blake. *The Rochester Historical Society Publication Series*. Vol. 21. Rochester, NY: Rochester Historical Society, 1943.

Melish, John. *Travels in the United States of America . . .* 2 vols. Philadelphia: Thomas & George Palmer, 1812.

Mellen, Grenville. *A Book of the United States . . .* New York: H. F. Sumner & Co., 1838.

Milman, H. H. *The History of the Jews, from the Earliest Period Down to Modern Times*. Vol. 1. 4th ed. London: John Murray, 1866.

Minutes of the General Assembly of the Presbyterian Church in the United States of America, From Its Organization A. D. 1789 to A. D. 1820 Inclusive. Philadelphia: Presbyterian Board of Publication, n.d.

Minutes of the General Assembly of the Presbyterian Church in the United States of America, Vol. VI, with an Appendix. Philadelphia: Jesper Harding, 1826.

Montulé, Edouard de. *Travels in America, 1816–1817*. Trans. Edward D. Seeber. Bloomington: Indiana University Press, 1951.

Morse, C. & M. *Charter and Directory of the City of Rochester*. New York: Marshall & Dean, 1834.

Nevins, Allan, and Milton Halsey Thomas, eds. *The Diary of George Templeton Strong: The Turbulent Fifties, 1850–1859*. New York: Macmillan Company, 1952.

Outler, Albert C., and Richard P. Heitzenrater, ed. *John Wesley's Sermons: An Anthology*. Nashville, TN: Abingdon Press, 1991.

Owen, Robert Dale. *Threading My Way*. New York: G. W. Carleton & Co., 1874.

Paine, Thomas. *Common Sense*. Philadelphia: W. and T. Bradford, 1776.

Parker, Joel. *The Signs of the Times: A Sermon, Delivered in Rochester, December 4, 1828*. Rochester, NY: E. Peck & Co., 1828.

Parsons, Israel. *The Centennial History of the Town of Marcellus, Delivered in the Presbyterian Church, of Marcellus, Onondaga County, N.Y., July 4, 1876*. Marcellus, NY: Reed's Printing House, 1878.

Passavant, William A. "A Visit to Economy in the Spring of 1840." *Western Pennsylvania Historical Magazine* 4, no. 3 (July 1921): 144–149.

Rapp, George. *Thoughts on the Destiny of Man, Particularly with Reference to the Present Times*. New Harmony, IN: Harmonie Society Press, 1824.

Recommendations of Worcester's Dictionaries; to Which Is Prefixed a Review of Webster's System of Orthography, from the United States Democratic Review, for March 1856. Boston: Hickling, Swan and Brown, 1856.

Rochester Historical Society Publication Fund Series Vol. I–XXIV. Rush Rees Library, University of Rochester, Rochester, New York.

Russell, Robert W. *America Compared with England.* London: Effingham, Wilson, and Royal Exchange, 1848.

Russell, William. *A History of Modern Europe, with a View of the Progress of Society from the Rise of the Modern Kingdoms to the Peace of Paris, 1763, Vol. III.* New York: J. & J. Harper, 1833.

Schoolcraft, Henry R. *Travels in the Central Portions of the Mississippi Valley...* New York: Collins and Hannay, 1825.

Sears, Robert, ed. *A New and Complete History of the Holy Bible, as Contained in the Old and New Testaments, from the Creation of the World to the Full Establishment of Christianity.* New York: Sears & Walker, 1845.

Seneca. *Seneca's Morals.* New York: Evert Duyckinck, 1817.

Shepard, Claude L. *The Connecticut Land Company and Accompanying Papers.* Cleveland, OH: Western Reserve Historical Society, 1916.

Snedeker, Caroline Dale, ed. *The Diaries of Donald MacDonald, 1824–1826.* Indianapolis: Indiana Historical Society, 1942.

Spencer, John C. *Circular by the Superintendent of Common Schools of the State of New York: To Trustees of School Districts, Librarians of District Libraries, Commissioners of Common Schools and Clerks of Counties, Containing "An Act Respecting School District Libraries" and Regulations for the Preservation of the Libraries...* Albany, NY: Hoffman & White, 1839.

State of Indiana. *Journal of the Senate of the State of Indiana,* 9th Session. Indianapolis: Douglass, 1825.

——. *Journal of the Senate of the State of Indiana,* 11th Session. Indianapolis: Douglass, 1827

Stilwell, Samuel. *Historical Sketches of the Rise and Progress of the Methodist Society, in the City of New-York.* New York: William Bates, 1821.

Swift, William, Jr. *Directory of the City of Rochester for 1838.* Rochester: C. S. Underwood, 1838.

Thatcher, B. B. *Indian Biography: Or, an Historical Account of Those Individuals Who Have Been Distinguished Among the North American Natives as Orators, Warriors, Statesmen, and Their Remarkable Characters.* Vol. 2. New York: Harper & Brothers, 1832.

Thoreau, Henry D. *Walden.* Annotated edition, with foreword and notes by Walter Harding. New York: Houghton Mifflin, 1995.

The Trade Circular Annual for 1871, Including the American Catalogue of Books Published in the United States During the Year 1870. New York: Office of the Trade Circular and Literary Bulletin, 1871.

Transactions of the New York State Agricultural Society. Vol. 31. Albany, NY: Argus Company, 1873.

Transactions of the New York State Agricultural Society. Vol. 32. Albany, NY: Jacob B. Parmenter, 1878.

Two Years Before the Mast, A Personal Narrative of Life at Sea. New York: Harper & Brothers, 1840. Nimitz Library, United States Naval Academy, Annapolis, Maryland.

United States Congress. *Annals of the Congress of the United States, 1789–1824.* 42 vols. Washington, DC: Gales and Seaton, 1834–1856.

——. *Serial Set.* Vol. 238. Washington, DC: U.S. Government Printing Office, 1834.

United States Department of Commerce. *Historical Statistics of the United States, Colonial Times to 1957.* Washington, DC: Government Printing Office, 1960.

Von Schweinitz, Lewis David. *The Journey of Lewis David von Schweinitz to Goshen, Bartholomew County.* Trans. Adolf Gerber. Indianapolis: Indiana Historical Society Publications, 1927.

Wakeley, J. B. *Lost Chapters Recovered from the Early History of Methodism.* New York: Carlton & Porter, 1858.

Watts, Frederick, ed. *Reports of Cases Argued and Determined in the Supreme Court of Pennsylvania.* Vol. 5. Philadelphia: James Kay Jun. and Brother, 1837.

Webster, Noah. *An American Dictionary of the English Language; Exhibiting the Origin, Orthography, Pronunciation, and Definitions of Words.* New York: Harper & Brothers, 1845.

Weed, Thurlow. *Life of Thurlow Weed Including His Autobiography and a Memoir.* Vols. 1 and 2. Boston: Houghton, Mifflin and Company, 1884.

Wesley, John. *The Nature, Design, and General Rules of the United Societies,* 5th ed. Bristol: Felix Farley, 1747.

——. *The Works of the Reverend John Wesley, Vol. 7.* New York: J. & J. Harper, 1826.

Woods, John. *Two Years' Residence in the Settlement on the English Prairie in the Illinois Country, United States.* London: A. & R. Spottiswoode, 1829.

Wright, Frances. *Biography, Notes and Political Letters of Frances Wright D'Arusmont, No. 1.* New York: J. Windt, 1844.

PERIODICALS

American Monthly Magazine (New York). HathiTrust.
American National Preacher (New York). ProQuest.

American Publishers' Circular and Literary Gazette (New York). Sabin Americana.

American Bookseller (New York). HathiTrust.

Boston Masonic Mirror. ProQuest.

Cayuga Free Press (Auburn, NY). Cayuga County Historian, Auburn, NY.

Cayuga-Patriot (Auburn, NY). Cayuga County Historian, Auburn, NY.

Cayuga Republican (Auburn, NY). Cayuga County Historian, Auburn, NY.

The Craftsman (Rochester, NY). Rush Rhees Library, University of Rochester.

The Critic (New York). HathiTrust.

Daily Atlas (Boston). America's Historical Newspapers.

District School Journal, for the State of New York (Geneva, NY). HathiTrust.

Eastern Argus (Portland, ME). America's Historical Newspapers.

Gospel Advocate and Impartial Investigator (Auburn, NY). Monroe County Public Library, Rochester, NY.

Harper's New Monthly Magazine. HathiTrust.

Harper's Weekly. HathiTrust.

The Jeffersonian (Albany, NY). HathiTrust.

The Knickerbocker (New York). McKeldin Library, University of Maryland, College Park, MD.

Ladies' Repository (Cincinnati, OH). HathiTrust.

Literary and Evangelical Magazine. ProQuest.

Louisville Public Advertiser (Louisville, KY). Nineteenth Century Newspapers.

Maryland Gazette (Annapolis). Nimitz Library, United States Naval Academy, Annapolis, MD.

National Preacher (New York). American Periodical Series.

New Hampshire Sentinel (Keene). America's Historical Newspapers.

New Harmony Gazette (New Harmony, IN). Center for Research Libraries.

New-London Gazette, and General Advertiser (New London, CT). America's Historical Newspapers.

New-York Commercial Advertiser. America's Historical Newspapers.

New-York Daily Times. ProQuest.

New York Evangelist. ProQuest.

New York Observer. Krauss Library, Lutheran School of Theology, Chicago, IL.

New-York Review. HathiTrust.

New Yorker. HathiTrust.

Niles' Weekly Register (Baltimore). HathiTrust.

Onondaga Register (Onondaga, NY). Onondaga Historical Association, Syracuse, NY, and New York State Library, Albany, NY.

Onondaga Register and Syracuse Gazette (Syracuse, NY). Onondaga Historical Association, Syracuse, NY.

Pittsburgh Daily Morning Gazette. http://archives.post-gazette.com/.

Pittsburgh Gazette. http://archives.post-gazette.com/.

Post Standard (Syracuse, NY). Onondaga Historical Association, Syracuse, NY.

Poulson's American Daily Advertiser (Philadelphia). America's Historical Newspapers.

Publishers' Weekly. HathiTrust.

Republican Star and General Advertiser (Easton, MD). America's Historical Newspapers.

Richmond Enquirer (Richmond, VA). America's Historical Newspapers.

Rochester Daily Advertiser. New York State Library, Albany, NY.

Rochester Daily Advertiser and Telegraph. New York State Library, Albany, NY.

Rochester Daily Telegraph. Rush Rhees Library, University of Rochester.

Rochester Observer. Monroe County Public Library, Rochester, NY, and Library of Congress, Washington, DC.

Salem Gazette (Salem, MA). America's Historical Newspapers.

Southern Literary Messenger (Richmond, VA). Making of America.

United States Democratic Review (New York). HathiTrust.

United States Literary Gazette (Boston). ProQuest.

United States Magazine and Democratic Review (New York). ProQuest.

Utica Sentinel and Gazette (Utica, NY). Center for Research Libraries, Chicago, IL.

Watch-Tower (Cooperstown, NY). America's Historical Newspapers.

Western Recorder (Utica, NY). Rush Rhees Library, University of Rochester.

SECONDARY SOURCES

Adams, David K., and Cornelius V. van Minnen, eds. *Religious and Secular Reform in America.* New York: New York University Press, 1999.

Adams, Herbert Baxter, and Frederick William Ashley. *Public Libraries and Popular Education.* Albany: University of the State of New York, 1900.

American Dictionary of Printing and Bookmaking. New York: Howard Lockwood & Company, 1894. Reprint, Detroit: Gale Research Co., 1967.

Amestoy, Jeffrey. *Slavish Shore: The Odyssey of Richard Henry Dana, Jr.* Cambridge, MA: Harvard University Press, 2015.

Andrews, Dee E. *The Methodists and Revolutionary America, 1760–1800.* Princeton, NJ: Princeton University Press, 2000.

Arndt, Karl J. R. *George Rapp's Harmony Society, 1785–1847.* Philadelphia: University of Pennsylvania Press, 1965.

——. "A Pious Fraud: Rapp's 1805 Harmony Society Articles of Association." *Western Pennsylvania Historical Magazine* 68, no. 3 (July 1985): 277–286.

——. "The Pittsburgh Meeting of General Lafayette, George Rapp, and Frances Wright." *Western Pennsylvania Historical Magazine* 62, no. 3 (July 1979): 281–295.

Arrington, Leonard J., Feramorz Y. Fox, and Dean L. May. *Building the City of God: Community and Cooperation Among the Mormons*. 2nd ed. Urbana: University of Illinois Press, 1992.

Balleisen, Edward. *Navigating Failure: Bankruptcy and Commercial Society in Antebellum America*. Chapel Hill: University of North Carolina Press, 2001.

Bangs, Nathan. *A History of the Methodist Church, Vol. IV.* New York: G. Lane and P. P. Sandford, 1841.

Banner, Lois W. "Religious Benevolence as Social Control: A Critique of an Interpretation." *Journal of American History* 60, no. 1 (June 1973): 23–41.

Baptist, Edward E. "Toxic Debt, Liar Loans, Collateralized and Secularized Human Beings, and the Panic of 1837." In *Capitalism Takes Command: The Social Transformation of Nineteenth-Century America*, ed. Michael Zakim and Gary J. Kornblith, 69–92. Chicago: University of Chicago Press, 2012.

Barnes, Joseph W. "Bridging the Lower Falls." *Rochester History* 36, no. 1 (January 1974): 1–24.

Bausman, Joseph H. *History of Beaver County, Pennsylvania and its Centennial Celebration*. Vol. 2. New York: Knickerbocker Press, 1904.

Bebchuk, Lucien A., and Roberto Tallarita, "'Stakeholder' Talk Proves Empty Again." *Wall Street Journal*, August 18, 2021. https://www.wsj.com/articles/stakeholder-capitalism-esg-business-roundtable-diversity-and-inclusion-green-washing-11629313759.

Becker, John E. *A History of the Village of Waterloo, New York and Thesaurus of Related Facts*. Waterloo, NY: Waterloo Library and Historical Society, 1949.

Beckert, Sven, and Seth Rockman, eds. *Slavery's Capitalism: A New History of American Economic Development*. Philadelphia: University of Pennsylvania Press, 2016.

Bellah, Robert N. *The Broken Covenant: American Civil Religion in Time of Trial*. New York: Seabury Press, 1975.

Bilhartz, Terry. *Urban Religion and the Second Great Awakening: Church and Society in Early National Baltimore*. Madison, NJ: Fairleigh Dickinson University Press, 1986.

Billington, Ray Allen. *The Protestant Crusade, 1800–1860: A Study of the Origins of American Nativism*. New York: Macmillan Company, 1938.

Bloch, Ruth. *Visionary Republic: Millennial Themes in American Thought, 1756–1800*. New York: Cambridge University Press, 1985.

Bodenhorn, Howard. *A History of Banking in Antebellum America: Financial Markets and Economic Development in an Era of Nation-Building*. New York: Cambridge University Press, 2000.

——. *State Banking in Early America: A New Economic History*. New York: Oxford University Press, 2003.

Boettner, Loraine. "Postmillennialism." In *The Meaning of the Millennium: Four Views*, ed. Robert Clouse, 117–141. Downers Grove, IL: InterVarsity Press, 1977.

Bole, John Archibald. *The Harmony Society: A Chapter in German American Culture History*. Philadelphia: Americana Germanica Press, 1904.

Brown, Candy Gunther. *The Word in the World: Evangelical Writing, Publishing, and Reading in America, 1789–1880*. Chapel Hill: University of North Carolina Press, 2004.

Brown, Dale. *Understanding Pietism*. Grand Rapids, MI: William B. Eerdmans, 1978.

Browning, Andrew. *The Panic of 1819: The First Great Depression*. Columbia: University of Missouri Press, 2019.

Bruegel, Martin. *Farm, Shop, Landing: The Rise of a Market Society in the Hudson Valley, 1780–1860*. Durham, NC: Duke University Press, 2002.

Bulthuis, Kyle T. *Four Steeples Over the City Streets: Religion and Society in New York's Early Republic Congregations*. New York: New York University Press, 2014.

Burrows, Edwin G., and Mike Wallace. *Gotham: A History of New York to 1898*. New York: Oxford University Press, 1999.

Bush, Charles P. "Historettes: The Bissells, Father and Son." In *Rochester Historical Society Publication Fund Series*, Vol. 6, ed. Edward Foreman, 333. Rochester, NY: Rochester Historical Society, 1927.

Bushman, Richard L. *The Refinement of America: Persons, Houses, Cities*. New York: Knopf, 1992.

Butts, Francis T. "The Myth of Perry Miller." *American Historical Review* 87, no. 3 (June 1982): 665–694.

Byrd, James P. *Sacred Scripture, Sacred War: The Bible and the American Revolution*. New York: Oxford University Press, 2013.

Campbell, Ted. *The Religion of the Heart: A Study of European Religious Life in the Seventeenth and Eighteenth Centuries*. Eugene, OR: Wipf and Stock Publishers, 2000.

Carey, Patrick, and Joseph Lienhard, eds. *Biographical Dictionary of Christian Theologians*. Westport, CT: Greenwood Publishing, 2000.

Carp, Roger E. "The Limits of Reform: Labor and Discipline on the Erie Canal." *Journal of the Early Republic* 10, no. 2 (Summer 1990): 191–219.

Carpenter, Delburn. *The Radical Pietists: Celibate Communal Societies Established in the United States Before 1820*. New York: AMS Press, 1975.

Carwardine, Richard. "Charles Seller's 'Antinomians' and 'Arminians': Methodists and the Market Revolution." In *God and Mammon: Protestants, Money, and the Market, 1790–1860*, ed. Mark Noll, 75–98. New York: Oxford University Press, 2002.

——. *Evangelicals and Politics in Antebellum America*. New Haven, CT: Yale University Press, 1993.

——. "Methodists, Politics, and the Coming of the American Civil War." In *Methodism and the Shaping of American Culture*, ed. Nathan O. Hatch and John Wigger, 309–342. Nashville, TN: Kingswood Books, 2001.

Cassedy, Tim. "'A Dictionary Which We Do Not Want': Defining America Against Noah Webster, 1783–1810." *William and Mary Quarterly* 71, no. 2 (April 2014): 229–254.

Charvat, William. *Literary Publishing in America, 1790–1850*. Philadelphia: University of Pennsylvania Press, 1959.

Chielens, Edward E., ed. *American Literary Magazines: The Eighteenth and Nineteenth Centuries*. Westport, CT: Greenwood Press, 1986.

Clouse, Robert, ed. *The Meaning of the Millennium: Four Views*. Downers Grove, IL: InterVarsity Press, 1977.

Cochran, Thomas. *Frontiers of Change: Early Industrialism in America*. New York: Oxford University Press, 1981.

Cole, Charles C., Jr. *The Social Ideas of the Northern Evangelists, 1820–1860*. New York: Columbia University Press, 1954.

Collections of Cayuga County Historical Society. No. 7. Auburn, NY: Jas. W. Burroughs, 1889.

Colombo, Ronald J. "Corporate Entanglement with Religion and the Suppression of Expression." *Seattle University Law Review* 45, no. 1 (Fall 2021): 187–239.

——. "Religious Liberty and the Business Corporation." *Journal of International Business and Law* 17, no. 1 (Winter 2017): 26–28.

Compton, John W. *The Evangelical Origins of the Living Constitution*. Cambridge, MA: Harvard University Press, 2014.

Connolly, William E. *Capitalism and Christianity, American Style*. Durham, NC: Duke University Press, 2008.

Costello, Augustine E. *Our Police Protectors: History of the New York Police from the Earliest Period to the Present Time*. New York: Augustine E. Costello, 1885.

Coulthard, Cheryl. "Frances Wright's Nashoba: Seeking a Utopian Solution to the Problem of Slavery." *Communal Societies* 39, no. 2 (2019): 58–74.

Creigh, Alfred, ed. *History of Washington County from Its First Settlement to the Present Time . . .* Harrisburg, PA: B. Singerly, 1871.

Cross, Whitney. *The Burned-Over District: The Social and Intellectual History of Enthusiastic Religion in Western New York, 1800–1850*. Ithaca, NY: Cornell University Press, 1950.

Cushing, John D. "Notes on Disestablishment in Massachusetts, 1780–1833." *William and Mary Quarterly* 26, no. 2 (April 1969): 169–190.

Daggar, Lori. *Cultivating Empire: Capitalism, Philanthropy, and the Negotiation of American Imperialism in Indian Country*. Philadelphia: University of Pennsylvania Press, 2023.

Dalzell, Robert F. *Enterprising Elite: the Boston Associates and the World They Made.* Cambridge, MA: Harvard University Press, 1987.

——. "The Rise of the Waltham-Lowell System and Some Thoughts on the Political Economy of Modernization in Ante-Bellum Massachusetts." *Perspectives in American History* 9 (1975): 229–268.

Davenport, Stewart. *Friends of the Unrighteous Mammon: Northern Christians & Market Capitalism.* Chicago: University of Chicago Press, 2008.

Davidson, Cathy N. *Revolution and the Word: The Rise of the Novel in America.* Expanded ed. New York: Oxford University Press, 2004.

Davis, John, Jennifer Greenhill, and Jason LaFountain, eds. *A Companion to American Art.* Malden, MA: Wiley-Blackwell, 2015.

Davis, Joshua Clark. *From Head Shops to Whole Foods: The Rise and Fall of Activist Entrepreneurs.* New York: Columbia University Press, 2020.

Dawdy, Shannon. *Building the Devil's Empire: French Colonial New Orleans.* Chicago: University of Chicago Press, 2008.

Dochuk, Darren. *Anointed with Oil: How Christianity and Crude Made Modern America.* New York: Basic Books, 2019.

Dolliver, Robert. *The Story of Old John Street Methodist Episcopal Church.* New York: John Felsberg, 1936.

Dreher, Rod. "Benedict Option," *American Conservative*, November–December 2013.

——. "Coming to Terms with a Post-Christian World." *Christianity Today*, November 2, 2015. http://www.christianitytoday.com/ct/2015/november/coming-to-terms-with-post-christian-world.html.

Durnbaugh, Donald F. "Work and Hope: The Spirituality of the Radical Pietist Communitarians." *Church History* 39, no. 1 (March 1970): 72–90.

Durrenberger, Joseph Austin. *Turnpikes: A Study of Toll Road Movement in the Middle Atlantic States and Maryland.* Cos Cob, CT: John E. Edwards, 1968.

Duss, John S. *The Harmonists: A Personal History.* Harrisburg, PA: Telegraph Press, 1943.

English, Eileen. *Demographic Directory of The Harmony Society.* 2nd ed. Clinton, NY: Richard W. Couper Press, 2016.

——. "The Life and Legacy of Count Leon: The Man Who Cleft the Harmonie." *Communal Societies* 33, no. 1 (June 2013): 45–82.

Esarey, Logan. "The First Indiana Banks." *Indiana Magazine of History* 6 (December 1910): 144–158.

——. "State Banking in Indiana, 1814–1873." *Indiana University Bulletin* 10, no. 2 (1912): 219–305.

Everill, Bronwen. *Not Made by Slaves: Ethical Capitalism in the Age of Abolition.* Cambridge, MA: Harvard University Press, 2020.

Bibliography 349

Exman, Eugene. *The Brothers Harper.* New York: Harper & Row, 1965.

——. *The House of Harper: One Hundred and Fifty Years of Publishing.* New York: Harper & Row, 1967.

Fea, John. *The Bible Cause: A History of the American Bible Society.* New York: Oxford University Press, 2016.

Feller, Daniel. "The Market Revolution Ate My Homework." *Reviews in American History* 25, no. 3 (September 1997): 408–415.

Fernandez, Kathleen. *Zoar: The Story of an Intentional Community.* Kent, OH: Kent State University Press, 2019.

Finke, Roger, and Rodney Starke. "How Upstart Sects Won America: 1776–1850." *Journal for the Scientific Study of Religion* 28 (1989): 27–44.

Fisher, Linford D. "Evangelicals and Unevangelicals: The Contested History of a Word, 1500–1950." *Religion and American Culture: A Journal of Interpretation* 26, no. 2 (2016): 184–226.

Fogleman, Aaron. *Hopeful Journeys: German Immigration, Settlement, and Political Culture in Colonial America, 1717–1775.* Philadelphia: University of Pennsylvania Press, 1996.

Foreman, Edward R., ed. *Centennial History of Rochester, New York.* Vols 1–3. Rochester, NY: Rochester Historical Society, 1931–1933.

——. *The Rochester Historical Society Publication Fund Series.* Vol. 6. Rochester, NY: Rochester Historical Society, 1927.

Foster, Charles I. *An Errand of Mercy: The Evangelical United Front, 1790–1837.* Chapel Hill: University of North Carolina Press, 1960.

——. "The Urban Missionary Movement, 1814–1837." *Pennsylvania Magazine of History and Biography* 75, no. 1 (January 1951): 47–65.

Foster, Lawrence. *Religion and Sexuality: Three American Communal Experiments of the Nineteenth Century.* New York: Oxford University Press, 1981.

French, Kara M. "Prejudice for Profit: Escaped Nun Stories and American Catholic Print Culture." *Journal of the Early Republic* 39, no. 3 (Fall 2019): 503–535.

Fuller, Wayne E. *Morality and the Mail in Nineteenth Century America.* Urbana: University of Illinois Press, 2003.

Gelles, David. "Benefiting Earth Through 'Hedonistic Altruism.'" *New York Times,* August 29, 2021, BU6.

Gelles, David, and David Yaffe-Bellany. "Shareholder Value Is No Longer Everything, Top C.E.O.s Say." *New York Times,* August 19, 2020. https://www.nytimes.com/2019/08/19/business/business-roundtable-ceos-corporations.html.

Gerson, Michael, and Peter Wehner. "The Power of Our Weakness." *Christianity Today,* November 2015, 40–46.

Giebelhausen, Michaela. *Painting the Bible: Representation and Belief in Mid-Victorian Britain.* Burlington, VT: Ashgate, 2006.

Gilje, Paul A. "The Rise of Capitalism in the Early Republic." *Journal of the Early Republic* 16, no. 2 (Summer 1996): 159–181.

Glaser, Rüdiger, Iso Himmelsbach, and Annette Bösmeier. "Climate of Migration? How Climate Triggered Migration from Southwest Germany to North America During the 19th Century." *Climate of the Past* 13 (2017): 1573–1592.

Goddu, Teresa A. *Selling Antislavery: Abolition and Mass Media in Antebellum America*. Philadelphia: University of Pennsylvania Press, 2020.

Goodman, Peter S. "Stakeholder Capitalism Gets a Report Card. It's Not Good." *New York Times*, September 22, 2020. https://www.nytimes.com/2020/09/22/business /business-roudtable-stakeholder-capitalism.html.

Gorski, Philip. *American Covenant: A History of Civil Religion from the Puritans to the Present*. Princeton, NJ: Princeton University Press, 2017.

Grainger, Brett. *Church in the Wild: Evangelicals in Antebellum America*. Cambridge, MA: Harvard University Press, 2019.

Grasso, Christopher. *Skepticism and American Faith: From the Revolution to the Civil War*. New York: Oxford University Press, 2018.

Gravely, Will. " '. . . Many of the Poor Affricans Are Obedient to the Faith': Reassessing the African American Presence in Early Methodism in the United States, 1769–1809." In *Methodism and the Shaping of American Culture*, ed. Nathan O. Hatch and John Wigger, 175–195. Nashville, TN: Kingswood Books, 2001.

Gray, Tim. "Aiming to Do Good, Not Just Well." *New York Times*, July 16, 2017, BU12.

Green, Steven K. *The Bible, the School, and the Constitution: The Clash that Shaped Modern Church-State Doctrine*. New York: Oxford University Press, 2012.

——. *The Second Disestablishment: Church and State in Nineteenth-Century America*. New York: Oxford University Press, 2010.

Greenberg, Joshua R. "The Era of Shinplasters: Making Sense of Unregulated Paper Money." In *Capitalism by Gaslight: Illuminating the Economy of Nineteenth-Century America*, ed. Brian P. Luskey and Wendy A. Woloson, 53–75. Philadelphia: University of Pennsylvania Press, 2015.

Griffin, Clifford. *Their Brother's Keepers: Moral Stewardship in the United States, 1800–1865*. New Brunswick, NJ: Rutgers University Press, 1960.

Griffin, Susan M. *Anti-Catholicism and Nineteenth-Century Fiction*. New York: Cambridge University Press, 2004.

Griswold, Wendy. *Cultures and Societies in a Changing World*. Thousand Oaks, CA: Pine Forge Press, 1994.

Gura, Philip F. *Man's Better Angels: Romantic Reformers and the Coming of the Civil War*. Cambridge, MA: Belknap Press of Harvard University Press, 2017.

Gutjahr, Paul C. *An American Bible: A History of the Good Book in the United States, 1777–1880*. Stanford, CA: Stanford University Press, 1999.

Guyatt, Nicholas. *Providence and the Invention of the United States, 1607–1876*. New York: Cambridge University Press, 2007.

Haanen, Jeff. "Investing in the Kingdom." *Christianity Today*, December 2016, 50–53.

Haas, Marilyn. "New York's School District Library Movement and Harper's School District Library Books, 1839–1846." Paper presented at Reading in America, 1840–1940, a Symposium, Strong Museum, Rochester, New York, November 22, 1986. Marilyn Haas Collection on the School District Library, 1812–2003, Box 1, Folder 16, Daniel A. Reed Library, State University of New York at Fredonia.

Hall, Henry. *The History of Auburn*. Auburn, NY: Dennis Brothers, 1860.

Halttunen, Karen. *Confidence Men and Painted Ladies: A Study of Middle-Class Culture in America, 1830–1870*. New Haven, CT: Yale University Press, 1982.

Hammond, Sarah. *God's Businessmen: Entrepreneurial Evangelicals in Depression and War*. Ed. Darren Dochuk. Chicago: University of Chicago Press, 2017.

Hardt, Philip F. *The Soul of Methodism: The Class Meeting in Early New York City Methodism*. Lanham, MD: University Press of America, 2000.

Harlow, Ralph V. *Gerrit Smith: Philanthropist and Reformer*. New York: Henry Holt and Company, 1939.

Harmon, Nolan B., ed. *Encyclopedia of World Methodism*. 2 Vols. Nashville, TN: United Methodist Publishing House, 1974.

Harper, J. Henry. *The House of Harper: A Century of Publishing in Franklin Square*. New York: Harper & Brothers, 1912.

Harrison, J. F. C. *Robert Owen and the Owenites in Britain and America: The Quest for the New Moral World*. New York: Charles Scribner's Sons, 1969.

Haselby, Sam. *The Origins of American Religious Nationalism*. New York: Oxford University Press, 2015.

Hatch, Nathan O. *The Democratization of American Christianity*. New Haven, CT: Yale University Press, 1989.

——. "The Puzzle of American Methodism." In *Methodism and the Shaping of American Culture*, ed. Nathan O. Hatch and John Wigger, 23–40. Nashville, TN: Kingswood Books, 2001.

——. *The Sacred Cause of Liberty: Republican Thought and the Millennium in Revolutionary New England*. New Haven, CT: Yale University Press, 1977.

Hatch, Nathan O., and John Wigger, eds. *Methodism and the Shaping of American Culture* Nashville, TN: Kingswood Books, 2001.

Hedstrom, Matthew. "The Commodification of Williams James: The Book Business and the Rise of Liberal Spirituality in the Twentieth-Century United States." In *Religion and the Marketplace in the United States*, ed. Jan Stievermann, Philip Goff, and Detlef Junker, 135–144. New York: Oxford University Press, 2015.

——. *The Rise of Liberal Religion: Book Culture and American Spirituality in the Twentieth Century*. New York: Oxford University Press, 2013.

Hempton, David, and John Walsh. "E. P. Thompson and Methodism." In *God and Mammon: Protestants, Money, and the Market, 1790–1860*, ed. Mark Noll, 99–120. New York: Oxford University Press, 2002.

Hill, Henry C. *The Wonder Book of Knowledge*. Philadelphia: John C. Winston Co., 1921.

Holcomb, Julie L. *Moral Commerce: Quakers and the Transatlantic Boycott of the Slave Labor Economy*. Ithaca, NY: Cornell University Press, 2016.

Holifield, E. Brooks. "Why Are Americans So Religious? The Limitations of Market Explanations." In *Religion and the Marketplace in the United States*, ed. Jan Stievermann, Philip Goff, and Detlef Junker, 33–60. New York: Oxford University Press, 2015.

Hood, Fred. "Presbyterianism and the New American Nation, 1783–1826: A Case Study of Religion and National Life." PhD diss., Princeton University, 1968.

——. *Reformed America: The Middle and Southern States, 1783–1837*. Tuscaloosa: University of Alabama Press, 1980.

Horowitz, Helen Lefkowitz. *Alma Mater: Design and Experience in Women's Colleges from Their Nineteenth Century Beginnings to the 1930s*. 2nd ed. Amherst, MA: University of Massachusetts Press, 1984.

Howe, Daniel Walker. *The Political Culture of the American Whigs*. Chicago: University of Chicago Press, 1979.

——. *Victorian America*. Philadelphia: University of Pennsylvania Press, 1976.

——. *What Hath God Wrought: The Transformation of America, 1815–1848*. New York: Oxford University Press, 2007.

Hurt, R. Douglas. *The Ohio Frontier: Crucible of the Old Northwest, 1720–1830*. Bloomington: Indiana University Press, 1996.

Ibrahim, Nabil A., Leslie W. Rue, Patricia P. McDougall, and G. Robert Greene. "Characteristics and Practices of 'Christian-Based' Companies." *Journal of Business Ethics* 10, no. 2 (February 1991): 123–132.

Innes, Stephen. *Creating the Commonwealth: The Economic Culture of Puritan New England*. New York: Norton, 1995.

Jenkyns, Richard. *Dignity and Decadence: Victorian Art and the Classical Inheritance*. Cambridge, MA: Harvard University Press, 1992.

Jennings, Chris. *Paradise Now: The Story of American Utopianism*. New York: Random House, 2016.

Jethani, Skye. *The Divine Commodity: Discovering a Faith Beyond Consumer Christianity*. Grand Rapids, MI: Zondervan, 2013.

——. "An Evangelical Case for Gay Wedding Cakes." *HuffPost*, February 20, 2014. https://www.huffpost.com/entry/an-evangelical-case-for-g_b_4476307.

John, Richard R. *Spreading the News: The American Postal System from Franklin to Morse.* Cambridge, MA: Harvard University Press, 1995.

——. "Taking Sabbatarianism Seriously: The Postal System, the Sabbath, and the Transformation of American Political Culture." *Journal of the Early Republic* 10, no. 4 (Winter 1990): 517–567.

Johnson, Curtis. *Islands of Holiness: Rural Religion in Upstate New York, 1790–1860.* Ithaca, NY: Cornell University Press, 1989.

Johnson, Elizabeth. "A Welcome Attack on American Values: How the Doctrines of Robert Owen Attracted American Society." *Constructing the Past* 8, no. 1 (2007): 87–106.

Johnson, Paul E. *Sam Patch, the Famous Jumper.* New York: Hill and Wang, 2004.

——. *A Shopkeeper's Millennium: Society and Revivals in Rochester, New York, 1815–1837.* New York: Hill and Wang, 1978.

Jordan, John W., ed. *Colonial and Revolutionary Families of Pennsylvania.* Vol. 3. New York: Lewis Publishing Company, 1911.

Kaser, David. *Messrs. Carey & Lea of Philadelphia: A Study in the History of the Book-trade.* Philadelphia: University of Pennsylvania Press, 1957.

Kamensky, Jane. *The Exchange Artist: A Tale of High-Flying Speculation and America's First Banking Collapse.* New York: Viking Press, 2008.

Kasson, John F. *Civilizing the Machine: Technology and Republican Values in America, 1776–1900.* New York: Grossman Publishers 1976. Reprint, New York: Hill and Wang, 1999.

——. *Rudeness and Civility: Manners in Nineteenth-Century Urban America.* New York: Hill and Wang, 1990.

Kelly, Catherine E. *Republic of Taste: Art, Politics, and Everyday Life in Early America.* Philadelphia: University of Pennsylvania Press, 2016.

Kendall, Joshua. *The Forgotten Founding Father: Noah Webster's Obsession and the Creation of an American Culture.* New York: G. P. Putnam's Sons, 2010.

Kern, Louis J. *An Ordered Love: Sex Roles and Sexuality in Victorian Utopias—the Shakers, the Mormons, and the Oneida Community.* Chapel Hill: University of North Carolina Press, 1981.

Kirk, Nicole C. *Wanamaker's Temple: The Business of Religion in an Iconic Department Store.* New York: New York University Press, 2018.

Knodell, Jane Ellen. *The Second Bank of the U.S.: "Central" Banker in an Era of Nation-Building, 1816–1836.* New York: Routledge, 2017.

Knoedler, Christiana F. *The Harmony Society: A 19th-Century American Utopia.* New York: Vantage Press, 1954.

Kocka, Jurgen. "Introduction." In *Capitalism: The Reemergence of a Historical Concept,* ed. Jurgen Kocka and Marcel van der Linden, 1–10. New York: Bloomsbury, 2016.

Kocka, Jurgen, and Marcel van der Linden, eds. *Capitalism: The Reemergence of a Historical Concept.* New York: Bloomsbury, 2016.

Kreitner, Richard. "Paterson: Alexander Hamilton's Trickle-Down City." *The Nation,* March 13, 2017, 18–24.

Krieger, Alex. *City on a Hill: Urban Idealism in America from the Puritans to the Present.* Cambridge, MA: Belknap Press of Harvard University Press, 2019.

Kring, Hilda Adam. *The Harmonists: A Folk-Cultural Approach.* Metuchen, NJ: Scarecrow Press and the American Theological Library Association, 1973.

Kruse, Keven. *One Nation Under God: How Corporate America Invented Christian America.* New York: Basic Books, 2015.

Ladd, George Eldon. "Historic Premillennialism." In *The Meaning of the Millennium: Four Views,* ed. Robert Clouse, 17–40. Downers Grove, IL: InterVarsity Press, 1977.

Larner, Jr. John W. "'Nails and Sundrie Medicines" Town Planning and Public Health in the Harmony Society, 1805–1840." *Western Pennsylvania Historical Magazine* 45 (June 1962): 115–138.

Larson, John Lauritz. *Internal Improvement: National Public Works and the Promise of Popular Government in the Early United States.* Chapel Hill: University of North Carolina Press, 2001.

——. *The Market Revolution in America.* New York: Cambridge University Press, 2010.

——. "The Market Revolution in Early America: An Introduction." *OAH Magazine of History* 19, no. 3. (May 2005): 4–7.

Lauer, Josh. *Creditworthy: A History of Consumer Surveillance and Financial Identity in America.* New York: Columbia University Press, 2017.

Lazerow, Jama. *Religion and the Working Class in Antebellum America.* Washington, DC: Smithsonian Institution, 1995.

Lehmann-Haupt, Hellmut. *The Book in America: A History of the Making and Selling of Books in the United States.* New York: R. R. Bowker, 1952.

Leja, Michael. "Issues in Early Mass Visual Culture." In *A Companion to American Art,* ed. John David, Jennifer Greenhill, and Jason LaFountain, 305–347. Malden, MA: Wiley-Blackwell, 2015.

Lepler, Jessica M. *The Many Panics of 1837: People, Politics, and the Creation of a Transatlantic Financial Crisis.* New York: Cambridge University Press, 2013.

Lepore, Jill. *A Is for American: Letters and Other Characters in the Newly United States.* New York: Vintage Books, 2002.

Leshem, Dotan. *The Origins of Neoliberalism: Modeling the Economy from Jesus to Foucault.* New York: Columbia University Press, 2016.

Leslie, E. Norman. *History of Skaneateles and Vicinity, 1781–1881.* Auburn, NY: Chas. P. Cornell, 1882.

Levine, Lawrence W. *Highbrow/Lowbrow: The Emergence of Cultural Hierarchy in America*. Cambridge, MA: Harvard University Press, 1988.

Levy, Jonathan. *Ages of American Capitalism: A History of the United States*. New York: Random House, 2021.

——. *Freaks of Fortune: The Emerging World of Capitalism and Risk in America*. Cambridge, MA: Harvard University Press, 2012.

Licht, Walter. *Industrializing America: The Nineteenth Century*. Baltimore: Johns Hopkins University Press, 1995.

Linton, W. J. "The History of Wood-engraving in America," *American Art Review* 1, no. 6 (April 1880): 236–242.

Littell, Franklin H. "Radical Pietism in American History." In *Continental Pietism and Early American Christianity*, ed. F. Ernest Stoeffler, 164–183. Grand Rapids, MI: William B. Eerdmans, 1976.

Lockwood, George Browning. *The New Harmony Communities*. Marion, IN: Chronicle Company, 1902.

——. *The New Harmony Movement*. New York: Augustus M. Kelley, 1905.

Long, Kathryn T. "Consecrated Respectability: Phoebe Palmer and the Refinement of American Methodism." In *Methodism and the Shaping of American Culture*, ed. Nathan O. Hatch and John Wigger, 281–307. Nashville, TN: Kingswood Books, 2001.

——. *Revival of 1857–58: Interpreting an American Religious Awakening*. New York: Oxford University Press, 1998.

Lossing, Benson John. *History of New York City, Embracing an Outline of Events from 1609 to 1830, and a Full Account of Its Development from 1830 to 1884*. New York: George E. Perine, 1885.

Loveland, Anne C. "Domesticity and Religion in the Antebellum Period: The Career of Phoebe Palmer." *The Historian* 39, no. 3 (May 1977): 455–471.

Luskey, Brian P., and Wendy A. Woloson, eds. *Capitalism by Gaslight: Illuminating the Economy of Nineteenth-Century America*. Philadelphia: University of Pennsylvania Press, 2015.

Lyford, James O., ed. *History of Concord, New Hampshire, from the Original Grant in 1725 to the Opening of the Twentieth Century*. Concord, NH: Mumford Press, 1903.

Marsden, George. *The Evangelical Mind and the New School Presbyterian Experience: A Case Study of Thought and Theology in Nineteenth-Century America*. New Haven, CT: Yale University Press, 1970.

——. *Fundamentalism and American Culture*. 2nd ed. New York: Oxford University Press, 2005.

——. *Jonathan Edwards: A Life*. New Haven, CT: Yale University Press, 2003.

Martin, Scott C., ed. *Cultural Change and the Market Revolution in America, 1789–1860*. New York: Rowman & Littlefield, 2005.

Matson, Cathy, ed. *The Economy of Early America: Historical Perspectives and New Directions*. University Park: Pennsylvania State University Press, 2006.

McCrossen, Alexis. *Holy Day, Holiday: The American Sunday*. Ithaca, NY: Cornell University Press, 2018.

McDannell, Colleen. *The Christian Home in Victorian America, 1840–1900*. Bloomington: Indiana University Press, 1986.

——. *Material Christianity: Religion and Popular Culture in America*. New Haven, CT: Yale University Press, 1995.

McGill, Meredith. *American Literature and the Culture of Reprinting, 1834–1853*. Philadelphia: University of Pennsylvania Press, 2003.

McKelvey, Blake. "Civic Medals Awarded Posthumously." *Rochester History* 22, no. 2 (April 1960): 1–24.

——. "Rochester Mayors Before the Civil War," *Rochester History* 26, no. 1 (January 1964): 1–20.

——. *Rochester: The Water-Power City, 1812–1854*. Cambridge, MA: Harvard University Press, 1945.

McLoughlin, William G. "Introduction." In *The American Evangelicals, 1800–1900: An Anthology*, ed. William G. McLoughlin, 1–27. Gloucester, MA: Peter Smith, 1976.

Merish, Lori. *Sentimental Materialism: Gender, Commodity Culture and Nineteenth-Century American Literature*. Durham, NC: Duke University Press, 2000.

Meyer, David R. *The Roots of American Industrialization*. Baltimore: Johns Hopkins University Press, 2003.

Mihm, Stephen. *A Nation of Counterfeiters: Capitalists, Con Men, and the Making of the United States*. Cambridge, MA: Harvard University Press, 2007.

Mitroff, Ian A. *A Spiritual Audit of Corporate America: A Hard Look at Spirituality, Religion, and Values in the Workplace*. San Francisco, CA: Jossey-Bass Publishers, 1999.

Moore, Joseph S. *Founding Sins: How a Group of Antislavery Radicals Fought to Put Christ Into the Constitution*. New York: Oxford University, 2016.

Moore, R. Laurence. *Selling God: American Religion in the Marketplace of Culture*. New York: Oxford University Press, 1994.

Moreton, Bethany. *To Serve God and Wal-Mart: The Making of Christian Free Enterprise*. Cambridge, MA: Harvard University Press, 2009.

Morgan, David. *Protestants and Pictures: Religion, Visual Culture, and the Age of American Mass Production*. New York: Oxford University Press, 1999.

Morris, Adam. *American Messiahs: False Prophets of a Damned Nation*. New York: Norton, 2019.

Mott, Frank Luther. *Golden Multitudes: The Story of the Best Sellers in the United States.* R. R. Bowker, 1947.

Moyer, Liz. "Funds Invoke Bible Values in Choosing Investments." *New York Times,* March 1, 2017, BU1.

Murphy, Andrew R. *Prodigal Nation: Moral Decline and Divine Punishment from New England to 9/11.* New York: Oxford University Press, 2009.

Murphy, Brian. *Building the Empire State: Political Economy in the Early Republic.* Philadelphia: University of Pennsylvania Press, 2015.

Murphy, Sharon. *Other People's Money: How Banking Worked in the Early American Republic.* Baltimore: Johns Hopkins University Press, 2017.

Nelson, Robert H. "Max Weber Revisited." In *Religion, Economy, and Cooperation,* ed. Ilkka Pyysiainen, 157–217. New York: Walter de Gruyter, 2010.

Nelson, Scott Reynolds. *A Nation of Deadbeats: An Uncommon History of America's Financial Disasters.* New York: Alfred A Knopf, 2012.

Nissenbaum, Stephen. *The Battle for Christmas: A Cultural History of America's Most Cherished Holiday.* New York: Vintage, 1996.

Noll, Mark A. *America's God: From Jonathan Edwards to Abraham Lincoln.* New York: Oxford University Press, 2002.

——, ed. *God and Mammon: Protestants, Money, and the Market, 1790–1860.* New York: Oxford University Press, 2002.

Noll, Mark A., David W. Bebbington, and George Marsden, eds. *Evangelicals: Who They Have Been, Are Now, and Could Be.* Grand Rapids, MI: Eerdmans Publishing Company, 2019.

Nord, David Paul. *Faith in Reading: Religious Publishing and the Birth of Mass Media in America.* New York: Oxford University Press, 2007.

Norris, James D. *R. G. Dun & Co., 1841–1900: The Development of Credit-Reporting in the Nineteenth Century.* Westport, CT: Greenwood Press, 1978.

O'Reilly, Henry. *Sketches of Rochester: With Incidental Notices of Western New York.* Rochester, NY: William Alling, 1838.

Ott, Alice T. *The Sunwoman in the Wilderness: The Religious Beliefs and Practices of George Rapp's Harmony Society.* Lexington, KY: Emeth Press, 2014.

Palmer, Richard F. *The "Old Line Mail": Stagecoach Days in Upstate New York.* Lakemont, NY: North Country Books, 1977.

Parker, Hershel. *Herman Melville: A Biography.* Vol. 1, *1819–1851.* Baltimore: Johns Hopkins University Press, 1996.

Peck, William E. *Semi-centennial History of the City of Rochester with Illustrations and Biographical Sketches of Some of Its Prominent Men and Pioneers.* Syracuse, NY: D. Mason & Co., 1884.

Perciaccante, Marianne. *Calling Down Fire: Charles Finney and Revivalism in Jefferson County, New York.* New York: State University of New York Press, 2003.

Perkins, Barbara M. "Harper's Monthly Magazine." In *American Literary Magazines: The Eighteenth and Nineteenth Centuries*, ed. Edward E. Chielens, 166–170. Westport, CT: Greenwood Press, 1986.

Perry, Seth. *Bible Culture and Authority in the Early United States.* Princeton, NJ: Princeton University Press, 2018.

——. "'What the Public Expect': Consumer Authority and the Marketing of Bibles, 1770–1850." *American Periodicals* 24, no. 2 (2014): 128–144.

Pessen, Edward. "Moses Beach Revisited: A Critical Examination of His Wealthy Citizens Pamphlets." *Journal of American History* 58, no. 2 (September 1971): 415–426.

Pilsworth, Edward S. *Electrotyping in Its Relation to the Graphic Arts.* New York: Macmillan, 1923.

Pitzer, Donald, ed. *America's Communal Utopias.* Chapel Hill: University of North Carolina Press, 1997.

——. "How the Harmonists Suffered Disharmony: Schism in Communal Utopias." *American Communal Societies Quarterly* 5, no. 2 (April 2011): 55–75.

Pitzer, Donald, and Josephine Elliott, "New Harmony's First Utopians, 1814–1824." *Indiana Magazine of History* 75 (September 1979): 225–300.

Pitzer, Donald, and Darryl Jones, *New Harmony Then & Now.* Bloomington: Indiana University Press, 2012.

Pomeroy, Jane R. "Alexander Anderson's Life and Engravings Before 1800, with a Checklist of Publications Drawn from His Diary." *Proceedings of the American Antiquarian Society* 100, no. 1 (April 1990): 137–230.

Porterfield, Amanda, Darren E. Grem, and John Corrigan, eds. *The Business Turn in American Religious History.* New York: Oxford University Press, 2017.

Prothero, Stephen. *God the Bestseller: How One Editor Transformed American Religion a Book at a Time.* New York: HarperOne, 2023.

Pyysiainen, Ilkka, ed. *Religion, Economy, and Cooperation.* New York: Walter de Gruyter, 2010.

Ratner, Lorman A., Paula T. Kaufman, and Dwight L. Teeter Jr. *Paradoxes of Prosperity: Wealth-Seeking Versus Christian Values in Pre–Civil War America.* Urbana: University of Illinois Press, 2009.

Richardson, Darcy G. *Others: Third-Party Politics from the Nation's Founding to the Rise and Fall of the Greenback-Labor Party.* New York: iUniverse, 2004.

Ringwalt, J. L. *Development of Transportation Systems in the United States.* Philadelphia: J. L. Ringwalt, 1888. Reprint, New York: Johnson Reprint Corporation, 1966.

Roberts, Alasdair. *America's First Great Depression: Economic Crisis and Political Disorder After the Panic of 1837.* Ithaca, NY: Cornell University Press, 2012.

Roberts, Kyle B. *Evangelical Gotham: Religion and the Making of New York City, 1783–1860.* Chicago: University of Chicago Press, 2016.

Robinson, Elwin C. "Heavenly Aspirations and Earthly Realities: Four Northeast Ohio Religious Utopias." *Timeline*, November–December 2000, 3–23.

Rogers, Raynor. *The Story of Old John Street Church*. New York: Raynor R. Rogers, 1984.

Rohrer, James R. "Sunday Mails and the Church-State Theme in Jacksonian America." *Journal of the Early Republic* 7, no. 1 (Spring 1987): 53–74.

Rokicky, Catherine. *Creating a Perfect World: Religious and Secular Utopias in Nineteenth-Century Ohio*. Athens: Ohio University Press, 2002.

Rothenberg, Winifred Barr. *From Market-Places to a Market Economy: The Transformation of Rural Massachusetts, 1750–1850*. Chicago: University of Chicago Press, 1992.

Rothman, Adam. *Slave Country: American Expansion and the Origins of the Deep South*. Cambridge, MA: Harvard University Press, 2005.

Rubenstein, Mary-Jane. *Astrotopia: The Dangerous Religion of the Corporate Space Race*. Chicago: University of Chicago Press, 2022.

——. "A Tale of Two Utopias: Musk and Bezos in Outer Space." *Metapolis*, March 2022. https://metapolis.net/project/a-tale-of-two-utopias-musk-and-bezos-in-outer-space/.

Ryan, Mary P. *Cradle of the Middle Class: The Family in Oneida County, New York, 1790–1865*. New York: Cambridge University Press, 1981.

Salguero, Gabriel, Rod Dreher, and Shirley Hoogstra. "Will the Wilberforce Option Work?" *Christianity Today*, November 2015, 47–49.

Samuels, Shirley, ed. *The Culture of Sentiment: Race, Gender, and Sentimentality in Nineteenth-Century America*. New York: Oxford University Press, 1992.

Sanchez, Maria Carla. *Reforming the World: Social Activism and the Problem of Fiction in Nineteenth Century America*. Iowa City: University of Iowa Press, 2008.

Sandage, Scott A. *Born Losers: A History of Failure in America*. Cambridge, MA: Harvard University Press, 2005.

Schocket, Andrew M. *Founding Corporate Power in Early National Philadelphia*. DeKalb: Northern Illinois University Press, 2007.

Seaman, Samuel. *Annals of New York Methodism, Being a History of the Methodist Episcopal Church in the City of New York*. New York: Hunt & Eaton, 1892.

Seavoy, Ronald E. *The Origins of the American Business Corporation, 1784–1855: Broadening the Concept of Public Service during Industrialization*. Westport, CT: Greenwood Press, 1982.

Sehat, David. *The Myth of American Religious Freedom*. New York: Oxford University Press, 2011.

Sellers, Charles. *The Market Revolution: Jacksonian America, 1815–1846*. New York: Oxford University Press, 1991.

Shankman, Andrew. "Capitalism, Slavery, and the New Epoch: Mathew Carey's 1819." In *Slavery's Capitalism: A New History of American Economic Development*, ed. Sven Beckert and Seth Rockman, 243–261. Philadelphia: University of Pennsylvania Press, 2016.

Shaw, Ronald E. *Canals for a Nation: The Canal Era in the United States, 1790–1860.* Lexington: University Press of Kentucky, 1990.

Shepard, Claude L. *The Connecticut Land Company and Accompanying Papers.* Cleveland, OH: Western Reserve Historical Society, 1916.

Sheriff, Carol. *The Artificial River: The Erie Canal and the Paradox of Progress, 1817–1862.* New York: Hill and Wang, 1996.

Shilling, Donovan A. "The Great Water Bridges: The Story of the Magnificent Genesee River Aqueducts." *Crooked Lake Review*, no. 75 (June 1994). https://www .crookedlakereview.com/articles/67_100/75june1994/75shilling.html.

Siddali, Silvana R. *Frontier Democracy: Constitutional Conventions in the Old Northwest.* New York: Cambridge University Press, 2016.

Slaughter, Joseph P. "A 'True Commentary': The Gendered Imagery of *Harper's Illuminated and New Pictorial Bible.*" *Journal of the Early Republic* 41, no. 4 (Winter 2021): 587–619.

——. "The Virginia Company to Chick-fil-A: Christian Business in America, 1600–2000." *Seattle University Law Review* 44, no. 2 (Winter 2021): 421–462.

Smith, Steven Carl. *An Empire of Print: The New York Publishing Trade in the Early American Republic.* University Park, PA: Penn State University Press, 2017.

Snow, Richard. *I Invented the Modern Age: The Rise of Henry Ford.* New York: Scribner, 2013.

Sorkin, Andrew Ross. "A Free Market Manifesto that Changed the World, Reconsidered." *New York Times*, September 11, 2020. https://www.nytimes.com/2020 /09/11/business/dealbook/milton-friedman-doctrine-social-responsibility-of -business.html.

Stansell, Christine. *City of Women: Sex and Class in New York, 1789–1860.* Urbana-Champaign: University of Illinois Press, 1987.

Stevens, Abel. *The Life and Times of Nathan Bangs.* New York: Carlton & Porter, 1863.

Stievermann, Jan, Philip Goff, and Detlef Junker, eds. *Religion and the Marketplace in the United States.* New York: Oxford University Press, 2015.

Stoeffler, F. Ernest, ed. *Continental Pietism and Early American Christianity.* Grand Rapids, MI: William B. Eerdmans, 1976.

——. *German Pietism During the Eighteenth Century.* Leiden, NL: E. J. Brill, 1973.

——. *The Rise of Evangelical Pietism.* Leiden, NL: E. J. Brill, 1965.

Storke, Eliot G. *The History of Cayuga County, New York.* Syracuse, NY: D. Mason & Co., 1879.

Storm, Jonathan. *Pietism and Community in Europe and North America, 1650–1850.* Boston: Brill, 2010.

Strom, Jonathan, Hartmut Lehmann, and James Van Horn Melton, eds. *Pietism in Germany and North America, 1680–1820.* Burlington, VT: Ashgate, 2009.

Sutton, William R. *Journeymen for Jesus: Evangelical Artisans Confront Capitalism in Jacksonian Baltimore.* University Park, PA: Penn State University Press, 1998.

Sutton, William R. " 'To Extract Poison from the Blessings of God's Providence': Producerist Respectability and Methodist Suspicions of Capitalist Change in the Early Republic." In *Methodism and the Shaping of American Culture,* ed. Nathan O. Hatch and John Wigger, 223–255. Nashville, TN: Kingswood Books, 2001.

Sweet, Leonard I. "The Female Seminary Movement and Woman's Mission in Antebellum America." *Church History* 54, no. 1 (March 1985): 41–55.

Sylla, Richard. "Forgotten Men of Money: Private Bankers in Early U. S. History." *Journal of Economic History* 36, no. 1 (March 1976): 173–188.

Taylor, George Rogers. *The Transportation Revolution, 1815–1860.* New York: Rineheart, 1951.

Taysom, Stephen C. *Shakers, Mormons, and Religious Worlds: Conflicting Visions, Contested Boundaries.* Bloomington: Indiana University Press, 2010.

Tebbel, John. *A History of Book Publishing in the United States.* Vol. 1, *The Creation of an Industry, 1640–1865.* New York: R. R. Bowker, 1972.

Temin, Peter. *The Jacksonian Economy.* New York: W. W. Norton & Company, 1969.

Temme, Willi. "From Jakob Böhme Via Jane Leade to Eva von Buttlar—Transmigrations and Transformations of Religious Ideas." In *Pietism in Germany and North America, 1680–1820,* ed. Jonathan Strom, Hartmut Lehmann, and James Van Horn Melton, 101–106. Burlington, VT: Ashgate, 2009.

Tanner, Kathryn. *Theories of Culture: A New Agenda for Theology.* Minneapolis, MN: Fortress Press, 1997.

Tanselle, G. Thomas. "The Sales of Melville's Books." *Harvard Library Bulletin* 18 (April 1969): 195–215.

Thornton, Tamara Plakins. "Capitalist Aesthetics: Americans Look at the London and Liverpool Docks." In *Capitalism Takes Command: The Social Transformation of Nineteenth-Century America,* ed. Michael Zakim and Gary J. Kornblith, 169–198. Chicago: University of Chicago Press, 2012.

Trowbridge, Francis Bacon. *The Champion Genealogy: History of the Descendants of Henry Champion of Saybrook and Lyme, Connecticut.* 2 vols. New Haven, CT: n.p., 1891.

Tucker, Barbara M. *Samuel Slater and the Origins of the American Textile Industry, 1790–1860.* Ithaca, NY: Cornell University Press, 1984.

Tuveson, Ernest Lee. *Redeemer Nation: The Idea of America's Millennial Role*. Chicago: University of Chicago Press, 1968.

Upham, Francis Bourne. *The Story of Old John Street Methodist Episcopal Church*. New York: John Street Methodist Church, 1932.

Vaca, Daniel. *Evangelicals Incorporated: Books and the Business of Religion in America*. Cambridge, MA: Harvard University Press, 2019.

Valeri, Mark. *Heavenly Merchandize: How Religion Shaped Commerce in Puritan America*. Princeton, NJ: Princeton University Press, 2010.

——. "Weber and Eighteenth-Century Religious Developments in America." In *Religion and the Marketplace in the United States*, ed. Jan Stievermann, Philip Goff, and Detlef Junker, 63–78. New York: Oxford University Press, 2015.

Van Deusen, Glyndon G. *Thurlow Weed: Wizard of the Lobby*. Boston: Little, Brown and Company, 1947.

Verde, Tom. "Investing Along Religious Guidelines." *New York Times*, July 2, 2017, BU3.

Vineyard, Ron. *Stage Waggons and Coaches*. Williamsburg, VA: Colonial Williamsburg Foundation Library, 2002.

Wallace, Anthony F. C. *Rockdale: The Growth of an American Village in the Early Industrial Revolution*. New York: Knopf, 1978.

Ward, F. De W. *Churches of Rochester: Ecclesiastical History of Rochester, N.Y.* Rochester, NY: Erastus Darrow, 1871.

Way, Peter. *Common Labor: Workers and the Digging of North American Canals, 1780–1860*. New York: Cambridge University Press, 1993.

Weber, Max. *The Protestant Ethic and the "Spirit" of Capitalism and Other Writings*. New York: Penguin, 2002.

Weeks, Andrew. *Boehme: An Intellectual Biography of the Seventeenth-Century Philosopher and Mystic*. Albany: State University of New York Press, 1991.

Weitenkampf, Frank. *The Illustrated Book*. Cambridge, MA: Harvard University Press, 1938.

Wetzel, Richard D. "J. C. Muller and W. C. Peters at Economy: A Reappraisal." *Communal Societies* 3 (1983): 158–174.

White, Harold. "Bassenheim Furnace." *Journal of Beaver County History* 26, no. 3 (Summer 2001). https://www.bcpahistory.org/beavercounty/BeaverCounty Topical/SteelandIron/BassenheimFurnace/BassenheimFurnace.html.

Wickenden, Dorothy. *The Agitators: Three Friends Who Fought for Abolition and Women's Rights*. New York: Scribner, 2021.

Wigger, John. *American Saint: Francis Asbury and the Methodists*. New York: Oxford University Press, 2009.

——. "Fighting Bees: Methodist Itinerants and the Dynamics of Methodist Growth, 1770–1820." In *Methodism and the Shaping of American Culture*, ed. Nathan O. Hatch and John Wigger, 87–133. Nashville, TN: Kingswood Books, 2001.

———. *Taking Heaven by Storm: Methodism and the Rise of Popular Christianity in America*. New York: Oxford University Press, 1998.

Wilentz, Sean. *Chants Democratic: New York City and the Rise of the American Working Class, 1788–1850*. New York: Oxford University Press, 1986.

Williams, Aaron. *The Harmony Society at Economy*. Pittsburgh: W. S. Haven, 1866.

Wilson, George. *Stephen Girard: America's First Tycoon*. Conshohocken, PA: Combined Publishing, 2000.

Wosh, Peter. *Spreading the Word: The Bible Business in Nineteenth-Century America*. Ithaca, NY: Cornell University Press, 1994.

Wright, Robert E. *Corporation Nation*. Philadelphia: University of Pennsylvania Press, 2015.

Wyatt-Brown, Bertram. *Lewis Tappan and the Evangelical War Against Slavery*. Cleveland, OH: Press of Case Western Reserve, 1969.

Yannessa, Mary Ann. *Levi Coffin, Quaker: Breaking the Bonds of Slavery in Ohio and Indiana*. Richmond, IN: Friends United Press, 2001.

Yacovazzi, Cassandra L. *Escaped Nuns: True Womanhood and the Campaign Against Convents in Antebellum America*. New York: Oxford University Press, 2018.

Young, Neil J. *We Gather Together: The Religious Right and the Problem of Interfaith Politics*. New York: Oxford University Press, 2016.

Zakim, Michael, and Gary J. Kornblith, eds. *Capitalism Takes Command: The Social Transformation of Nineteenth-Century America*. Chicago: University of Chicago Press, 2012.

Zboray, Ronald. *A Fictive People: Antebellum Economic Development and the American Reading Public*. New York: Oxford University Press, 1993.

Index

Page numbers in *italics* refer to figures. Those followed by n refer to notes, with note number.

Abercrombie, John, 176
abolitionism: Bissell and, 282n5; Harmony and, 49–50; Harper brothers and, 125, 162, 193; and reform CBEs, 92, 134
Adams, Isaac, 182, *183*, 208, 319n63, 330n83
Adams, John Quincy, 140, 176
Adams, Joseph, 199, 206
Akin, James, *140*, 141
Albany and Michigan Six Day Line, 118
Albany Christian Register, 136
American Anti-Slavery Society, and reform CBEs, 92
American Dictionary (Webster): Harper & Brothers' adoption of orthography of, 193–94; Harper & Brothers publication of, 193
American Hotel (Auburn), *134*, 134–35
American identity, Webster's *American Dictionary* and, 193–94

American Monthly, 190
American Publishers' Circular and Literary Gazette, 206
American Republican Party, 194–96, 324n23
American Society for the Diffusion of Useful Knowledge (ASDUK), 177, 317n32
American System, Rapps' support for, 78
amillennialism, 22, 240n27
Anderson, James, 88
Arminianism: Bissell and, 144; rise in influence in America, 5; on salvation and free will, 5, 152; scholarship on, 15; views on marketplace, influence of, 6. *See also* Methodism
Arminius, Jacobus, 5
Arndt, John, 20
Arndt, Karl, 237n12

Asbury, Francis: asceticism of, 159; on business and wealth, 158; as guest in Harper family's home, 158; and John Street Church building, 171; sermons at John Street Church, 165–66

ASDUK. *See* American Society for the Diffusion of Useful Knowledge

Atkinson, Elizabeth, 117, 291–92n41

Atkinson, William: background and career of, 99; Calvinism and postmillennialism of, 147–48, 219; church attended by, 114–17; and collapse of Pioneer Line, 142; death of, 291–92n41; and founding of Pioneer Line, 121, 122; friendship with Bissell, 100; and funding of Pioneer Line, 126; and goals of reform CBEs, 147–48; merging of business and spiritual life, 101; as Pioneer Line commissioner, 94, 99, 122; religious life of, 99–100; and Sabbatarian movement, 101, 105, 108

Auburn Convention, 121–22

Awful Disclosures by Maria Monk (Monk), 196–97, 325n35, 325–26n37

Baker, John L., 42, 61, 68, 249–50n10

Baker, Romelius L., 61, 79, 80, 87, 249n10

Baker v. Nachtrieb (1856), 74

Bangs, Nathan, 163, 168–69

banknotes: costs and delays in redemption of, in early 19th century, 60, 68, 260n96; introduction of clearinghouses for, 60

Bank of the United States, First, 42–43, 45

Bank of the United States, Second, 45, 46, 57, 80, 259n89

Bank of Vincennes, 45, 47, 57, 253n36

banks: Atkinson as bank director, 99; counterfeiting, 251n25; failures, Harper and, 185; Harmony Institute Bank, 45, *46*, 252n31; inadequacy in early 19th century, 44–46; inadequacy in Indiana, as handicap for George Rapp & Associates, 44–47, 60, 80–81, 252n27, 260n96, 276n121; in Indiana, George Rapp & Associates' investment in, 45–47, 253n36; number in Pennsylvania *vs.* Indiana, 80–81, 276n121; and Panic of 1819, 57, 259n89; wildcat banks, 45. *See also* banknotes

Barnes, Albert, 107

Barra, Mary, 222

Beach, Moses, 198, 326n43

Bedford, John, 51

Beecher, Lyman, 106–7, 119, 173

Bernhard, Duke of Saxe-Weimar-Eisenach, 71–72

Beyond Meat, 221–22

Bezos, Jeff, 221

Bible, changing status in mid-19th century, 200. *See also Harper's Illuminated and New Pictorial Bible*

Biddle, Nicholas, 80

Billington, Ray, 196–97 325n37

Bimber, A., 275n113

Bissell, Champion Aristarchus, 100

Bissell, Henrietta, 98–99, 143–45

Bissell, Josiah Jr.: as anti-Mason, 129; attacks on Old Line, 135–36; background and business ventures of, 98; and backlash against Sabbatarians, 1, 129, 131, 135, 137, 138, *140*; Calvinism and postmillennialism of, 113, 135, 147–48, 219; and capitalism, attitude

366 *Index*

toward characteristics of, 10; character of, 131, 135; and Charles Finney, 93, 99, 110; Christian reform capitalism of, 109; churches attended by, 113–14, *115*; and collapse of Pioneer Line, 142; and covenant theology, 109, 110, 113; as cultural warrior, 1, 135–36; death of, 143–44; donations to Christian causes, 131; and Erie Canal, damage to home from construction of, 97, 282n2; estate, disposition of, 144–45; and Finney's revival movement, 93, 99; and founding of Pioneer Line, 119, 121, 122, 125–26; friendship with Atkinson, 100; and fundraising, 125–27, 142; and goals of reform CBEs, 147–48; on importance of Christian values pervading life, 112–13; life financial troubles, 100, 142, 299n47; and marketplace reform, 1–2, 118, 119; merging of business and spiritual life, 101; modern connections, 221–22; and Pioneerism, 1–2; as Pioneer Line commissioner, 94, 99, 122, 124–25; and Pioneer Line financial troubles, 141–42; and Pioneer Line's bid for Post Office contract, 132, 138, 140; and Presbyterian General Assembly, 114, 291n32; reform activism of, 8–9; and religious controversy, 114; religious life of, 98–99, 283n6; and Sabbatarian movement, 1–2, 94, 98, 101–2, 105, 108; Sabbath-breakers, attacks on, 135–36; on Sabbath violations, dire effects of, 101–2, 108, 110; on Sam Patch, 105; and temperance, 99

Bissell, Josiah W. (son): career of, 145–46, 303n85; on damage to family home from Erie Canal construction, 282n2; and father's will, 144, 302n83; and Genesee Suspension Bridge, *145, 146*; home of, *144, 145*

Blane, William, 62, 257n71

Blue Origin, 221

Bodmer, Karl, *79*

Böhme, Jakob, 28

Boston Recorder, 117

Broadway Journal, 206–7

Brown, Ethan, 221–22

Brownson, Orestes Augustus, 137–38

Buckingham, J. S., 12, 54, 83, 85–86, 275n114

Bulwer-Lytton, Edward, 169, 185, 214–15, 305n13

Burned-Over District, Bissell's reform efforts and, 93

Bush, Charles, 101

business and morality: as issue from 19th century until today, 218, 220–21; and reexamination of business goals, 222–23

business and religion in America: Democratization School of scholarship on, 7, 235n24; Social Control School of scholarship on, 7, 234n22

businesses of Protestant fundamentalists: and Christian virtue capitalism, 218; continued engagement with society, 217–18. *See also* Christian business enterprises (CBEs); Christian virtue capitalism

Business Roundtable, 222–23

Byron, Lord, 30

Calvin, John, 5

Calvinism: and Christian reform capitalism/Pioneerism, 91, 113–14,

Index 367

Calvinism (*continued*)
219; dominance and decline in America, 5; and reform CBEs, 94–95; on salvation and free will, 5; scholarship on, 15; views on marketplace, influence of, 6

canal building, waves of, 66. *See also* Erie Canal

capitalism: American, Methodism and, 155–56, 306n27; analytic value, 6–7; definition of, 2; emergence in 19th century, 2–3; scholarship on, 3–4; 21st century, 219–24. *See also* Christian business enterprises (CBEs); Christian communal capitalism; Christian virtue capitalism; conscious capitalism

Carey, Mathew: as economist, 50–51, 255n55; as publisher, 12, 13–14

Carey & Hart, publishers, 169, 314n71

Carey & Lea, publishers, 190, 312–13n53

Catholic immigration: and battle over educational materials, 154; nativist backlash against, 194–95, 197

Cayuga Lake Bridge, toll records, 141–42 *142*, 301n67, 302n75

CBEs. *See* Christian business enterprises

Chambers, Robert, 180

Champion, Aristarchus: background and career of, 100–101, 284nn20–21; Calvinism and postmillennialism of, 147–48, 219; character of, 101, 284n24; church attended by, 111–13; and collapse of Pioneer Line, 142; and covenant theology, 111–12; and founding of Pioneer Line, 121, 122; friendship with Bissell, 100; funding for Pioneer Line, 125–26; and goals of reform CBEs, 147–48; home of, *100*; merging of business and spiritual life, 101; move to Rochester, 128; origin of wealth, 126–28, *128*; as Pioneer Line commissioner, 94, 99, 100, 122; religious life of, 101; and Sabbatarian movement, 101, 105, 108

Champion, Aristobulus, 101

Champion, Henry, 101, 126–27, 128

Chapin, Moses, 119

Chapman, John Gadsby, 199

Charleston Gazette, 177

Chick-fil-A, 220

children in Harmony Society: births, 29, 30; confirmation, 22; education, 22; family conflict, 32; indentured, as source of dispute, 72–73; jobs done by, 55, 71; membership rules, 54, 258n76

Christian business enterprises (CBEs): backlash against, 137; and capitalism, central role in emergence of, 3, 4, 7, 8, 9; continuum with modern businesses' moral concerns, 218, 220–21; as controversial, 7–8, 224; defining characteristics of, 8–9, 235n26; definition of, 232n4; echoes of, in modern business ventures, 220–22; and faith-based approach to markets, 8; focus on, as alternative to standard views, 7; Harper & Brothers as, 8, 9, 157; history of activism by, 2; modern forms of, 220, 224; prominence in 19th century, 7–8; scholarship on, 2, 92; and three Protestant approaches to larger culture, 218; tight governance of, 8; as under-studied, 3, 9, 10; and "virtuous" consumer goods, 4–5

Christian business enterprises dedicated to market reforms, 91; Calvinism and, 94–95; and covenant

368 *Index*

theology, 94–95; examples of, 118; Gerrit Smith and, 125; goals of, 93, 147–48; and postmillennialism, 94–95; predating of voluntary reform associations, 91; range of causes of, 118; Sabbatarian transportation lines, 146–47; scholarship on, 92; success of many, 148; support for capitalist system within constraints of God's moral law, 94; targeting of specific evils, 92; as template for Sabbatarian movement, 119

Christian communal capitalism, 11–15; advantages of model during economic downturns, 60–61; examples in 19th century, 12, 88; Harmony Society as, 88, 218. *See also* Harmony Society

Christian reform capitalism, 91–95; Calvinism and, 91, 219; and covenant theology, 109; standard historiographic narrative of, 91. *See also* Pioneer Line

Christian Spectator (New Haven), 118

Christian virtue capitalism, 151–56; and fundamentalist engagement through business, 218; publishers of 19th century and, 151–53; Wanamaker's department store and, 156. *See also* Harper & Brothers

Clark, Davis W., 167, 212–13

Clay, Henry, 78, 325n32

CLC. *See* Connecticut Land Company

Clinton Line, 146

Columbiana commune. *See* Society of United Germans

Commercial Line, 146

Committee to Ministers of the Gospel and Christians and Patriots in Massachusetts, 9–10

Common Sense (Paine), 139–40

Congress: Harmony and Post Office, 43; Harmony petition, 24; Harmony testimony on tariffs, 78; Rapp's testimony on wool manufacturing, 77–78; Sabbatarian movement's protests and petitioning of, 103, 105, 140; support for Sunday mail service, 142

Connecticut Land Company (CLC), 126–27

conscious capitalism, 6, 151, 220

Cook, Calvin W., 89

Cook, Tim, 222

copyright protection in early 19th century, 9, 169, 186

Correct Craft, 218

covenant theology: Bissell's rhetoric on, 135–36; in churches beyond Congregationalists and Presbyterians, 111–13; Covenanters, 287–88n2; increase in diversity of population and, 110; Presbyterian Church and, 109–10; and reform CBEs, 94–95, 119, 121, 219; Sabbatarian movement and, 94–95, 107–8, 109–11; and Sabbath observation, 111

The Craftsman newspaper, 129, 131, 137, 139, 146

The Critic, 215

culture, definition of, 304n1

Dana, Richard H. Dana Jr., 180–81, 186–88, 189

Dana, Richard H. Dana Sr., 180–81, 186–88

de Leon, Count (Maximillian Bernhard Mueller): collective founded on former Harmony Society land, 76; and crisis at Economy, 74–76, 271n80

Index 369

democratization, and Arminianism, 5

Derby, James C., 158, 167, 168

Dexter, Andrew Jr., 61

Dimon, Jamie, 222

Disney Corp., 220

Don Juan (Byron), 30

Dun, R. G., 87, 92, 101, 146, 160, 280n8

du Pont family, and Frederick Rapp, 37

Duyckinck, Evert, 166–67, 169–70

Eckensperger, Frederick, 31–32, 61

Eckensperger, Jacob, 31–32

Eclipse Line, 146

Economy, Pennsylvania. *See* Harmony
Society in Economy, Pennsylvania

Economy, Rapp's Colony on the Ohio
(Bodmer), 79

ecumenicalism, of Pioneerism, 118–19

electrotyping, 199

Ely, Elisha, 98

Ely, Ezra Stiles, 112–13, 138

Emerson, William, 197

Engels, Friedrich, 13, 86–88

Erie Canal: aqueduct across Genesee
river, 145; disruption caused by, 97,
145; and East-West travel times, 60;
and growth of manufacturing, 41;
Harmonie community in Indiana
and, 66; and Harper & Brothers
growth, 190; impact on surrounding
communities, 97, 101, 104–5; land
sales, 99, 115, 282n2; as part of
infrastructure construction boom,
66, 98; and Protestant social order,
3, 91, 104; public meeting to
condemn Sabbath violations of, 119,
121; reform CBE's interest in, 94;
sparking of competition in
transportation infrastructure, 48;
and turn to seven-day business

week, 92, 101–2, 103–4;
unscrupulous competition between
boat lines, 130

ESG (environmental, social, and
corporate governance), 220

evangelicals: approach to culture, 2, 94,
117, 125, 148, 151, 155, 168, 205, 217,
223–24; contested definition of,
232n8; thesis, 2, 232n6

Eventide, 220

Exman, Eugene, 155, 188, 306n23

Express Stage Line, *147*

Farkas, Alexander, 89, 268n44

Fay, Theodore Sedgwick, 188–89

Featherstonhaugh, George, 84, 277n133

fiction, 19th century concerns about,
153, 211–12, 215

Finney, Charles Grandison: and
Arminianism, 5; Bissell and, 93, 99,
110, 143–44; and Burned-Over
District, 93; and Elizabeth
Atkinson, 117, 291–92n41; and
emergence of capitalism, 3, 91;
revival movement, and reform
CBEs, 93–94; revival movements
preceding market changes, 7

First Methodist Episcopal Church. *See*
John Street Church

First Presbyterian Church of Rochester,
113

Flower, Richard, 14, 67

Francis, John, 153

General Union for Promoting the
Observance of the Christian
Sabbath: and backlash, 138; and
covenant theology, 106, 111;
ecumenicalism of, 118–19, 292n48;
focus on economic leverage, 106;

370   *Index*

formation of, 94, 104, 117, 281n11; mass distribution of its inaugural address, 118; and Pioneer Line, 124

George Rapp & Associates: access to markets through Post Office, 37, 43; administrative structure of, 34, 87; agents for, across trading network, 58, 68–69, 79; agriculture and textile businesses of, 12, 36–37, 43, 48, 59, 77, 85, 89; and banking, 46, *46*, 80–81; as business entity of Harmony Society, 13, 30, 33, 34, 88; as CBE, 8, 9, 14; disruption of, during Count de Leon dispute, 75–76; disruption of, during move back to Pennsylvania, 68; Frederick Rapp as head financial manager of, 15, 33–34; Golden Rose trademark of, 30–31, *31*, 244n64; hiring out workers, 36; integration into market economy, 14; labor of, 53, 72, 76, 83; litigation, 32, 76, 245n73; loan policy of, 47, 253–54nn36–38, 254nn40–41; local complaints about, 73; management after George Rapp's death, 87; marketing of products by, 39; as model for Christ's millennial kingdom, 30; and Panic of 1819, 60–61; and Panics of 1937/39, 85–86; patents and trademarks filed by, 88–89; reinvestment of profits into Harmony Society, 60–61; success after George Rapp's death, 86–87; success of, 37, 77; trade network of, 39, *58*; and trade with slaveholding states, 41–42, 49–50, 59; turn to investment capitalism, 30, 87; value of assets, 79, 87. *See also* Harmony Society

Germany (Württemberg): abuse of migrants from, 54, 257–58nn73–74;

economic decline and emigration in early 19th century, 53–54, 239n8; George Rapp's life in, 19; Harmony Society motives for leaving, 20–21, 22; and Pietism, 20–23, 241n31; tracking down inheritances from, 266n32

Gontgen, John George, 75

Goodrich, Samuel, 216

Gospel Advocate and Impartial Investigator, 131, 137

Gould, Edward S., 194, 323n17

Gould, Jacob, 142, 303n85

Gowans, William, 310n28

Graham, Billy, 2, 217

Great Awakening, Second, 3, 113, 174

Greene, Asa, 184, 319–20n64

Green Tavern (Waterloo), 118

Hamilton, Alexander, 11

Harmonie, Pennsylvania. *See* Harmony Society in Harmonie, Pennsylvania

Harmony Institute Bank, 45, *46*

Harmony Society: accusations of block voting by, 61, 73, 78, 261n102; Articles of Agreement/Association, 25–26, 34, 74, 87, 242–43n3; beliefs of, 21–22; births, 1805–1859, 28, 29, 30; and charges of unfair practices because of unpaid labor, 62; and Christian communal capitalism, 4, 10, 17, 218; clothing worn by, 54–55; communalism of, *vs.* Shakers or Mormons, 279n164; communal ownership of wealth, 13, 21; critics' views on, 26, 32, 89, 259n83; decline in population from celibacy teaching, 30, 83; disaffected members' efforts to recover property, 15, 27–28, 74, 272n88; discouragement of sex and

Index   371

Harmony Society (*continued*)
marriage, 18, 28–30, 83, 244n60; "divine economy" of, 13, 18, 30, 40–41, 67, 238n13; as early Christian communal capitalist society, 88; embrace of technological advances, 18, 37, 41, 56, 88–89; families separated by departures from, 32, 245n72; hierarchical structure of, 37, 55, 258n79; house and livestock assigned to families, 34; indentured children, dispute over, 72–73; integration into market economy, 13, 14; international interest in, 12, 13, 14, 17, 37, 50–52, 64, 247n96; lack of private property, Christian values and, 25, 52; longevity of, 18, 88; management after George Rapp's death, 87, 275n111; marriages, 1805–1900, 28, 29, 247n57; Marx and Engels' views on, 86–87; members' lack of voice in management of, 33, 34, 75; as model for productive assimilation of immigrants, 53–54; motives for leaving Germany, 20–21, 22, 23; and not serving in militia, 49; and orphans, 55–56; outsiders' criticisms of, 31–32; probation period for new members, 54, 258n76; prosperity of, 35–36, 87, 268n44, 273n92, 275n114; Rapp & Associates as business entity of, 12; rationing of clothing, 34; relations with other communal groups, 236–37n9; religious beliefs as essential to success of, 90; replication of early Christian communalism as goal, 17, 21; rules on children admitted to Society, 54; scholarship on, 237n12; secrecy of

finances, 81, 83; and slavery, 18, 49–50; social isolation to prevent corruption from society, 18, 39, 40, 218; sophisticated business practices of, 33–34, 88; spying on departed members, 275n113; textile manufacture, slavery and, 41–42; usefulness as case study, 13–15; and U.S. Supreme Court, 74, 270n70; visitors' failure to grasp role of Pietism in, 14–15. *See also* Christian communal capitalism; George Rapp & Associates; Rapp, George

Harmony Society, premillennialism of, 22–23, 30; and avoidance of corruption, 18; and importance of purity over membership numbers, 83; as key concept in beliefs of, 219; and pointlessness of helping doomed neighbors, 47, 63

Harmony Society in Economy, Pennsylvania, *84*; and access to money in circulation, 70; agents sent to tour East Coast textile mills, 83–84; and available banks, 80–81; Baker home in, 82; businesses and industries at, 17, 71; common reservoir of milk, 35; and conflict between George and Frederick Rapp, 73–74; continued prosperity despite setbacks, 77; decline in population over time, 83; departure of one-third of members, 76; disaffected members' efforts to recover property, 74, 76, 272n88; dispute over Count de Leon, 74–76, 271n80; dispute with ex-Harmonists in Society of United Germans, 72–73, 74; embrace of innovation, 77, 83–84; emergence of class hierarchy in, 81;

372 *Index*

fame for manufacturing expertise, 77–78, 79, 83; former members' attack on, 76; and Frederick Rapp's financial speculation, 69–70; George Rapp's home in, 81, 82; George Rapp's oversight of construction at, 68; growth in manufacturing, 83; international interest in solutions of, 72; local complaints about business practices of, 62, 73; loss of woolen factory to fire, 76–77; manufacturing output, 85; as most materially successful Christian industrial town of 19th century, 12, 13; naming of, 67; new Articles of Association for, 74; outsiders' criticism of leadership, 83; process of moving to, 66–67, 68–69; prosperity of, 17; purchase of site for, 65; Rapps' reasons for move to, 65–66, 263n9; second-generation members' grievances, 75; self-sufficiency in times of crisis, 85–86, 88; silk production, 70–71, 83, 85; structures and town layout, 71; textile production, 70–72; as third Harmonist location, 13; value of assets, 79, 273n92, 275n114; visitors' impressions of, 83; wool factories and production, 71, 76, 77

Harmony Society in Harmonie, Indiana: access to markets through Post Office, 43; advantages of model during economic downturns, 60–61; beauty of town, 55, 56; children and work in, 55, 71; churches in, 43, *43, 44*, 55; community houses at, 34–35, *35*; early construction and businesses, 43, 251nn22–23; embrace of technology, 56; engagement with local politics, 48–49; enslaved

persons admitted under indenture, 49, 255n52; fame of, 64; Frederick Rapp's management of sale of, 33; gendering of work in, 53; George Rapp's house in, 55; governor as customer of, 57; and Harmony Riot of 1820, 61–62; Harmony Society's move to, 13; hierarchy at, 55, 258n79; Indigenous people and, 41, 250n12; industry at, 55, 60, 259n88, 261n98; international interest in solutions of, 50–52; lack of adequate banking sector and, 44–47, 60, 80–81, 252n27, 260n96, 276n121; layout of town, 55, *56*; leasing of peripheral farmland, 63, 262n114; and machinery, delays in delivery of, 48; mail services delays, 48–49; military-style defenses against attacks from neighbors, 63; as most impressive industrial center in West, 60; move to, 13; natural resources available in, 42; orphans taken in by, 55–56; and Panic of 1819, 60; payments to excuse members from military service, 49; purchase of land, 42; Rapps' decision to move back to Pennsylvania, 47, 65–66, 263n9; Rapps' later sale of smaller properties near, 76, 265n28; sale of site to Owen, 13, 17, 64, 67–68, 265n28; search for land for move to, 40, 42; as second Harmonist location, 13; singing at, 53, 266n30; site along Wabash River, 42; some local supporters of, 63; specialization and efficiency at, 53; stores and tavern opened in nearby communities, 62–63, 76; and tension between social separation

Index　373

Harmony Society in Harmonie, Indiana (*continued*) and economic engagement, 49, 62–63, 66; trade network, *58*, 59; transportation costs and delays, 47–48, 57, 59, 60; value of assets, 268n44; views on helping neighbors, 63; visitors' impressions of, 50–57, 256n56, 259n83; visits from curious neighbors, 256n60; waves of German migrants taken in by, 54; whiskey and beer production, 62–63; wine cellar in church building, 55; workers' control over work schedules, 52–53; work in, 52–53, 55, 71

Harmony Society in Harmonie, Pennsylvania: acreage owned by, 37; curiosity of outsiders about, 28–30; disaffected members' efforts to recover property, 27–28; economic disruption at time of move to, 42–43, 45; as first Harmonist location, 13; founding of, state of U.S. economy and, 18; hiring out of skilled laborers, 36; lack of adequate banking sector and, 44–45; large homes of George and Frederick Rapp, 37, *38*; members' turnover of all assets to Rapp, 25–26, 242n43; purchase of land for, 23–25; reasons for moving from, 40–41; sale of site, 13, 42–43, 252n31, 265n28; sense of entitlement of largest contributors, 27; sources of income, 36; state's refusal to grant incorporation, 26–27; structures, businesses, and industries at, 35–37, 246n81; and tension between social separation and economic engagement, 39, 40–41; transportation network expansions and, 41; value of assets, 37; whiskey production by, 36, 39

Harper, Elizabeth, 158, 307n3

Harper, Fletcher: addition to the firm, 166; on contract terms offered to authors, 188; death of, 307n1; dinner parties for clergy and authors, 167–68; on *Harper's New Monthly Magazine*, 210; and John Street Church, 185, 192–93, 322n10, 330n81; meeting with John C. Spencer, 178; religious faith of, 167; role at Harper & Brothers, 166. *See also* Harper brothers

Harper, James: on criteria for Harper publications, 154, 157; daily routine of, 161; death of, 307n1; death of wife, 207, *208*, 329–30n80; early life of, 161; generosity of, 310n28; and marketing of Harper School District Library, 178; marriage, 174; mayoral campaign, 194–95; as mayor of New York, 168, 195–96; Methodist influence on, 161; move to Lewis Tappan's former home, 193; move uptown, 207, *209*; and nativism, 195–98, 324n23, 324n26, 324n28, 325n30; religious faith of, 167, 168; reputation for business acumen, 309n25; rise to social prominence, 174; and temperance movement, 195; and Thurlow Weed, 163–64, 178; as trustee of Vassar College, 168; uncontroversial virtue capitalism of, 168; willingness to run for governor, 325; work ethic of, 163–64. *See also* Harper brothers

Harper, James, and John Street Church: attendance through 1840s, 192–93, 322n10; as class leader, 174, 186,

374　*Index*

320n79; donations to, 163, 172, 185; early attendance at, 161, 163–64, 309n26; prayer meeting at home of person of color led by, 161–62; rise in leadership of, 174, 186, 191–92, 193, 322n7; withdrawal from, 207–8, 330n81

Harper, J. Henry, 158, 161, 167, 168, 199

Harper, John: death of, 307n1; early career of, 166, 167; and John Street Church, 163, 172; move uptown, 193; religious faith, characteristics of, 168; reputation for ardent religious faith, 167; role at Harper & Brothers, 168. *See also* Harper brothers

Harper, Joseph (father), 158, 307n3

Harper, Maria Arcularius, 174, 207, *208*, 329–30n80

Harper, Wesley: death of, 307n1; and Edgar Allen Poe, 184, 185; as John Street class leader, 186; move uptown, 193; religious faith of, 167; role at Harper & Brothers, 166; and Webster's American orthography, 194. *See also* Harper brothers

Harper & Brothers: adoption of Webster's American orthography, 193–94; attitude toward market, 214; and battle over educational materials, 154; and Bulwer-Lytton, controversy over works by, 185, 214–15; as CBE, 8, 9, 154, 157, 158–59, 166; change of name from J. & J. Harper, 166, 182, *182*; and Christian virtue capitalism, 152, 156, 157, 198, 214, 312–13n53; closing on Sabbath, 8, 157, 167, 214, 311–12n53; common account of, 161; core principles of, 159–60; and creation of middlebrow culture, 151–52, 184; criteria for

publications, 154, 157, 169–70, 173, 184–85; critics' accusations of sharp practices by, 187–89; cultural power of, 214–16; destruction by fire of facilities, 212, 319n63, 331n94; dominance in mid-19th century publishing, 210, 216, 330n84; ecumenical culture of, 168; and Eugene Exman, 155, 306n23; first printing jobs, 168–70; five characteristics defining "order" of, 154; and formation of American identity, 194; founding of, 166; growth of, 173, 182, 186, 190, 198, 208–10, *211*, *213*; honoring of foreign copyrights, 169; influence of, 153, 155, 157, 190–91; investments in printing technology, 173, 182, *183*, 199, 208–10, *209*, 212, 319n63; loan from John Street Church, 208; longevity of, 214; long-term success of, 154; marketing by, 173–74, 315n6; Methodism and, 152–53, 155, 159–60, 219; and Methodists' education goals, 169; move into more-elevated works of culture, 198–99; and *National Preacher* magazine, 173; negotiations for Dana's *Two Years Before the Mast*, 180–81, 186–88, 189; new building after 1853 fire, *211*, 212, *213*; as one of many Protestant publishing companies, 153; output in new facilities (1850s), 212, 213–14; and Panic of 1837, 185, 198; poor recordkeeping by, 159, 188; power to influence reviewers, 215; and Protestant middle-class values, 153, 157, 181–82; publication of *Awful Disclosures by Maria Monk*, 196–97, 325–26n37, 325n35; publication of

Index 375

Harper & Brothers (*continued*)
Bibles containing Apocrypha,
197–98; publication of Webster's
American Dictionary, 193; and
public's exposure to uplifting books,
155; records of, 159, 308n7; and
redemption of society through
engagement (Naaman Option), 219;
reputation as Christian firm, 167, 198,
215–16; reputation for quality and
influence, 190–91; scholarship on,
151, 154–55; shrewd business sense of,
184, 185, 186–89; success, factors in,
190; transformation of American
culture as goal of, 152–53; transition
from printing to publishing firm, 173,
182, 314n72; types of contracts
offered to authors, 186–87; as
unconstrained by conservative
religious values, 184–85, 212;
virtuous print culture as goal of,
153–54; volumes published per year,
182, 213, 331n91; workers, as skilled
and well paid, 212–13
Harper brothers: and abolitionism, 162;
close relations between, 161; deaths
of, 307n1; donations to John Street
Church, 185; faith in capitalism, 10;
family and early life of, 158, 307n3;
as functional postmillennialists,
219–20; and John Street Church,
159, 161–65, 172, 174; and keeping of
Sabbath, 167; lack of conflict
between principles and business
practice, 159; Methodist influence
on, 158, 161; and nativism, 195–98,
324n26; opening of J. & J. Harper,
Printers, 166; religious tolerance of,
168, 184–85; reputation as good
Christians, 166–67, 215; reputation

for hard work and integrity, 159, 160,
188–89; social rise of, 182
Harper's Family Library series, 175–77;
benefits to American authors, 177;
and books of dubious moral tone,
180–81; broad view of instructive
books in, 181–82; contract terms
offered to authors, 188; financial
success of, 198; modest prices to
broaden audience for, 175, 176, 177;
reviews of, 176–77, 181; types of
books included in, 175–76
*Harper's Illuminated and New Pictorial
Bible*, 199–207; artist and engraver
of images, 199; and Bible as status
symbol, 205–6; claimed authenticity
of images in, 201–2; cost of, 200,
327n56; errors in, 200, *205*; as
financial risk for Harper & Brothers,
206; gentrification of Methodism
and, 207; high quality of, 157;
images' function as commentary in,
200–202, *201*; initial serial release
of, 199–200; as luxury gift, 206;
marketing of, 199; maternal
Protestantism of images in, 202,
203; number of images in, 199,
327n52; presentation of women in,
202–4, *203*, *204*, 328n64; printing
technology for, 199; reference
materials included in, 200; reviews
of, 205–7; as "sacred token" to be
displayed in middle-class parlor,
204–6; sales of, 157; targeting of
female consumers, 204; as U.S.'s
first richly illustrated book, 199
Harper's New Monthly Magazine,
210–12
Harper's School District Library series,
177–79; broad view of instructive

376 *Index*

books in, 181–82; contract terms offered to authors, 187, 188; controversial works in, 179–81; criteria for books in, 177; expansion from New York to other states, 179, 318n48; financial success of, 198; number of volumes in, 178; partnership with ASDUK in, 177, 317n32; pricing of, 178, 317n36, 318n49; reviews of, 178, 179; use in New York public libraries and schools, 177–79; works included in, 178

Harper's Weekly, 161–62, 166

Henrici, Jacob, 79, 87, 275n111

The History of the Jews (Milman), 175–76, 179–80, 318–19n50

Holmes, Oliver Wendell, 194, 318n40

"The 'Holy Alliance'" (Akin), *140*, 141

The Holy Bible (Kinnersley's edition), 203, *204*

Hopkins, John Henry, 74, 270n69

Hopkins, Mark, 107

Hudson & Erie line: advertisement for, *124*; as inspiration for Pioneer Line, 119, 124; as reform CBE, 118, 119; success of, 146

immigrant workers, perceived impact on surrounding communities, 104

Indiana: banking, 44–46; constitutional convention, Frederick Rapp at, 49, 255n49; inferior infrastructure, 66, 254n42; loan to, by Harmony, 47, 253nn36–37; number of banks/currency *vs.* Pennsylvania, 80–81, 252n27, 276n121; and slavery, 49–50. *See also* Harmony Society in Harmonie, Indiana

Indigenous peoples of America: Harmony Society and, 24, 41,

250n12; and Western Reserve land development, 127

industrial towns in America: Christian social systems of, 12; effort to avoid squalor of English mill towns, 11, 12; examples outside New England, 11–12; international interest in solutions of, 12; scholarship on, 236n8. *See also* Harmony Society

inequality, modern increase in, and reexamination of business goals, 222–23

Jackson, Andrew, 74–75, 78, 80

James, William, 114

J. & J. Harper, Printers, 166, 168–69, 170, *182*, 212. *See also* Harper & Brothers

Jefferson, Thomas, 24

The Jeffersonian, 178, 318n40

Jennings, Jonathan, 48–49, 253n36

Johnson, Elisha, 99, 115–16, 142

John Street Church (First Methodist Episcopal Church): Asbury's sermons at, 165–66; declining membership in mid-19th century, 192–93; first building, 161, *162*; Fletcher and James Harper's attendance through 1840s, 192–93, 322n10; Fletcher Harper and, 185, 192–93, 322n10, 330n81; and Francis Asbury, 165–66, 171; gender segregation in, 174; growth of, 164; Harper brothers and, 161–65, 166, 172, 185; and Harper brothers' views on capitalism and Christianity, 159; increased wealth of members with city growth, 166, 174; James Harper as class leader in, 174, 186, 320n79; James Harper's early attendance at,

Index 377

John Street Church (*continued*)
161, 163–64; James Harper's rise in
leadership of, 174, 186, 191–92,
320n79; and James Harper's vision
of class unity, 195; James Harper's
withdrawal from, 207–8, 330n81;
loan to Harper & Brothers, 208, 210,
330n82; and Maria Harper, 207, *208*,
329–30n80; meetings in rigging loft,
164, *164*, 172; and Methodist turn to
focus on family, 174; mix of wealthy
and working-class members,
164–66, 193, 195; and race, 161–63,
310–11n31; second building,
controversy over, 170–72, *171*,
314n79; third building, *191*, *192*, 193,
322–23n12; and U.S. Methodism,
161, 163, 207, 310n28
Jones, Bob, 217

Kauffman and Bissell, engineers, 146
Kinnersley, Thomas, 203, *204*
The Knickerbocker, 178, 179, 205,
318n40
Krimmel, Georg Friedrich, 53–54

Lafayette, Marquis de, 69, 266n30
laissez-faire capitalism, support and
critiques of, 223–24
Law, John, 19
Lesueur, Charles Alexandre, *43*, *44*
Lewis, Tayler, 211
liberal Christian authors, influence in
mid-19th century, 198–99
Lieber, Francis, 188–89
List, Friederich, 78, 86–87
Little & Brown publishers, 188
London Pictorial Bible, 206
Longfellow, Henry Wadsworth, 185,
318n40

Louisiana land, marketing in Europe,
19
Lutheran Pietists: Christian communal
capitalism of, 4; Harmony Society
as, 19, 20

Macaulay, Zachary, 92
MacDonald, Donald, 53, 259n83
Magie, David, 106, 109
Main Line Canal, 66
manufacturing, U.S., expansion in
early 19th century, 41
market revolution, and emergence of
capitalist system, 3, 232–33nn9–10
Marx, Karl, 13, 86
Masonic Mirror, 182
Masons, attacks on Sabbatarians, 129,
137
McCulloch v. Maryland, 46
McIlvaine, Charles P., 116–17, 291n38
McLean, John, 132
Meigs, Return J., Jr., 285n35
Melish, John, 37, 256m56
Mellen, Grenville, *84*
Meloon, Walt, 218
Melville, Herman, 152, 175, 187, 305n6
Mercantile Agency, 93, 148
Merchants and Millers' Line, *148*
Methodism: and American capitalism,
155–56, 306n27; and classes, 161,
310n29; and embrace of middle-
class culture, 153, 163; evolution
from society to denomination, 174;
evolution into large, middle-class
denomination, 163, 174, 207, 214;
faction seeking improved
refinement of members, 169; and
gender, 174, 205; growth in New
York City and nationally, 214,
311n32; and Harper & Brothers'

378 *Index*

Christian virtue capitalism, 152–53, 155, 156, 159, 161, 219; and the Harpers' upbringing, 154, 167; higher education institutions of, 174; and Nathan Bangs, 169; in New York, class conflict in, 171–72; in New York, influence of, 193; and race, 161–63; turn from focus on personal sanctification to community renewal, 174; turn to focus on family, 174–75; and Weber, 156, 160, 161, 165, 306n29 (*See also* John Street Church (First Methodist Episcopal Church))

Methodist Book Concern, 152, 153, 168–69, 211–12

millennialism: different views, 219, 240–41n28, 240n27; and Harmony, 18; modern residue of, 220–21; and reform capitalists, 95. *See also* postmillennialism; premillennialism

Milman, H. H., 175–76, 179–80, 318–19n50

Mississippi Bubble, 19

"Mister Bissell! Mister Bissell!" (anon.), 1

Mitchell, Donald, 211

Mormons: communalism of, *vs.* Harmony Society, 279n164; former Harmonists joining, 76; sexuality, 244n60

Morse, Richard, 9

Morse, Samuel F. B., 9, 194–95, 324n23

Morse, Sidney, 9

Mott, Frank Luther, 330n84

Mount Tambora eruption, 53–54, 251n24

Mueller, Maximillian Bernhard. *See* de Leon, Count

Muller, D. B., 24

Murray, John, 175, 180

Musk, Elon, 221

Mutschler, Hildegard, 73, 269n66

Napoleon and Napoleonic Wars, 19, 20, 22, 23, 53, 75

Nashoba, Tennessee, 69

National Magazine, 211–12

National Preacher magazine, 173

National Road, 41, 60

New England Palladium, 176, 181

New Harmony, Owen's community at: failure of, 69, 78–79, 90; purchase of site from Harmony Society, 13, 17, 64, 67–68, 265n28

New Philadelphia Congregation, 75

New York Commercial Advertiser, 182

New York Daily Times, 213–14, 331n94

New York District Library system, 177–79

New Yorker magazine, 161, 190–91

New York Evening Post, 193–94

New York Gazette, 176–77, 181

New York Journal of Commerce, 92, 118

New York Observer, 9–10, 131, 168, 316n24

New York Review, 186

New York *Sun*, 198

New York Times, 211

New-York Tribune, 211

Niles Weekly Register, 52, 87

Noah, Mordecai, 263n6

Old Line: Auburn as headquarters of, 134; ownership of, 123, 298–99n35

Old Line competition with Pioneer Line, 123, 124, 129–35, 141–42; and battle for hotel affiliations, *134*, 134–35; and Bissell's attacks, 135–36; and competition for speed, 130, 133,

Index 379

Old Line competition with
Pioneer Line (*continued*)
298n29; and inherent danger of
stage coach lines, 133; Post Office
contract as competitive advantage
for, 132–33, 298–99n35; public
relations campaign in, 131–32,
297n20; success in, 142; as
unscrupulous, 129–30
Onderdonk, Henry U., 116–17, 291n38
Opposition Lines, 146
Order of United Americans, 196, 198
O'Reilly, Henry, 295n80
Owen, Richard, 78–79
Owen, Robert: ideology of, 64, 65;
impressions of Harmonie, Indiana,
55; interest in Harmony's successes
in Indiana, 64–65; and labor
movement, 267n37; meetings with
Rapps, 67; purchase of Harmony
Society's Indiana location, 13, 17, 64,
67–68, 265n28
Owen, William, 266n34

Paine, Thomas, 139–40
Palmer, Phoebe, 205
Panic of 1819, 57, 59, 60, 259n89
Panic of 1837, 80, 85–86, 185, 198,
253–54n38
Parker, Jason, 132, 298–99n35
Parker, Joel, 113, 137, 142, 290n27
Patch, Sam, 105
Paul, Abraham, 161
Pennsylvania: agents from, targeting
German immigrants, 20; economy
in early decades of 19th century, 18,
36, 44; governor's compliments
toward Harmony, 37; improvements
in transportation in first half of
19th century, 66; legislature's refusal

to incorporate Harmony, 14, 26–27,
74; number of banks/currency *vs.*
Indiana, 44–45, 80–81, 251n25,
252n27, 276n121; population growth,
256n58; supreme court, 74. *See also*
Harmony Society in Economy,
Pennsylvania; Harmony Society in
Harmonie, Pennsylvania
Pennsylvania-Ohio Canal Company
stock, Rapp & Associates purchase
of, 78
Penny, Joseph, 114
Pietism: beliefs and practices of, 6;
definition of, 239n17; in Germany,
and alchemy, 73; importance in
Harmony Society, 14–15, 90, 218;
influence in North America, 6, 219,
239n22; spread in Europe, 20; as
under-studied, 15; views on
marketplace, influence of, 6. *See also*
Spener, Philipp Jakob
Pioneerism: beginnings of, 117–28,
303n90; Bissell and, 1–2; criticism
of, 114, 139; and fight for reform
(Wilberforce Option) in Protestant
engagement with society, 218–19;
goals of, 93; as term coined by
critics, 93
Pioneer Line, 132–33; advertisement of,
125; all new coaches used by, 122,
123, *123*, 124; and backlash against
Sabbatarians, *139*, 139–40; bid for
Post Office contract, 132–33, 138,
140, 143; Bissell as public face of, 99,
136; boycott of, 139; as CBE, 7, 8, 9,
138, 147; churches attended by
founders of, 111–17; commissioners
of, 99–101, 122; and competition for
speed, 133; as component of larger
movement, 146, 148; and context of

380   *Index*

larger political battles, 129; and covenant theology, 111; criticism, charges of misconduct and hypocrisy against, 130–31, 136–38, 235n28; debate on, 301n72; and debate on reform capitalism, 93; demise of, 129, 141–44; ecumenical leadership of, 118–19, 123, 292n48; establishment of, 117–18, 295n80; excellence of service as goal of, 93; fare policies, 123–24; and formation of General Union for Promoting the Observance of the Christian Sabbath, 94; fundraising for, 121, 122–23, 125–27; godly drivers as goal of, 93, 122, 130–31; and hotels, *134*, 134–35; Hudson and Erie line as model for, 119, 124; and incorporation, 294n72; and inherent danger of stage coach lines, 133; launch of, 124–25; major donors to, 126, 295n18; market share of, 141; meetings leading to founding of, 119–22; organized opposition to anti-Sabbatarian goals, 131; other successful Sabbatarian transportation lines, 146–47; and postmillennialism, 147–48, 219; principles of, 122; promotion of dry lodging and dining, 92–93, 122; reform activism of, 8–9; as reform CBE, 92, 94–95, 118, 148; relative inexperience of drivers, 133, 143; Rochester commissioners of, 94; Sabbath closing as goal of, 1–2, 92, 94, 214; scholarship on, 93, 281n8, 302n80; short, unprofitable life of, 93; significance of, 93–94, 146, 303n90; statement of principles, 122; target launch date for, 122, 124–25;

Telegraph Line and, 132–33; total investment in, 126, 295n80; unscrupulous agents misleading customers of, 129–30. *See also* Old Line competition with Pioneer Line

Pittsburgh and Wheeling Packet (steamboat), 77

Poe, Edgar Allen: and Harper & Brothers publishers, 184, 185–86; *The Narrative of Arthur Gordon Pym, of Nantucket*, 185–86; and *Southern Literary Messenger*, 184, 320n65; *Tales of the Folio Club*, 184, 320n68

Porter, Noah, 107

postmillennialism, 22, 240–41n28; and Church doctrine, 240–41n28; reform CBEs and, 94–95, 148

Post Office, U.S.: Congress's support for Sunday mail service, 142; controversy over Sunday deliveries, 103, 109, 139, *140*, 140–41, 147, 149, 285n35; and importance of Sunday mail for businesses, 103; importance to George Rapp & Associates, 37, 43; limitations, costs, and growth, 60; as male social scene, 103; Pioneer Line's bid for contract with, 132, 138, 140; services delays in Indiana, 48–49; turn to seven-day business week and, 92, 98, 102–3

Powell, Thomas, 298–99n35

premillennialism, 22, 240–41n28, 282n16. *See also* Harmony Society, premillennialism of

Presbyterian Church: Aristarchus Champion's will and, 101; Bissell nominated to General Assembly of, 114, 291n32; General Assembly of, and covenant theology, 109–10; and

Index 381

Presbyterian Church (*continued*)
Hugh Wylie Sunday work
controversy, 103; upheaval of early
19th century, 113–14. *See also*
Second Presbyterian Church of
Rochester; Third Presbyterian
Church of Rochester
Prescott, William H., 188–89
"Priest Parker! Priest Parker!" (anon.),
137
Prime, Samuel I., 168
print culture, evangelical, and for-
profit publishing companies, 151.
See also Harper & Brothers
printing presses, technological
advances of early 19th century, 173,
182, *183*, 199, 208, *209*
Producerists, 165, 311n39
Proli, Maximillian Ludwig. *See* de
Leon, Count
Protestants, American, approaches to
larger culture: complex response to
markets, 3–4; long debate on, 2, 217;
three types of, 2, 217. *See also*
Christian business enterprises
(CBEs); Christian communal
capitalism; Christian reform
capitalism; Christian virtue
capitalism
Protestants, fundamentalist: and
evangelical support for laissez-faire
capitalism, 223–24; narrative of
withdrawal as inapplicable to
business, 2, 217–18
publishing companies, Christian: and
Christian virtue capitalism, 151–53;
and creation of middlebrow culture,
151–52; and creation of virtuous
print culture, 153; and public's
exposure to uplifting books, 155;

relation to secular world, 152. *See
also* Harper & Brothers
publishing companies, 19th century:
and battle over educational
materials, 154, 177–79; and cost of
books, 178, 206, 305n16; lack of
copyright protection for foreign
authors, 169; Protestant, examples
of, 153. *See also* Harper & Brothers
Putnam, G. P., 213

Quakers, free produce movement, 92

Ramage printing press, 208–10, *209*
Randolph, A.D. F., 153, 154
Rapp, Frederick: as adopted son of
George Rapp, 33; and alchemy, 73;
on business progress in Indiana,
56–57; on communal life, necessity
of Christian values for, 52, 234n18;
correspondence with Henry Clay,
78; death of, 79, 275n111; decline in
health, 77; on donation to departing
member, 27; embrace of new
technology, 37, 77, 247n93; as
exempt from Harmony Society
rules, 34; on factors for selecting
new site in Indiana, 42; on fame of
Harmonie, Indiana, 64; fined for
Harmony Riot of 1807, 32; Frances
Wright and, 69; friction with father,
68–69, 73–74; on frustrations of
doing business in Southwestern
Indiana, 43–44, 48–49, 56–57, 65,
263n7; frustrations with western
Pennsylvania, 40; on goals of
Harmony Society, 234n18; and
Harmonist-owned steamboats,
66–67, 77, 264n18; and Harmony
Riot of 1920, 61–62; and Harmony

382 *Index*

Society loan policy, 47; and Harmony Society wool business, 36–37; as head financial manager of George Rapp & Associates, 33; at Indiana constitutional convention, 49, 244n46; involvement in Indiana banks, 45–47, 253n33, 253n36, 259–60n90; large homes of, 37, 38, 258n79; lawsuits against neighbors to recover debts, 61; and leasing land, 63; and lending, 47, 253n36; meetings with Robert Owen, 67; and move to Economie, Pennsylvania, 68; on Panic of 1819, 60; political engagement in Indiana, 48–49; and postal delays, 48–49, 255n46; and Rapp & Associates' wool business, 36–37; relationships with prominent businessmen, 37; reliance on trusted members as agents, 68–69, 79, 249n10; and sale of Harmonie, Indiana, 67–68; and sale of Harmonie, Pennsylvania, 42–43; scholars' downplaying of business success of, 87; secret speculation in stocks and commodities, 69–70, 80, 267n41, 275n114; as shrewd, hard-bargaining businessman, 33–34, 61; on silk manufacturing, 70–71, 83; and slavery, 49–50; support for Whig policies, 50, 78; testimony to Congress on wool manufacturing, 77–78

Rapp, George: and alchemy, 73; autocratic, patriarchal rule of Harmony Society, 31–32, 34, 53, 73, 74, 75; charisma of, as glue holding Harmony Society together, 86; on communal life, necessity of Christian members for success of, 14, 25–26; control of Rapp & Associates after Frederick's death, 79–80, 275n111; and Count de Leon crisis, 75–76; cultivation of autocratic image, 69; death of, 86, 278n152; and development of Economie, Pennsylvania, site, 68; discouragement of sex and marriage, 28–30; as economist-philosopher, 14; embrace of innovation, 83, 84–85, 89; as exempt from Harmony Society rules, 34; faith in capitalism, 10; founding of Harmonie, Pennsylvania, 18; founding of Harmony Society, goals of, 14; friction with Frederick in Economie, Pennsylvania, 73–74; on Harmony Society beliefs, 21–22; hiding of Harmony assets' value from members, 79, 81–83; on immanent return of Christ, 23, 26, 30; and isolation of Harmonists from worldly influences, 66–67; large homes of, 37, 38, 55, 71, 81, 82, 258n79; life in Germany, 19; meetings with Owen, 67; modern counterparts of, 221; motives for leaving Germany, 20–21, 22; and naming of Economy, Pennsylvania, 67; and new Articles of Association in Economy, Pennsylvania, 74; as Pietist, 20; powerful presence of, 31, 32; premillennialism of, 23; purchase of Pennsylvania-Ohio Canal Company stock, 78; reasons for move, search for land in Indiana, 40, 42; on reasons for return to Pennsylvania, 65; relationship with Hildegard Mutschler, 73; reluctance to admit new members, 83; scholars'

Rapp, George (*continued*)
downplaying of business success of, 87; search for land for Harmony Society, 19, 23–24; some Harmonists' resentment of leadership, 15; stockpiling of gold and silver, 80, 81; strained relations with Frederick during move to Economy, 68–69, 266n33; struggle to impose communalism, 26–28; support for Whig policies, 50, 78; theology of self-will, 25; *Thoughts on the Destiny of Man*, 14; views on helping neighbors, 63; violent opposition to autocratic rule of, 32

Rapp, Gertrude, 85, 277n143

Rapp & Associates. *See* George Rapp & Associates

Raymond, Henry J., 210–11

Redding & Co., 216

redemption of society through engagement (Naaman Option): Harper & Brothers and, 219; as one of three Protestant responses to society, 2, 217

Redfield, J. S., 206

reform, Protestants' fight for (Wilberforce Option): as one of three Protestant responses to society, 2, 217; Pioneerism and, 218–19

reform CBEs. *See* Christian business enterprises dedicated to market reforms

Religious Advertiser and Journal, 118–19

Religious Right, as part of myth of reemergence of fundamentalist Protestants, 217

R. G. Dun & Company, 87, 92, 101, 146, 160, 280–81n8

R. Hoe and Company, 199

Richmond Advertiser, 200

Riley, A. W., 144

Rochester, Nathaniel, 138

Rochester, New York, Erie Canal's impact on, 92, 101, 104–5

Rochester, William, 138, 139

Rochester Daily Advertiser, 139

Rochester Daily Advertiser and Telegraph, 128

Rochester Observer, 94, 98, 104, 110, 118, 119, 139, 144

Sabbatarian movement, 102–8; backlash against, 137–41, *140*; canal and stage lines voluntarily ceasing Sunday service, 121–22; and context of larger political battles, 129; cultural impact of Erie Canal and, 104–5; first phase of, 103, 117; focus on economic leverage, 106; influence on transportation lines, 146–47; objections to Sabbath violation, 103–4; origin of, 98; petitioning of Congress, 103, 105, 285n33; on Sabbath observance, benefits of, 105–6, 107; on Sabbath violations, dire effects of, 101–2, 105, 106–7; on Sabbath violations' damage to America's covenantal status, 94–95, 107–8, 109–11, 218–19; spread of, 303–4n92; success of, 147, 149. *See also* Bissell, Josiah Jr.; General Union for Promoting the Observance of the Christian Sabbath; Sabbath, closing of businesses on

Sabbatarian movement, second phase of: Auburn Convention, 121–22; ecumenicalism of, 118–19, 292n48;

384 *Index*

focus on mass media campaign, 117–18; and meetings leading to Pioneer Line, 119; petitioning of Congress, 105

Sabbath: importance in covenant theology, 111; and Post Office, 103, 140, 285n35; strict observance, origin of, 102; variations in definition of, 102

Sabbath, closing of businesses on: Harper & Brothers and, 8, 157, 167, 214, 312–13n53; importance of issue in early 19th century, 94; as key issue for conservative Protestants, 102; opponents of, 285n35; as Pioneer Line goal, 1–2, 92, 94

St. Luke's Episcopalian Church (Rochester), 115, 116, 291n34

St. Paul's Episcopalian Church (Rochester), 99–100, 114–17, *116*

Schaal family, 245n72

Schieck, Jacob, 32

Schnee, Jacob, 45, 252n31

Schnee, John, 252n31

Schoolcraft, Henry, 53, 249n3

Second Great Awakening, and emergence of capitalism, 3

Second Presbyterian Church of Rochester, 113, 114, 290n28

Sedgwick, Theodore Jr., 187

Sellers, Charles, 3–4, 156, 233n11, 307n30

separation of Protestants from society (Benedict Option): Harmony Society and, 218; as misleading conventional narrative, 2–3, 232n6; as one of three Protestant responses to society, 2, 217

Seymour, Jonathan, 161, 164, 166, 289n21

Shakers: as Christian communal capitalists, 12, 14, 21, 86, 88, 218; *vs.*

Harmony Society, 18, 28, 244n60, 279n164; move westward, 42; relations with Harmony Society, 236–37n9

Sherwood, Isaac, 297n20, 298–99n35

Sherwood, John, 131–35, 297n20, 298–99n35

Shields, David, 42–43

Ski Nautique, 218

Slater, Samuel, 11

slavery: and Aristarchus Champion's family, 111–12; Bissell and, 144; and capitalism, 92, 255n55; Harmony Society and, 18, 41, 49–50, 69; Methodism and, 162–63, 310–11n31; Presbyterians and, 113–14; reforming CBEs and, 92, 118, 218

Smith, Gerrit, 99, 101, 125–26, 283n7

Society for the Establishment of Useful Manufactures, 11

Society of United Germans, 72–73, 74, 269nn59–60

Solms, J., 69–70, 80, 263n6, 267n42

Southern Literary Messenger, 176, 179, 184, 190, 320n60

SpaceX, 221

Spencer, John C., 178

Spener, Philipp Jakob, 20, 23, 240n18

stagecoach lines: inherent danger of, 133; lines voluntarily ceasing Sunday service, 122; part of market's expansion, 98, 103. *See also* Hudson and Erie line; Old Line; Pioneer Line; Telegraph Line

steamboats: and cost of river transport, 59; Harmony not welcoming toward passengers of, 84; operating on Sundays, 10; owned by Harmony Society, 56, 66–67, 77, 264–65n18, 265n20; Sabbatarian line on Hudson

Index 385

steamboats (*continued*)
  River, 122; sinking of *Mechanic*,
  266n30; transporting Harmony
  specie, 68
Stilwell, Samuel, 314n81
stock sales, in 19th century, 274n106
Suffolk System, 60
Sunday as day of rest. *See* Sabbath
Supreme Court, cases involving
  Harmony, 74, 270n70
Swartwout, John, 301n67

Tappan, Arthur, 125
Tappan, Lewis, 92, 93, 126, 148, 193
technological innovation: and
  emergence of capitalism, 3;
  Harmony Society's embrace of, 18,
  37, 41, 56, 88–89; Harper & Brothers'
  investments in, 173, 182, *183*, 199,
  208–10, *209*, 212, 319n63
Telegraph Line, 132–33
telegraph service, and reduced need for
  Sunday mail service, 147
Tersteegen, Gerhard, 25
Teutonia. *See* Society of United
  Germans
Third Presbyterian Church of
  Rochester, 98, 99, 105, 113, 114, 115,
  115, 142, 144, 290n27, 291n33
Thompson, E. P., 155
Thoreau, Henry David, 216
Thoughts on the Destiny of Man (Rapp), 14
trade in early 19th century,
  specialization and modernization
  of, 57–59
transportation in Pennsylvania,
  improvements in first half of
  19th century, 66
transportation in Western U.S.: costs
  and delays in, 47–48, 57, 59, 60; poor

or nonexistent roads, 47–48; river
  transportation, 48, 59. *See also* Erie
  Canal
Travels in the United States of America
  (Melish), 37, 256n56
Treadwell, Daniel, 182, *183*
Troy and Michigan Lake Boat Line, 118
Two Years Before the Mast (Dana), 176,
  180–81, 186–88
Tyler, John, 78

United States: economy and
  demographics in early 19th century,
  18; population growth, first half of
  19th century, 51
United States Democratic Review, 194
*United States Magazine and
  Democratic Review*, 206
Utica Circular, 121

*Vestiges of the Natural history of
  Creation* (Chambers), 180
voluntary associations, fundamentalist
  Protestants' social action through,
  218
von Schweinitz, David, 32, 245n69

Waltham-Lowell system, 11
Wanamaker, John, 156
Wanamaker's department store, and
  Christian virtue capitalism, 156
War of 1812, and economic disruption
  in U.S., 42, 45
Wayne and Cuyahoga Turnpike
  Company, 128
Weber, Max, 6, 7, 156, 161, 165, 234n20,
  306n29
Webster, Noah, 193–94
Weed, Thurlow, 163–64, 178, 196,
  311n36

Weingartner, W., *56*

Wesley, John: on business and wealth, 158–59, 160; on free will, 307–8n5; *General Rules* of, 160; on work ethic, 165

Westchester Congregational Church (Connecticut), 101, 111–13, 289n16

Western Exchange Hotel (Auburn), 118, 134, *134*

Western Recorder (Utica), 101–2

Western Reserve of Connecticut, 127, *127*

Whey Station(ary) restaurant, 220, *221*

Whig party: Harper brothers' support of, 195–96; and James Harper, 196, 325nn31–32; Rapps' support for, 50, 78; support for business, 50

White and Sheffield, publishers, 193–94

William I (king of Württemberg), 53–54

William Penn (steamboat), 66–67, 265n20

Williams, Peter, 162–63, 310–11n31

Winthrop, John, 109

women: Auburn as site of women's rights organizing, 134; as audience, 205; in Harmony Society, 23, 34, 45, 53, 71, 72, 268n49; mistreated on stagecoaches, 235n28; portrayal of, in *Harper's Illuminated Bible*, 202–4, *203*, *204*, 328n64; priest-like role in Methodist middle class homes, 205; working at Harper's, 208, 213

Worcester, Samuel, 52

work, changing nature in early 19th century: and international interest in Harmony Society model, 12, 13, 14, 17, 37, 50–52, 72; shift toward manufacturing and specialization, 51; and U.S. desire to avoid squalor of English mill towns, 11, 12

Wright, Frances, 50, 69, 267n37

Wylie, Hugh, 103

Young America movement, 166, 312n51

Ziegler, Abraham, 42–43, 45, 252n31

Printed and bound by CPI Group (UK) Ltd, Croydon, CR0 4YY
08/01/2024

08219036-0003